GW01372979

The King and The People

The King and The People

Sovereignty and Popular Politics in Mughal Delhi

ABHISHEK KAICKER

OXFORD
UNIVERSITY PRESS

OXFORD
UNIVERSITY PRESS

Oxford University Press is a department of the University of Oxford. It furthers the University's objective of excellence in research, scholarship, and education by publishing worldwide. Oxford is a registered trade mark of Oxford University Press in the UK and certain other countries.

Published in the United States of America by Oxford University Press
198 Madison Avenue, New York, NY 10016, United States of America.

Library of Congress Cataloging-in-Publication Data
Names: Kaicker, Abhishek author.
Title: The king and the people : sovereignty and popular politics in Mughal Delhi / Abhishek Kaicker.
Description: New York : Oxford University Press, 2020. |
Includes bibliographical references and index.
Identifiers: LCCN 2019035558 (print) | LCCN 2019035559 (ebook) |
ISBN 9780190070670 (hardback) | ISBN 9780190070694 (epub)
Subjects: LCSH: Mogul Empire—Politics and government. | Mogul Empire—Kings and rulers. |
Delhi (India)—Politics and government—17th century. |
Delhi (India)—Politics and government—18th century. | Massacres—India—Delhi—History.
Classification: LCC DS461 .K216 2020 (print) | LCC DS461 (ebook) | DDC 954/.56025—dc23
LC record available at https://lccn.loc.gov/2019035558
LC ebook record available at https://lccn.loc.gov/2019035559

1 3 5 7 9 8 6 4 2

Printed by Integrated Books International, United States of America

الناس على دين ملوكهم

For my family, and in memory of my father.

Contents

Acknowledgments

The prehistory of the ideas developed in the following pages lies in formative encounters with my various teachers: Shahid Amin, Tim Brook, John Roosa, and Jim Stewart. Though its origins reside in a doctoral dissertation submitted at Columbia University in 2014, itself the product of questions that Janaki Bakhle and Nick Dirks asked me, the bulk of this book was written between my time at Harvard University and the University of California, Berkeley, from 2015 to 2018. My foremost gratitude is to those whose familial care enabled my work at the Society of Fellows at Harvard, particularly Diana Morse, Kelly Katz, Yesim Erdmann, and Ana Novak; and I thank Wally Gilbert for enabling my sojourn there. During my time in Cambridge I benefited immensely from the companionable friendship and intellectual solidarity of many remarkable colleagues, including Julien Ayroles, Alexander Bevilacqua, Michaela Bronstein, Idan Dershowitz, Stephanie Dick, Sivan Goren-Arzony, Len Gutkin, Daniel Hochbaum, Alisha Holland, Daniel Juette, Florian Klinger, Marika Knowles, Ya-Wen Lei, Jed Lewinsohn, Naomi Levine, Rohan Murty, Andrew Ollett, Paris Spies-Gans, Alma Steingart, Amartya Sen, Daniel Williams, and Nur Yalman. I thank Adam Mestyan, with whom much serious rethinking and interpretation happened over smoke breaks in the dead of winter at the Yellow House. I am particularly grateful to Noah Feldman for his intellectual generosity and helpful guidance at various stages of this book's gestation, and to Andy Strominger for always reminding me of the bigger picture. Sunil Sharma has been a constant mentor and friend during my years in Cambridge, and I express my warmest gratitude to him. I am likewise grateful to Francesca Orsini for her never-ending stream of encouragement and intellectual engagement.

I am also grateful for the seemingly inexhaustible wellsprings of sustenance and enrichment of my colleagues and dear friends across two continents: I thank Manan Ahmed, Eric Beverley, Gabriella Boulting, Danielle Callegari, Divya Cherian, Muriam Davis, Farhat Hasan, Kelly Hammond, Nishita Jha, Aparna Kapadia, Sumayya Kassamali, Mana Kia, Rajeev Kinra, Sanjay Krishnan, Naveena Naqvi, Luther Obrock, Diego Pirillo, Teena Purohit, Aman Sethi, Shuddhabratta Sengupta, and Nir Shafir for their friendship and support through the vicissitudes of book-writing. I am proud to call Aarti Sethi a comrade-in-arms for as long as I can now remember, and Poulomi Saha for being a bedrock of intellectual kinship and familiality at Berkeley.

I thank Ali Anooshahr, Christine Philliou, Taymiya Zaman, and Qamar Adamjee, Victoria Frede, and Harsha Ram for their invaluable comments on my various attempts to formulate some of the key ideas in this book. Imperfect though it remains, this book would have been much worse yet but for the patient scrutiny, careful criticism and correction, and generous assistance of Muzaffar Alam, Janaki Bakhle, Munis Faruqui, Noah Feldman, Ethan Shagan, Samira Sheikh, Mary Woolsey and Peter Zinoman, all of whom have commented on various full drafts of this work. I am humbled their generosity which I can never hope to repay. I likewise bear a very special debt of gratitude to Barbara and Tom Metcalf, my ideal audience, who read an early draft of this book chapter by chapter.

The guidance and, at various critical moments, active intercession of Muzaffar Alam, Shahid Amin, Janaki Bakhle, Nick Dirks, and Partha Chatterjee have given my intellectual life the shape it bears. I am also profoundly grateful to my friend and interlocutor Hasan Siddiqui, whose constant engagement has fundamentally shaped my work.

I have been deeply privileged to call the department of history at UC Berkeley a home during the writing of this book. Whether they recognize it or not, this book has been profoundly improved by conversations with my colleagues in Dwinelle Hall, particularly Diliana Angelova, Andrew Barshay, Beth Berry, Brian DeLay, Carla Hesse, Susanna Elm, Stefan-Ludwig Hoffman, Marty Jay, Bob Goldman, Sally Goldman, Tom Laqueur, Michael Nylan, Carlos Noreña, Mark Peterson, Caitlin Rosenthal, Daniel Sargeant, Peter Sahlins, Jonathan Sheehan, Elena Schneider, Nicolas Tackett, James Vernon, Wen-hsin Yeh, and Peter Zinoman. I am very grateful to Hannah Archambault for casting her eye and her pen over this book. At Berkeley, I also thank Anurag Advani, Aparajita Das, Nicole Ferreira, Sourav Ghosh, Shaivya Mishra, Brent Otto, Omar Qashoa, and Mariam Sabri. Research for this book has been generously supported by the Milton Fund at Harvard and the Institute of International Studies at Berkeley.

I am grateful to Theo Calderara and Macey Fairchild at Oxford University Press, and the anonymous reviewers for their very careful and helpful comments. I likewise thank Prabhu Chinnaswamy for shepherding this book to publication, and George Chakvetadze for making the maps. This book would never have been possible without my family, on whose love I have relied at every turn, and who have given me all that I possess: Geeta and Aparajita Kaicker; and Stacey Van Vleet, who has shared the joys and eased the burdens of this book from the very beginning. My greatest regret is that my father Sudhir Kaicker, who made the scholar that I am, is not alive to see this book in print. It is in his memory that I leave this memento on the page of time. While I am profoundly aware of the great and unselfish help of so many friends, colleagues, and teachers all around the world, the inevitable errors which remain are mine alone.

Chronology

1526	The Central Asian prince BABUR defeats the ruler of Delhi and establishes a nascent Mughal empire in India
1556–1605	The empire and its institutions take shape under the emperor AKBAR
1605–1627	The reign of JAHANGIR
1628	SHAH JAHAN comes to power
1648	After a decade of construction, a new city of Delhi, called SHAHJAHANABAD, is inaugurated
1658–1659	SHAH JAHAN is overthrown by his son; AURANGZEB comes to power, killing his brother DARA SHUKOH; the people of Delhi express their disapproval of AURANGZEB
1666	SHAH JAHAN dies in captivity
1680	AURANGZEB leaves Delhi to campaign in the Deccan
1707	AURANGZEB dies and is succeeded by BAHADUR SHAH
1711	BAHADUR SHAH's attempted alteration of the Friday sermon (*khutba*) provokes an uprising in Lahore
1712	BAHADUR SHAH is dead; JAHANDAR SHAH comes to the throne
1713	JAHANDAR SHAH is overthrown; FARRUKH SIYAR comes to power with the support of the clan of the SAYYIDS OF BARHA
1719	FARRUKH SIYAR is overthrown by the SAYYIDS OF BARHA in the midst of an uprising in Delhi
1719	MUHAMMAD SHAH comes to the throne
1729	The shoemakers' riot rocks Delhi
1739	NADIR SHAH invades India and occupies Delhi; the people revolt and are massacred
1748	MUHAMMAD SHAH dies
1756	Delhi is sacked by an Afghan army
1757	The East India Company-backed contender wins the battle of Plassey, inaugurating the British rise to power in India
1803	The arrival of an East India Company Army in Delhi marks the British takeover of the city

A Note on Transliteration and Sources

Given the seemingly insuperable difficulties in creating a perfectly coherent system of transliteration, I have imposed only a lenient form of standardization in this work. A simplified form of the transliteration used in Steingass's *Dictionary* is used to denote words in Persian; I maintain diacritics marking long vowels to aid pronunciation but exclude all other diacritical markers except for ʿain and hamzaʾ. Familiar places and persons are rendered in their usual form—thus Aurangzeb, not Aurangzib, and Delhi, not Dihli.

In citations, I distinguish between printed Persian texts and their English translations by appending [FA] or [EN] as necessary. When I have consulted several manuscripts of a text, I denote them as [A], [B], and so forth. In citing Urdu and Persian texts, all translations are my own unless noted otherwise. For quotations from the Qurʾan I rely on the translation of Muhammad Asad.

To facilitate ease of discovery, I have not attempted to standardize the transliterations into English of the names of books in my bibliography, and leave them in the form they appear on WorldCat. For the same reasons, I treat the second part of authors' names as last names in my citations. Thus Mirza Muhammad appears as "Muhammad" in the footnotes, and Shakir Khan as "Khan." Full references are provided in the bibliography.

Since the original dates of composition of Persian manuscripts are frequently missing, I have provided them when available, or when I have felt sufficiently confident to hazard a guess. Dates from the Islamic calendar have been converted to the Gregorian.

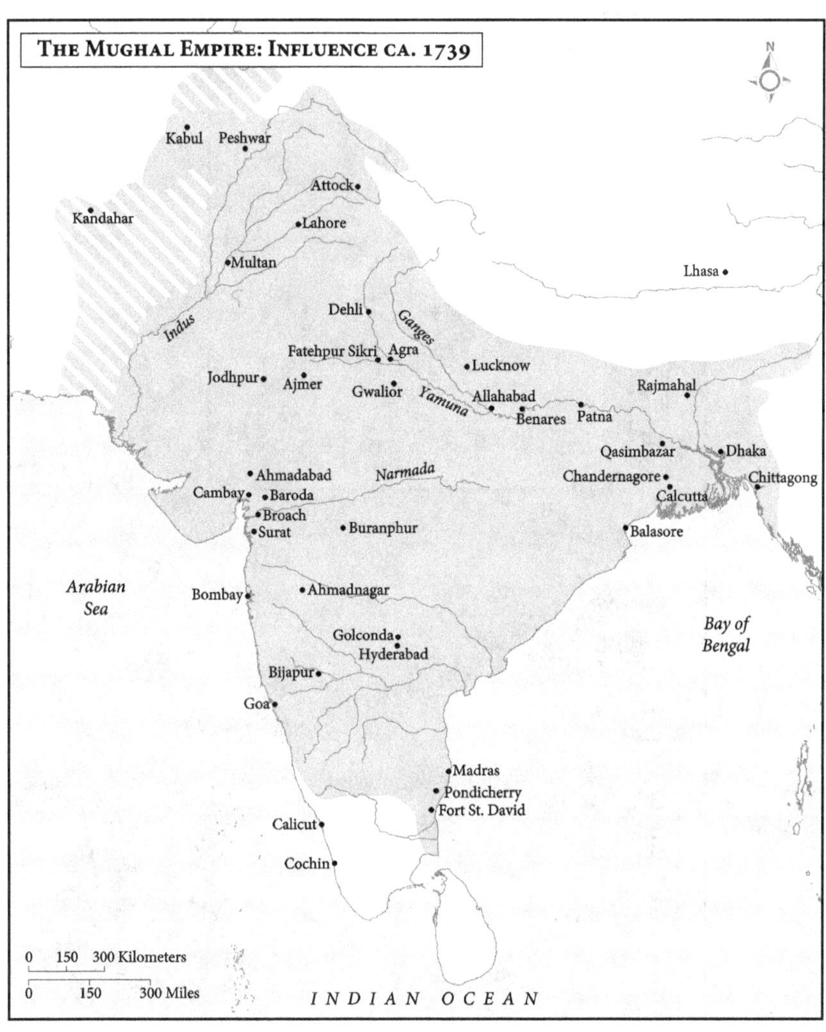

THE MUGHAL EMPIRE: INFLUENCE CA. 1739
N
Kabul
Peshwar
Attock
Lahore
Kandahar
Multan
Lhasa
Indus
Dehli
Ganges
Fatehpur Sikri
Agra
Lucknow
Jodhpur
Ajmer
Gwalior
Yamuna
Allahabad
Benares
Patna
Rajmahal
Qasimbazar
Dhaka
Chandernagore
Chittagong
Calcutta
Ahmadabad
Narmada
Cambay
Baroda
Broach
Surat
Buranphur
Balasore
Arabian
Sea
Bombay
Ahmadnagar
Bay of
Bengal
Golconda
Hyderabad
Bijapur
Goa
Madras
Pondicherry
Fort St. David
Calicut
Cochin
0 150 300 Kilometers
0 150 300 Miles
INDIAN OCEAN

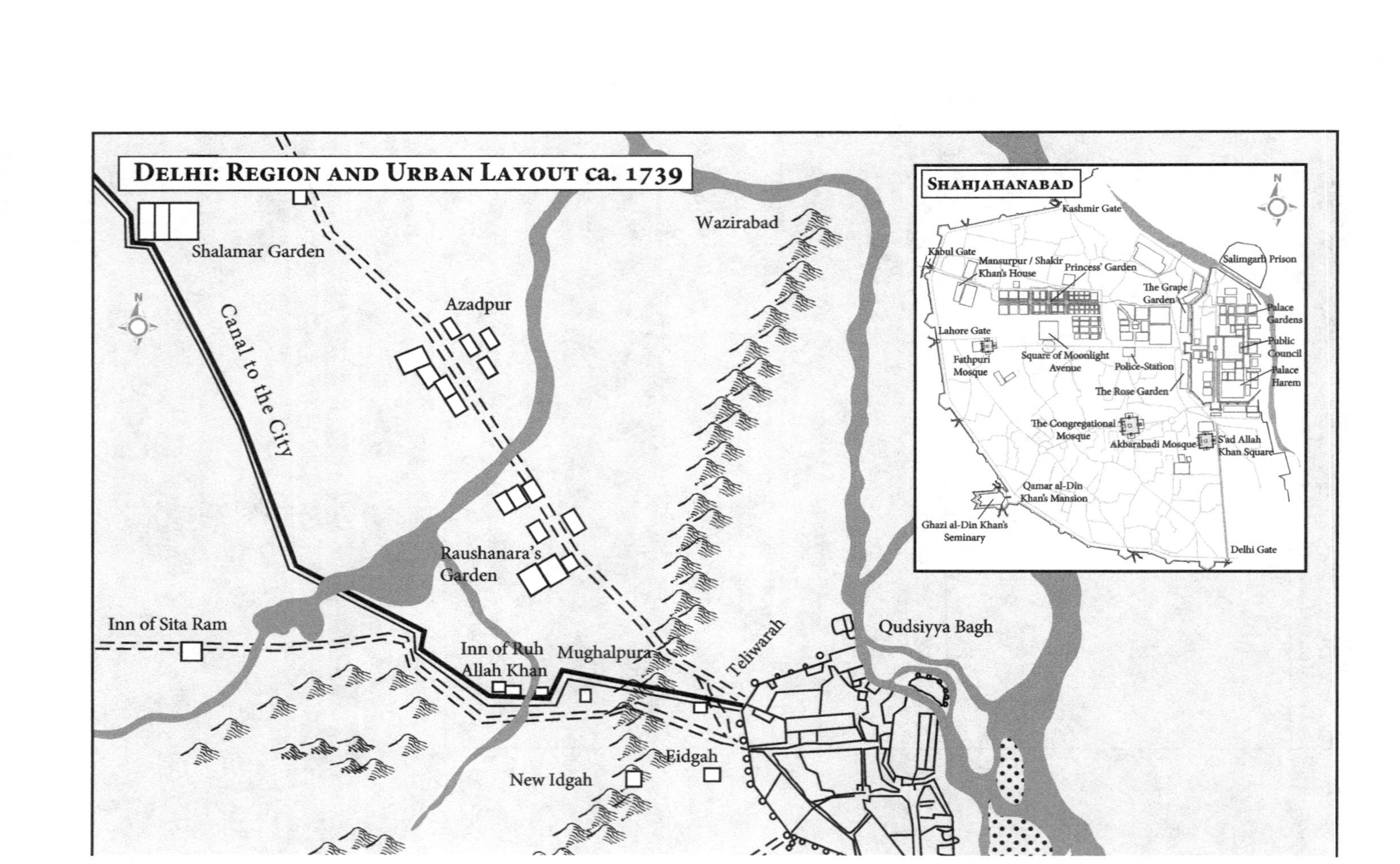
Delhi: Region and Urban Layout ca. 1739
Shalamar Garden
Canal to the City
Azadpur
Wazirabad
Raushanara's Garden
Inn of Sita Ram
Inn of Ruh Allah Khan
Mughalpura
Teliwarah
Qudsiyya Bagh
Eidgah
New Idgah
Shahjahanabad
Kashmir Gate
Kabul Gate
Mansurpur / Shakir Khan's House
Princess' Garden
Salimgarh Prison
The Grape Garden
Palace Gardens
Lahore Gate
Fathpuri Mosque
Square of Moonlight Avenue
Police-Station
Public Council
Palace Harem
The Rose Garden
The Congregational Mosque
Akbarabadi Mosque
S'ad Allah Khan Square
Qamar al-Din Khan's Mansion
Ghazi al-Din Khan's Seminary
Delhi Gate

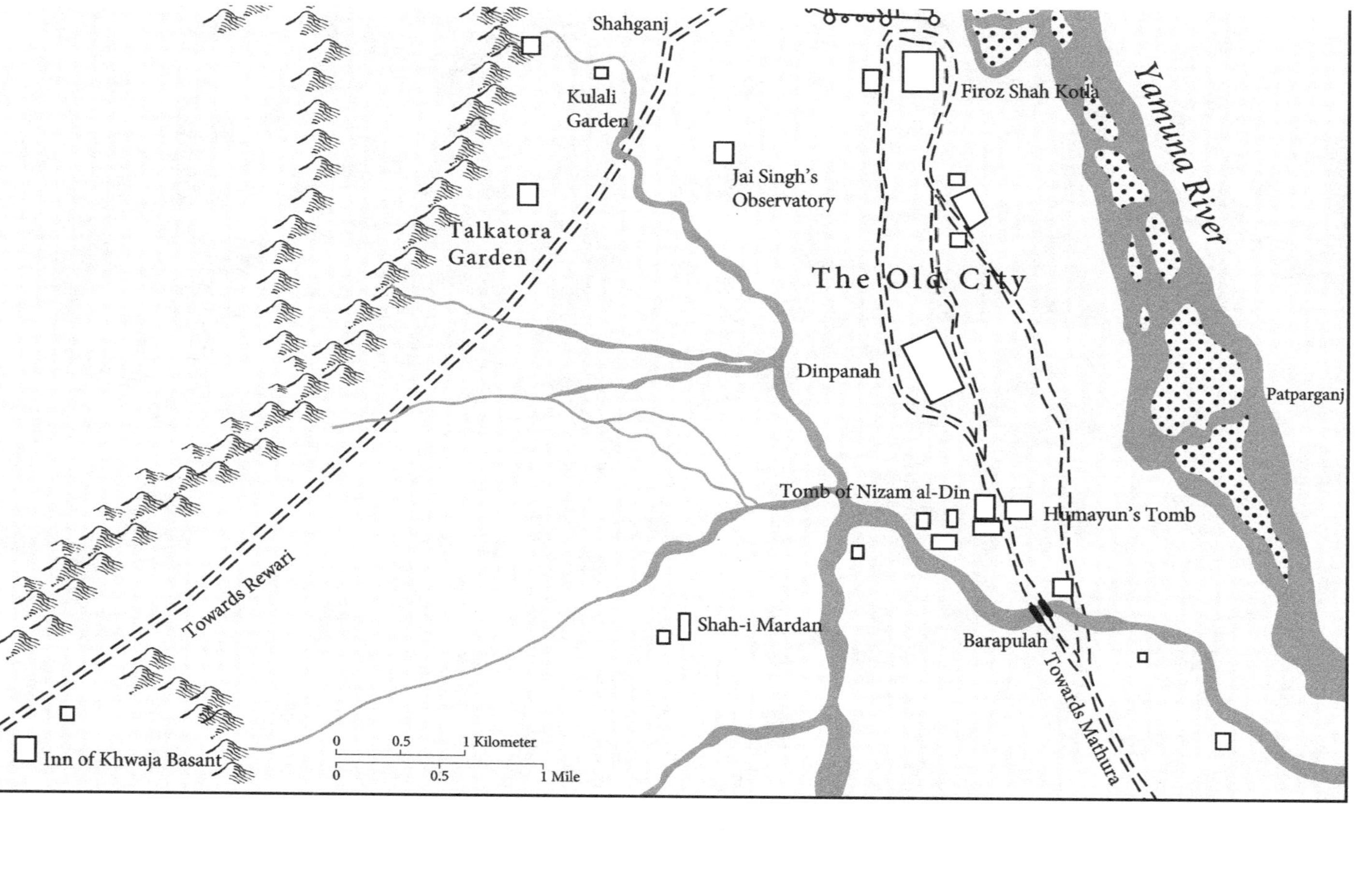
Yamuna River
Patparganj
Shahganj
Kulali Garden
Firoz Shah Kotla
Jai Singh's Observatory
Talkatora Garden
The Old City
Dinpanah
Tomb of Nizam al-Din
Humayun's Tomb
Shah-i Mardan
Barapulah
Towards Mathura
Towards Rewari
Inn of Khwaja Basant
0 0.5 1 Kilometer
0 0.5 1 Mile

Introduction

Seeing the People

That the people were merely the passive objects of sovereign authority has long served as a chief axiom in the study of precolonial India. The enduring power of this presumption manifests in two recurrent notions, which continue to color the vision of even the largest and most sophisticated premodern polity in the subcontinent, the Mughal empire. The first is that ordinary folk did not exercise any say in matters of politics: an unquestioned truth, encapsulated in the comment of Jadunath Sarkar, one of the founding figures of its modern study, that "[t]he mass of the people remained 'human sheep'" until the coming of British colonial rule.[1] Secondly, when confronted with the lengthy record of popular violence and rebellion, particularly in cities, historians have traditionally insisted the people's actions were driven by no causes other than economic discontent or blind religious passion.

To be sure, scholarship on the Mughal empire has advanced enormously in the century since the labors of Sarkar and others established this bedrock of scholarship. The pathbreaking work of Irfan Habib decisively turned the focus of historians from the questions of high politics toward the countryside.[2] Subsequent research by scholars of a revisionist bent has challenged prevailing views of economic crisis and political decline and turned instead to the closer study of regions and local groups across the subcontinent, particularly in the eighteenth century.[3] In the last few decades, a more capacious sense of the languages and texts that might constitute an archive for the history of the region has reinvigorated scholarship on premodern South Asia, as has the sustained inquiry into the connections forged by the movement

[1] Sarkar, *The Mughal Administration*, 75.

[2] Habib, *The Agrarian System of Mughal India, 1556–1707*.

[3] Bayly, *Rulers, Townsmen, and Bazaars*; Alam, *Crisis of Empire*; Singh, *Region and Empire: Panjab in the Seventeenth Century*; Eaton, *The Rise of Islam and the Bengal Frontier, 1204–1760*; Dhavan, *When Sparrows Became Hawks*; Barnett, *Rethinking Early Modern India*; Alavi, *The Eighteenth Century in India*; Travers, "The Eighteenth Century in Indian History."

The King and The People. Abhishek Kaicker, Oxford University Press (2020). © Oxford University Press.
DOI: 10.1093/oso/9780190070670.001.0001

of people, commodities, books, and ideas between the subcontinent and the wider world.[4]

And yet, in the general turn from matters of high politics and the agrarian system to those of cultural history, ordinary people—and particularly urbanites—have received little attention. While it has long been suggested that the *Pax Mughalica* of the sixteenth and seventeenth centuries stimulated urbanization, the social and cultural history of the empire's cities remains generally unbroached.[5] The growing body of scholarship in premodern cities in the subcontinent remains organized by schematic divisions between themes of economy, religion, and culture.[6] Because it has been taken for granted that urbanites were incapable of political representation, questions of urban politics have remained broadly absent, but for a very few notable exceptions, from the horizon of historians.[7]

The inability to see the political capacity of city-dwellers has a storied provenance. Given the formal lack of legal autonomy, Weber discounted the possibility that such a thing as a city might exist in India, to say nothing of its politics.[8] In this vein, it was until recently asserted that "relations between the urban population and the Mughal state were determined in large measure by the fact that the traditional Indo-Muslim city, like the traditional Islamic city in north Africa and the Middle East, lacked any kind of corporate or municipal institutions."[9] Because urban populations were "parasitically" dependent on the wealth drained from the countryside and on the whims of the ruling class, their grievances were only "economic" in nature, and transitory at that: thus, concludes Irfan Habib, "the scope and intensity of protest by the urban poor was limited."[10] Such conceptions have undergirded the study of

[4] Subrahmanyam, "Connected Histories"; Narayana Rao, Shulman, and Subrahmanyam, *Textures of Time: Writing History in South India*; Alam and Subrahmanyam, *Indo-Persian Travels in the Age of Discoveries, 1400–1800*.

[5] A recent exception is Dadlani, "The City Built, the City Rendered."

[6] Chaudhuri, "Some Reflections"; Gillion, *Ahmedabad*; Gokhale, *Surat in the Seventeenth Century*; Das Gupta, *Indian Merchants and the Decline of Surat: C. 1700–1750*; Grewal et al., *Studies in Urban History*; Singh, *Town, Market, Mint, and Port in the Mughal Empire, 1556–1707: An Administrative-Cum-Economic Study*; Gokhale, *Poona in the Eighteenth Century*; Sharma and Malekandathil, *Cities in Medieval India*.

[7] Hasan, *State and Locality*.

[8] Weber, "The Nature of the City," 45–46.

[9] Hambly, "Towns and Cities," 447; such a conception also shapes Blake's discussion of politics in the city: Blake, *Shahjahanabad*, 161–73. For a critique of the Weberian approach, see Subrahmanyam, "The Mughal State—Structure or Process?"; Subrahmanyam, "Parody and Public Space in an Early Modern Society," 244–45.

[10] Habib, "Peasant and Artisan Resistance in Mughal India," quote on 28, 30.

even the Mughal capital of Delhi, arguably the most significant of precolonial cities in the subcontinent.[11]

This book offers an argument to the contrary. It contends that, in the first decades of the eighteenth century, the city's common people—artisans, from haughty jewelers to humble shoemakers, soldiers, obscure preachers, minor clerics, wandering mendicants, unnamed idlers, vagrants, vagabonds, and spectators—emerged as subjects in a regime that had no conception of their place in politics. In these tumultuous years, otherwise known for the rapid collapse of imperial power, even the humblest of urbanites developed the ability to assert themselves, in exceptional circumstances, in the very highest affairs of state. And, in a more everyday sense, the people of the city both invoked the king's authority and challenged it in terms of the commitments to Islam which were central to the expression of imperial sovereignty. In this way, the practices and gestures by which Islamic community was evoked—prayers, Friday sermons, festivals, and funerary rights—were forged into a language of popular politics. To trace this coming of the people into politics in relation to imperial sovereignty is the key objective of the pages that follow.

That the denizens of so wealthy and populous a city as early eighteenth-century Delhi emerged as political subjects should come as no surprise to historians. It is now well established that the period ranging from the early sixteenth to the mid-eighteenth century saw the rise of large states and the intensification of global connections across Eurasia, including across the Indian subcontinent.[12] Less remarked is the fact that this was also the period of the rise of urban centers, which, serving as hubs of manufacture, entrepôts of trade, and the favored residences of intellectuals and literati, were the spatial hub in which the effects of these integrative phenomena were concentrated. It was in the great cities across Eurasia and its southern rim that people from hinterlands and distant parts came to trade commodities, and urbanites strolled in gardens and gathered in taverns and coffee-houses to discuss strange news of distant parts and the newest works of rising poets.[13] While from the perspective of the twenty-first century, the total volume of exchanges between these cities may have been minuscule, the movement of

[11] Spear, *Twilight of the Mughuls; Studies in Late Mughul Delhi*; Hambly, *Cities of Mughul India*; Frykenberg, *Delhi through the Ages: Essays in Urban History, Culture, and Society*; Blake, *Shahjahanabad*; Chenoy, *Shahjahanabad, a City of Delhi, 1638–1857*; Chenoy, *Shahjahanabad.*

[12] Richards, "The Seventeenth-Century Crisis in South Asia"; Subrahmanyam, "Connected Histories"; Richards, "Early Modern India and World History"; Parker, *Global Interactions in the Early Modern Age.*

[13] Berg et al., *Goods from the East, 1600–1800.*

people, commodities, books and ideas had profound effects on local cultures across Eurasia.[14] London and Paris, Istanbul and Cairo, Suzhou and Edo all emerged as vital nodes in an increasingly interlinked world even if they were not yet directly or tightly connected to one another. With Shah Jahan's building of Shahjahanabad immediately to the north of the older city (begun in 1638 and more or less concluded in the next two decades) the new conurbation of Delhi must be included among these Eurasian capitals. As the newly christened "Abode of the Caliphate," Delhi became the most important urban center in the Mughal empire of the seventeenth century. While the absence of population data preclude the estimation of its size, the French visitor Bernier's oft-cited comparison between Delhi and Paris indicates the city's population may have roughly ranged between 300,000 and 500,000 inhabitants in the mid-seventeenth century.[15]

The commercial vitality and growing cultures of consumerism and leisure in urban centers was also accompanied by the increasing political assertiveness of city-dwellers. Though historians of the premodern world have been slow to integrate the insights of urban theorists on the space of the city as a frame for politics, cities across Eurasia shared characteristics with corresponding similarities in urban political cultures.[16] As much scholarship has shown, the denizens of not only Paris and Amsterdam but also those of Istanbul, Cairo, and Damascus played an instrumental role in shaping their political order.[17]

Although the designation of this era as an "early modern" period has remained subject to vigorous debate, such periodization offers a valuable opportunity to historicize features of the present that are conventionally regarded as the hallmarks of our modernity.[18] Viewing the Mughal empire as an early modern polity thus allows us to inquire into the local origins and

[14] Vries, "The Limits of Globalization in the Early Modern World."

[15] Habib, "Population."

[16] Soja, "Cities and States in Geohistory"; an important essay in this regard is Friedrichs, "What Made the Eurasian City Work? Urban Political Cultures in Early Modern Europe and Asia."

[17] To name only a few works I have found helpful in this vast literature: Rudé, *Paris and London in the Eighteenth Century: Studies in Popular Protest*; Hunt, *Politics, Culture, and Class in the French Revolution*; Darnton, *The Great Cat Massacre and Other Episodes in French Cultural History*; Te Brake, *Regents and Rebels*; Nussdorfer, "Politics and the People of Rome"; Te Brake, *Shaping History*; Harris, *The Politics of the Excluded, c. 1500–1850*; Shagan, *Popular Politics and the English Reformation*; Pincus, *1688*; Jacob and Secretan, *In Praise of Ordinary People*; Sariyannis, "Mob, Scamps and Rebels in Seventeenth-Century Istanbul"; Kafadar, "Janissaries and Other Riffraff of Ottoman Istanbul: Rebels without a Cause?"; Elbendary, *Crowds and Sultans*; Gara, Kabadayi, and Neumann, *Popular Protest and Political Participation in the Ottoman Empire*; Anastasopoulos, *Political Initiatives "from the Bottom up" in the Ottoman Empire.*

[18] Chakrabarty, "The Muddle of Modernity"; Subrahmanyam, "Waiting for the Simorgh: Comparisons, Connections, and the 'Early Modern.'"

aspects of what are today experienced as global phenomena. Take, for instance, the idea of popular sovereignty, surely a feature of political modernity with a global and indeed hegemonic reach. Few would dispute the now-commonsensical belief that absolute authority derives from, and should reside in, the people of any given political entity. Yet the historical vision of this momentous and foundational shift in the locus of power from the body of the king to the body politic remains resolutely centered on the Atlantic world at the end of the eighteenth century.[19]

Do the disorderly urbanites of eighteenth-century Delhi have anything to contribute to this history of the political modernity of our present? It is remarkable that the political actions and aspirations of the faceless masses who breathed and died in the shadow of the Red Fort have generally gone unrecognized in the history of Delhi and the Mughal empire.[20] This inability to see has marked treatments of even the vast cataclysms which so obviously disturbed urban life. A prime example, with which this book begins, is that of Nadir Shah's occupation of Delhi and his massacre of its residents in 1739. Following Sarkar's determination that only the city's "hooligans and low people" rose up against Nadir Shah's soldiers on the basis of a misguided rumor, later historians generally dismissed the action of the people as the mindless violence of the mob, perhaps occasioned by a spike in prices of grain.[21] The possibility that the city's people may have been motivated by cherished ideals and beliefs to gamble with (and, as it turns out, lose) their lives in resisting an occupying army has never been seriously entertained.

In much the same fashion, the many everyday instances of urban violence recorded from the period have been dismissed as occasioned by some admixture of irrational religious fanaticisms and economic rivalry. The paradigmatic instance of such an event is the so-called shoemakers' riot of 1729,

[19] Thus, a recent collection of essays on the idea leaves one with the distinct sense that popular sovereignty was birthed in the Hellenic world, matured in Enlightenment Europe, and came to its troubled end in the colonies: Bourke and Skinner, *Popular Sovereignty in Historical Perspective*; but see also the lone essay on South Asia by Karuna Mantena. A valuable contrast is apparent in Ben-Dor Benite, Geroulanos, and Jerr, *The Scaffolding of Sovereignty*. The editors' belief that "modern developments concerning democracy, balance of power, law and popular sovereignty are (or derive from) fundamentally European practices" (6) is, however, questionable. A criticism of such views was already made in Chatterjee, *Nationalist Thought and the Colonial World: A Derivative Discourse?*; see also the thoughtful remarks in Pocock, "On the Unglobality of Contexts: Cambridge Methods and the History of Political Thought."

[20] By contrast, historians of the city in the colonial period have been more sensitive to these issues. See Gupta, *Delhi between Two Empires, 1803–1931: Society, Government and Urban Growth*; Pernau, *Ashraf into Middle Classes*.

[21] Sarkar, *Nadir Shah*, 62–63.

which was sparked by an altercation between a group of shoemakers and a passing jeweler, and culminated in a confused melee in the courtyard of Delhi's congregatory mosque. For William Irvine, the colonial administrator who in conjunction with Sarkar was the first to fully describe the event, the question of the people's motivations did not arise. The riot was significant only in its consequences for courtly politics, and the decline of the empire demonstrated by such unchecked unruliness.[22] In such vein, later historians regarded it as a "Hindu-Muslim riot," again symptomatic of a larger economic crisis: an instance of the increasingly strident assertion of religious communities, which unleashed long-standing intercommunal tensions that could no longer be contained by a collapsing empire.[23] Again, the question of the motivations of the shoemakers at the center of the story has remained irrelevant to the meaning of the event.

Instances of everyday urban violence, historians have pleaded, did not in any case represent widespread sectarian resentments, and should not be seen as originating the modern "communalism" of South Asia, which is ascribed to colonial rule.[24] More generally, this historical vision has been shaped by insufficient attention to the craft and artifice of the late-Mughal elites who wrote the memoirs, chronicles, and histories from which modern historians have synthesized their narratives. The commitment to a positivist practice of reading, central to the discipline since its birth at the hands of Irvine and Sarkar, has seamlessly rendered the contempt of late-Mughal elites for the people of the city into the prose of modern historians. As equally for the shoemaker in 1729 as the resistant urbanite in 1739, the result (to borrow the words of Ranajit Guha) has been the denial of "recognition as a subject of history in his own right even for a project that was all his own."[25]

By placing the people at the heart of the narrative, this book claims an altogether different significance for events such as the ones noted above, which, over the turn of the century, came to increasingly shake the city. It contends that while idealizations of the people may have preceded the establishment of Mughal imperium, those individuals who took to the city's streets were constituted as subjects by a distinctively Mughal discourse of sovereignty and acted in relation to it. As this book will show, the politically activated urban

22 Irvine and Sarkar, *Later Mughals*, I:257–63.

23 Rizvi, *Shah Wali-Allah and His Times*, 197–202; Bayly, *Empire and Information*, 196–97; Rezavi, "The Dynamics of Composite Culture"; Alam, *The Crisis of Empire in Mughal North India*, lviii–lix.

24 Pandey, *Construction of Communalism*.

25 Guha, *Elementary Aspects of Peasant Insurgency*, 3.

populace of the eighteenth century was the inadvertent and unanticipated product of Mughal imperial hegemony and its expressions of sovereignty, shaped as much by intensifying commercialization as by the increasingly systematic imposition of imperial law. Through the experience of the political crises of the early eighteenth century, Delhi's urbanites would forge a dual practice of politics: one that challengingly invoked the king's authority in everyday struggles, but rose to his defense when imperial hegemony was endangered.

Such a dual practice of urban politics cannot become visible until we suspend our modern conceptual schema that demarcate some sacred and mystical realm of religion from the canny and hard-nosed realities of urban politics. In this light, it will be argued that the everyday disorders regarded as outbreaks of "communal violence" with economic undertones—such as those of the shoemakers of 1729—instead saw the creative use of the gestural and symbolic vocabulary of Islam by subordinate groups to forge communities and generate solidarities over the course of an urban political struggle. Yet, though the people might confront the ruler in these ways in everyday urban conflicts, they would rise unambiguously to his defense when the institution of Mughal rule was itself threatened by forces perceived as external to the city: as will become evident in the scarcely noticed urban uprisings in defense of the ruler in 1719 and 1739 that reveal a popular investment in the ideals of Mughal kingship. This book offers no neat linear story from popular quiescence to defiance. But what the challenging invocations and defenses of imperial power show together is a growing ability in the people for assertion against sovereign power which regarded them as merely the objects of rule.

Terms and Sources

Some terminological specification is necessary here. Sovereignty, emerging as a much-debated juridical and philosophical concept contested from Jean Bodin to Jean-Jacques Rousseau, finds no direct coeval or parallel in Mughal intellectual culture, where no equivalent term merited similar theoretical discussion.[26] Though the term has long been freely applied to Mughal

[26] See the remarks in Al-Azmeh, *Muslim Kingship*, 113–14.

rule, its unqualified use is therefore misleading.[27] To explain the changing dynamic between the king and the people in Mughal Delhi, we must understand the ways in which political authority was constructed in its own terms. Indeed, notwithstanding the absence of the theorization of anything equaling sovereignty, the conception of an absolute ruling imperial power is readily discernible in the ethical treatises (*akhlāq*) produced by courtly intellectuals.[28] More broadly, this conception of power, which undergirded the Mughal dynasty's new and enormous claims to authority, was expressed at imperial centers across a range of textual genres, paintings, architectural features, practices, ceremonies, customs, and gestures. Such expressions are collectively described in this book as a *discourse of sovereignty*. Though they varied in emphasis from reign to reign, these expressions all relied upon longstanding ideals familiar from the "circle of justice" regarding the disposition and use of power, including prominently the principles of justice (*ʿadālat*), prosperity (*faiz*), and felicity (*iqbāl*) among others.[29]

A key concept in this complex of enunciations on which this work focuses is the Perso-Arabic term *daulat*.[30] Though a word of many meanings, for Mughal intellectuals *daulat* particularly connoted "fortune," both in the sense of the divine endorsement to rule, and the possession of worldly wealth. In giving the king the supreme power to ensure the greatest virtue of justice, the possession of *daulat* related the body of the king to the body politic. The shifting uses and conceptions of this ubiquitous ideal illustrate how successive articulations of royal power worked on its objects of governance, and offer insight into how the political transformations of the period were perceived, justified, and debated by observers. Because questions of justice were central to the relation between the ruler and the ruled, the violent and public stripping of *daulat* from kingly bodies in the upheavals of the eighteenth century would catalyze the development of a contestatory popular politics.

What, however, might constitute a popular politics in the era before mass participation in representative democracy? Joining recent scholarship on premodern South Asia, this book pleads for a broader conception of politics

[27] Moin, *The Millennial Sovereign*; see the debate in Fancy, "Of Sovereigns, Sacred Kings, and Polemics"; Gilmartin, "Imperial Sovereignty in Mughal and British Forms"; Moin, "Millennial Sovereignty, Total Religion, and Total Politics"; my own views in this regard are shaped by Sheehan, "Problem of Sovereignty"; Ben-Dor Benite, Geroulanos, and Jerr, *The Scaffolding of Sovereignty*.

[28] Alam, "A Muslim State in a Non-Muslim Context: The Mughal Case."

[29] Darling, "Do Justice, Do Justice, For That Is Paradise"; Darling, *A History of Social Justice and Political Power in the Middle East*.

[30] For a recent analysis of *daulat* in the discourse of sovereignty see Yılmaz, *Caliphate Redefined*; see also Markiewicz, "The Crisis of Rule in Late Medieval Islam," particularly chaps. 8–9.

than the machinations of elites for resources and position at court.[31] The work of Farhat Hasan has been of profound importance in reshaping our understanding of local politics in the Mughal empire.[32] But where Hasan sees the emergence of an increasingly inclusive "public sphere" created by an imperial sovereignty expanding to incorporate local elites and intermediaries, this book takes a somewhat different approach. It emphasizes instead the dynamic and contingent nature of the practices that enabled the assertive and frequently transgressive participation of even the lowest members of society in affairs seen as above their station. It is through these practices, by which individuals and groups looked to exercise, invoke, or contest power—often beginning in, and expanding from, the context of local struggles for "justice" against their neighbors—that the people of the city emerged as properly political subjects.

But who were the people? I am aware that the idea of "The People" is an act of imagination that imposes a fictitious unity on heterogeneous and fragmented collectivities in order to grant legitimacy to a political projection.[33] Yet the category has been a foundational one in the intellectual traditions of the Islamic world, whether construed as "the common" (*ʿāmm, ʿawāmm*) who are contrasted with "the special" (*khāss*), or as "God's creation" (*khalq-i Allāh*), the "flock" (*raʿiyat*) entrusted to the pastoral care of the ruler. Unlike their rulers, the ordinary folk of Delhi who are the subject of this book have left few traces in the Mughal archive, which, for historical reasons of its own, is fragmented beyond reconstruction. Though this book relies in part on broadly underutilized collections of news reports (*akhbārāt*) which described the daily doings of the king and his court, the kinds of administrative records through which historians have reconstructed the everyday life of premodern cities do not appear to be extant in our case.[34] Thus we must rely on a wider corpus of literary sources, including chronicles, memoirs, essays, epistolary collections, biographical compendia, and works of poetry.

The men who produced the works on which this book is based were all in some way associated with the imperial court and to varying degrees, their writings were hued in its values. Many authors of the seventeenth century were closely tied to the imperial throne. The scribe Chandar Bhan, whose

[31] Chandra, *Parties and Politics*; Ali, *The Mughal Nobility under Aurangzeb*; Ali, "The Mughal Polity: A Critique of Revisionist Approaches."

[32] Hasan, *State and Locality*; Hasan, "Forms of Civility and Publicness in Pre-British India."

[33] Badiou et al., *What Is a People?*

[34] See, for instance, Canbakal, *Society and Politics in an Ottoman Town*; Zarinebaf, *Crime and Punishment in Istanbul.*

writing fully embodied the imperial discourse of sovereignty, was personally proximate to the emperor Shah Jahan.[35] Others, like the merciless satirist Niʿmat Khan-i ʿAli, or the politically maladroit Mirza Iradat Khan Wazih, belonged to the nobility and held courtly ranks and titles. The authors of the next generation, particularly those who produced the "admonitory" histories (*ʿibratnāma*-s) of the early eighteenth century, stand at a greater remove from the centers of imperial power. Thus, expectedly elite authors such as Shakir Khan, a nobleman whose father had held important positions in the imperial household of the emperor Muhammad Shah, are now joined by more indistinct figures, many of whom remain anonymous to us. To some degree coevals of their contemporaneous "nouveau literate" writers of history in the Ottoman empire described by Dana Sajdi, such men hailed from the cities and small towns of north India and belonged to a striving service gentry of unstoried provenance.[36] Steeped in a common canon of classical prose and poetry in schoolhouses across the empire's cities and small towns, and combining in varying proportions the ideals of the "mastery of the pen" and the "mastery of the sword," they had prepared for a life of peripatetic service in the administrative establishments of the empire's elites.

In many instances, the collapse of their prospects in the bitter political turmoil of the 1710s stimulated the historicizing impulses of this middling gentry of precarious status. Among their numbers we might count figures like Mirza Muhammad, a highly educated scholar and scion of a formerly noble family fallen upon hard days, and his nephew, Mirza Muhammad Bakhsh "Ashob," an officer and poet who would produce memoirs of his days in Delhi for officials of the East India Company.[37] Of others, such as the scribes Kam Raj and Muhammad Qasim Lahori, we know little more than their names and the fact that they served the noblemen whose conduct they vociferously defended. Then came the pen-pushers of the bureaucracy, many of whom were Hindus of the Khatri and Kayastha castes, who wrote reams of poetry and fat chronicles in their evenings. Among their ranks fall the high administrator Anand Ram "Mukhlis," a noted intellectual who moved in Delhi's highest literary circles; and, far below him in prominence, the financial administrator Khwush Hal Chand, who produced a vast universal history of which only fragments survive.[38] Despite their very different places

[35] Kinra, *Writing Self, Writing Empire*.

[36] Sajdi, *The Barber of Damascus*.

[37] For a short autobiography of Ashob, see his "Sawānih-i ʿUmrī."

[38] Not to be confused with his more famous contemporary, the Rai Khwush Hal Chand. Irvine, "Two Proposed Corrections in the 'Catalogue of Persian MSS. in the British Museum' of Dr. C. Rieu."

in the social order, such men participated in what has been described as an "Indo-Persian 'republic of letters.'"[39] Indeed, the numbing sameness of their prose is tribute to the powerful homogeneity of the empire's intellectual culture, which integrated individuals across boundaries of ethnic, sectarian, or regional affiliation.[40] Common to this literary culture was an orientation toward the affairs of the imperial court and nobility, and, as a corollary, an active distaste and contempt for the category of the ruled.

It is therefore an unavoidable fact that the people who are the object of examination in this book are a figure constructed in the imagination of those intellectuals who were moved to consign their acts to paper. Given their implacable condescension for the vast majority of humanity, our relatively miniscule group of elite male authors used a narrow palette and a broad brush to outline the heterogeneity of the multitudes beneath them. It is only garbed in literary abstraction that the masses of the city were allowed entry into the stately pages of elite writing. In general, Mughal chroniclers resolutely refused to besmirch their pages with mention of ordinary folk, let alone their given names or recorded speech: for if the recognition of speech marks the assent to political participation, as Jacques Rancière has it, then it is surely significant that the people, however fleetingly they appear in the pages of the elite chronicles, do so almost always as an inarticulate collectivity, capable only of moaning in hunger or crying out in pain.[41] While I do not wish to suggest a binary opposition between mass and elite—for the great social variegation and dynamism will be readily apparent in the pages which follow—it must be emphasized that we can only glimpse this social reality by sensitivity to the terms by which elites saw their world.

Thus cloaked in silence and stripped of specificity, the people are only ever depicted in caricature, whether as "Hindu" or "Muslim," "pious" or "unbeliever," properly submissive or pridefully rebellious. Such terms, however, do not encompass social realities. They are an artifice of Mughal textuality, by which a rightfully agitating 'Community of Muslims' described on one page of a chronicle could mutate into a "ruffianly mob" overleaf, when, in the eyes of the author, it transgressed the codes of deference; or praise of a dear Hindu friend in one line might be succeeded by bitter polemics against "the infidels" in the next. Moreover, such tropes and rhetoric appear as freely used

[39] Alam and Subrahmanyam, "Eighteenth-Century Historiography," 411.
[40] Kia, "Adab as Literary Form and Social Conduct."
[41] Rancière, *Disagreement*, chap. 2.

by authors with Hindu names as those with Muslim ones: a testament, again, to the deeply intermingled milieu of the Mughal period—one that befuddled and infuriated colonial historians who could not understand why a Hindu scribe might dub an enemy co-religionist an "infidel."[42]

Such perplexities have continued to persist because few historians have seriously considered the implications of the challenges to the idea that "Hindu" and "Muslim" were fixed, exclusive and timeless communities that fully determined the behaviors of their members in accordance with religious texts and dogmas.[43] Given the craftiness of our Mughal writers, it would be folly indeed to confidently assume fixed identities for the people who flit through their pages, particularly given the fluid relationship of lowly groups to denominational communities of faith.

But, as this book will repeatedly argue, it is only in suspending the (always artificial) distinction between some sacral and transcendental realm of "religion" and the earthly and secular world of "politics" that we might begin to see *how* ordinary people conjured communities of faith and enacted gestures of belief in order to build solidarities and invoke higher powers in local struggles. To advocate this indistinction is not to give primacy to one category over the other: It is rather to show how features we now see as properly confined to the category of "religion" have historically also served as a *language* through which political struggles have been waged by the lowly.

Given the elite and literary nature of the surviving texts, discerning such popular actions poses a grave interpretive challenge. And yet, the very reluctance of elite chroniclers to record the doings of their inferiors offers an opportunity to the historian. The rare occasions on which Mughal observers were forced to record the doings of ordinary folk, despite their unseemliness, mark the forceful irruption of the people into the realm of elite historiography. Though the violence of such actions is invariably delimited and constrained by the artifice of the chroniclers' craft, behind the seductive rhythms of their prose it is still possible to hear a distant clamor from the streets. Given that those encompassed in the category of "the people" have left us almost no trace of themselves in their own words, even the most selective, vague, hostile, generic, brief, and contradictory statements on their

[42] Elliot and Dowson, *History of India*, I:xxi–xxii.

[43] For the sharpest statements of this point, see Cynthia Talbot, who has argued that "supra-local identities did exist in pre-colonial India and that these identities themselves were historically constructed and hence constantly in flux." Talbot, "Inscribing the Other, Inscribing the Self," 694; and Subrahmanyam, "Before the Leviathan"; see also the suggestive speculations in Smith, "Crystallization of Religious Communities."

doings offer a chance to reconstruct, howsoever imaginatively, the originary act of popular assertion that shook the observer enough to record it. Our objective therefore will be to inhabit the world posed by this elite literary tradition in its own terms, to unearth within it the fleeting traces of the people's actions, and to reconstruct from these fragments their practice of politics, given the varying perspectives of different commentators, and without presuming the fixity of identity implied by the language of their representations.

Limitations

The argument of this book operates under several limitations. For one, it is not my claim that the Mughal court inaugurated a totally new discourse of sovereignty, or that it witnessed an unprecedented appearance of politically active urbanites, or that the relation between sovereign power and the people was an invention of the Mughal empire.[44] Quite to the contrary: What was distinctive and novel about the period was perhaps merely borne of the intensification in scale of long-running economic and social processes already well evident in the preceding centuries. What this book will suggest, however, is that a historical conjuncture of the early modern period, combining characteristically Mughal visions of sovereignty with the stimuli of global trade and transregional migrations, inadvertently produced the conditions for the birth of an assertive urban public in its capital and elsewhere. Though it draws on evidence from several other cities, my focus on the new Mughal capital of Delhi, even to the exclusion of the surrounding countryside, similarly constrains the scope of the argument. As a result, my claim that the practices of Islam served as a language of popular politics is limited to the urban areas of North India directly under consideration in this work, although some will doubtless discern echoes in other times and places.

The model of urban popular politics in this book is proposed by a broad reading across a fragmented archive, which limits the perspective to the writings of a group of literate Hindu and Muslim intellectuals who were affiliated in some way with the imperial establishment. Their language, idioms,

[44] On the recognition of the dangers of disgruntled urbanites in ancient India, see Singh, *Political Violence in Ancient India*, 111, 121–22; violently rebellious urbanites are recorded from as far back as ancient Takshashila, in the third century BC, if not earlier. Marshall, *Taxila*, I:20–23.

and ideas refracted the high tradition of Persophone writing and the discourse of imperial sovereignty. I have sought to maintain a fidelity to the terms in which late-Mughal observers expressed themselves in order to glimpse their world through their own eyes, even if their language might sometimes strike us as numbingly ornate or gratingly harsh. But it is certain that very different perspectives on politics (particularly of those groups who are not described as Muslim) will come to light from sources in other languages, just as the particular histories of other cities, towns and regions may modify the picture that I present here.

It is also important to delimit the interpretation offered of the violent and agonistic struggles that are the object of this work. In an everyday sense, I consider those acts as political that invoked varying forms of community to exercise power in local struggles around questions of justice, and sought the involvement and support of the powers-that-be. But I do not suggest that the religious passions that periodically appear to have animated confrontations were merely the instruments of a cynical and calculating political logic. As we shall repeatedly see, symbolic acts of violence gained their hurtful power through a deep understanding of the sentiments of the other, and must be taken seriously as such.[45] If, however, the power of godly passion in forging solidarities and rousing acts of violence cannot be discredited, it is also impossible to speculate about the feelings and beliefs of long-dead individuals and groups, especially those who left no account of themselves. Instead of reproducing the unproductive dichotomy between "religion" and "politics," this work suggests that the beliefs, practices, and gestures that constituted Islam were fundamental to the way in which justice was popularly imagined and demanded from the sovereign power that claimed to be its guarantor. Though this work does not dispute the fact that statements of belief, faith, and worship are central to any definition of Islam, my primary interest lies in the *practices* by which belief and faith were evoked in the course of urban struggles. Similarly, I do not intend to suggest that the practices of Islam were the *only* possible language of a popular politics, though they are the focus of this work. What this book does hope to illustrate more generally, however, is that the politics of the people was intertwined with, and in relation to, the highest form of sovereign power on their horizon.

[45] My approach in this regard owes much to Amin, *Conquest and Community*.

Structure

A conventional way to frame this narrative would be to place it in the familiar arc of birth, growth, decay, and demise. Such neat histories of the empire inescapably deliver us to the larger question of what came after: colonialism and the Indian nation-state. But neither were a prospect on the mental horizons of those shoemakers who challenged Muhammad Shah's authority in 1729, or the masses who rose to defend him against overthrow ten years later. The popular politics we seek to recover are elusive, contradictory, and multiple. Given their tantalizingly brief mention in hostile accounts, we will always have more questions than answers about the motivations of those who caused the little everyday disturbances that roiled the city of the eighteenth century. Rather than attempt to (yet again) tame the obscurity, violence, suddenness, and contingency of the people's actions in a smooth chronological narrative, I have tried to preserve the complexity and the asynchronicity of the historical processes that produced the dual politics of the people.

The book proceeds broadly from the mid-seventeenth to the mid-eighteenth century, with chapters alternating between the close study of events and thematic analyses. The usual narrative of the period is one of imperial decline, which is seen as setting in with Aurangzeb's departure in 1680 to wage a fruitless war on the Deccan frontier for thirty years.[46] In memoirs and histories they dubbed "Books of Admonition," minor noblemen and service officials recorded the disorder of the years after Aurangzeb's fifty-year reign came to an end in 1707. His son Bahadur Shah won a war of succession but died suddenly in 1712. Jahandar Shah, the victor of the next war, barely reigned for a year before he was overthrown by his nephew Farrukh Siyar. Supporters of the new claimant to the throne papered over the unorthodoxy of this succession by claiming that Jahandar Shah was unfit to rule because of his obsession with the lowly singer Lal Kunwar. But Farrukh Siyar fared no better. His reign was marred by tension with the two noble brothers who led the clan of the Sayyids of Barha and had been instrumental in placing him on the throne. In 1719, these noblemen took the unprecedented step of deposing the unobliging ruler and replacing him with another prince. Both brothers would lose their lives for these actions in the next few years; and Muhammad Shah, who became king in 1719, could derive only vestigial authority from

[46] Richards, *Mughal Administration in Golconda.*

the famed Peacock Throne until Nadir Shah carted it too away with him to Iran in 1739.

These facts of high politics will serve only as the backdrop for our analysis of the evolving relation between sovereignty and popular politics in the period. To lay out in the starkest terms the heretofore-unrevealed potential of Delhi's urbanites for concerted action in extraordinary circumstances, this book begins with a moment of ending: Chapter 1 argues that Nadir Shah's conquest of Delhi in 1739 should be treated not as a moment decided on a battlefield but as a persistent state of relation between powerful if unequal forces. Seeing conquest as a *state of being* reveals that the primary opposition in the city lay not between natives and invaders, but between Iranian and Mughal elites and the common people of the city, who rose to protect their king.

What drove ordinary people to embark on such a forceful and dangerous course of action? To understand their motivations, Chapter 2 explores the relationship between the Mughal discourse of sovereignty, its staging in the new city of Shahjahanabad built in 1648, and its implied audience: the people. Indeed, the people were a product of Mughal sovereignty insofar as an unintended consequence of Shah Jahan's vision of the city as a center of commercial prosperity was the growth of a deeply stratified urban society with a teeming underclass. Chapter 3 describes the changing expression of sovereignty under his successor Aurangzeb, and his attempts to create an idealized 'Community of Muslims' submissive to his rule. At the same time, the forces of commerce fired the growth of an urban sphere in which popular criticism of the powers-that-be and their policies became increasingly audible, particularly through satirical poetry. Chapter 4 argues that Aurangzeb's efforts to discipline his variegated and fractious subjects by application of the law politicized them in unanticipated ways, stimulating them to challenge imperial authorities in terms of the king's expression of sovereignty.

The development of the practices of popular politics was catalyzed by events after Aurangzeb's death, in the 1710s. Two chapters consider these foundational moments in the making of this dual politics: Chapter 5 shows how the exceptional moment of the regicide of Farrukh Siyar in 1719, an elite attempt to wrest the substance of sovereignty from the king, provoked an uprising of the people, who would brook no such change: an event which foreshadowed the great uprising against Nadir Shah in 1739. Chapter 6, by contrast, shows how, in more everyday situations, the practices of Islam came to serve in the hands of ordinary people as a language with which to both invoke and challenge imperial authority, its key gesture forged in response to the emperor Bahadur Shah's theological innovations in 1711. Chapter 7 proves the potential of this everyday practice of popular politics through a detailed study of the shoemakers' riot of 1729. In the epilogue, I briefly discuss the fate of sovereignty and the practices of popular politics in the decades after Nadir Shah's departure from Delhi. No individuals have yet been found in the historical record to claim sovereignty on behalf of the people as the power of the Mughal scion waned to nothingness over the eighteenth century. But the practice of popular politics in relation to expressions of imperial sovereignty would remain of consequence under colonial rule and was most dramatically evidenced in the resurrection of Mughal kingship in the great uprising of 1857; And perhaps yet later still.

1

Anatomy of a Massacre

Nadir Shah in Delhi, 1739

In 1922, the historian Jadunath Sarkar delivered six lectures at Patna University on the Persian ruler Nadir Shah's invasion of the Mughal empire in 1739, his plunder of the capital Shahjahanabad, and the massacre of its inhabitants. His exposition of this obscure event would initially have seemed of little interest to an audience intent on a future in which the outline of a nation independent of British colonial rule was becoming discernible. But there was a contemporary charge to Sarkar's acrid critiques of Muhammad Shah (r. 1719–1748) and his squabbling courtiers, who succumbed to the invader with the barest resistance. As Gandhi's non-cooperation movement reached a crescendo in North India, Sarkar pointedly emphasized the internecine conflict that doomed the Indian side in 1739. Lack of solidarity within the empire's ruling class, in his view, allowed the invader to defeat the larger Mughal army without much loss of life; to occupy and loot Delhi; to remove and reappoint the hapless Muhammad Shah from the throne as he saw fit; and ultimately to depart Delhi with wagons creaking under its treasures. Sarkar thus implied the impossibility of any kind of nation emerging from the Mughal state, which he thought a cause for pessimism about the possibilities of mass anticolonial nationalism in India.[1]

Central to Sarkar's narrative was the terrible bloodbath of the "general massacre" that Nadir Shah inflicted on the city's people on the day after his entry into Delhi. The historian, however, had no sympathy for those killed. Following the contemporary Mughal observers on whom he based his account, he blamed the city's "idle talkers" and "mischief makers" for spreading a foolish rumor that excited the city's "hooligans and low people" to rise up against the invading army. Sarkar noted that the upper classes did not participate in the uprising. This was not a mark against them. In fact, he bemoaned their failure to restrain the urban rabble, which derived from the autocratic

[1] Chakrabarty, *The Calling of History*, 210–11.

The King and The People. Abhishek Kaicker, Oxford University Press (2020). © Oxford University Press.
DOI: 10.1093/oso/9780190070670.001.0001

nature of Mughal government that permitted no "opportunity of corporate action and municipal self-government" to a gentry otherwise divided by "caste, creed, race and profession."[2]

Though he was disavowed by later historians, Sarkar's views were enormously influential in shaping subsequent scholarship on the events of 1739. Following Sarkar, historians have paid scant attention to Nadir Shah's massacre in Delhi and even less to the preceding popular uprising. In the chapter on Nadir Shah in his classic treatment of late-Mughal politics, Satish Chandra dismisses the events of the occupation of the city with a single sentence: "The story of the subsequent massacre and exactions is only too well known."[3] Stephen Blake's otherwise detailed study of the city of Delhi during the period only notes that "when a disturbance arose over grain prices," many of Nadir Shah's men were killed.[4] Zaheeruddin Malik disregards the events as "mob violence" motivated by "hostile feeling against the foreigners."[5] Yet another simply fails to notice the uprising while dwelling briefly on the horrors of the massacre in his account of the "decline of Delhi."[6] Only recently, by demonstrating the viability of a new post-Mughal polity under Nadir Shah, Sanjay Subrahmanyam has offered a note of caution against the facile conclusion that the invasion represented some terminal decrepitude in South Asia.[7]

In the pages that follow, however, it will be our contention that the events of 1739 reveal not decline and death, but rather the vitality of late Mughal politics, in which the common people had emerged as an assertive and independent force. Through a close examination of the occupation's central moments of uprising and massacre, we will see that the most powerful and productive division was not between natives and foreigners but rather between those whom Mughal chroniclers described as the "high" (*khāss*) and the "low" (*'āmm*). The extraordinary moment of the occupation of Delhi can thus be seen to delineate two political formations in the city. The first is that of the traditional elite of the realm, who saw themselves as the natural and rightful arbiters of the destiny of the empire. But the events of 1739 also reveal that those expected to be docile subjects were now unafraid to express views on, and intervene in, the domain of political action that was

2 Sarkar, *Nadir Shah*, 62–63.
3 Chandra, *Parties and Politics at the Mughal Court, 1707–1740*, 290.
4 Blake, *Shahjahanabad*, 162.
5 Malik, *The Reign of Muhammad Shah, 1717–1748*, 166.
6 Umar, *Muslim Society*, 621–23.
7 Subrahmanyam, "Un Grand Dérangement."

formally restricted to elites. The existence of these two distinct formations is evidenced by their very varying responses to the conquest.

To perceive the existence of the people, however, we must rethink the conquest that has been seen as accomplished with the Iranian military victory on the battlefield of Karnal, on February 24, 1739. The outcome of the battle has been thought to reflect the superiority of a disciplined and cohesive Iranian force against an incompetent and enfeebled Mughal opponent. For Sarkar, and those who have followed him, Nadir Shah's conquest had an air of inevitability, because it revealed the Mughal empire, thought by the world to be "a strong man," to be nothing more than "a gorgeously dressed corpse."[8] But, as historians of warfare remind us, what the "rhetoric of battle history" conceals is that military engagements are in their nature contingent.[9] If Nadir Shah's victory represented the superiority of his artillery or tactics and the inferiority of Indian organization, then what might we say if a stray shell had killed him at the outset of the battle? Such a possibility was entirely present at the battlefield of Karnal. Recognizing that the battle could have gone in many different ways in turn requires us to reconsider the idea of conquest as a foreordained event that merely revealed inevitable realities.

In this light, Nadir Shah's conquest should not be seen as established on the battlefield of Karnal. Conquest was not a *moment* that carried the self-evident significance of the event (as it was for Sarkar and others) but as a *state*, a duration defined by a relation of power between the invader and the invaded that produced varying possibilities for all participants. This state of conquest was shaped, on the Mughal side, by a dynamic of elite acquiescence and popular resistance, which, as subsequent chapters will show, had long preceded Nadir Shah's arrival in the plains of North India. Well before the first shot had been fired at Karnal, and at every turn from there on, Mughal elites were keen to establish cooperative relations with the invading power. The terms and conditions of the occupation and the exaction of tribute were likewise made by Mughal elites in close conjunction with the victors. Meanwhile resistance to this joint complex of Iranian and Mughal elites came from the city's commoners. In this context, it is crucial to recognize the riot that shook the Iranian army on the first day of the occupation of Delhi was not a mindless but a motivated action of the people; likewise, the massacre of the next day

[8] Sarkar, *Nadir Shah*, 1
[9] Keegan, *The Face of Battle*.

was not an act of Iranians against Indians, but one of military power against popular resistance. The consequences of the massacre fell predominantly on the people, not the empire's elites. The fines and plunders that followed marked the hard limit of the possibility of Mughal and Iranian cooperation; but even here, as we will see, members of the Mughal elite influenced and shaped the very processes of exaction. From before the battle of Karnal to after Nadir Shah's departure from Delhi, Mughal elites modulated the state of the conquest by both extending and limiting its reach.

It would be easy to cast this vision of the conquest in terms of a foreign imperial elite collaborating with the invader and betraying their native Indian subjects. Nothing, however, could be further from the truth. Imperial elites were able to cooperate with the invading army because they were deeply connected through kinship and culture to their Iranian counterparts. But this was only one facet of their success. More importantly, what separated the Mughal elite from their subjects were their fundamentally distinct positions on the nature of Mughal sovereignty. By 1739, Mughal elites had become indifferent as to who sat on the peacock throne. By contrast, the occupation of the Red Fort by a scion of the Timurid dynasty was central to the conception of a just political order for the city's common folk.

Elite Responses to Nadir Shah's Victory

Among historians there is general consensus that Nadir Shah needed no invitation to invade India.[10] But it is striking that in the popular imagination of the eighteenth century, the invasion was seen as caused by the disloyalty of a fractious nobility to a hapless king. A late-eighteenth century commentator recalled Muhammad Shah's era as the one in which discord and treachery became widespread. Blame was laid at the king's doorstep for his sensual indulgences, which are described with relish: the emperor drew deeply from the "goblet of negligence," spending days in the company of dancers, singers, and reciters of the vernacular "mixed speech" (*naghma-gūyān wa rīkhta-gūyān*), and nights in bed with "moon-faced" beauties. Having donned "the crown of negligence," the king had no time to manage the provinces

[10] Lockhart, *Nadir Shah*, 124; Chandra, *Parties and Politics at the Mughal Court, 1707–1740*, 285; Malik, *The Reign of Muhammad Shah, 1717–1748*, 171; Mathee, "Nādir Shāh in Iranian Historiography: Warlord or National Hero?."

or respond to the oppressed who sought his justice. So the great nobleman Nizam al-Mulk (a "seasoned old wolf") invited Nadir Shah to conquer the realm.[11]

The lively language of these criticisms was not intended to convey historical fact. Accusations of sexual indulgence and negligence of justice, as we shall see in Chapter 5, were standard tropes that inverted the Mughal discourse of sovereignty. The idea that the king's most powerful minister had invited Nadir Shah to conquer the land, however, was very widely held. Two poems in the polyglot vernacular (*hindawī*), which are suggestive of the popular perceptions of the event across North India in the decades following the invasion, claim that Nizam al-Mulk became discontented when the king indiscreetly likened his visage and gait to that of a "black monkey."[12] Others, however, defended the actions of the nobility. An anonymous account, much circulated in the Deccan provinces where Nizam al-Mulk had been carving out his autonomous domain, deflected the blame on the king and his newly elevated (*nau-daulat*) courtiers.[13] Yet, by offering in way of analogy the tale of a cunning thief who saves the ruler from death at the hands of a brainless servant (which proved the adage that a wise enemy is better than a foolish friend), even such stout defenses tacitly acknowledged the minister's hostility toward his king.[14]

Endlessly recombining images of monkeys, thieves, and rulers, such stories were a means by which those far removed from the machinations of high politics made sense of them.[15] Colorful though they are, these tales nevertheless testify to a widespread understanding that the king had angered his nobleman, who spitefully invited an invader to come and ruin Delhi. They encapsulate a widespread understanding of the nature of elite politics in the early eighteenth century: the crown had been hollowed out, and the empire's elites no longer cared who ruled in Delhi.

Such popular convictions about the faithlessness of the empire's nobility were not without foundation. At the other end of the social spectrum,

[11] Daulat Ra'i, *Inshā-yi Daulat Rām [sic]*, 17–18.

[12] Irvine, "Nādir Shāh and Muhammād Shāh, a Hindi Poem by Tilok Dās," 48; Amar, "Hālāt-i Nādir Shāh," fols. 1b–2a.

[13] Anonymous, "Waqā'i'-yi Kharābī-yi Dihlī"; Anonymous, "Hādisa-yi Nādir Shāhī."

[14] Anonymous, "Waqā'i'-yi Kharābī-yi Dihlī," 19–22.

[15] Thus the story of the king of Kashmir, who is protected from his foolish friend, a monkey, by a wise thief, recorded in *The Asiatic Journal and Monthly Register for British and Foreign India, China, and Australia*, 272–74; that a wise enemy is to be preferred to a foolish friend is proverbial from the Arabic *Kalīlah wa Dimnah*, itself a refraction of the early Indic Panchatantra. Al-Kashifi, *The Anwár-i-Suhailí*, 139.

a sense of the attitude of the nobility can be derived from the voluminous reminiscences of the Mughal nobleman Shakir Khan, who had lived through the invasion as a young man. In them, he defends the conduct of his father Lutf Allah Khan, an important courtier who would be forced to retire in disgrace after Nadir Shah's invasion. Shakir Khan leaves us a remarkably detailed account of the events leading up to the clash with Nadir Shah at Karnal, near Delhi, in 1739. On the eve of battle, Lutf Allah Khan had been granted a small contingent of cavalry and charge of the province of Delhi, along with the responsibility of safeguarding the captive persons of royal blood (*salāṭīn*) and the imperial harem. He was also given charge of an envoy of Nadir Shah named Muhammad Khan Turkman, who had been detained in Delhi as the court prevaricated over a course of action. As Shakir Khan, his father, and the detained envoy proceeded to join the camp near Panipat before the battle, they all stopped to admire a garden built by Lutf Allah Khan's brother. In the privacy of the garden Lutf Allah Khan and the envoy had a delicate conversation. The envoy began by praising Shakir Khan's comeliness and beauty to his father. Lutf Allah Khan responded,

> If, like ʿAli, I had a hundred such sons for the emperor's purposes, I'd consider it the acme of happiness. And if the friends of our *daulat* (*auliyāʾ-yi daulat-i mā*) win, I would seek favor for you without being disloyal to my masters. But if heaven has decreed that our side loses, then your highness must remain steadfast in his previous commitments and keep this discussion under consideration [too].[16]

Sighing mournfully, the envoy declared his own inability to intercede with Nadir Shah. Though Shakir Khan vehemently denied the conversation progressed beyond these pleasantries, rumors of his family's disloyalty immediately reached the already despondent Mughal court.

What was the standard of loyalty in such circumstances? Shakir Khan seems to have thought there was nothing dishonorable about planning for the worst contingency by privately hedging one's bets on the eve of battle. This was not a view shared by other Mughal noblemen, for when Shakir Khan arrived at court, explanations were demanded of him. At about the same time, his father reprimanded (for his disloyalty) a former Mughal

[16] Khan, "Hadīqa," fols. 142b–143a.

official who had crossed over to Nadir Shah and now appeared as the invader's emissary.[17] Yet after Nadir Shah's departure, Shakir Khan's father would fall from grace: he was accused of giving custody of the entire body of royal descendants (*salātīn*) to the invader, despite explicit instructions to the contrary, thus enabling him to end the dynasty at a stroke if he so desired.[18]

Nadir Shah's defeat of the Mughal army at Karnal exposed the fragility of the ideal of noble loyalty in the eighteenth century, which is further evident in Shakir Khan's doings in the immediate aftermath of the battle. Though Lutf Allah Khan had tearfully importuned his son to accompany him to Delhi before the battle, Shakir Khan had elected to stay at court. But the young nobleman did not participate in the Mughal army's disastrous sally on the day of battle, and returned to his tent at dusk, apparently without having unsheathed his sword. As Shakir Khan threw himself on a humble meal of kababs, braised meat (*roghan josh*), and rice-and-lentil stew (*khicharī biryān*), his elder brother burst agitatedly into the tent with news that the king would retreat to the Deccan, while the army would launch a night assault. Though urged by his brother to leave immediately for their nearby estates in Panipat, Shakir Khan still insisted on remaining by the king's side.[19] The terrible spectacle he beheld as he emerged from the tent to wash his hands changed his mind. None of his troop (*misl*) remained in sight. Most had run away into the biting cold, abandoning meals half-eaten and tents still standing. The great noblemen's contingents were fleeing toward Delhi in complete disarray. It was as if a voice resounded from the heavens, proclaiming the Qur'anic verse "All that lives on earth or in the heavens is bound to pass away: but forever will abide thy Sustainer's self, full of majesty and glory."[20]

Now that the *daulat* of the dynasty, preserved for three hundred years, seemed ruined in the blink of an eye, Shakir Khan abandoned the imperial cause. Taking charge of several thousand dispirited soldiers, he and his brother marched painfully through the night to their hometown of Panipat. Yet his memory of the next day was not of the shock of defeat or preparations of resistance, but rather the basket of confections and fruits he received, with a letter, from a lady-friend (*marghūba*).[21] Despite the valorization of loyalty

[17] The official for his part plaintively responded that the task had been forced upon him on pain of death. Khan, "Hadīqa," fol. 143a.

[18] Kishor, "Rūydād-i Nādir Shāh," 2; for imperial instructions to safeguard the princes, see Khan, "Hadīqa," fol. 151b.

[19] Khan, "Hadīqa," fol. 147a.

[20] Qur'an 55:26–27; Khan, "Hadīqa," fol. 147a.

[21] "From these happy tidings," he recalled, "I expanded in myself so that the garments on my body became tight." Khan, "Hadīqa," fols. 146b–148b.

to the emperor, the prospect of dynastic collapse moved Shakir Khan not into an act of tragic defiance but to a retreat to the homeland, where the nobility to which he belonged occupied a dominant position. His actions typify the pragmatism that tempered the influence of imperial ideology on the nobility by the early eighteenth century, and explains their attitude during the subsequent occupation of the city.

The autonomy of the nobility and their indifference to who sat on the Peacock Throne in Delhi is emblemized by Raja Jugal Kishor, a high-ranking financial administrator and representative (*wakīl*) of the governor of Bengal Shujaʿ al-Din at the imperial court.[22] Obscure though his family's origins may have been, by 1739 Jugal Kishor was established in a vast mansion near the main square of the Moonlight Avenue, near an alley that still bears his name.[23] Jugal Kishor described his own considerable role in the wheelings and dealings in Delhi after the massacre in a letter to his patron in Bengal written shortly thereafter. Like others, Jugal Kishor suggests that Nadir Shah was originally content to turn back from the battlefield of Karnal with a war indemnity of 30 million rupees. But jealousies within the Mughal court led Burhan al-Mulk, the governor of Awadh, to offer the invader a huge tribute and to invite him to Delhi with promises of even more.[24]

Though his sources of information are unclear, Jugal Kishor represented the situation as one in which high noblemen such as Burhan al-Mulk were actively clearing the ground for the establishment of a new dynasty. Far from criticizing such behavior as disloyal or unworthy, Jugal Kishor described to his own employer how he had immediately established a relationship with Nadir Shah's chamberlain by presenting him with a gift of shawls and fine cloth worth 20,000 rupees, besides 1,000 rupees in cash. Jugal Kishor realized that such behavior might be construed as disloyal. But he justified it by claiming that he "sacrificed his honor in the service of faithfulness" in order to secure the "eastern domains" of Bengal from Nadir Shah's depredations.[25]

The immediate cooperativeness of Delhi's nobility was born of a distinct disinterest in who might occupy the throne in Delhi. It betokened their

[22] Raja Jugal Kishore's financial dealings and disbursements are evidenced in the administrative documents held at the Uttar Pradesh Regional Archives, Allahabad; see documents no. 2159, 2179, 2226.

[23] Jugal Kishor is first reported being presented at court at the beginning of Muhammad Shah's reign, in 1721. Lakhnavi, *Shāhnāma*, 134; He appears to have inherited the position of the agent of the governor of Bengal at court on his father's death in 1736. See Alam, *Crisis of Empire*, 172.

[24] Kishor, "Rūydād-i Nādir Shāh," 1–2.

[25] Kishor, "Rūydād-i Nādir Shāh," 2.

confidence in the stability and solidity of their local sources of power, which sprang from two sources. One was the nobility's recently acquired ability to receive and maintain land grants in their own areas of origin and putting down local roots—the prevention of which had been a long-standing principle of imperial administration.[26] The second was the recent experience of the years after the emperor Aurangzeb's death in 1707: Though kings had risen and fallen in dizzying succession, there had been no large-scale reallocation of land grants within the ranks of the nobility.

At the same time, in 1739, the actual control of this imperial nobility over the region's populace was tenuous. Local communities of settled peasants, herdsmen, and itinerant peoples exhibited scant regard for Delhi's authority. Jats, Gujars, Minas, Meos, and Mewatis, long held in contempt by Delhi's elites, maintained a perennially antagonistic relationship with Mughal authority. The primary manifestation of this opposition involved the plundering of travelers on the imperial highways and the raiding of settlements. Despite the application of spectacular violence, imperial agents seemed unable to staunch the stream of outrages that were regularly reported at court in Delhi in the previous decades. Predictably, such groups sprang into action as Nadir Shah's army marched into the plains. Shakir Khan described how his retreating party of soldiers repeatedly encountered raiders mounting ambushes and ranging across the countryside to pillage those who were fleeing.[27] Again, these freebooters did not come from elsewhere; they were simply the region's populace, equipped with arms and horses and led by the local landholders (*zamīndār*-s) who opportunistically turned to plunder when Delhi's agents were unable to exert control.[28] Their behavior reveals the generalized resistance of caste and clan groups who were only partially incorporated into the Mughal system of governance, and maintained their own forms of distributed social organization.[29]

That the region's barely contained refractory peoples aroused a greater fear in the nobility than the invading army can be sensed in the writings of Anand Ram "Mukhlis" (d. 1751), a high-ranking official in the vizier's establishment.

[26] This manifested in the early-eighteenth-century innovation of the "homeland grants" (*jāgīr-i mahal-i watan*) discussed in Alam, *Crisis of Empire*, 124–33. It is not a coincidence that Shakir's Khan's family grants were clustered in and around his hometown of Panipat.

[27] Khan, "Hadīqa," fols. 147a–148a.

[28] Habib, "Forms of Class Struggle in Mughal India"; the proliferation of gunpowder weapons in the countryside enabled local notables and their retainers to increasingly challenge central authorities in the eighteenth century. Khan, "Muskets in the Mawas: Instruments of Peasant Resistance."

[29] Mayaram, *Against History, Against State*, 59–64, 100–125; Bhardwaj, *Contestations and Accommodations*.

Like his other contemporaries, Anand Ram did not let his bureaucratic duties interfere overly with the epicurean lifestyle of his rarified set of noble bon vivants and intellectuals. He is exceptional, however, for his voluminous and intimately detailed memoirs, which serve as an elegant and lively record of his everyday pleasures in literature and poetry, conversation and conviviality, over the 1730s and 1740s. But in relating the events of 1739, Anand Ram's otherwise carefree tone became grave. He described how he took measures to secure his neighborhood of Wakilpura even before the battle had taken place, by setting up checkposts in its alleys, hiring extra gunners, and dispatching his women and children to an alternate residence.[30] The fear here was not of the invading army but the city's people; and even after Nadir Shah's victory, Anand Ram was more worried by Delhi's "seditious folk" (*fitna-ārāyān-i shahr*), who might combine with peri-urban malcontents (*hangāma-pīrāyān-i qarb o jawār*) to loot the city. Only the constant exertions of the chief of police Faulad ("The Iron") Khan preserved Delhi from plunder.[31] The imperial commander of the guard (*darogha-yi chaukī*) also set his Mewati cavalry to nightly patrolling the markets, and personally inspected troubled areas on some evenings. Since it was no longer possible to safely leave the city, Anand Ram redoubled his efforts to secure his neighborhood. He restored a degree of confidence among his neighbors by procuring and distributing lead, gunpowder, and rockets among them, while continuing to spend his days in idle chatter and poetry (*gap o sha'r*) with friends, and his nights in vigilance.[32]

Coffee and the State of Conquest

The circumstances that greeted elites like Shakir Khan and Anand Ram were bewildering, for Nadir Shah's conquest was unusual by any standards. In defeating the Mughal army and occupying Delhi, he proclaimed his absolute dominion over the land. Yet, from the very beginning, Nadir Shah received the advice of the highest Mughal noblemen Burhan al-Mulk (who was captured or defected on the battlefield) and Nizam al-Mulk (who visited him to make terms). We do not know what counsel these noblemen offered, or

[30] Mukhlis, "Waqā'i'," 38–39.
[31] Mukhlis, "Waqā'i'," 39; another contemporary also praised the chief of police for his patrimonial care of the populace and his efforts to protect them from the depredations of the mob. Khwush Hal, "Nādir al-Zamānī [B]," fol. 196a.
[32] Mukhlis, "Waqā'i'," 39–41.

how they might have influenced Nadir Shah's plans. But instead of ending the Mughal dynasty, Nadir Shah evinced a notable keenness to preserve the prevailing imperial order. The conqueror's declarations of victory were balanced by protestations of his desire to restore the Mughal empire to even keel, evidenced in the careful respect with which he treated the defeated Mughal ruler Muhammad Shah. Such seemingly contradictory responses were undoubtedly shaped by the realities of the situation, in which the putative victor faced a defeated but potent enemy in a hostile landscape.

What would thus emerge in the aftermath of the battle of Karnal was a *state* of conquest: a relation of power that balanced the interests of the Mughal elite against that of Nadir Shah. On the one hand, members of the Mughal nobility were happy to cooperate with the invader if it preserved or advanced their interests, individually or collectively. On the other hand, Nadir Shah required the cooperation of the conquered elite to secure the tribute he desired while not becoming entangled in the complexities of this fractious realm.

The inauguration of the state of conquest is marked in Mughal accounts by the first meeting between Muhammad Shah and Nadir Shah. A recurring motif in descriptions of this encounter is in the dilemmas of hospitality, for instance, in the serving of coffee. When coffee is served, who should be the first to receive it, and what relationship is thereby implied?[33] Some believed that Nadir Shah was first offered the drink, but declared his subordinate status by serving it to the defeated Mughal emperor with his own hands.[34] In Shakir Khan's rendition, Nadir Shah presented himself as a supplicant, expressing distress at unanswered requests for aid against the "accursed Afghans," which had led to "regrettable errors unworthy of exalted rulers." In this vein, Nadir Shah declared:

> Blessed be the *daulat* of rule (*daulat-i sultanat*) on the Sublime Presence (*ʿĀlī Hazrat*), for its robe of honor suits the garments of your [Timurid] family. I am merely the law-enforcer (*yasāwal*) of this throne, and am at your service to punish whoever opposes the orders of the Sublime Presence.

Nadir Shah went on to pass his hookah to Muhammad Shah "by his own hands," and instructed his nobility to refer to Muhammad Shah by no title

[33] This was not a question without significance in the Iranian case. On the importance of coffee in Safavid courtly culture, see Matthee, "Coffee in Safavid Iran," particularly 18–19.

[34] ʿAbd al-Karim, *Bayān-i Wāqiʿ*, 33.

other than "the Sublime Presence, for I am his younger brother." In light of future events, for Shakir Khan such words only indexed Nadir Shah's deviousness and cunning.[35]

For the financial administrator Khwush Hal Chand, who produced a mammoth chronicle of the reign, however, the story of coffee was used to meditate on the problem of loyalty. To whom should the Indian nobleman first serve coffee? Would it not be a violation of the "protocols of loyalty" (*haqq-i namak*) if it were not served first to one's own ruler? But to snub Nadir Shah in this way would surely excite his wrath and result in immediate death. In this version, the perplexed nobleman brilliantly resolved his quandary by taking the coffee cup to Muhammad Shah, and then asked him to present it "with his own hands" to Nadir Shah.[36] The Mughal nobility, here, were seen as successfully reconciling the requirements of long-standing loyalty under circumstances of conquest.

However apocryphal they may be, stories of the coffee ritual are significant. They indicate a resolution to the crisis of conquest, the reassertion of the protocols of civilized relation over naked violence, and the foreclosing of the possibility of Mughal collapse. Both absolute powers find a balance (however unequal) through the ritual, which in its controlled politeness is the precise opposite of courtly insult that so often prefigures historical bloodlettings in the Indian subcontinent.[37] Henceforth the language of interaction between the conqueror and the conquered would be that of hosting and visiting, gifting and entertaining. The delicate navigation of the coffee ritual is thus symbolic of the establishment of the peculiar state of conquest, in which Nadir Shah would first claim sovereignty over the realm and then restore the previous order.

In considering such stories of the conquest from both sides, Ernest Tucker notes that "each writer uses idealized visions of elements of the other empire to criticize his own," and concludes, rightly, that this indicated "a growing self-critical awareness in eighteenth-century Indo-Persian historiography."[38] But the successful resolution of the coffee dilemma also reflects the fact the encounter on the battlefield of Karnal was one of not simply commensurate polities. In fact, they were interwoven. Not only did conqueror and conquered speak the same language and abide by the same cultural codes; in

[35] Khan, "Hadīqa," fol. 150b.
[36] Khwush Hal, "Nādir al-Zamānī [B]," fol. 216a.
[37] Subrahmanyam, *Courtly Encounters*, chap. 1, "Courtly Insults."
[38] Tucker, "1739," 217.

many instances they were related by affiliations of ethnicity, clan, and homeland, as in the case of the high Mughal nobleman Danishmand Khan, whose brother arrived with Nadir Shah as his chief jurist (*mullā-bāshī*).[39] A less dramatic but more instructive case is that of the powerful Mughal provincial governor Burhan al-Mulk, who had capitulated with suspicious ease to Nadir Shah's famed Qizilbash troops on the battlefield of Karnal. Burhan al-Mulk was himself born of a Qizilbash mother in Nishapur in Iran sometime around 1680. He immigrated to the Mughal realm at the comparatively advanced age of twenty-seven and rose rapidly from his obscure beginnings in the imperial service during the turmoil of the 1710s. Immigrant noblemen like Burhan al-Mulk continued to keep close ties with family members in their places of origin. Burhan al-Mulk invited his nephew from Nishapur to India in 1724 and married his eldest daughter to him. This nephew, later known as Safdar Jang, would in turn go on to succeed Burhan al-Mulk as governor of Awadh and serve as an important player in the imperial politics of the mid-eighteenth century.[40]

Burhan al-Mulk and many others in the Mughal nobility of the early eighteenth century thus belonged to an imperial elite with links spanning the Mughal, Iranian, and central Asian realms. These horizontal connections between victor and vanquished would play a crucial role in mediating the processes of conquest, occupation, and exaction. Ties of shared language, culture, and kinship enabled the seamless fusing of the Mughal and Iranian administrative establishments, and the smooth transfer of power to Nadir Shah also signified by stories of the coffee ritual. As the figure of the nobleman bearing a cup of coffee suggests, the Mughal elite naturally assigned themselves a central role in shaping the state of conquest, seeking to both extend its reach and modulate its violence to fit their own interests. Their self-conception as the arbiters of power is perfectly expressed in Shakir Khan's account of Burhan al-Mulk's initial conversation with Nadir Shah. Burhan al-Mulk urged Nadir Shah to extract a tribute from India. But he also complained showily of his millions spent and decades wasted in "smiting" (*shamshīr-zanī*), which had failed to quell the unending sedition of Jats, Rajputs, Bundelas, Chandelas, and Sikhs across the vast and disordered realm of India. Thus, even as he congratulated Nadir Shah on his historic conquest, Burhan al-Mulk's veiled threats of perpetual resistance declared India to be barren ground for a new

[39] Fraser, *History of Nadir Shah*, 204.
[40] Srivastava, *The First Two Nawabs*, 87–89.

dynasty. The thankless task of subduing India's refractory peoples must only fall on noblemen such as Burhan al-Mulk himself.[41]

No doubt seeing the wisdom in such advice, even as Nadir Shah set about establishing his rule, he signaled that the reign of the Timurid dynasty was not at an end, but merely in abeyance. When, on March 7, 1739, Nadir Shah took Muhammad Shah prisoner, he was treated with every courtesy.[42] On March 11, Nadir's chief general Tahmasp Khan Jalayir and Burhan al-Mulk jointly entered Delhi with their armies, proclaiming peace to the beating of drums. The Iranian and the Mughal grandees proceeded to the city's congregational mosque, to which judges, jurisprudents, and other notables of the Muslim community had been summoned with due respect and honor. The sermonizer (*khatīb*) ascended the pulpit (*mimbar*) and recited the proclamation in adherence with conventional Sunnism, enjoining prayer for the four rightly guided caliphs and then for Nadir Shah, thus confirming his rule to the assembled populace in the customary manner.[43] On March 18, Muhammad Shah returned to Delhi, albeit without his ceremonial music and insignia.[44] Two days later, on March 20, Nadir Shah entered the Red Fort in Delhi, and ordered coins be struck in his name bearing the verse:

> He is ruler above the rulers of the world
> King of Kings, Nadir, Lord of the Conjunction[45]

The performance of these key symbolic acts, observed a chronicler, made it clear that Nadir Shah had conquered Hindustan, and no one had the capacity to resist him.[46] Yet Nadir Shah's dual intentions of both securing his paramountcy and not altering the Mughal order are revealed in these very coins. Despite bearing the conqueror's name, such coins were produced in the same weight and measure as the Mughal imperial rupee. In fact, the new monetary system that Nadir Shah instituted after his return from India was designed to integrate with the prevailing imperial system and adopted its weights, measures, denominations, and terminology.[47] Such efforts indicate that Nadir Shah had neither the intention nor perhaps the imagination to found

[41] Khan, "Hadīqa," fol. 149b.
[42] Lockhart, *Nadir Shah*, 143.
[43] Ashob, "Tārīkh-i Shahādat [A]," fol. 260a; Ashob, "Tārīkh-i Shahādat [B]," fol. 243b.
[44] Anonymous, "Delhi Chronicle," 4.
[45] Ashob, "Tārīkh-i Shahādat [A]," fol. 262a.
[46] Ashob, "Tārīkh-i Shahādat [A]," fol. 262a.
[47] Matthee and Floor, *The Monetary History of Iran*, 150–67.

a new dynasty in South Asia. His primary objectives were limited only to "establish[ing] a broad political framework that could tie him, more closely than his Safavid predecessors, to both Ottomans and Mughals."[48]

In minimizing his disruptions to the established Mughal order, Nadir Shah also aimed to curtail the resistance that Burhan al-Mulk had attributed to India's troublesome peoples. Great precautions were accordingly taken to avoid any provocation to Delhi's folk. The historian Warid claimed that the combined Indian-Iranian force was first stationed outside Delhi's walls, and members of the invading army were thwarted in three attempts during the night to raid the city. According to an account recorded by James Fraser, Nadir Shah himself did not enter the city in the night "having heard that the People of the City were of a seditious and turbulent temper."[49] When they did enter, the Iranians were sequestered in the large mansions of the nobility. Those few soldiers who attempted crimes against the city's residents were severely and publicly punished: Warid reported that "two or three hat-wearers [Iranians] had their bellies slit open and were hanged in front of the police station" soon after the army's entry.[50] Fraser noted that Nadir enjoined his military police (*nasaqchī*-s) "to spare no Punishments, such as cutting off Ears and Noses, and bambooing to Death, whoever molested the *Indians*."[51] Such harsh discipline was apparently maintained even after the massacre in Delhi: Warid noted that "from time to time" "twenty or thirty" of the hat-wearers had their bellies split open or were hanged in public.[52]

The Popular Uprising against Nadir Shah

Though well-founded, such precautions proved to be woefully insufficient. Where the Mughal nobility had quickly acquiesced to Nadir Shah's rule, the attitude of the common people of the city was one of marked opposition. All were unanimous in blaming the origins of the violence of March 21 on Delhi's inhabitants. It is significant that both the festival of Eid and Holi fell at about this time: Mughal observers expected popular violence on intercalendrical conjunctions such as this.[53] The violence apparently

[48] Tucker, "Nāder Shah."

[49] Fraser, *History of Nadir Shah*, 178. For a detailed account of Fraser's life and scholarship, see Subrahmanyam, *Europe's India*, chap. 3.

[50] Warid, *Tārīkh-i Nādirshāhī*, 188–89.

[51] Fraser, *History of Nadir Shah*, 179.

[52] Warid, *Tārīkh-i Nādirshāhī*, 220–21.

[53] Anonymous, "Delhi Chronicle," 4.

began just outside the city's Southwestern Ajmer Gate in the King's Quarter (*shāhganj*), a provisioning market which already had a reputation for fractious folk.[54] Fraser reported that Nadir's chief lieutenant had sent nine mounted military policemen (*nasaqchī*-s) to raid the granaries there so as to reduce the price of grain, which tended to shoot up at moments of political uncertainty. Displeased by these severities, the grain-traders "towards the Evening . . . assembled the Mob, and a great many disaffected People joining them, they killed the abovesaid *Nissikhchis* [*nasaqchī*-s] with several *Kuzzlebash* [*qizilbāsh*], who had come over to buy corn."[55] Another recalled Nadir's soldiers going to buy grain in the King's Quarter, but "paying less than the price and taking by force."[56] In his letter to his master in Bengal, Jugal Kishor attributed the outbreak of violence to the sudden withdrawal of the Iranian army from the market by Nadir's military police "on the basis of a request" (*hasb al-ʿarz*), indicating that the court was already apprehensive about the occupiers mingling with an armed and resentful populace.[57]

The late-eighteenth-century memoiristic history by Mirza Muhammad Bakhsh Ashob, the minor scion of a great family, offers some insight into the violence unleashed against the occupying army on that night. Ashob had returned from the battlefield of Karnal to his family mansion by the city's Northwestern Kabul Gate, at the edge of the city canal's northern branch. Nearby stood the newly constructed palatial complex of Burhan al-Mulk, with its several floors of shops, chambers, and a vast caravanserai capable of housing 10,000 horsemen. Having led Nadir Shah to Delhi, Burhan al-Mulk had died on the preceding day, either of cancer, or, as some whispered, by his own hand in remorse for his disloyalty.[58]

It was the evening of Eid. Ashob had just sat down to enjoy the feast of the sacrifice, eager for the steaming meat and rice after the deprivations of the campaign. As he waited for his meal to cool, he heard a strange, loud noise in the alley outside. At first, he thought it was merely the comings and goings of Burhan al-Mulk's rowdy soldiers. But the clamor became louder, and cries of "Grab ahold! Strike! Kill!," were followed by the clangor of metal and the crack of gunshots. A voice cried out piteously: "O Muslims, I am a stranger and a traveler and a Sunni and a follower of the four caliphs (*chahār yār*). For

[54] Das, "Chahār Gulzār-i Shujāʿī," fol. 91a
[55] Fraser, *History of Nadir Shah*, 181;
[56] Khwush Hal, "Nādir al-Zamānī [B]," fol. 197a.
[57] Kishor, "Rūydād-i Nādir Shāh," 3.
[58] Ashob, "Tārīkh-i Shahādat [A]," fols. 263b–264a.

the sake of God and his prophet, have mercy on me, and let me return to the company of Fath ʿAli Khan Sistani, which is stationed in this neighborhood!" Running up to his rooftop, Ashob saw a solitary Iranian soldier running for his life from the direction of the Kabul Gate. The man was quickly surrounded by a swarm of people. They appeared to be Burhan al-Mulk's soldiers, "generally from among the lowly folk of Kabul and Peshawar." Paying no attention to his implorations of shared faith, the men in the street fell upon the Iranian in revenge (thought Ashob) for their comrades slain in the battle of Karnal. The Iranian was cut to pieces in an instant, and a man quickly stripped him of his money-belt, dividing its contents among his friends. His corpse, naked and bloody, hands and feet severed from the torso, lay in the mud and filth of the alley, while the group squatted in wait for further prey. Ashob began to curse and harangue these men: didn't they realize that there would be a price to pay for the unjust (*nā-haqq*) killing of this man? Weren't they afraid that Nadir would order a retributive massacre, and the city would be plundered? But they paid him no heed, and just at this moment another fleeing Iranian appeared and was likewise cut down in the twinkling of an eye. The same fate befell two more men, and all four corpses remained lying about the alley in front of Ashob's door.[59]

A wide gulf separated the world of someone like Ashob from the men who crouched in the shadows and struck down the soldiers of the occupying army. Ashob came from a family, which, if no longer regarded as particularly influential, had nonetheless been ennobled by generations of imperial service. His values were the precise opposite of those he ascribed to the nameless, vulgar (*arāzil*) murderers, who were "refractory" (*shora-pusht*), "tyrannical by temperament," (*zālim tabʿīat*), and "tormenting of strangers" (*gharīb āzār*).[60] Yet Ashob's account makes it clear that the disaffected soldiers he criticized for their lawlessness were also seeking revenge for their defeated comrades. Their attitudes toward the occupying army were far from the gentlemanly acquiescence with which Ashob and others of his class regarded the occupation.

Ashob's experience of such retributive violence was limited to his alley, but Mughal observers were shocked (if not surprised) by its extent and intensity. To one, it seemed that "one became two, and two became four."[61]

[59] Ashob, "Tārīkh-i Shahādat [A]," fols. 264a–265a.
[60] Ashob, "Tārīkh-i Shahādat [A]," fol. 264b; Ashob, "Tārīkh-i Shahādat [B]," fol. 247a.
[61] Khwush Hal, "Nādir al-Zamānī [B]," 197b.

For another, even though the events fit the sadly routine pattern of an "uprising of the villainous ruffians of Hindustan" (*balwā'ī-yi aubāsh-i bad ma'āsh-i Hindūstān*), he was still awed by its ferocity, which left the startled Iranians "powerless even to take a breath."[62] Yet another noted that the darkness of the night, the twisting, unfamiliar alleys, and the rage of the people all contributed to the terror of the occupying army.[63] The poet Gulshan, a lowly retainer of an uncle of Shakir Khan, described how "barbarous and wicked" commoners, particularly young beggars (*luccha-hā-yi gadā*), lurked in these alleys and killed about five hundred of the occupying army.[64] Like "a body without a head or an arrow without a bow," the paralyzed Iranians were everywhere "beheaded by the Indians' unrelenting swords."[65]

Nor was the violence confined to the dark alleys and obscure corners of the city. Fraser described "all the idle Vagabond and disaffected People" who joined into a mob "from all quarters, with what arms they could most readily find, [and] poured like a torrent towards the Castle." Some of Nadir Shah's troops posted by the fort fled toward the sandbank on the river, where they met their end. Cannons and muskets were shot all night from the castle and the mansions in which the Iranians were garrisoned to keep the crowds at bay; but "all this Time they were increasing, and became more and more furious."[66] Another remembered how the volleys fired all night long by the five or six thousand Iranians at the foot of the fort would not deter the raging crowds until dawn.[67]

Accounts such as these had provided the evidence for Jadunath Sarkar's contention that "the higher classes and all good men held aloof" from the violence of the riot.[68] Though Sarkar was not wholly correct in this assessment (as we shall see), belief in the unfitness of the people for autonomous action was the cornerstone of Mughal administrative thought. There existed no terms for the masses that did not connote something pejorative. At their best and most fitting, the common people were only a part of God's creation (*khalq-i Allāh*), supine objects of rule like the birds and the beasts. This attitude is evident in the commentary of the historian Warid on the rabble that attacked Nadir Shah's soldiers, in which he sharply delineated the domain of

62 Warid, *Tārīkh-i Nādirshāhī*, 202.
63 Mukhlis, "Waqā'i'," 45.
64 Jaunpuri, "Sūrat-i Hāl," fol. 32a; on his service of Sher Afkan Khan, see ff. 11b-12a.
65 Warid, *Tārīkh-i Nādirshāhī*, 197–98; Khwush Hal, "Nādir al-Zamānī [B]," fol. 197b.
66 Fraser, *History of Nadir Shah*, 181–82.
67 Warid, *Tārīkh-i Nādirshāhī*, 202.
68 Sarkar, *Nadir Shah*, 63.

elites from the popular. He claimed that no member of the Indian nobility was aware of the doings of the people during the riot, who acted completely autonomously, "without the approval or consultation of even a single nobleman." Therefore, "not even a single" wellborn Indian had any part in the uprising, which was the product of "pedestrians" (*rajāla*) and "the common mob" (*aubāsh*). In so disclaiming the uprising, Warid recognized it as something outside the normal order of things, as a spontaneous act of the people. But it derived from their characteristic short-sightedness: "[R]emaining negligent of the end of the affair, they focused only on its beginning." Warid was moved to compose a poem on the theme of the foolishness of the weak assaulting the mighty ("How can a mosquito equal an elephant? / How can a gutter match the Nile?"). He elaborated: the wise, the experienced, the elders had said that "one should extend one's foot according to the quality of one's carpet." Only he who adhered to this maxim could be considered a human, while those who lived violation of this precept—such as the mob of Delhi, for example—"lie outside the circle of humanity."[69]

The Role of Rumor

In portraying it as an inhuman act driven by greed, short-sightedness, and barbarity from which all men worth mentioning abstained, elite observers sought to strip the riot of any political significance. And yet it is possible to discern the traces of the people's motivation within these very narratives, for rumors, here as elsewhere, symptomize the activation of popular politics.[70] In this instance, they reveal the presence of a popular perspective on Mughal kingship that is quite at odds with that of the Mughal nobility. Consider the importance ascribed by all observers to "false rumor" (*afwāh-i kāziba*) in firing the people's fury.[71] No one, however, was quite sure as to what the rumor was.

A critic of Burhan al-Mulk thought the people began to riot on seeing his bier.[72] Jugal Kishor reported that when the Iranian military police came to effect the withdrawal of the army, some "ill-fortuned provocateurs" (*badbakhtān-i wāqiʿa-talb*) began to spread a falsehood that someone had

69 Warid, *Tārīkh-i Nādirshāhī*, 192, 198, 199.
70 See for instance Shagan, "Rumours and Popular Politics in the Reign of Henry VIII."
71 Warid, *Tārīkh-i Nādirshāhī*, 199.
72 Anonymous, "Risāla-yi Muhammad Shāh," fol. 131b.

shot Nadir Shah in the Red Fort and "seated" Muhammad Shah on the throne.[73] This portrayal of the king as an inanimate object to removed and placed at will itself says much about the place of the ruler in the imagination of a high-ranking Mughal courtier of the period. Bitterly castigating rumormongers of "womanly temperament" (*zan tabaʿān*) who "loudly proclaimed" falsehoods, another was nevertheless compelled to list all their words: Nadir had been given poison in his food, or slipped a poisoned electuary by the imperial doctor; or that he had fallen deathly ill, or been stabbed by a servant.[74] Yet others heard that Nadir Shah had been wounded in the eye or killed by a member of the emperor's elite personal bodyguard, staffed by Central Asian Qalmaq women, or even killed by the emperor himself.[75]

How are we to interpret these rumors? In his treatment of the forms of "transmission" which undergirded peasant insurgency in colonial India, Ranajit Guha noted the predominance of sacred idioms in rumors and the apotheosis of insurgent leaders. Through such rumors, Guha demonstrated the existence of "sacralized political action" and "political thinking" among peasants, though one that marked their "false consciousness" and produced self-alienation. Thus, even as Guha argued strongly against the Marxist orthodoxy of his day, which designated peasant insurrection as "pre-political," he nevertheless thought that self-alienation led (for instance) the "Maratha peasant to do the very opposite of what he thought he was doing."[76] Except in the sense that the rabble of Delhi were not establishing a people's republic, such a characterization seems difficult to apply to those who were risking life and limb on the basis of the false news on that evening in March 1739. And "trigger and mobilizer" though the rumor in Delhi was, it is striking that observers did not attribute a sectarian motive to the events. On the one hand, no tension between Shiʿa and Sunni was seen as fueling the riot. On the other, declarations of adherence to Sunni orthopraxy (as we have seen) did not save the Iranians who were attacked.

Notwithstanding their variegation, all recordings of these rumors share certain essential features. Nadir Shah, who had just occupied the Red Fort, is overthrown, whether by guile or outright force. The agents of his overthrow are usually the king's loyal servants, and Muhammad Shah is restored to the

[73] Kishor, "Rūydād-i Nādir Shāh," 3.
[74] Warid, *Tārīkh-i Nādirshāhī*, 191.
[75] Mukhlis, "Waqāʾiʿ," 44–45; Khwush Hal, "Nādir al-Zamānī [B]," fol. 197b; ʿAbd al-Karim, *Bayān-i Wāqiʿ*, 35; Lockhart, "De Voulton's Noticia," 237; Siddiqi, "Jauhar-i Samsām," fol. 56b.
[76] Guha, *Elementary Aspects of Peasant Insurgency*, 256, 266, 268, 270, 272; see 250–77 more broadly.

throne. The king's enemies are now, at a stroke, to be defeated. Then as now, the rumors of the invader's fall and the king's return, whether true or not, reflected what the people of the city wanted and desired. The intensity of this desire is reflected in Khwush Hal's puzzlement at the fact that even when palace officials returned from the fort to their own houses and emphatically denied the rumor, "no one gave their ears to these admonitions, and all remained trapped in their senselessness."[77] Despite Nadir Shah's precautions and his careful adherence to Mughal practice in issuing his coins and proclamations, the symbolic displacement of the Mughal order produced a powerful popular backlash. The city's folk wished only a descendant of the exalted lineage of Amir Timur to sit on the peacock throne.

The Shape of the Massacre

It is surely the vehemence of the popular uprising and the existential danger it posed to the occupying army that spurred Nadir Shah to take the step for which he would be long remembered in Delhi. Early the next morning, he rode from the Exalted Fort to the newly built little seminary at the heart of the city's central promenade, Moonlight Avenue. From its roof, he ordered his soldiers to set out in all directions, to kill and plunder all whom they encountered. Many thousands of Delhi's residents were slaughtered in the next few hours. By the time the killing was concluded, the most conservative commentators estimated twenty thousand dead. Elite chroniclers insisted on Nadir Shah's initial resistance to ordering the massacre, which only broke under the severe and continuing provocation of the rioters. They wrote of the ensuing bloodshed in apocalyptic terms, describing how Nadir's soldiers slaughtered not just men and women, old and young, but even horses and camels, dogs and cats. But this portrait of the violence, derived from the chronicles by Sarkar and Irvine, and reproduced by generations of historians since, is at best misleading. Such bright contrasts between Indians and Iranians, between unrelenting killers and helpless victims, were the literary artifice through which the rhetorical power of history was conjured. They conceal the fact that the killing was neither indiscriminate nor unresisted.

[77] Khwush Hal, "Nādir al-Zamānī [B]," fol. 197b.

To see this essential feature of the violence, we must pry apart the narrative of the "general massacre." In the case of Delhi, the more literal rendition of the term *qatl-i ʿāmm* as "the massacre of the commoners" better captures its nature. Nadir Shah, as indeed his official chronicler, recognized that the uprising was an act of popular assertion; even though some noblemen were implicated in the uprising, the weight of the conqueror's sanguinary retribution fell overwhelmingly on the city's common folk.[78] And it was the Mughal elite who shaped the course of this punishment, both in guiding the violence and in moderating and limiting its effects.

Though unusual in its scope, Nadir Shah's violence was not unprecedented. In ordering a *qatl-i ʿāmm*, he drew on a hallowed technique of subjugating resistant urban populations made notorious by Chinggis Khan and Amir Timur, on whom he modeled himself.[79] His armies had already brutally sacked the small towns ("which had become like cities because of their plentiful population") in the plains of Punjab on his way to Delhi.[80] Aside from the lachrymose descriptions of chroniclers, an unusually detailed account of the actual violence in Delhi is again offered by the soldierly Ashob, who related the prized testimony of his superior officer Sʿad al-Din Khan, the commander of the Mughal artillery. The commander's memories of the massacre offer unprecedented insight into its working, and show that the violence was neither without control nor without direction.

In the aftermath of the battle of Karnal, the two armies' artillery forces had been combined under the shared (if unequal) control of the Mughal Sʿad al-Din Khan and the Iranian general Yar ʿAli Sultan. Both commanders quickly became "embroiled in all each other's affairs, good and bad."[81] The Mughal commander was summoned in haste to the fort in the early hours of the day following the uprising. According to him, Nadir Shah initially attributed the uprising to the people of the Turani Mughal community (*qaum*). Accordingly, the Iranian general was ordered to proceed to the mansion of the vizier, who was regarded as the Turani Mughals' leader; if he did not submit, instructed Nadir Shah, "then you will enact a great butchery." He further ordered that the Indian commander was to be treated as a brother by the Iranian general. Although he had no contingent of his own, the Indian was to

[78] Astarabadi, *Tārīkh-i Jahāngushā-yi Nādirī*, 240–41.

[79] Aubin, "Comment Tamerlan Prenait Les Villes"; Welsford, *Four Types of Loyalty in Early Modern Central Asia the Tūqāy-Timūrid Takeover of Greater Mā Warā Al-Nahr, 1598–1605*, 100–101.

[80] Mukhlis, "Waqāʾiʿ," 21.

[81] Ashob, "Tārīkh-i Shahādat [A]," fol. 267b; Ashob, "Tārīkh-i Shahādat [B]," fol. 249b.

assist in "questioning and answering, words and senses, and the meaning of the Indians' speech," and warned ominously against wavering in this task.[82]

Under the claim of compulsion, the Mughal commander accompanied the massacre party on its course from the square of Moonlight Avenue, first south toward the congregational mosque and next west toward the vizier's palatial complex near Ajmer Gate. Ashob resorts to the most extreme hyperbole to represent the destruction inflicted by the massacre party, describing how blood flooded the streets and splattered on walls and rooftops like rainwater, and how the severed heads of men and women rolled about like black earthenware pots.[83] Such images suggest that the victims of the massacre went unresistingly to their deaths. Ashob went so far as to claim that the Iranian force raged through the city in silence, because their victims did not even have the courage even to utter a cry of opposition. On the same page, however, he mentions two occasions on which rockets were fired at the Iranian party, causing them to scatter in fear.[84] He did not find it fit to speculate on who might have launched these rockets, but he and other chroniclers related stories of the noblemen who did resist the Iranian soldiers.[85] And when the massacre party finally reached the vizier's complex in the southwest of the city, they were a confronted by a force they could not overcome. Exhausted by their plunder of the overflowing shops of the money-changers, clothiers, and brewers, the Iranians espied the vizier's Turani Mughal retainers, "numerous as ants and locusts," dotting the rooftops with muskets, and commanding fields of fire with their small cannons. So the Mughal general persuaded his Iranian counterpart (who had temporarily lost his senses in a war-fever) to negotiate with the vizier under a flag of truce.[86]

This was not the only instance when discretion proved the better part of valor on the day of the massacre. One chronicler noted that the raiding parties only attacked those who were defenseless or unguarded, withdrawing in the face of the slightest opposition.[87] In Ashob's neighborhood, some men managed to drive off a party of raiders simply by brandishing mock firearms

[82] Notwithstanding his protestations of being "the only Indian" who assisted in the killing, it is difficult to conceive how the massacre parties dispatched in other directions could have proceeded without the assistance of similar native informants. Ashob, "Tārīkh-i Shahādat [B]," fols. 250b–251a; Ashob, "Tārīkh-i Shahādat [A]," fols. 268b–269a.

[83] Ashob, "Tārīkh-i Shahādat [A]," fols. 269b–270a; Ashob, "Tārīkh-i Shahādat [B]," fols. 251b–252.

[84] Ashob, "Tārīkh-i Shahādat [A]," fol. 270b.

[85] Ashob, "Tārīkh-i Shahādat [A]," fols. 277a–278a.

[86] Ashob, "Tārīkh-i Shahādat [A]," fols. 273b–275a; Ashob, "Tārīkh-i Shahādat [B]," fols. 254b–256b.

[87] Warid, *Tārīkh-i Nādirshāhī*, 206–07.

fashioned from bamboo and iron implements.[88] Despite the unreliability of his statistics, the very fact that Fraser noted the death of "above 400" Qizilbash during the massacre is suggestive of the continuing resistance.[89]

The Extent of the Massacre

Nadir Shah's retribution fell heavily but unevenly on the city. The Dariba, which was populated by money-changers and jewelers, bore the brunt of the violence because it was adjacent to the square of Moonlight Avenue from where the massacre parties had set forth. The denizens of such places were caught off-guard when their houses were set aflame by the attackers. Prone to accidental conflagrations at the best of times, these neighborhoods proved death-traps for their residents. Many were unable to escape their burning homes and buried beneath collapsing walls and beams. In many other areas, however, Nadir's troops made little or no impact. The Old City remained unaffected, as did the suburb of Wakilpura, and the Vizier's Quarter near the Ajmer Gate.[90]

The unevenness of the destruction was not only produced by the configuration of the city's space. More importantly, the city's elites suffered far less than the poor did, because of a striking fact that has escaped histories of the event: The houses of the rich were assigned guards of Iranian military policemen at the outset of the killing. By contrast, the common folk suffered disproportionately: many of the poor were saved only because they happened to live near the mansions of the nobility.[91] In fact, of those elites who died, many were felled not by Iranians but their own hands. Fearing dishonor, the city's finer folk preemptively killed their wives and dependents (*jauhar*)—a practice observed with dismay by their contemporaries.

Such self-inflicted violence aside, the city's elites largely escaped the brunt of the massacre. Shakir Khan recalled that his father Lutf Allah Khan, bitterly decrying the "wretchedness" and "infamy" of the Indian people, personally accosted Nadir Shah in the Red Fort and sought his protection. After briefly toying with him, the conqueror granted him immunity from the massacre, and assigned him twenty guards. Lutf Allah Khan distributed these men

[88] Ashob, "Tārīkh-i Shahādat [B]," fol. 262b.
[89] Fraser, *History of Nadir Shah*, 185.
[90] Warid, *Tārīkh-i Nādirshāhī*, 218; Mukhlis, "Waqāʾiʿ," 45–50.
[91] ʿAbd al-Karim, *Bayān-i Wāqiʿ*, 39.

among the four residences of his extended family. The five assigned to his own house, claimed Shakir Khan, ensured the protection of the entire stretch from the Fort to the Kashmir Gate in the North.[92] Other families also received protection. The mansion of the powerful financial administrator Jugal Kishor was adjacent to the square of Moonlight Avenue from where the massacre parties first set out. The five hundred Qizilbash troops who had broken into his compound with their rope-ladders were halted in their looting by the appearance of an Iranian officer with fifty gunners sent by Nadir Shah.[93] Mirza Zaman, the secretary to the nobleman Sar Buland Khan, likewise claimed that his master turned back a massacre party near his home at the southern Delhi Gate of the city with the promise of money, thus preserving his entire quarter.[94]

Far below Jugal Kishor and Shakir Khan in the social hierarchy, even minor elites such as Ashob were insulated from the fate that befell the city's lowly inhabitants. Ashob and his brothers had fortified themselves in their mansion and planned to fight to the death in defense of their honor. An Iranian party approached their house, fired a few rounds at their door, and tried to set it afire. Just then a man in the garb of the Iranian military police appeared and shooed them away. It turned out to be an acquaintance, a minor Indian official, who on the previous night had come to warn them of the impending massacre, but who now appeared in the distinctive clothing of a servant of Nadir Shah. The Iranian military policeman he installed to guard their house appeared overjoyed to accept a gift of thirty rupees and a shawl. From that time on, claims Ashob, his family suffered no molestation at the hands of the conquering army.[95]

The protection extended to Ashob derived from the same network that linked Mughal and Iranian elites and enabled the state of conquest. Ashob's protector was the chamberlain (*khān-i sāmān*) to the tutor of the son of the governor of the province of Punjab, who, after the fall of Lahore, had accompanied Nadir Shah's army. This was not a unique occurrence. Later, the nobleman Anand Ram would be similarly saved from dishonor by the intercession of a minor official, the tutor to the son of his employer, the vizier. This man too arrived in the nick of time "wearing that very Qizilbash garb, which was wisely donned after the coming of Nadir Shah."[96] In this context, another

[92] Shakir Khan, "Hadīqa," fols. 153a–154b.
[93] Kishor, "Rūydād-i Nādir Shāh," 3–4.
[94] Fraser, *History of Nadir Shah*, 184–85.
[95] Ashob, "Tārīkh-i Shahādat [B]," fols. 262b–263a.
[96] Mukhlis, "Waqāʾiʿ," 63–64.

chronicler scornfully noted that "even Hindus" trusted by Nadir Shah were given his army's scarlet caps to wear.[97] It would be easy to see such changing of clothing as craven acts of affiliation with the conquering power, and perhaps not wrong either. Doubtless many people made difficult compromises with their conscience when threatened with extinction. But such cases suggest how even minor elites facilitated the extension of Nadir Shah's power precisely to insulate their families, friends, and acquaintances from its worst effects.

The individuals who comprised Delhi's ever-tumultuous mob, of course, were only thinly connected (if at all) with the networks which linked their betters. For all the nobility were concerned, the city's unruly folk had brought the massacre upon themselves. Thus, even as they deplored his excesses, Mughal observers exculpated Nadir Shah for the massacre. One chronicler tells us how Nadir Shah at first blamed his own soldiers for the tumult and resisted mobilizing them.[98] Many others claimed that a stone or a bullet narrowly missed him as he surveyed the scene from Moonlight Avenue's square.[99] So when Nadir finally succumbed to immoderation, it was clear where the fault lay. "If the crafty folk of the city had not acted in this erroneous way," declared a writer, "the plunder would not have taken place, and the terror of Nadir Shah would not have befallen the people of India." He was forced to act because the multitudes were "a breeze of sedition," and the "flame of revolt would not subside without chastisement."[100] "If one were to consider the matter carefully and fairly," reflected Ashob, "he would discover that Nadir Shah was not at fault in giving the order for the massacre." Nadir's retributive violence was justified precisely because of the intolerable willfulness of Delhi's common people: "Because of slackness in matters of administration and the abandonment of the protocols of aristocracy and punishment" he declared, "negligent rulers had permitted the people to drink the waters of obstinacy and self-willedness without bridle or rein." Now they no longer "extended the head of submission and the neck of docility of their own accord." This was the source of the "longstanding self-assertiveness" that they demonstrated on the night of the riot.[101]

[97] Warid, *Tārīkh-i Nādirshāhī*, 248.
[98] ʿAbd al-Karim, *Bayān-i Wāqiʿ*, 35–36.
[99] Warid, *Tārīkh-i Nādirshāhī*, 192.
[100] ʿAbd al-Karim, *Bayān-i Wāqiʿ*, 38.
[101] Ashob, "Tārīkh-i Shahādat [A]," fols. 288b–289a; Ashob, "Tārīkh-i Shahādat [B]," fols. 267b–268a.

Writing of news from Delhi soon after the massacre, an anonymous author wryly invented a term to describe exactions on Delhi's gentlefolk. "Before there was a *qatl-i ʿāmm*," he remarked ruefully, "and now occurred a *qatl-i khāss*"—a massacre of elites.[102] In this way he unveiled a new meaning for the phrase *qatl-i ʿāmm*: where it usually connoted a "general massacre," it now implied a "massacre of the commoners," a sanguinary assault on the common people. As we have seen, our nameless author's contemporaries would have found the usage apposite. To the elite imagination, what befell the city may have been woefully excessive, but it was nevertheless well-deserved. It was as if the body politic had developed a lamentable distemper of chronic independence and self-assertiveness that only a vigorous bloodletting could purge. On this point both conquered and conquerors were agreed: the "undoubtedly wretched" people of Delhi were behaving according to an established tradition of political assertion, one for which massive retribution was long overdue.

The Aftermath of the Massacre

The aftermath of the massacre presented a dreadful spectacle. Bodies, gnawed on by dogs and cats, choked the streets. The administration struggled to cope. Five days after the killing, the city's people were impressed into dragging the corpses beyond its walls.[103] Observers lamented the impossibility of conducting proper funeral rites, because the burnt and rotting corpses of the Hindus and Muslims who had intermingled in life were now indistinguishable in death.[104] Some who were "imagined to be Hindus" were cremated with the timbers of ruined buildings in piles of forty or fifty.[105] Nadir Shah ordered the chief of police to throw the remaining corpses in the river, downstream from the city, where they became fodder for the Jamuna's fish and crocodiles.[106] Despite the vigorous efforts of the police chief, putrefying corpses littered the streets for more than a month, until at least May 19.[107] The remains of many who had been trapped inside their burning

[102] Anonymous, "Bayāz-i Yūsufī," fol. 220a; for a translation see Askari, "A Contemporary Correspondence Describing the Events at Delhi at the Time of Nadir Shah's Invasion."

[103] Fraser, *History of Nadir Shah*, 189.

[104] Warid, *Tārīkh-i Nādirshāhī*, 204–5.

[105] Fraser, *History of Nadir Shah*, 189.

[106] Ashob, "Tārīkh-i Shahādat [B]," fol. 265b.

[107] Fraser, *History of Nadir Shah*, 214.

houses could not be excavated from the rubble, and the stench of death "was a source of discomfort to the people" in some neighborhoods for six months or a year.[108]

How many were dead it was impossible to say. Khwush Hal surely represented popular sentiment more than empirical veracity when he claimed that two hundred thousand were killed (he also claimed that the Iranians kidnapped and consumed children).[109] An anonymous letter-writer from Delhi thought that eighty to ninety thousand, fully one-third of the city's population, had been murdered.[110] Ashob said that fifty thousand souls were killed, since the palace gave 50,000 rupees to Shah Kallan, leader (*dhāvat?*) of the "vagrants and vagabonds" (*shuhda-hā, luccha-hā*) who huddled in their multitudes "on the steps of the congregational mosque and in every neighborhood and alley of the city," and who were now tasked with disposing of the dead.[111] Shakir Khan, while not otherwise careful about dates or numbers would nevertheless have had access to official records, casually claimed 42,000 were killed.[112] ʿAbd al-Karim believed that 20,000 died.[113] Warid said merely that the number of the dead throughout the city could be estimated by the fact that 682 bodies were brought out of the congregational mosque, which had been stormed by the massacre party accompanied by the Mughal commander.[114]

Though it is impossible to establish the numbers killed, the fact that death did not winnow the ranks of Delhi's people impartially is evident from the *History of Muhammadans*, an antiquarian project that Ashob's uncle Mirza Muhammad, a historian of some note who we shall encounter again, had begun in 1712.[115] For the year of the massacre, Mirza Muhammad listed only sixteen names: they include two theologians, two doctors, a famed

[108] Ashob, "Tārīkh-i Shahādat [A]," fol. 270a; Ashob, "Tārīkh-i Shahādat [B]," fol. 251b.

[109] Khwush Hal, "Nādir al-Zamānī [B]," fol. 199b.

[110] Anonymous, "Bayāz-i Yūsufī," fols. 217b–218a.

[111] Ashob, "Tārīkh-i Shahādat [A]," fol. 286a; Ashob, "Tārīkh-i Shahādat [B]," fol. 265b; for the meaning of *shuhda* and *luccha*, now obscure, see Gilchrist, *Oriental Linguist*, 42. I thank Pasha Khan for this reference.

[112] Khan, "Hadīqa," fol. 154b.

[113] ʿAbd al-Karim, *Bayān-i Wāqiʿ*, 37.

[114] Warid, *Tārīkh-i Nādirshāhī*, 204.

[115] Originally Mirza Muhammad had planned to produce a book that recorded the dates of death for all the worthy and learned folk of Islam from its earliest days, a task that led him to develop an intricate system of abbreviation and citation for the sixty-odd works he would consult. But by the time his work arrived in his century, he had begun to record the everyday deaths of the empire's notables, Hindus and Muslims both. Mirza Muhammad, "Tārīkh-i Muhammadi," fols. 1a–6a.

calligrapher, and a few minor Hindu and Muslim notables. By contrast he named thirteen notable dead in the abortive battle of Karnal.[116] Even if Mirza Muhammad named only a fraction of the noble dead, it is clear that the commoners who died in their multitudes far outnumbered their betters.

Retribution after the Massacre

Nadir Shah's retribution did not end with the massacre, though again it was mediated through the state of conquest and shaped by the city's disciplinary institutions and elites. The conqueror's first priority was to identify resisters and make an example of them. But who they were was far from obvious. On March 23, two days after the massacre, the Mughal nobleman Azim Allah Khan and the city's police chief were sent to the King's Quarter (*shāhganj*), where the conflict between the Iranians and the Indians had begun. Khwush Hal said that when on investigation the police chief discovered the bodies of slain Qizilbash soldiers concealed in shops, he ordered the arrest of the "bystanders and gawkers who are absent at no event," so that two thousand innocent folks "encountered the angel of death." Of these, five hundred escaped with the mutilation of their ears, noses, or fingers, but the rest were executed.[117] Warid, attributing the same fate to the more reasonable number of number of 40 killed and some 360 mutilated, also blamed the officials for not conducting a proper investigation. Like Khwush Hal, he felt that most of those punished were decent folk (*nujabā'*) who had nothing to do with the uprising.[118]

Three days after the massacre, Nadir Shah ordered the combined artillery force on a "righteous war" (*jihād*) to conduct a "minor massacre" against the European suburb of Firangipura, to the northwest of the city. According to the eyewitness Ashob, its numerous European inhabitants, led by the imperial servants "Firangi Khan" and "Fransis Khan," were accused of having deceived and killed Nadir Shah's military policemen during the massacre, or turned on his forces when they sought to seize the Mughal park of artillery stationed there. The beheaded bodies of three hundred of these resistant

[116] Mirza Muhammad, fols. 286a–289b.
[117] Khwush Hal, "Nādir al-Zamānī [B]," fols. 202b–203a.
[118] Warid, *Tārīkh-i Nādirshāhī*, 218.

artillery officers were publicly displayed at the usual site of the city's river bank.[119]

Claims that the "true" instigators of the violence vanished unknown represent the elite inability or refusal to recognize the autonomous and distributed nature of popular uprisings.[120] The logic of Mughal governance required that leaders be found and publicly punished. No doubt as a result of the investigations of Azim Allah Khan and the police chief, three noblemen were found worthy of punishment. These were Sayyid Niyaz Khan, Shehsawar Khan, and the imperial servant Raiman. Sayyid Niyaz Khan appears to have been well-born but obscure, and is described only as the son-in-law of the vizier. His social elevation had led to his recent appointment as administrator of the grain market. It was said that some of his gunners had shot Iranians during the riot.[121] He was captured and executed on the second day after the massacre. Similarly, Shehsawar ("Mounted by the King") Khan had married well, and was the son-in-law of the high-ranking nobleman Qarra Khan, and a leader of the "community of the Turani Mughals" (*firqa-yi mughaliyya-i tūrānī*). His crimes are unspecified, but perhaps he was seen as orchestrating the Turani Mughal resistance which Nadir Shah had blamed before the massacre. Others killed or punished included Mir Mubarak Khan, and Jamal Allah Khan, the tax collector (*karori*) of the Grain Market.[122]

The most intriguing of these figures, however, is the female harem servant given the title Raiman. The causes of her execution are nowhere stated. But the unexplained execution of a high-ranking palace servant tasked with the protection of the emperor's person raises the possibility that an assassination attempt had in fact been made on Nadir Shah during his first day in the fort. Such an event, if indeed it occurred, would go some way in explaining the persistence of rumors of the invader's death and ferocity of the popular uprising against the Qizilbash on the night of March 21.

But, in contrast to the popular rebellion, the resistance of these minor elites was sporadic and uncoordinated. There is no indication that they acted in concert or had any other than a peripheral role in the agitation. Shehsawar Khan and Sayyid Niyaz Khan were low-ranking officials and noblemen of recent provenance. Their status derived from their far worthier fathers-in-law. And it is noteworthy that their motives—self-preservation? patriotism?

[119] Ashob, "Tārīkh-i Shahādat [A]," fols. 286a–87b; Ashob, "Tārīkh-i Shahādat [B]," fols. 266a–267b; Fraser, *History of Nadir Shah*, 187–88.

[120] Das, "Chahār Gulzār-i Shujāʿī," fol. 91a.

[121] Khwush Hal, "Nādir al-Zamānī [B]," fol. 204b.

[122] Ashob, "Tārīkh-i Shahādat [A]," fol. 276a-b; Ashob, "Tārīkh-i Shahādat [B]," fol. 268a-b.

loyalty to the king?—were not widely shared by their peers in the lower or the middle echelons of the elite. This was to say nothing of the higher nobility, whose failure to resist was criticized by some commentators.[123] And Nadir Shah cannily forestalled further resistance by conciliating and even rewarding some of the elites who had violently resisted the massacre, such as Oghuz Khan and Hakim Khan.[124]

Exactions from the City

The destruction of the city and the murder of its inhabitants appears to have quelled the overt resistance of the people to Nadir Shah's control. Nadir Shah nevertheless accelerated the levying of tribute on the nobility and the city's people in its aftermath. These financial exactions—the "massacre of the nobility," as an anonymous correspondent had described it—denuded the polite fictions of "hosting" and "visiting," which had enabled the state of conquest thus far. And yet, even in this stark moment of expropriation, members of the Mughal nobility were intricately involved in every aspect of the process.

The sanguinary violence of the massacre did not dampen the appetite of the city's elites to make the best of the new regime. The nobleman Jugal Kishor again serves as the paradigmatic example of this tendency. Jugal Kishor's mansion, as we have seen, was partially plundered by Iranian troops on the day of the riot. Despite his losses, he strove hard for Nadir Shah's approval. He presented the four thousand gold coins which remained in his treasury as tribute to Nadir Shah the next day. He did not flinch when the initial demand to pay 125,000 rupees levied against him was doubled. He protected his patron Shujaʿ al-Din from the exaction of a large tribute, arguing that since the Bengal revenues had always been sent without peculation to Delhi, no more than 5 million rupees remained in the provincial exchequer.[125] So when Nadir Shah ordered the imposition of a tribute on the people of the city, Jugal Kishor naturally came to play an important role. Of the five high officials assigned to extract this money, Jugal Kishor assisted the Mughal noblemen Sar Buland Khan and ʿAzim Allah Khan. In his letter to the governor of Bengal, he castigated them for their incompetence and tyranny, which resulted in inaccurate assessments levied on the city's people. By

123 Khwush Hal, "Nādir al-Zamānī [B]," fol. 199b.
124 ʿAbd al-Karim, *Bayān-i Wāqiʿ*, 40–41; Ashob, "Tārīkh-i Shahādat [A]," fol. 277b.
125 Raja Jugal Kishor, "Rūydād-i Nādir Shāh," 4–5.

contrast, Jugal Kishor proudly noted how he produced a far more accurate assessment within two days and was praised by Nadir Shah for his efficiency.[126]

In these efforts, Jugal Kishor cut quite a different figure from Majlis Rai, the vizier's financial administrator, who had his ear cut off before Nadir Shah for his obstinate refusal to give up his master's money. Majlis Rai went on to pay nine hundred thousand of the 1.5 million rupees demanded of his master by Sar Buland Khan and ʿAzim Allah Khan before killing himself.[127] The official found popular acclaim for this act of loyalty. A balladic poem in the "mixed" (*rekhta)* vernacular praises Majlis Rai's fidelity (though it mistakenly remembers its object as not the vizier but the king).[128] Jugal Kishor, by contrast, was not recalled so warmly. Ashob thought that Jugal Kishor acted on the belief that the massacre was the prelude to the conquest of Hindustan. This explained why he had been very punctilious in extracting the sums which had been whimsically assigned to respectable people by the noblemen he assisted. But the limits of Jugal Kishor's collaboration were made clear when, one day, on being perceived lax in his collections, he was publicly caned like a dog, and rudely mocked for his weepings and wailings.[129]

In relating this story, Ashob illustrated the limits of the state of conquest. There was a widespread sense that Jugal Kishor was responsible for the heavy taxes that befell the people of Delhi. Scorning him as a "scoundrel (*shirrīr*) . . . cursed by all rich and poor," the anonymous correspondent blamed him for "starting this fire" of exaction after the massacre, and predicted a harsh fate for him after Nadir Shah's departure.[130] In the event, however, Jugal Kishor does not appear to have been called to account for the sufferings he inflicted. Twelve years after the conquest, we find him among the chief noblemen in Delhi, receiving the most valuable robes of honor at court and being assigned to the imperial mint (*sarf-i khāss*).[131] Where the vizier's manager had demonstrated his stubborn adherence to an old-fashioned sense of loyalty and paid the price, the opportunistic Jugal Kishor thrived in his wheelings and dealings until his death in a freak elephant accident in 1757.[132]

Though it is true that many were unable to pay the demanded tribute, and gentler souls than Jugal Kishor committed suicide after the dishonor of

126 Raja Jugal Kishor, "Rūydād-i Nādir Shāh," 6.
127 Anonymous, "Bayāz-i Yūsufī," fol. 218b; Kishor, "Rūydād-i Nādir Shāh," 7.
128 Irvine, "Nādir Shāh and Muhammād Shāh, a Hindi Poem by Tilok Dās," 81–83.
129 Ashob, "Tārīkh-i Shahādat [B]," fol. 270a-b.
130 Anonymous, "Bayāz-i Yūsufī," fol. 219a.
131 Anonymous, "Delhi Chronicle," 35, 36.
132 For further references to Jugal Kishor, see Umar, *Islam in Northern India*, 385, 90.

the bastinado, there is an element of hyperbole to recitations of the travails of Delhi's elites.[133] For even now, the hybrid nature of the Indo-Iranian elite mediated and moderated the exaction of tribute. Consider the case of Anand Ram, who has left us a full account of how his difficulties at the time were ultimately resolved. The author and his cousins were assigned to pay their share to the nobleman Sar Buland Khan (Jugal Kishore would have been involved).[134] Anand Ram managed to pay off his initial demand of 137,000 rupees (after a remission) by scraping together his reserves and dipping into the "internal treasury" (*toshakhāna-yi andarūn*), no doubt the financial resources managed by the ladies of his house. But just as he was given a letter of release, Sar Buland Khan revoked his initial remission and placed his house under guard.

Again, hysterical negotiations followed. The vizier's son stood surety for part of the sum; the family jewels were mortgaged and loans taken at 5% and 6% from the financier Indar Sen, whose avarice the author bitterly likened to that of "a pelican, [which] has no gullet."[135] The last 11,000 rupees were borrowed from one of Nadir Shah's own generals, whom Anand Ram's neighbor had befriended. Our author clearly found the soldier too coarse for his company but held his nose on the (dubious) principle that "there's a nobleman in every commoner" (*dar har ʿāmmī khāssī ast*). After several flagons of wine consumed and much poetry recited, the general happily consented to lending the author the remaining amount, which the author had returned to him by the time the departing army reached Lahore.

There is no doubt that the exactions placed Anand Ram in a situation of considerable financial hardship. Yet, far from being pauperized, he does not seem to have suffered any lasting troubles. The series of negotiations, reductions in demand, sureties, mortgages, and loans all indicate that the state of conquest mediated and mitigated the huge transfer of wealth from Indian to Iranian elites. What befell Delhi's ordinary people is unrecorded.

Conclusion

> Then said Nadir Shah: "Listen, O King! Wear the dress which I have donned,"
> "And consider me granting you rule from Delhi to Attock."

[133] Warid, *Tārīkh-i Nādirshāhī*, 215–17.

[134] The following account is derived from Mukhlis, "Waqāʾiʿ," 61–75; Warid blamed Sar Buland Khan for the idea of imposing the tax. Warid, *Tārīkh-i Nādirshāhī*, 213–15.

[135] Mukhlis, "Waqāʾiʿ," 72.

> It was then that Muhammad Shah put on [his] clothes:
> donning the robe and hat, he adopted the Durrani fashion.[136]

Perhaps a decade or two after Nadir Shah's departure from Delhi, the obscure poet Tilok Das sang these verses for an equally indeterminate audience somewhere in North India. The poet's distance from the events he described is evident in his mistaken attribution of the later "Durrani" fashion of the later invader Ahmad Shah Abdali to Nadir Shah. Such confusions, trivial in comparison with the bard's more egregious flights of fancy, led Jadunath Sarkar's mentor and fellow historian William Irvine to dismiss the poem as bearing "no historical value," its only use being to demonstrate "how rapidly in the East, even in modern history, fact and fiction are blended. We see, as it were, myth in the making."[137]

Despite this judgment, Irvine was not unaware of the significance of such poems. Manifest inaccuracies notwithstanding, they were the vehicle of an oral transmission that recorded and conveyed the essential features of a distant political event. The bard Tilok Das would not have known of the particular details of Nadir Shah's last formal audience in Delhi, which Jugal Kishor recorded for his patron in Bengal: how Nadir Shah gave robes of honor to the leading members of the Mughal nobility; how the famed Peacock Throne was turned over to him by way of "the expenses of brotherly hospitality"; how he in turn gifted Muhammad Shah with 7 million rupees worth of jewels and fastened his own turban-ornament and a jeweled sword to Muhammad Shah's person; and, finally, how he sternly enjoined obedience to India's recalcitrant nobility.[138]

Yet Tilok Das's verses succinctly captured the essence of the event for his listeners. The gift of clothes signified incorporation and subjugation on favorable terms.[139] His audience would have understood that an important change had occurred at the highest levels of the imperial polity. But given that Tilok Das and other bards also related how Nadir Shah had been forced to turn back after being bested in a spiritual contest by a naked mystic who resided in Moonlight Square, they would know too that the essential order of their world remained unchanged, that divine favor still preserved a Mughal emperor on Delhi's throne.[140]

136 Irvine, "Nādir Shāh and Muhammād Shāh, a Hindi Poem by Tilok Dās," 45–46; 55–56 (Irvine's translation amended).

137 Irvine, "Nādir Shāh and Muhammād Shāh, a Hindi Poem by Tilok Dās," 25.

138 Kishor, "Rūydād-i Nādir Shāh," 7–8.

139 Gordon, *Robes of Honour: Khil'at in Pre-Colonial and Colonial India.*

140 Irvine, "Nādir Shāh and Muhammād Shāh, a Hindi Poem by Tilok Dās," 46, 56; Amar, "Hālāt-i Nādir Shāh," f7b.

Such beliefs would of course become increasingly hard to sustain in the face of the warfare that shook the land over the coming decades. Yet Tilok Das's poem reminds us of the vast world beyond the narrow vision of the chronicles on which our account of the events of 1739 has relied. Mughal commentators were acutely aware of the existence of a capacious realm of popular opinion. What did Delhi's common folk make of the occupation, the uprising, and the massacre? Because their views were not recorded and have not survived for posterity, such a question is not easy to answer. Yet, as Tilok Das's verses suggest, the views of the people were at some variance with those of Mughal elites. Perhaps the criticisms that Khwush Hal attributes to the stunned imperial secretaries who had to hand over the palace treasures to Nadir Shah were shared more widely:

> Astonished at this wealth (*daulat*) beyond count or reckoning, sometimes they uttered praises of the miraculous power of God, and sometimes of the fortune of this eternal dynasty; and sometimes they hurled curses and vulgar reproaches at the disloyalty of imperial officials and the unworthiness of the highest nobles. They used to say that despite their great fortune and vast armies, these short-sighted men ruined all their great pomp and splendor.[141]

For Mughal elites, there was something bewilderingly alien about popular responses to the invasion. For instance, Fraser's informant Mirza Zaman noted with disbelief:

> The Inhabitants, from the Terror of this Calamity, like people poessess'd, and in Fits, are quite stupefied and not yet come to themselves, and what is still more strange . . . [is the fact that] The indecent Expressions and beastly Actions of his [Nadir Shah's] Soldiers, are the constant Subjects of Discourse, in all Companies, related with a seeming Satisfaction and Pleasure, and by way of Jest and Drollery; not being in the least affected with a Reflection on their past Disgrace and Misfortunes.[142]

A sense of what such flippant talk might have entailed is given by the small note which the chronicler ʿAbd al-Karim apologetically includes at the end of his account of Nadir Shah's presence in Delhi. He describes an

[141] Khwush Hal, "Nādir al-Zamānī [B]," fol. 205b.
[142] Fraser, *History of Nadir Shah*, 216–17.

exchange between "a friend" and Delhi's leading courtesan Nur Bai, who had entertained Nadir Shah. The friend asked Nur Bai how she felt on the occasions that Nadir Shah had sexual intercourse with her. Nur Bai instantly responded, "I imagined that my vagina had also been included in the general massacre."[143] This unseemly repartee exhibited the quick wit so valued among the city's elites and had established Nur Bai's status as Delhi's most desired courtesan. It also cautions the modern reader not to take the exaggerated lamentations of elite chroniclers at face value and is suggestive of a popular perception of the event as marked as much by resilience as by trauma.

Indeed, those who bewailed the destruction sometimes paused in their keenings to remark on the surprising hardiness of the city's ravaged people. One observer noted Nadir's astonishment at the fact that Delhi's folk returned to purchase the very things that had been looted from them in the massacre, so that the vast mounds of booty thrown in front of the gate of the fort had quite vanished in three days. Moreover, the Indians thoroughly fleeced their persecutors, "buying jewels worth fifty thousand for merely a hundred." This observer believed this led to a vast social reorganization, so that those who had once been poor "became the equal of noblemen" and remained so even after the passage of years.[144] Such exaggerations convey a sense of the social upheaval "and indicate the continuing rise of new groups to wealth and power" in the wake of the conquest.

Nadir Shah thus departed from a profoundly divided polity, one in which a great divergence in thought and belief had arisen between an independent-minded nobility that no longer cared who reigned in Delhi so long as their perquisites were not touched, and an assertive populace that, in rising in defense of Muhammad Shah, evinced distinctly contrary views. This was a fact that elite chroniclers were loath to acknowledge: no history of the event, for instance, finds it pertinent to mention the fact that in 1719, only two decades previously, the people of Delhi were animated by (true) rumors of the overthrow of a king to (successfully) rise up and defeat an occupying army. Such repeated uprisings show that urbanites held forceful convictions about the proper nature and locus of sovereignty. To understand this emergence of the people of Delhi as political actors, and their relationship with the king, we must begin at the moment of the foundation of their world: the making of a new city of Delhi almost a century earlier, in 1648.

143 ʿAbd al-Karim, *Bayān-i Wāqiʿ*, 44.
144 Warid, *Tārīkh-i Nādirshāhī*, 202, 205–206, 200–201.

2

Sovereignty, City, and the People

One day in 1718/19, a master painter began to outline on paper a scene he had doubtless witnessed many times in life: the arrival of an imperial procession—almost certainly that of emperor Farrukh Siyar—at Delhi's "world-revealing" mosque of congregation on a Friday, to hear the sermon (*khutba*) recited in his name (Fig. 2.1).[1] This lavishly painted single leaf, probably a gift to the king himself, offers an unusual depiction. From the perspective of an onlooker in the square before the mosque, we see Farrukh Siyar, readily identifiable by his halo, accompanied by a panoply of objects laden with symbolism: fly whisks and golden parasols; the standards of the hand of ʿAli and the dragon, which marked the venerable dynastic ancestor Timur's conquest of India; and a variety of other flags and insignia.[2] Surrounding the king are an equally diverse array of imperial servants. From the onlooker's perspective, we espy sweepers ready to clear the path with their brooms; a bevy of court officers bearing golden maces and staffs; well-dressed gentlemen and courtiers on horseback stiffly facing the king; his gunners, mounted on camels; trumpeters and pious officials; and the many units of imperial guards and servants, demarcated by their red, green, or blue uniforms. In the background looms the mosque, surrounded by the densely packed houses of the city and crowded with worshipers.

The aura of a Mughal conception of sovereignty radiates from this painting. Entranced, as all onlookers, by the seductive allure of the court's glittering rhetoric and otherworldly allusions, historians too have long been mesmerized by the spectacle of the king's procession. Yet, we might ask, for whose benefit were the elaborate performances of ceremony and ritual such as the

[1] I have not encountered scholarly discussion of this painting, recently acquired by the Louvre museum (MAO2091). The painter is not identified, but the rear of the painting bears a calligraphic inscription of poetry declaring an aging courtier's plea to be liberated from service, and bears the date of 1131 AH (1718/19 AD). Given the lavish nature of the painting, it perhaps served as both gift and petition to the reigning ruler, Farrukh Siyar. It seems therefore probable that the image it bears is meant to represent the ruler himself. In style the painting appears similar to the illustrations in an undated copy of the *Emperor's Book (pādishāhnāma)* of Shah Jahan held at the Library of Congress, available online: https://lccn.loc.gov/50045639, Image 361, accessed June 5, 2019.

[2] Irvine, *The Army of the Indian Moghuls*, chap. 3, particularly 31–32.

The King and The People. Abhishek Kaicker, Oxford University Press (2020). © Oxford University Press.
DOI: 10.1093/oso/9780190070670.001.0001

Figure 2.1. Farrukh Siyar's procession arrives at the congregational mosque for Friday prayers. (ArtRes Image)

imperial procession staged? As the simply dressed stragglers who are hastening up the steps of the mosque remind us, the audience of these dramatic displays of imperial pageantry in the theater of the city were its inhabitants, the nameless masses of subjects who were the proper objects of the discourse of sovereignty: the common people who comprised the flock enjoined to the ruler's pastoral care. What the painting seeks to convey to us as viewers is what the procession conveyed to its onlookers: a kingly claim to an absolute power, legitimized by divine sanction, exercised in conformance with faith over the people at large. Such claims are expressed in a distinct vocabulary of concepts, symbols, and gestures that this book describes as a discourse of sovereignty, of which the painting itself is a visual enunciation.

Yet there is also something poignant about this image, for its maker could hardly have been unaware of the storm clouds that loomed over the capital at that time. Within months of the painting's completion, the king's highest ministers would violently dethrone Farrukh Siyar and throw his mutilated corpse out in the Red Fort's forecourt for all to see. "[T]he body is always the site of sovereign power," observe the anthropologists Hansen and Stepputat.[3] By so desacralizing the kingly body, the nobility would offer an unprecedented challenge to the imperial discourse of sovereignty that had located supreme power in his inviolable person. And the nobility's attempt to alter the dispensation of imperial power by claiming it for themselves would provoke a response from an unlikely quarter: the people of the city. Though they would prove to be unable to defend Farrukh Siyar, the people's intervention marked their transformation from spectators to actors on the stage of imperial politics. How did the people, who appear in the painting only as the faint and inconsequential backdrop to the performance of imperial sovereignty, gain the capacity for political action? To understand their emergence as political subjects in a regime that conceived of no place for them, we must first examine the relationship between the sovereign, the city, and the people as it evolved over the course of the Mughal empire.

Sovereignty

Without sovereignty there could be no people. It is true, of course, that North India was thickly inhabited long before the arrival of the Mughals, or even

[3] Hansen and Stepputat, "Sovereignty Revisited," 297.

before the establishment of the Sultanate of Delhi in 1206.[4] Yet the many residents of the thriving villages and populous cities of the region were imagined as the subjects of a king. The sovereign and the people came into existence together in a discourse, which saw the king's subjects neither existing prior to sovereignty nor anywhere outside its purview.[5] The contours of this discourse are encapsulated in the first sentence of a political tract by Ziya᾿ al-Din Barani, the fourteenth-century courtier and theorist of kingship in the Delhi Sultanate: "praised be the creator, for adorning faith-nourishing rulers with justice, and giving creation the . . . fortune (*daulat*) of subjection to their commands."[6] Barani's words encapsulate an entire vision of sacral and human order: as Barani explains elsewhere, God alone appoints true kings, who adhere to the faith and preserve by their justice "the weak, the obedient, and the helpless" from the claws of "oppressors, tyrants, the powerful."[7]

Though the idea of the people is clear, what constituted sovereignty is less obvious.[8] Courtly intellectuals in the Islamic world did not concern themselves with the debates of their European contemporaries over the distinction between *summum imperium* and *administratio*—sovereignty, as the right to enact laws and government, as the means of their imposition.[9] For Barani, as indeed for his successors, the right and the duty to enforce God's law fell upon the kings He chose. Such thinkers were keenly aware of the violence by which kingly authority was established and maintained.[10] For them the question was not *where* the right to impose the laws lay, but *how* the king who enforced them should conduct himself.

Its answers were repeatedly articulated in what is described in this book as a *discourse of sovereignty*. While the term discourse is sometimes seen as connoting an ether of ideas with little relation to reality, we regard the discourse of sovereignty as a productive arena in which kings and courtly intellectuals articulated, debated, justified, defended, and contested the proper disposition and regulation of power. As we shall see, traces of this discourse are evident not only in the ethical treatises produced at court, but also

[4] Jha, *Urbanisation in Early Medieval North India*; Siddiqi, *Delhi Sultanate*.

[5] On the history and political dynamics of the Sultanate, see Kumar, *The Emergence of the Delhi Sultanate, 1192–1286*.

[6] Barani, *Fatāwā-yi Jahāndārī*, 1; Haider, "Justice and Political Authority."

[7] Cited in Sarkar, "An Urban Imaginaire," 411.

[8] See the remarks in Anooshahr, "On the Imperial Discourse of the Delhi Sultanate and Early Mughal India."

[9] Tuck, *The Sleeping Sovereign*.

[10] Habib, "Barani's Theory," 104.

in para-courtly histories and chronicles, visual texts and architecture, and the bodies of its objects.

Daulat in the Discourse of Sovereignty

The fountainhead of this discourse was the ideal of *daulat:* a word of wide semantic range, but one which primarily implied "fortune," both in the sense of heavenly favor and wealth.[11] It was *daulat*, as a mark of God's approbation, which established kings over the earth for the enactment of justice. It must be emphasized that *daulat* was not an exact coeval of the classical notion of sovereignty, and had never in the historical period connoted anything resembling absolute authority over a definite territory.[12] The ideal of *daulat*, however, was integral to the discourse of sovereignty; it endowed the king with limitless authority to fulfill the heavenly mandate of maintaining justice on earth. Long before it came to assume its present meaning of "state" in modern Arabic, the word *daulat* had first implied rotation, then the fortune to rule, and, by the eleventh century, a notion of dynasty.[13] For Sultanate intellectuals like Barani, *daulat* meant fortune; thus he describes the people of the world enjoying the *daulat* of obedience to their appointed rulers. But more conventionally it was the secular, earthly, and material object, forming, with the sacred faith, the conventional dyad of *dīn o daulat* possessed and safeguarded by rulers.[14]

The idea of *daulat*, however, appears to have evolved in the aftermath of Amir Timur's (d. 1405) conquests, now becoming more infused with mystical overtones that derive from Turco-Mongol ideas of divinely sanctioned rule.[15] A joke that is more than a joke, included in a work of the mid-eighteenth century, recounts how Amir Timur, the ancestral founder of the Mughal dynasty, had a blind woman named Daulat brought before him on his entry into his capital Samarqand. On hearing her name, Timur wittily asked, "How can *daulat* be blind?" To this, the woman retorted, "If *daulat* were not blind, how would she choose a lame ruler?"[16] Fortune was blind and could

[11] See Najm-Sani, *Advice on the Art of Governance*, 42 fn. 9.

[12] For a similar critique of the equivalence of Dawla with "State," see Rouighi, *The Making of a Mediterranean Emirate*, "Introduction."

[13] Rosenthal, "Dawla,"; Meisami, *Persian Historiography*, 281.

[14] Barani, *Fatāwā-yi Jahāndārī*, 9.

[15] Inalcik, "The Ottoman Succession and Its Relation to the Turkish Concept of Sovereignty."

[16] Rai, "Malāhat-i Maqal," fol. 3b.

come to anyone, but the *daulat* that accrued to Timur and his descendants was something special. Perhaps absorbed from Timur, the idea of *devlet* in the Ottoman context of the fifteenth century suggested a sacral authority to rule.[17] While it is unclear when the term began to demarcate a sense of "state" as distinct from the person of the ruler, it appears that until the seventeenth century, *devlet* was a power "particular to the Prince or Sultan, which cannot in any way be delegated."[18] Farther afield, in Melaka, the idea of *daulat* connoted the sense of the mystical, supernatural power of the ruler, which could strike down rebels and cause them to "suffer agonizing deaths."[19]

A similar sense is evident in the delusions of grandeur of Timur's descendant Babur (d. 1529), which were exacerbated by his conquest of North India.[20] Babur readily came to believe that his rule was divinely ordained and inhered to him alone. So he recounts with astonishment the "peculiarity" of Bengal, where any regicide could seize the throne without opposition from his subjects, who held that, " 'We are the legal property of the throne, and we obey anyone who is on it.' "[21] Such thinking was anathema in the Timurid tradition, where the divine sanction to rule resided in the body of the king. But a distinctively imperial discourse of sovereignty was perhaps first coherently enunciated in the writings of Abu al-Fazl, the preeminent intellectual at the court of the third emperor Akbar (r. 1556–1605), who merged Islamic conceptions of kingship with Mongol views of heavenly favor.[22] Thus Akbar, the vice-regent of God, was not only the perfect man, as the Sufis had it, but also a manifestation of the divine light that had impregnated Alanquwa, the mythical progenitor of the Mongol clans and the Mughal dynasty.[23] This light, he tells us, was frequently observed radiating from Akbar's mother's forehead before his birth, and even fell into the lap of his future wet-nurse.[24] It is this divine light, (Turkish: *kut*) which the lexicographer Mahmud al-Kashgari had already glossed in the eleventh century, among other things, as *daulat*.[25]

[17] Tezcan, *The Second Ottoman Empire*, 60.

[18] Sariyannis, "Ruler and State, State and Society in Ottoman Political Thought," 96.

[19] Moy, "The 'Sejarah Melayu' Tradition," 70–71; Andaya and Andaya, *A History of Early Modern Southeast Asia, 1400–1830*, 102.

[20] Dale, *Garden of Eight Paradises*, 457–67.

[21] Babur, *The Baburnama*, 332.

[22] Richards, "The Formulation of Imperial Authority under Akbar and Jahangir."

[23] Tripathi, *Muslim Administration*, 136; Lal, "Settled, Sacred and All-Powerful"; Truschke, "The Mughal Book of War," 19.

[24] Abu al-Fazl, *The history of Akbar*, I:48–49, 50–51.

[25] Inalcik, "The Ottoman Succession and Its Relation to the Turkish Concept of Sovereignty," 41–42.

For the theorists of the previous Sultanate, the king had the fortune to rule and the people the fortune of obedience. For the theorist of the nascent empire, *daulat* acquired a subtle new tint. While the ruler remains, as formerly, endowed with the formulaic "faith and fortune" (*dīn o daulat*), the substance adheres to his lineage (*dūdmān-i daulat*) and physical person (*hazrat badaulat*).[26] The idea recurs in the discourse of the next emperor Jahangir, who, in renaming his rebel son Khurram "sans-*daulat*" (*bī-daulat*), proclaimed his inability to rule. The slight must have stung, for it is on Khurram's accession to the throne as Shah Jahan in 1628 that *daulat* finds its fullest expression (see Fig. 2.2). In the *Foursquare Garden*, a work of elegant prose by the king's secretary and ideologue Chandar Bhan Brahman, *daulat* is now closely associated with the body of the ruler.[27] Shah Jahan's *daulat* is "God-given" and "increases every day." He sits on the "seat of *daulat*"; his

Figure 2.2. The mystical substance of kingship falls pointedly on Shah Jahan and not his minister. (Arthur M. Sackler Gallery, Smithsonian Institution, Washington, DC: Purchase – Smithsonian Unrestricted Trust Funds, Smithsonian Collections Acquisitions Program, and Dr. Arthur M Sackler, S1986.03.)

[26] Abu al-Fazl, *The history of Akbar*, I:26–27, 42–45, 32, 46, 20–21.

[27] Brahman, *Chahar chaman*; the comprehensive study of Chandar Bhan and his literary production is Kinra, *Writing Self, Writing Empire*, 2015.

residence is described as the "hall of *daulat*"; his servants are the "friends of *daulat*."[28] In one form or another, the word occurs one hundred and seventy-five times in an almost equal number of pages. The significance of the term for the author becomes apparent by its contrasting absence from a short genealogy of Delhi's rulers attributed to him. Composed after Shah Jahan was overthrown by his son Aurangzeb, Chandar Bhan now takes a more distant view of things. From the legendary Raja Judhishtir to his beloved king, on whose end he dwells with resignation, kings are endowed with the power to rule (*hukūmat*) but never *daulat*.[29]

By Shah Jahan's reign, the presence of *daulat* had come to be indicated through a multitude of signs which drew upon disparate symbolic vocabularies. The locus in which *daulat* was concentrated, and from which it visibly emanated, was the body of the king. Its otherworldly effulgence was represented in the halos that, from Akbar's reign, had begun to adorn images of the emperor.[30] Its personal nature was marked in the king's speech, for he alone joined the phrase "*badaulat*" to his personal pronoun, implying that his every action was conducted with it. It was signified by his standards, and, drawing on an older language of Indic kingship, was enveloped by a parasol and protected by a fly-whisk, and proclaimed by the gigantic kettledrums beaten in his procession.[31] Items reserved for his person or associated with it were denoted the term "*khāss*"; the same term referred broadly to the class of the nobility who depended on him.

The emperor's authority was thus exercised through his body. Symbolic contact with the kingly body, mediated through robes of honor that had been adorned or even touched by it, gave something of its legitimacy to the grantee: a long-standing practice that became utterly routinized at the Mughal court.[32] But even as bureaucratization drained robes of their charismatic capacity, the imperial body retained its aura of sacrosanctity. It was inconceivable to touch the king, or the things that he touched, without his permission. Aurangzeb made this point with characteristic sharpness in ordering a general to wear spectacles for three days, when the latter's elbow inadvertently touched the emperor's seat as he bent to kiss his foot.[33] In the

[28] Brahman, *Chahar chaman*, 33, 39, 40, 41 and passim.

[29] Brahman, "Tārīkh-i Rājāhā-yi Dihlī-yi Hindūstān." I am deeply grateful to Rajeev Kinra for sharing his copy of this rare manuscript with me.

[30] Stronge, *Painting for the Mughal Emperor*, 151; Franke, "Emperors Of Ṣūrat and Maʿnī:"

[31] Khare, "Emblems of Royalty."

[32] Gordon, "Robes of Honour."

[33] Khan, *Ahkām-i ʿĀlamgīrī*, 37–39.

same way, the minor nobleman who was given the remnants of his cup of coffee by Aurangzeb (to be consumed in the privacy of an antechamber) thought this so patent a mark of honor as to require no explication.[34]

The fashioning of this sacrosanct kingly body as an object of display and veneration by the people at large was also given impetus by Akbar. The emperor's grand palace complex at Fatehpur included a "window of presentation" (*jharoka*), a window mimicking in form the alcoves in which idols were kept in temples.[35] In these windows, which proliferated in the imperial complexes from the late sixteenth century, the king ritually presented himself before the eyes of his subjects, invoking the sacral experience of beholding a temple deity. His successor Jahangir elaborated this representative code by constructing the distinctive arched roofs (*bangala*) in which the emperor's figure came into the popular gaze. Jahangir's son Shah Jahan, most voluble of all in enunciating the discourse of sovereignty in architecture, took pains to ensure that his figure appeared before his subjects as an otherworldly, angelic being: when the emperor appeared below the gilded arched roof of his palace windows, the light of the morning sun enveloped his figure in the same sort of golden shimmering halo which surrounded his image in portraits.[36]

The idea that fastened the body of the king to the body of the people was that of justice, the central virtue promulgated by the ethical treatises popular among the Mughal elite.[37] In 1579, having himself declared superior to any independent theological authority (*mujtahid*), Akbar indicated himself as not subject to the law and possibly above it.[38] His son elaborated on this idea by presenting himself as the final and absolute source of justice to the people at large. Following the tradition of the pre-Islamic Sassanid ruler Anushirwan the Just, Jahangir had a chain of gold-plated bells installed from where he dispensed popular justice, to be rendered personally accessible to any petitioner.[39] More than a symbolic claim to divine legitimacy, such acts of regular and unmediated contact between ruler and ruled were seen as necessary in ministering the body politic. So a thinker at Jahangir's court advised the ruler to not be disheartened by the "loquacity" of his supplicants: "if the

[34] Wazih, *Memoirs of Eradut Khan*, 3.
[35] Asher, "Sub-Imperial Palaces"; Asher, "A Ray from the Sun"; Koch, "The Hierarchical Principles of Shah Jahani Painting," 133.
[36] Asher, *Architecture of Mughal India*, 186; Moin, *The Millennial Sovereign*, 219–20.
[37] Alam, "State Building under the Mughals," 113–17.
[38] Moin, *The Millennial Sovereign*, chap. 5; Buckler, "A New Interpretation of Akbar's 'Infallibility' Decree of 1579."
[39] Koch, "Shah Jahan and Orpheus," 127 fn. 142.

patient does not fully explain his condition, the physician cannot apprehend his disease."[40] Likewise, another felt that "the speech of the people translates the writings of divine fate; future conditions and outcomes can be discerned from their rumors (*afwāh*)."[41] Unsurprisingly, therefore, Jahangir was regular in appearing twice a week at the window of presentation in order to hear petitioners and directly give them justice.[42]

By the reign of Shah Jahan, the discourse of sovereignty had thus become rather more elaborate and totalizing than Barani's time some three centuries before.[43] Its basic contours remained the same: the king was appointed by God to nurture his flock by his nourishment of the faith and his dispensation of justice. But unlike Barani's day, the mark of heaven's favor was solely concentrated in the receptacle of the king's body (Fig. 2.3). Significantly, the king's nobility, who had no independent *daulat* of their own, are described by Chandar Bhan as simply appended to that of the king (*amīrān-i daulat-i ʿuzama*); or in war, as the companions of the conquering *daulat*; or, most picturesquely, as the "stars of the firmament of *daulat*." And as with Jahangir, since the notion of heavenly fortune required the king to personally ensure justice for his subjects, Shah Jahan's court ideologue unsurprisingly emphasizes how he set aside one day a week to tend to petitioners, despite the plethora of judicial officials appointed for the task.[44]

Beyond the prime virtue of justice, the king's ideologues saw him as granting prosperity to his obedient subjects. Again, Akbar had begun the tradition of distributing gold and foods equal to his weight twice a year among the worthy poor. This ritual, which replicated the form of kingly gifts in pre-Islamic South Asia, was one way in which the fortune carried in the king's body translated into sustenance for the poor.[45] His son Jahangir appears to have begun the practice of minting special coins to be strewn from his hand among the people observing his procession.[46] Shah Jahan represented himself as conveying divine prosperity (*faiz*) to his subjects and the world at large. So, thought Chandar Bhan, in his era "the limitless ocean of *faiz*

[40] Najm-Sani, *Advice on the Art of Governance*, 46.
[41] Dihlawi, *Risāla-i nūrīyya-i sultāniyya*, 44.
[42] Faruqui, *Princes*, 268.
[43] Though nowhere nearly as pronounced, the sense of *daulat* as heavenly illumination was however not absent in the earlier period. See for instance Barani, *Tārīkh-i Fīroz Shāhī* p. 582 for a reference to the "radiance of the daulat" (*farr-i daulat*) of Firoz Shah (d. 1388).
[44] Brahman, *Chahar chaman*, 129, 70, 39, 99.
[45] Mangalam, "Tulāpurusha Mahādāna"; Veluthat, "Status of the Monarch"; Heim, *Theories of the Gift in Medieval South Asia*.
[46] Hodivala, *Mughal Numismatics*, 177–85.

Figure 2.3. Heavenly approbation permits the ruler to rule with justice over lion and lamb alike. (Freer Gallery of Art, Smithsonian Institution, Washington, DC: Purchase – Charles Lang Freer Endowment, F.1939.49a.)

of this unbounded *daulat* is boiling over." Emanating from the imperial gaze (*nazar-i faiz asar*), this virtue came to imbue the court, which was the "arrival-hall of eternal *faiz*"; from here it radiated out to the traders at his door, and all the world's inferior rulers beyond. And, in the same way, Shah Jahan's routine sponsorship of public illuminations and fireworks, were all orchestrated for the people's pleasure and repose.[47] In this way, the idea of the people emerged most fully in the discourse of sovereignty elaborated in the reign of Shah Jahan, albeit only as its requisite and necessitating object. They were expected to be the recipients of the king's justice and prosperity; nothing more than obedience and gratitude was needed of them.

In its textual expression, the discourse of sovereignty was limited to elite circles, which had however been expanding to integrate new social groups across the empire by the mid seventeenth century.[48] Not content with this constrained arena of representation, Shah Jahan required a more expansive theater of sovereignty for himself, in which the people would play a more prominent role. These ambitions would be enacted, in the middle of the seventeenth century, by the making of a new imperial capital in his own name: Shahjahanabad.

The City as the Insignia of Sovereignty

Writing a short essay on Shahjahanabad almost a century later, a certain Haji Khair Allah discerned this connection between the expression of imperial sovereignty and the city. "Praise be to God!," he marveled, "what a feat of construction it is! Luxuriating glory, it sits radiating moist freshness on the sublime royal diploma of the earth like an imperial insignia (*tughrā*)."[49] While the making of the new city has been seen as an act of incorporating the city into the king's patrimonial household, the following pages suggest that Shahjahanabad was an architectural expression of Shah Jahan's discourse of sovereignty.[50] The principle features of the new city represented in stone the values by which imperial rule claimed legitimacy. Encoded in the city's gardens, fountains, squares, and mosques, these values would shape the subjectivity of the common multitudes who appear

[47] Brahman, *Chahar chaman*, 88, 59, 83, 92, 122–23.
[48] Alam and Subrahmanyam, "The Making of a Munshi."
[49] Khair Allah, "Tausīf-i Dār al-Khilāfat Shāhjahānābād," fols. 75b–76a.
[50] For the former view, see Blake, *Shahjahanabad*.

with increasing frequency in the early eighteenth century. Yet the city did not simply serve as a conduit from the king's mouth to the people's ear. On the one hand, the space in which Shahjahanabad was built was not freshly-made paper on which Mughal power could be freely inscribed: the land was manifestly a palimpsest, from which the traces of the engraving—and effacing—of older symbols of power and authority were never eradicated.[51] The values of the imperial discourse of sovereignty thus did not reach the people in an unmediated form. And, on the other hand, Shah Jahan's new capital became transformed by its own success in ways the king could not have imagined: The prosperity that the city was designed to engender created both a complex stratification of wealth and a large underclass of the urban poor. It is these urban masses, shaped but not dominated by the discourse of imperial sovereignty, who, in the eighteenth century, would rise as much to defend the king in exceptional circumstances as they challenged his everyday rule in the city.

That the capital city was the key site for the expression of imperial ambition is evident in an official chronicle of Shah Jahan's reign, which compares the existing capital of Akbarabad favorably to Baghdad in the era of the great Caliphs.[52] But Akbarabad, a much older town, bore the name of Shah Jahan's grandfather, and did not afford a canvas expansive enough for the ambitious monarch, who would lavish incredible sums of money on his architectural projects.[53] After much consultation and discussion, a site was selected north of the existing city of Delhi, and the architects Ustad Ahmad and Ustad Hamid, scions of a family of architects and mathematicians, were assigned to execute the court-approved plan. In 1638, at an astrologically propitious moment, excavations for the new fort's foundations were inaugurated.[54] The new city was built immediately to the north to the existing urban complex of Firozabad, never fully rebuilt since Timur's sack of Delhi in 1398, which now came to be regarded as "old Delhi."[55]

Recent scholarship has showed that Shah Jahan's palace architecture was built with heavenly and cosmological significations in mind.[56] This insight

[51] A notion explicated in Corboz, "The Land as Palimpsest."

[52] Lahori, *Bādshāhnāma*, I:106.

[53] Koch, "Agra"; Koch, "Mughal Agra: A Riverfront Garden City"; Moosvi, "Expenditure on Buildings under Shah Jahan."

[54] Kambuh, *'Amal-i Sālih*, 20; Chaghtai, "A Family of Great Mughal Architects."

[55] Verma, *Dynamics of Urban Life in Pre-Mughal India*, chap. 7; Koch, "The Delhi of the Mughals."

[56] Hasan, "The Morphology of a Mediaeval Indian City: A Case Study of Shahjahanabad in the 18th and Early 19th Century"; Koch, "Shah Jahan and Orpheus"; Moin, *The Millennial Sovereign*, chap. 7. See also the essays and very helpful map in Ehlers and Krafft, *Shâhjahânâbâd*.

applies equally to the new city as a whole. Shahjahanabad's design and layout, its architectural features and templates, all reflected the values and ideals central to its maker's vision of kingship. The following pages briefly describe four central values of the discourse of sovereignty, and their spatial expression in the city. These include an assertion of universal sovereignty in relation competing claims; a commitment to Islam as the principle form of access to the divine, which ordered the world and to justified the dynasty's rule; the quality of prosperity, which the king as beneficent master bestowed upon his subjects; and the cultivation of pleasure, the natural product of an urbanity under imperial rule.

Power

The power of the empire was most clearly represented by the fort, which dominated the city's eastern side, and held palaces named the "house of *daulat*" (*daulat-khāna*). Poets and essayists heaped words of rhythmic praise on its firm foundations, lofty battlements, and soaring towers, all of which were linked to Shah Jahan's excellence as a ruler. The imperial chronicler spends several pages in minute description of the palace's gardens and pavilions, a grand theater of imperial ritual designed to overwhelm those who approach the royal presence.[57] While later paintings present depictions of the palaces within, the earliest known plan of the fort, from about 1750, depicts only the periphery of the building, with the center a perfect blank, as if "suggesting that what went on there within the . . . [fort] was too other-worldly to be depicted in reality or to a mundane audience."[58]

If the pavilions and gardens within the fort served as an otherworldly theater of imperial pageantry, its looming red walls stood for the solidity and awesomeness of imperial power, one inscribed in the abject bodies of rebels left for all to see at its gate. The poet ʿHunarwar Khan ʿAqil likened the fort, among other things, to a circle of fire; its red sandstone battlements appeared to him as jeweled teeth in betel-stained lips; its cannons were dragons without head or feet; its moat was animated by the glittering flash of fish and crocodiles.[59] Enabled by the king's *daulat*,

[57] Waris, "Bādshāhnāma (Vol. III)," fols. 31a–42a; Koch, "Diwan-i ʿAmm and Chihil Sutun"; Rezavi, "The Mighty Defensive Fort."
[58] Losty, "Delineating Delhi: Images of the Mughal Capital," 19.
[59] ʿAqil, "Jalwa-yi Dīdār," fols. 22b, 23a, 24a.

the purpose of this power was to ensure justice, which lay symbolically at the heart of the fort. As Ebba Koch has shown, the mobilizing of such diverse images as of Orpheus taming the beasts, Solomonic thrones, and heavenly scales, all of which appear at key sites of public visibility within the fort, and are repeated as motifs in imperial albums, was to represent the king as the fountain of justice for all his subjects.[60] Thus the emperor appeared at the golden-domed "window of presentation," at the center of the eastern façade of the fort, bound personally to his subjects through the provision of justice (Fig. 2.4).

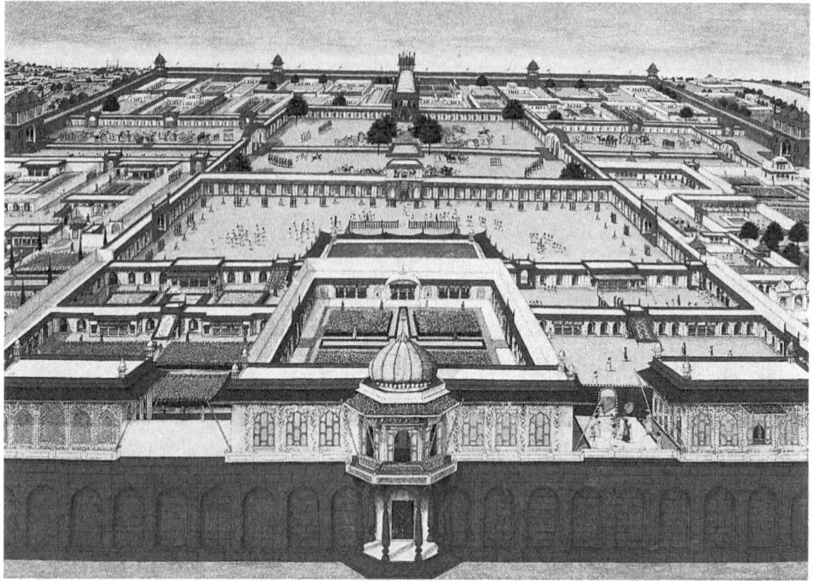

Figure 2.4. An idealized bird's-eye-view of the fort from the East, from the late eighteenth century. (ArtRes.)

Piety

As the complex of palaces, offices and gardens behind the red sandstone walls of the fort marked the rule and purpose of the dynasty, so the new city's "world-revealing mosque," built on its highest feature, established Shahjahanabad as a bastion of Islam.[61] With peristyles on three

[60] Koch, "The Mughal Emperor as Solomon, Majnun, and Orpheus."
[61] On the architecture of this mosque, see Asher, *Architecture of Mughal India*, 202.

sides surrounding an immense central courtyard, the mosque's three gates not only facilitated access from all sides, but also marked an airy and self-confident openness to the city's population, whether of Muslims or potential converts. Shah Jahan's courtly ideologue, the Hindu official Chandar Bhan, reveled in the mosque's sense of height and purity of line. "Heavenly spirits come to prostrate themselves there," he rhapsodized, "while mortals do not [even] raise their heads from their prostrations"—neatly expressing the imperial vision of a docile populace praying behind, or perhaps to, their God-like king.[62] The same ambiguity of representation is to be seen in the elaborate engravings above the eleven arches leading to the prayer chamber. Given their use of the naskh script, a casual visitor might easily mistake them for God's word of verses from the Qur'an. But a closer look reveals a single long inscription in Persian (with Qur'anic quotations), styled by a certain Nur Allah Ahmad, which heaps flowery praise on the emperor: as "a manifestation of divine power," and, crucially, "the founder of the regulation of justice and punishment."[63] The inscription ends with the hope:

> May the heads of the pulpits of the populated world continue to be decorated with the proclamation (*khutba*) of the eternal *daulat* which adorns this just and pious monarch, the benedictions of whose blessed and sanctified self have opened the doors of peace and tranquility on the face of time.[64]

Visitors were thus inexorably led to associate the intertwining of imperial *daulat*, justice, and Islamic piety in the courtyard of the mosque. For just as Shah Jahan's palace audience-halls evoked the mosque where the people prostrated before their God, so the mosque's architectural features and engravings evoked the looming fort to the east, indelibly linking king and justice to the temporal sovereignty of Islam in India (Fig. 2.5). This was a relationship ritually reenacted on every Friday, when the king's grand procession conveyed him to the mosque, to hear the sermon (*khutba*) which publicly affirmed his role as the temporal ruler of the realm, and to offer the obligatory noontime prayers in congregation with the assembled community of Muslims.

[62] Brahman, *Chahar chaman*, 164.
[63] Baig, *Sair al-manāzil*, 14.
[64] Baig, *Sair al-manāzil*, 17.

Figure 2.5. The Mosque, as seen from the Red Fort. (The British Library board: Add. Or. 4126 Section 4.)

Prosperity

The importance attached by Shah Jahan to the ideal of abundance was encapsulated for his courtly ideologues in the idea of *faiz*, which has been described as "a name for the gradual but steadily descending creative development of the world out of God and its maintenance through his providence."[65] The importance of the ideal in the discourse of sovereignty was already evident in Shah Jahan's father's claim that agricultural prosperity was the "fruit of [kingly] justice."[66] To promote *faiz* was an immediate objective of the construction of Shahjahanabad, and is evident in the nomenclature of two of the city's most notable features: the channels of water that traversed the city's two main thoroughfares and were named the "Channel of Abundance" (*nahr-i faiz*) and the "Bazar of Abundance" (*faiz bāzār*) which stretched south from the fort to the city's Delhi gate.

Given the connection between water and wealth in a land dependent on the vagaries of the monsoon rain for agricultural production, the building of a canal was a potent assertion of imperial beneficence. As part of developing

[65] de Boer, "Faiḍ."
[66] Jahangir, *Jahāngīrnāma*, 275.

Shahjahanabad, the Iranian émigré nobleman ʿAli Mardan Khan was tasked with repairing and extending an older canal, built in the reign of Firoz Shah (d. 1388), which brought water from the foothills of the Himalayas to Safidon, north of the city.[67] While the official chronicler is silent on the work this entailed, an early-nineteenth-century colonial surveyor admired the result, which conveyed water through elevated mounds, aqueducts, and a sixty-foot-deep channel cut through the solid stone of the ridge into the northwest of the city. Flowing into the fort, this water was dispersed overground in the two main streets and in the city's central park, while subterranean ducts conveyed it to the mansions of the nobility and to neighborhood wells.[68] The link between the king's generosity, urban prosperity, and water is evident in the praise of Farrukh Siyar by the poet and bureaucrat ʿAbd al-Jalil Bilgrami:

> His hand's a river and every finger a channel
> Each wave of which makes a city flourish.[69]

For Shah Jahan's courtly ideologue Chandar Bhan, the flow of water was mingled with the city's economic vibrancy:

> Ample and plentiful delicacies, shops with chairs, filled to the brim with coin and jewels, merchandise and fabrics and delicacies and rarities of every land, and canals of flowing water, pools and step-wells and wells of sweet-tasting water, markets and alleys and inns and quarters and vegetable-markets and houses and suburbs have all been built to the apogee of beauty for the rest of those coming and going.[70]

The key site of commercial vitality in the new city was to be Moonlight Avenue (*chāndnī chauk*); the 1,300-meter-long thoroughfare ran due west from the Lahore Gate of the fort toward the Lahore Gate of the city. An eighteenth-century drawing of the street renders it as a long promenade

[67] Waris, "Bādshāhnāma" vol. III, fol. 31a; Siddiqui, "Water Works and Irrigation System in India during Pre-Mughal Times"; Blake, *Shahjahanabad*, 64–65.

[68] "[M]oney must have been expended with a most lavish hand" on making the canal, noted Colvin. He adds, "During the long period that it did flow, the system of irrigation from its waters appears to have been most extensively diffused." Colvin, "On the Restoration of the Ancient Canals in the Delhi Territory," 109–10.

[69] Bilgrami, *Maṣnawī*, 3.

[70] Brahman, *Chahar chaman*, 125.

with two octagonal squares leading to the Fathpuri Mosque. Though not an accurate architectural plan, the image nevertheless conveys its essential features. The first square contained the city's police office (*kotwālī*), with a railed platform and a public wooden whipping-post (*lakrā*) named after a certain Laʿl Khan.[71] Further up the avenue was a larger square; on one side of its central pool lay the public baths (*hammām*); on the other a caravanserai constructed by the princess Jahan Ara, which lay next to the grand "Princess's Garden" (*bāgh-i begam*), also endowed by her. Most strikingly, on either side of the street were 1,560 shops of regular size, behind which lay the mansions of their owners.[72]

Through the center ran the water which gave Moonlight Avenue its distinctive character (Fig. 2.6). The poet ʿAqil captured its significance perfectly in a line of verse:

> The channel of water runs through its middle
> Like an artery filled with the water of life.[73]

Were the designers of the Moonlight Avenue mindful of the biblical vision of the new Jerusalem, endowed with "the river of the water of life, clear as crystal, flowing from the throne of God and of the lamb, down the middle of the main street of the city"?[74] Such eschatological allusions were perfectly in tenor with the messianic overtones of the Mughal court under Shah Jahan.[75] But even Mughal observers unschooled in Bibliology marveled at the sight of water flowing through the city's streets. A late-seventeenth-century gazetteer noted the canal brought healthful water "to every street and square."[76] At about the same time, the visitor Nek Rai praised the sweetness of the water that the canal carried "to every heart's door" of the city, dwelling particularly on its role in sustaining a large population in this otherwise dry region.[77]

For Shah Jahan, *faiz* was ensured by securing the flow of commerce through his realm. Of course, the excitations of the empire's markets had already been

[71] Mirza Sangin Baig, *Sair al-manāzil*, 40. The early-nineteenth-century author of the text also informs us that a wheel on which murderers were broken was in use here in previous times.
[72] Blake, *Shahjahanabad*, 55–56.
[73] ʿAqil, "Jalwa-yi Dīdār," 35b.
[74] Revelations 21:1–2.
[75] Moin, *The Millennial Sovereign*, chap. 6.
[76] Bhandari, *The Khulasatu-t-Tawarikh*, 30.
[77] Nik Raʾi, "Tazkīrat al-Safar wa Tuhfat al-Zafar," fol. 13b; Alam and Subrahmanyam, "The Making of a Munshi," 66.

established as the subject of poetic praise before Delhi was remade. For the high nobleman and poet Ahsan somewhat earlier, the market's erotic charge derived not only from drapers, jewelers, betel-leaf sellers and tradesmen, but also the comeliness of Hindustan's "native" communities: (Hindu) Rajputs, Afghans, and (Muslim) Shaikhzadas.[78] For Shah Jahan's courtly ideologue Chandar Bhan, abundance was manifested in the cosmopolitanism of the new city's many bustling markets:

> Iraqis and Khorasanis beyond counting
> Place before themselves their stock
> Franks have come from Frankistan
> With select fineries from many a port
> Because the king is aware of his affairs
> A highway links East to West.[79]

Imperial power ensured the economic vitality of everyday life in the city. The path that linked the East of the Mughal domains to the West of the foreign lands was forged and protected by a vigilant and alert ruler, and the empire's greatness was evidenced by the exotic foreigners drawn to it.[80]

Charged by a sense of competitiveness against the Ottoman and Safavid empires, Chandar Bhan's sentiments became widely shared beyond the court as his writings circulated through the realm at the end of the seventeenth century. This is why the gazetteer Sujan Rai, an obscure local intellectual in the provincial town of Batala, quotes Chandar Bhan's above poem, though he omits the ending about the king and instead adds verses celebrating the presence of the wares of all the world in Delhi's shops: a telling lack of emphasis on imperial authority and an amplification of the praise of commerce. Like the courtly ideologue, Sujan Rai emphasizes the presence of foreigners in the city, coming from the faraway realms of France, England, and Holland, the more familiar lands of Khwarazm, Turkistan, Zabulistan, Khita, Khotan, Chin and Machin, Kashgar, Qalmastan, and Tibet—besides, of course, people from other parts of the Mughal domains. The abundance of peoples was a sign of the empire's prosperity. All these foreign folk, we are told, had learned the "manners and the speech of Hindustan," and were "freely practicing their

[78] Ahsan, "Jalwa-yi Nāz/Wasf-i Kashmīr," fols. 11a–12a.
[79] Brahman, *Chahar chaman*, 125.
[80] On Chandar Bhan's idealization of Shah Jahan, see Kinra, *Writing Self, Writing Empire*, chap. 3.

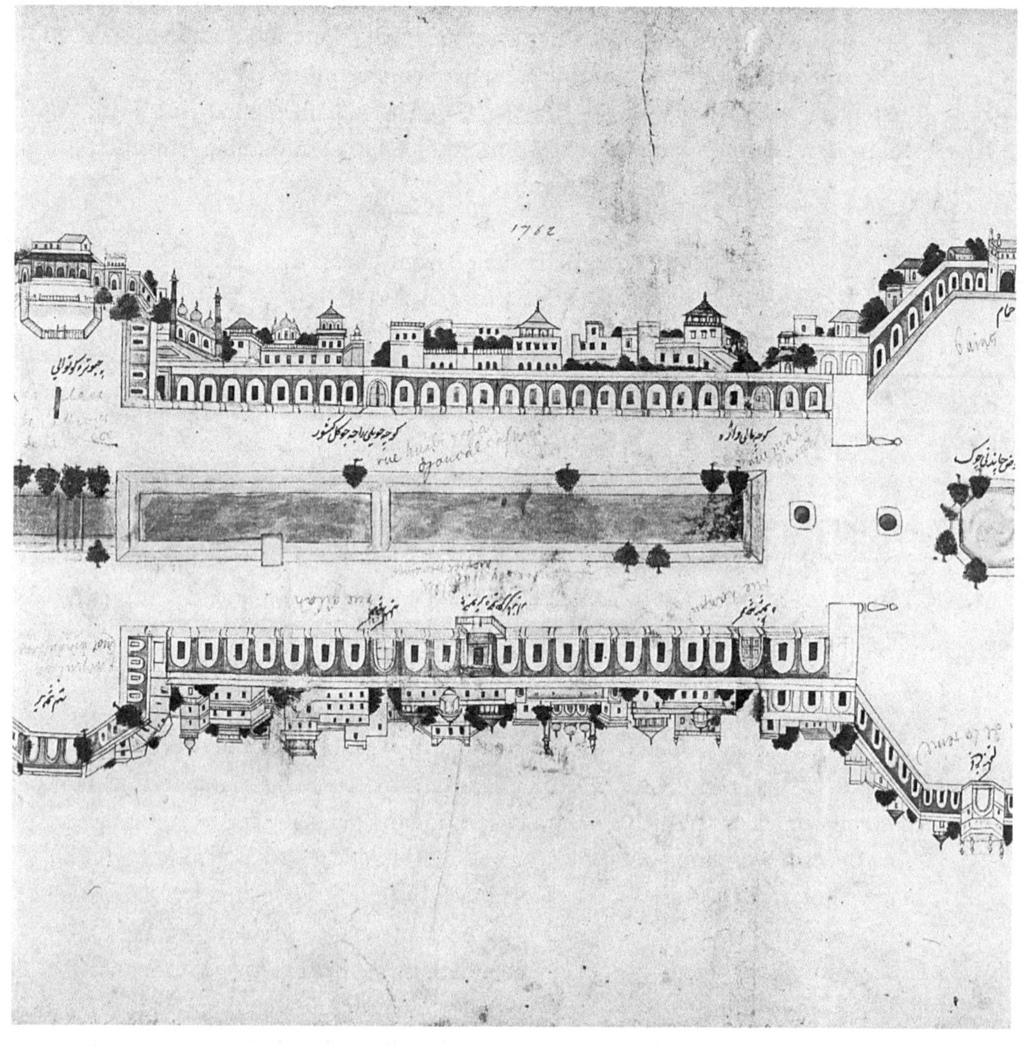

Figure 2.6. Shops on either side of the square of Moonlight Avenue. (Victoria & Albert Museum.)

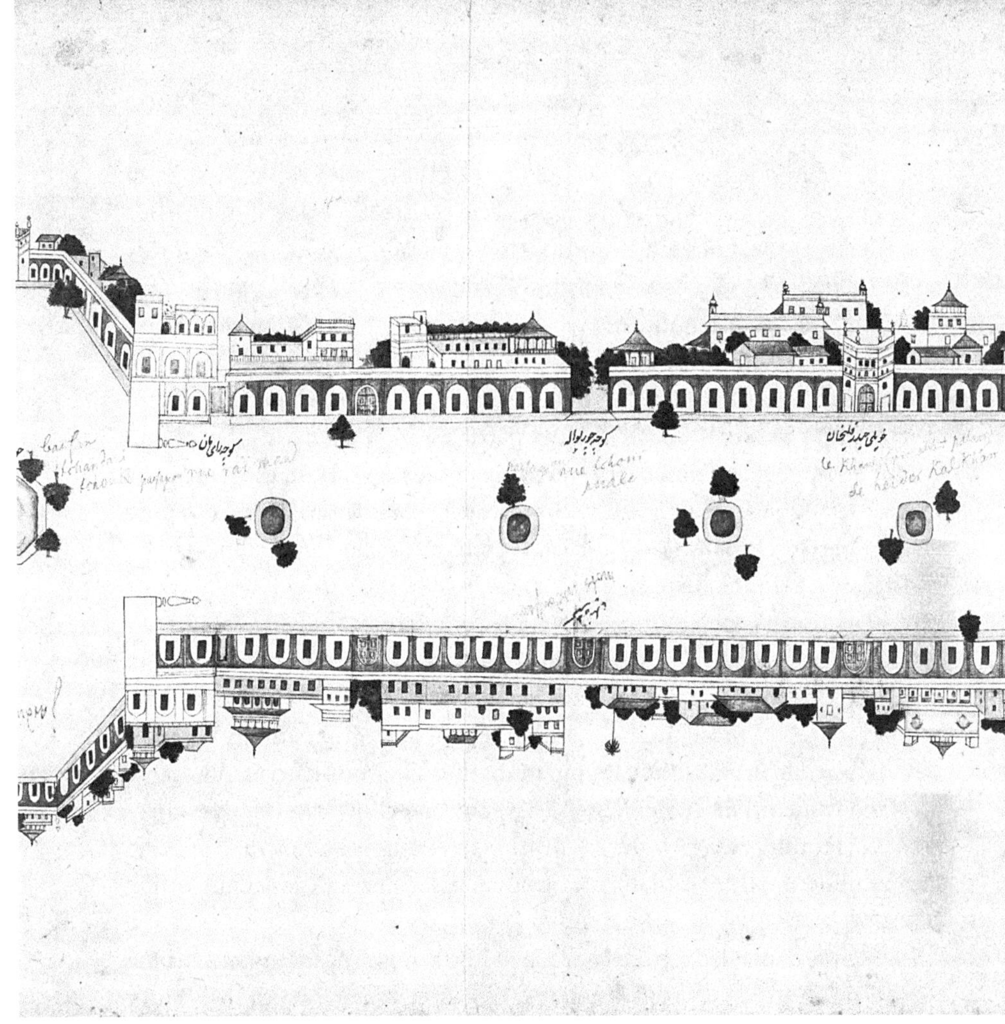

own trades" in markets where "all the luxury items and clothes required for the imperial warehouses could be acquired in a single day."[81]

Pleasure

The final component of imperial ideology was the pursuit of pleasure, associated in India with kingship from the early medieval period if not earlier. The courtly context of such kingship has been described as a "*kāma* world," an aesthetic realm of sensual pleasures that included the erotic, but also the consumption of commodities (exotica, perfumes, flowers, fabrics, gems, wine, and betel-nut to list only a few) and the practices of music and dance, games and poetry.[82] Such ideals of kingship appear to have been rapidly integrated into Mughal courtly culture, particularly in the early seventeenth century.[83] An explicit aim of the founding of the new city, in the words of a chronicler associated with Shah Jahan's court, was the provision of repose and the pleasures of life (*firāgh, lazzat-i zindagī*) for the king's subjects.[84]

The key site for the experience of pleasure was the garden, itself a visual representation of the natural abundance produced by imperial power. As Koch has argued, Shah Jahan's palace-gardens were built "as an image of his reign and empire, as garden paradises of the ideal king whose good government . . . had brought about a new golden age of unending spring."[85] Beyond their palaces, Mughal emperors built pleasure-gardens in scenic locales outside urban centers. In the new city of Delhi, however, the court's architects produced a striking innovation, creating the Sahibabad Garden immediately north of Moonlight Avenue and running the length of the street.[86]

Though founded by members of the imperial family, gardens such as the Sahibabad were not restricted to imperial use.[87] A late-eighteenth-century

[81] Bhandari, *The Khulasatu-t-Tawarikh*, 30; in this way his views appear to stand in some contrast to the rather narrow conception of local patriotisms in South Asia suggested in Bayly, *Origins of Nationality*, chaps. 1–3.

[82] Ali, "Rethinking the History of the 'Kāma' World in Early India"; McHugh, "The Incense Trees of the Land of Emeralds."

[83] Balabanlilar, "The Emperor Jahangir and the Pursuit of Pleasure."

[84] Kambuh, *'Amal-i Sālih*, 20.

[85] Koch, "Mughal Palace Gardens from Babur to Shah Jahan (1526–1648)," 165.

[86] Baig, *Sair al-manāzil*, 35.

[87] Cf. Blake, "The Khanah Bagh," 188.

observer remarked on how gardens in Delhi and elsewhere were "without exception free and open to all the world" for entertainments or stay.[88] Only the eastern portion of the Sahibabad garden appears to have been limited for royals. The produce of imperial gardens belonged to the king, and was sold to the populace at large.[89] That the part adjoining the square of Moonlight Avenue was open to public access is evident from the praise showered on it by the poet ʿAqil, who describes its trees, flowers, canal, and particularly the grand fountain at its heart, which he sees as the lamp placed at the center of the lively salon (*majlis*) of the city.[90] From the writings of the nobleman and poet Faʾiz, it is clear that even imperial gardens had become sites of elite conviviality by the late seventeenth century. Thus, in a literary epistle, he reproves a person for missing an assignation in a garden full of revelers, where peacocks trailed their feathers in pathways among canals murmuring with sweet water. In another, he bemoans the high-handedness of an administrator in the cutting of the water supply to the Shalamar garden, causing the faces of the roses to become dusty like that of a Hindu mendicant boy (*sanāsī-pasar*).[91]

The intent of placing the Sahibabad garden in the midst of the city was unambiguous. As the king had his private gardens, so gardens were given also for the benefit of the people. A similar impetus lay behind the endowment of other urban institutions, such as the city's public hospital and baths, the latter of which were also endowed by the princess Jahan Ara. Unmentioned in Chandar Bhan's narrative of the court's doings, these baths were much celebrated by less-exalted authors. While the late-seventeenth-century gazetteer praises its medicinal and recreational virtues, ʿAqil mentions the presence of the city's well-born, and Ottomans, Africans, Iraqis, and Tatars all gathered in convivial warmth under the bathhouse's dome: its cosmopolitanism again reflecting the virtues of empire.[92]

[88] Khan and Mustepha, *Sëir Mutaqherin*, 74, fn. 68. Robert Travers has recently identified Haji Mustepha, the enigmatic translator and annotator of Ghulam Husain Khan's history, as Dominique Lhomaca, from a Latin Christian dragoman family in service of the French and Ottoman states. See Travers, "The Connected Worlds of Haji Mustapha (c. 1730–91)."

[89] For instances of conflicts which reduced garden revenue, and gifts of garden produce, see Anonymous, "Akhbārāt, Farrukh Siyar, RY 6-7/II," 34, 85; Habib, "Notes on the Economic and Social Aspects of Mughal Gardens."

[90] ʿAqil, "Jalwa-yi Dīdār," fol. 28a.

[91] Faʾiz, "Kulliyāt-i Fāʾiz," fols. 151b–152a.

[92] ʿAqil, "Jalwa-yi Dīdār," fols. 36a–37b.

The City in the Eighteenth Century

Sometime in 1706/7, the poet Hunarwar Khan "ʿAqil" put his finishing touches to a long panegyric called *A Lustrous Vision*, which had occupied his attention for a week. Much of the poem was directed at the nobleman Nizam al-Mulk, whose arms and accoutrements the author dutifully extolled. But then ʿAqil's attention turned to the imperial metropolis, a place he knew both as the ancient site of "Delhi, the Dignified," (*hazrat-i Dihlī*) and as the new city of Shahjahanabad.[93] ʿAqil was astounded by the vastness of the city, and marveled at the huge amounts of earth and stone marshalled in the making of this new "Abode of the Caliphate." The profuse, tangled alleys of the new city reminded him of the curving tresses of Ayaz, the famously handsome figure of myth. Its streets were as the paths of a garden, whose fountains and lights greeted the eye wherever one turned; its shops glittered with lamps like rubies. The soldiers and traders who lived here were both masters of the pen and the sword: just as delicately composed at the gathering as they were quick and ferocious on the battlefield. They were, of course, natives, but there were also immigrants from Iraq and the Tatar lands, drawn to the country by its riches: he who could not afford a single square meal in his homeland lived grandly in Delhi. In fact, rhymed ʿAqil, India was a kind of magical mirror, one which hid the defects of those who perused it; it exerted a benevolently civilizing influence, making humans of even the most worthless lumps of clay. Its two communities, the Muslims and infidels, lived together in a "comprehensive peace" (*sulh-i kull*), without argument or strife. For "what difference between rose and thorn, born as they are on the same branch?" So the poet advised his reader: muss up your hair a little bit, and slant your hat at a jaunty angle, for no reproachful gazes were to be encountered in India. Indeed, hatred and discord did not weigh upon hearts in this land, and no one troubled another.[94]

Though Shah Jahan was a distant memory as ʿAqil put pen to paper, his enunciation of sovereignty had, by the early eighteenth century, become natural and indeed integral to the way both city and empire were imagined: this is why visions of Delhi and India smoothly telescope into one another in this poem as indeed elsewhere. But ʿAqil's glittering panegyric also papered over

[93] On such praise-filled descriptions of the city, see Sharma, "The City of Beauties in Indo-Persian Poetic Landscape."

[94] ʿAqil, "Jalwa-yi Dīdār," fols. 20a–22a.

a slightly seamier reality. For, by the early eighteenth century, the unintended consequences of the waves of silver that washed through Moonlight Avenue were becoming manifest, both in the rise of new elites and the growth of an increasingly turbulent new underclass. It is to this wealthy and turbulent city of the eighteenth century that we must now turn.

How rich was the city by the early eighteenth century, and how was its wealth distributed? Historians have long believed that the fruits of empire were concentrated in the hands of the emperor and a tiny elite of noblemen: a logical corollary of the fact that both city and empire were "one big household workshop" in the hands of the ruler.[95] Others have argued that a "middle-class" of well-to-do mercantile and professional groups had already emerged in the Mughal realm by the early decades of the seventeenth century.[96] An important vein of scholarship has also argued that the economy of the empire, expanding in concert with growing inter-regional trade, caused the dramatic increase in imports of silver into the subcontinent, though scholars differ as to its extent and effects.[97] Much of this silver, it appears, streamed into Delhi. As we shall see, the intensification of the processes of economic expansion and integration desired by Shah Jahan had, by the early eighteenth century, produced a city with a complex, layered, and mobile hierarchy of wealth.

While evidence is sorely lacking, even stray documents offer a glimpse of the money streaming through the city's streets by the reign of Muhammad Shah. Consider the evidence of a clutch of sale-deeds that are now preserved in the National Archives of India. On May 13, 1729, two noblemen set their seals to initiate a legal transaction of sale for a mansion in the neighborhood of Mirza Sultan, in Delhi, near the passage by the "Dhar-i Mahabat Khan," just south of the city walls. The seller Mirza Baqir Khan was in the court's employ, as were his witnesses. The buyer, one Ghulam Ahmad Khan, also a courtier, was purchasing a well-appointed mansion, built of

[95] Blake, *Shahjahanabad*, 120–21; Ali, *The Mughal Nobility under Aurangzeb*, 170; for a note of caution against generalizations, see Subrahmanyam, "The Mughal State—Structure or Process?" 312 et passim.

[96] Khan, "The Middle Classes in the Mughal Empire"; Rezavi, "Representation of Middle-Class Professionals in Mughal Visual Art."

[97] Of this vast literature see Raychaudhuri, Habib, and Kumar, *The Cambridge Economic History of India*, chaps. 12, 13; Perlin, "Growth of Money Economy"; Richards, *The Imperial Monetary System of Mughal India*; Moosvi, "The Silver Influx"; Richards, "The Seventeenth-Century Crisis in South Asia"; Haider, "Precious Metal Flows"; Subrahmanyam, *Money and the Market in India, 1100–1700*, "Introduction"; Satyal, "The Mughal Empire, Overland Trade, and Merchants of Northern India, 1526–1707."

stone and brick. Behind the house's imposing north-facing doorway stood a large porticoed courtyard. On the north side, there were two rooms, a bathroom, and a dressing-room; to the east, a walled-off section with eight private rooms, a sunken well, and a toilet. In addition, the house came with an attached shop, and four Mulsari, Kinar, and Gondi trees. Six weeks later, the sale was completed between the agents of Mirza Baqir Khan and Ghulam Ahmad Khan with the payment of a staggering 11,133 rupees and four annas.[98] Given that a hypothetical sale-contract from an instructional manual for secretaries from the 1740s describes the sale of a mansion in the small town of Sultanpur for only 300 rupees, it is clear that Ghulam Ahmad's new mansion derived its primary value not only from its size and furnishings, but also from its location near the main southern road leading to the walled city.[99]

Who were the principals involved in this transaction? Though the sum exchanged was immense, both buyer and seller are obscure men who did not belong to the uppermost nobility. Mirza Baqir Khan appears to have been a descendant of the district's eponymous founder, Mirza Sultan Safawi. The family of Mirza Sultan had been declining steadily since the death of his son Shah Nawaz Khan in the war of succession of 1712, and perhaps financial necessity drove Mirza Baqir Khan to sell his ancestral home.[100] By contrast, the buyer, Mirza Ghulam Ahmad, was the descendant of one Muhammad Saʿid, more likely a nobleman with large estates around Kol (Aligarh) rather than the more famous Muhammad Saʿid Saʿadat Allah Khan, the long-standing administrator of the far southern districts of Karnatak.[101] Systematically buying houses in the same neighborhood, Ghulam Ahmad purchased an even grander mansion in the next year, this time for the sum of 14,500 rupees (with Mirza Baqir Khan serving as a witness to this transaction).[102] Muhammad Saʿid himself bought a smaller adjoining mansion in the same neighborhood for 350 rupees in the year of his death.[103]

[98] National Archives of India, Oriental Documents, Acc. No. 1295, 1296. Perti Doc. No. 160. Moosvi, "Urban Houses And Building."

[99] Khan, "Tārīkh," fols. 124a–125a.

[100] Muhammad, *Tārīkh-i Muhammadī*, 30; Aurangabadi, *Maʾāsir al-Umarāʾ [En]*, 2:772–73, 909–10.

[101] Confusingly, both men died in the same year. Muhammad, *Tārīkh-i Muhammadī*, 83, 85. I thank Hannah Archambault for discussing this with me.

[102] Tirmizi, Perti, and National Archives of India, *Calendar of Acquired Documents 1352–1754*, 89 Item 169, Acc. No. 1297.

[103] Tirmizi, Perti, and National Archives of India, 96 no. 182, Acc. No. 1304.

What was the value of a rupee in the early eighteenth century? A freshly minted silver rupee coin in Aurangzeb's reign weighed 180 grains (11.66 grams), of which the alloy did not comprise more than four per cent.[104] A list of the price of wheat in Delhi between 1763 and 1835, shows that only in conditions of famine or insecurity did a rupee purchase less than 20 *sir*-s (approximately 40 pounds) of wheat.[105] A rupee was a vast sum of money. There must have been many in Ghulam Ahmad's day who had never felt the touch of silver in their hands, who lived precariously on the verge of starvation, and who were driven to death by the slightest increase in prices; and it is no doubt their corpses that were to be seen "heaped in every market and alley" of the city during the great famine of 1713–1714.[106] But even the lower rungs of the bureaucracy were not immune from such privations, because a modest gentleman's life in Delhi could require more than a rupee a day. Arriving in Delhi the midst of this scarcity, the minor bureaucrat and poet ʿAbd al-Jalil Bilgrami confessed to his son that, having fallen into the "Red Sea of the Court," he found himself spending three rupees a day to keep up appearances while receiving a daily stipend of only two rupees from his patron.[107] Where ʿAbd al-Jalil was consigned by his relative poverty to live in a squalorous inn, the rather more aristocratic Iʿtimad ʿAli Khan, on reaching Delhi at much the same time, put up instead at the great Serai on Moonlight Avenue's central square. Spending a week there, Iʿtimad ʿAli Khan went on to rent the mansion of the doctor (*hakīm*) Muhammad Rafiʿ, situated on an equally prime location, for two rupees a day.[108]

ʿAbd al-Jalil's genteel poverty can be discerned from his counsel of frugality to his son, urging him reduce his expenses and pay off their debts in the hometown, and to copy manuscripts of interest by hand.[109] By contrast Iʿtimad ʿAli Khan belonged to the class who would have been able to afford manuscripts of interest to a connoisseur, such as the manuscript *de luxe* of Shah Jahan's imperial chronicle, which passed from a book-seller to a buyer for 215 rupees in 1727.[110] This did not place him in the uppermost

[104] Raychaudhuri, Habib, and Kumar, *The Cambridge Economic History of India*, 360.
[105] Roy, "A Rare Document on Delhi Wheat-Prices 1763–1835," 96–97.
[106] Kam Raj, "ʿIbratnāma," fol. 53a.
[107] Bilgrami, "Original Letters, &c.," 168–69; 278–79.
[108] Khan, "Majmaʿ al-Fawāʾid / Masdar-i Akhbār," fol. 133a.
[109] eg. Bilgrami, "Original Letters, &c.," 139–43.
[110] See the "Shah Jahan Nama" (no. 565) described in Khuda Bakhsh Oriental Public Library, *Catalogue*, VII:67–70.

ranks of book-collectors: the most expensive manuscript known from Shah Jahan's own library, priced by the emperor himself in 1628, was worth 20,000 rupees.[111]

Even Delhi's criminals were spectacularly wealthy. When the famed thief Khannan, a beef-butcher by profession, was apprehended in 1722, 20,000 rupees in cash besides stolen goods were recovered from his house (among his accomplices was an imperial servant who had a land grant of his own).[112] A final statistic, however, should bring us down to earth again: on August 14, 1744, a certain Nura Singh sold a nameless girl to one Dundi Mir for the sum of one-and-a-half rupees in the town of Allahabad. The sale was legal, and confirmed by the seal of the official ʿAbd al-Wahid.[113] To buy or sell a hundred such children would have meant nothing to Ghulam Ahmad, though he would have remained unable to afford Shah Jahan's most valuable book. In this context, Ghulam Ahmad's purchase of the mansion is suggestive of a stratospheric hierarchy of wealth in the city, in which the buyer himself was by no means in the uppermost echelon.

It is surely tales of such riches that drew Nadir Shah to the Mughal empire in 1739, and his depredations provoked commentators to reflect on the greatness of Delhi's wealth in general. One, for instance, imagined Nadir Shah asking about the state of Delhi's affairs since the Timur's brutal destruction of the city in 1398, an ominous foreshadowing of what would soon befall the city at his hand. He learns in response that though Delhi had not been much populated in previous eras, "the justice of its emperors and tranquility of the times" for three hundred years had caused the city to become swollen with the peoples of the seven climes.[114] Delhi's prosperity was recognized as markedly different, even shocking, to those unused to it. This is why many drew a sharp distinction between the people of Delhi and Nadir Shah's rough soldiery, who were ridiculed as guileless nomads and rustics, incapable of even conceiving the quantities of gold and silver that inadvertently fell into their hands during the sack of the city.[115] Even as another chronicler bewailed the expropriation of great quantities of buried treasure that had accumulated

[111] Seyller, "The Inspection and Valuation of Manuscripts in the Imperial Mughal Library," 270. See also the excellent discussion of the production and circulation of books in Habib, "Persian Book Writing."

[112] Lakhnavi, *Shāhnāma*, 152.

[113] National Archives of India, Oriental Documents, Acc. 2382/27

[114] Khwush Hal, "Nādir al-Zamānī [B]," fol. 196a–b.

[115] ʿAbd al-Karim, *Bayān-i Wāqiʿ*, 38.

in private residences over "four generations," he marveled at how the city's inhabitants also cunningly fleeced the naïve invaders of their looted jewels.[116]

The lamentations of chroniclers of Nadir Shah's exactions perversely offer us an unprecedented view into the complex stratification of wealth in the city. European observers breathlessly reported that incredible sums had been taken from Delhi, ranging from 40 to 100 million rupees.[117] A more accurate number is probably 21.2 million rupees, estimated by the Raja Jugal Kishor, who enthusiastically helped prepare the tax-rolls of the tribute from the city. Yet even this number could only be a poor proxy for the actual wealth of the city. While the rich sought at every turn to conceal their wealth, incompetent or corrupt assessors assigned exorbitant sums of money or deliberately undervalued receipts.[118]

Although the tax-rolls produced for Nadir Shah do not appear to have reached us, from statistics reported by Mughal observers, it appears that the highest stratum of the wealthy after the king was, predictably, that of the upper echelon of the nobility. Among the richest of these was the nobleman Nizam al-Mulk, who paid 1.5 million of the 3.3 million rupees he was to extract from his assigned ward of the city, quite aside from his personal tributes to Nadir Shah. Below this group stood the Hindu financial administrators at court. Their wealth can be estimated from the fact that Sita Ram, the leaseholder for revenue collection in the imperial demesne and the vizier's treasurer, paid 600,000 rupees. Majlis Rai, the vizier's financial administrator who killed himself after having his ear cut off for his obstinacy, was said to have paid either 400,000 or 900,000 rupees of the sums variously recalled as assigned to him.

Lesser noblemen such as Jugal Kishor paid 250,000 rupees. Anand Ram paid more than 200,000 rupees but with extreme difficulty. Far below them stood their scribes such as Lallu Mal, the accountant (*naqdī-nawīs*) of the imperial demesne, who could pay only 50,000 rupees before committing suicide. Jugal Kishor's own managers were assessed at 8,000 rupees. Finally came the merchants, imperial guards (*wālā-shāhīyān*) and jewelers of the Princess' Quarter (*katra-yi begam*) who, despite the greatest duress, could only muster 150,000 of the 217,000 rupees demanded.[119] Taken together, these numbers

[116] Warid, *Tārīkh-i Nādirshāhī*, 225–28, 205–06.
[117] Subrahmanyam, "Un Grand Dérangement," 362; Fraser, *History of Nadir Shah*, 202.
[118] Anonymous, "Muhāriba-yi Nādir Shāh," fol. 12a.
[119] These statistics have been assembled from Kishor, "Rūydād-i Nādir Shāh," 7–8; Anonymous, "Muhāriba-yi Nādir Shāh," fols. 13a–14a; Anonymous, "Bayāz-i Yūsufī," fols. 218b–219a.

also indicate not only the considerable financial resources available to the upper echelons of the nobility in a period that has long been imagined as one of imperial decline, but also the wide dispersal of such resources through many distinct social strata.

If the distribution of wealth in the city was much more complex than has been previously allowed, it was also generated by means other than revenue extraction. Certainly, many of the officials named above derived their wealth from their association with the imperial court, which enabled access to stipends, land grants, and revenue leases. Mirza Ghulam Ahmad's family could afford such expensive mansions perhaps because of their extensive landholdings. On the latter's death in 1732, these grants were not resumed to the imperial fisc (as had once been the custom), but simply inherited by his sons and grandsons. Among them, Ghulam Ahmad received land grants in Kol (Aligarh) and Jalali worth as much as 45,000 rupees annually.[120]

Yet such grants were not the only means of income in eighteenth-century Delhi. Despite their reticence in such matters, it would appear that another importance source of wealth for Delhi's elites was trade. Attitudes toward trade in the empire were complex. As we have seen, the centrality of the shops of Moonlight Avenue represented an imperial commitment to commercial prosperity. More particularly, the networks of seaborne trade through Gujarat and Bengal and the overland trade with Iran and Central Asia, through which textiles were exchanged for precious metals and horses respectively, were vital to the running of the empire.[121] Yet, even though traders might find honorable welcome at court, such as one Shaikh ʿIsa who appears presenting six bottles of perfume to Farrukh Siyar in October 1718, the work of the bazar was broadly regarded as unbefitting the respectable.[122] Mughal guides to gentlemanly conduct of the seventeenth century stridently disapproved of anything that might smack of the trader's ethos. "When purchasing a thing wanted by him," suggested one, "he [the gentleman] should not make any difficulty about the price, and ought not to buy like traders."[123] Another did not believe that a person who had acquired wealth through his labor could ever be a gentleman. While he acknowledged that there existed

[120] Tirmizi, Perti, and National Archives of India, *Calendar of Acquired Documents. 1352–1754*, 119. Item 226, Acc. No. 1309.

[121] Das Gupta, *Indian Merchants and the Decline of Surat: C. 1700–1750*; Das Gupta, "Trade and Politics in Eighteenth Century India"; Maloni, "The Monetary Realm of Surat in the Seventeenth Century"; Subrahmanyam, "The Hidden Face of Surat."

[122] Anonymous, "Akhbārāt, Farrukh Siyar, RY 6-7," 137.

[123] Hidayat Husain, "Mīrzā Nāmah," 4–5.

"people who have accumulated some wealth and are in quest of digging more of it out of the earth," he was sure that "their *mīrzā*-hood can have no durability."[124]

Nevertheless, as Satish Chandra has suggested, the Mughal peace of the seventeenth century caused members of the royal family, noblemen, and bureaucratic officials to "become more commerce-minded."[125] This only added impetus to the already vibrant networks of trade and exchange that had linked parts of the subcontinent to central and west Asia overland.[126] By the seventeenth century, the *khatrī* communities of North India, whose precursors had been involved in trading with Central Asia since the fourteenth century, also came to staff the imperial bureaucracy and came to identify with it.[127] North Indian noble households also came to engage in trade "as a by-product of military power and office."[128] This was certainly true of Muhammad Saʿid's house, whose records include the termination of a trade investment contract with the financier (*sāhūkār*) Gobind Rai of Panipat after the former's death in 1736.[129]

The ubiquity of such arrangements is apparent in a set of document templates which the nobleman Shakir Khan joined to the end of his memoirs. Among them he added a template for a co-investment partnership (*muzārabat*), which stipulated that half the profits generated through trade on borrowed principal would be given to the lender.[130] Elsewhere, Shakir Khan proudly recalled how the emperor Muhammad Shah had praised his father as one of the only two members of his court "from whose clothes the stench of the tailor's urine (*bū-yi baul-i bazzāz*) does not offend my nose."[131] The comment marks both the unseemliness of commerce and its pervasiveness in the early eighteenth century.

Muhammad Shah's reference to tailors was not accidental. Though studies of the production of cloth in the subcontinent focus on the major export-oriented centers of the Coromandel Coast, Gujarat, and Bengal,

[124] Ahmad, "British Museum Mīrzānāma," 100.

[125] Chandra, *Medieval India*, 383.

[126] For the reach of Mughal traders, see Dale, *Indian Merchants and Eurasian Trade, 1600–1750*; Habib, "Merchant Communities in Precolonial India"; Habib, "The Mercantile Classes of India During the Period of the Delhi Sultanate"; Rezavi, "Mercantile Life in Mughal India"; Rezavi, "Bazars and Markets in Medieval India."

[127] Alam, "Trade, State Policy and Regional Change," 211, 216–17.

[128] Subrahmanyam and Bayly, "Portfolio Capitalists," 415; Subrahmanyam, "Of Imarat and Tijarat."

[129] Tirmizi, Perti, and National Archives of India, *Calendar of Acquired Documents 1352–1754*, 109. Item 206, Acc. No. 1305.

[130] Khan, "Tārīkh," fol. 133a–b.

[131] Khan, "Hadīqa," fol. 141b.

Delhi had become a major center of the cloth trade with Central Asia and Iran by the eighteenth century if not well before.[132] Some of this may have indeed been stimulated by the presence of the court. The king's predecessor Farrukh Siyar was remembered for his preference for ostentatious gold-embroidery and lace (*zar-dozī, bādila, kinārī*), so much so that the lace-makers (*kinārī-firoshān*) of Delhi were said to have entered a severe mourning on his death.[133]

But it also appears that Delhi's elites actively participated in the city's cloth trade. It is revealing that Mukhlis, when pressed for cash by Nadir Shah's tax-men, had 10,000 rupees worth of fine cashmere (*pashmīna*) and brocade (*kimkhwāb*) in his house ready to offer by way of payment.[134] Mukhlis may have received it as a share of profit from an investment contract, or purchased it to sell for a shop of his own. Shops were built into mansions for this very purpose, as we have seen in the case of the one purchased by Ghulam Ahmad in 1729. A striking example of this phenomenon writ large was the new complex of residences and shops constructed by Burhan al-Mulk, the governor of Awadh, within the city walls of Delhi, just next to the Kabul gate. Named Mansurpur, the edifice was designed around the canal which entered the city from the northwest. A panegyrist praised its golden-domed tower (*burj*), the gateway, square, and fountains; he dwelt on the canal with shops on both sides, and the Shiʿi theologians and intellectuals to be encountered there.[135]

The extent of elite participation in the scorned activity of shopkeeping, and the great sums it might yield, is also evident in Raja Jugal Kishor's description of Nadir Shah's sack of Moonlight Avenue, on which his own huge mansion sat. The Raja reported that when Nadir's Shah's soldiers partially burned and plundered his mansion and shop as they rampaged down the street, he lost 200,000 rupees worth of materiel, and 50,000 rupees in cash. But Jugal Kishor's private treasury (*tosha-khāna*), containing cloth, jewelry, and 4,000 gold coins remained safe. Of course, as a financial agent recently risen from a lowly background, Jugal Kishor was expected to dirty his hands in trade and was held in contempt for it.[136] But even if Jugal Kishor

[132] Alam, "Trade, State Policy and Regional Change," 206.

[133] Khwush Hal, "Nādir al-Zamānī [B]," fols. 83b–84a.

[134] Mukhlis, "Waqāʾiʿ," 62.

[135] Ashob, "Tārīkh-i Shahādat [A]," fol. 263b; Husaini, "Kulliyāt-i Husainī," fols. 110b–112b; the building of Mansurpur was a significant investment in Delhi for a nobleman, who, by 1739, had created the foundations of his personal successor-state in Awadh. Cf. Srivastava, *The First Two Nawabs*.

[136] Alam and Subrahmanyam, "Eighteenth-Century Historiography," 414–15.

exaggerated his losses, the numbers indicate the significance of the cloth trade in making and maintaining the fortunes of Delhi's elites.[137]

The confusions of pleasure produced in Mughal culture by the intensification of commerce in the streets of Delhi is apparent from the glowing recollections of the young nobleman Dargah Quli Khan, who had arrived in Delhi from Hyderabad on the eve of Nadir Shah's invasion.[138] Dargah Quli Khan's *Delhi Album* (*Muraqqaʿ-i Dihlī*) has been much-cited as an account of the culture of the city during the early eighteenth century. But it is worth considering how much his writings reflect the wonderment of a youthful aristocrat at a market in which he (perhaps hyperbolically) imagined 100,000 rupees might easily be spent in a day. Where Bernier had complained of generally unadorned and boring shops some seventy years before, the youth was now buffeted by the sensuous power of the commodity. Walking along Moonlight Avenue and its "paradisiacal" canal, our author spied jewelers reclining haughtily on their cushions; rather more crude peddlers of cloth who called out to buyers; and sellers of fine arms and weapons. Such objects produced an erotic response in the author: the finest products of every land "wink hotly from every corner" and "the wave of the coquettish delicacy of every item . . . tugs at the heartstrings." It was no longer the "arching eyebrow of the beloved" which he likened to a fine sword, but the reverse. Observing the variegated wares of the manufactories of China was "to have the glass-house of restraint struck by the stone of astonishment." Similarly, the glass water-pipes, colorful flagons and cups, so enticingly arranged in front of the shops, "would move even a hundred-year-old ascetic with the lust for wine."[139]

The unanticipated success of Shah Jahan's vision of the radiating *faiz* of commerce came to exercise its disorienting influence on every aspect of the urban milieu in the eighteenth century. A powerful acknowledgement of this transformation is offered in a poem by the nobleman and poet Sadr al-Din Faʾiz, through which he criticizes the entire order of urban society, starting at the top. Faʾiz begins with the objects that bear such significance in the

[137] Kishor, "Rūydād-i Nādir Shāh," 4; on the value attached to shawls in precolonial elite culture more broadly, see Bayly, *Rulers, Townsmen, and Bazaars*, 72–73.

[138] My approach here owes much to Brook, *Confusions of Pleasure*.

[139] Khan, *Muraqqaʿ-yi Dihlī*, 61–62; such stylized representations of erotic markets were common in the period. See, for instance, ʿAsi, "Bahr Al-Maʿāni," fols. 8b–13a; but celebrations of markets and market-folk were already common in the poetry of the seventeenth century. Sharma, *Mughal Arcadia*, chap. 3.

discourse of sovereignty: the parasol, the crown, the throne—for him, they signify only that the king wants money. The poet then attributes the same motivation to all the king's officers: the vizier, the paymaster, the chamberlain, and the nobility as a whole. The same desire percolates down to lowly imperial servants: the censor, who examines weights or clears the road, who harangues the poor or imprecates the rich, wants only money. Likewise, the chief of police is hand-in-glove with the thieves he is supposed to arrest. Silver's lure has caught the lower orders: the pious mendicant, the haughty macebearer, the dextrous barber, the butcher who slaughters a hundred animals for his daily bread, the cheating goldsmith, the story-teller, the clown, the thief, the gardener, the mendicant—all are moved solely by the lust for money. The poet concludes:

> Fa'iz, whoever of the world's people comes into sight
> The desire for money is engraved in their heart as a coin
> Save for dinars and dirhams they have no other desire
> [And] losing honor is their work, all day and night
> All of this, for the love of money[140]

Sour though it is, Fa'iz's vision reflects an awareness of the abstract forces of the market that had come to exercise such a powerful influence on all orders of imperial society, from the highest to the lowest.

The Rise of Non-Elites and the Disorderly City

Though the youthful aristocrat reveled in the erotics of commerce, the percolation of wealth through the lower orders caused much disturbance to his contemporaries. For ʿAli, a resolutely noble poet of the seventeenth century, the place of commoners was clearly and unambiguously demarcated:

> In mixing with the lowly, take care that the cotton
> Of their rags and garments does not strike your satin.[141]

140 Fa'iz, "Kulliyāt-i Fā'iz," fols. 68b–72b; quote at 72b. I am grateful to Hasan Siddiqui for directing me to this reference.
141 ʿAli, *Dīwān-i ʿĀlī*, 102.

But by the early eighteenth century, the lowly were not only mingling among elites but wearing satin themselves. As we might expect, Faʾiz was disturbed enough by this phenomenon to write a poem of twenty couplets titled the "Allegory on the Condition of the Lowly." Premised on asserting distinctions where they have begun to blur, Faʾiz's poem demonstrates how far things had changed since ʿAli's day, only a few decades earlier. If a crow were to master a skill, rhymes Faʾiz, it would still not be respected by the male eagle. No one considers what is gilded to be gold. A lamp at night cannot match daylight. In the same way, although a beggar's son may rise high, he cannot be admired by the knowledgeable. If, "for example," a lowly man became a nobleman (*amīr*), he is still to be regarded as (coarse as) barley. Some of this resentment appears directed rising Hindu elites, for we are told that a financier (*sarrāf*), though rich, will not be liked by the great, and

> Although a statue of stone may a man resemble
> It cannot feel pain, nor from love's pangs tremble

Though Faʾiz ends with the claim that there can be no substitutes for either accomplishment or lineage, his defensiveness indicates precisely how much the sons of those who were recently scorned as beggars or traders now counted among the educated and elite.[142]

Nor was it only that a small number of *nouveaux riches* had arrived on the scene. To the eyes of the thirty-year-old poet Shaikh Zuhur al-Din Hatim, it looked like all of Delhi had gone topsy-turvy in 1729. Hatim begins by claiming that the emperor is no longer just and his nobility has given up its generosity, that the judge and the jurisprudent are corrupt and administrators are all thieves. Shocked at their impoverishment, the descendants of the nobility wander about in a daze in search of money, though without losing their hauteur. But the lowly (*razālē*) are intoxicated by their newfound wealth; they strut about wearing their golden clothes, which they display for all to see.

> The money-changer flings rupees and gold coins day and night
> The lace-maker is drowning in golden wire
> Those who inherited libraries now bind books for free

[142] Faʾiz, "Kulliyāt-i Fāʾiz," fol. 96a-b.

The stew-seller prattles mindlessly at his shop
The goldsmith plays all the time in gold and rupees[143]

The poet then proceeds to list all the city's upstarts, which serves as an opportunity to mention every profession. The barbers are all puffed up, and the wick-makers have grown corpulent eating the butcher's meat. The baker and the kabab-maker have grown bold, the grocer is verdantly rich, the smith asserts the strength of his lock, and even the meanest weavers now dare to mock everyone all the time. The oil-pressers who now stride through town are perfumed with the oil of jasmine, and are masters of money and mansions, having quite forgot the coarse grains that were their staple until recently. Those who sold coarse cloth have been granted shawls of honor, and even the city's ruffians (*luccha*) are eating full meals. The men who used to carry palanquins on their shoulders now ride in them. The prostitute laughs at the noble lady. Shoemakers brandish their shoes at everyone. The trunk-maker has filled boxes full of gold. Everyone is now a king in their own alley. But Hatim's own reasons for such laments are made amply clear in the last lines of the poem, which betray only his own humiliating dependence on the men beneath his station whom he mocks.[144]

The rise of the lowly was accompanied by the expansion of the city's underclass, generically dubbed the populace (*'awāmm*). It is difficult to derive a picture of social variegation within this broadest of categories. It is clear, however, that the broad group of market-people (*ahl-i bāzār*) or artisans (*ahl-i hirfa*) who were noted as swarming through Delhi encompassed a wide social variety: from rich and powerful jewelers, brokers, financiers, and traders, to more humble makers of golden lace (*kinārī*) and fine cloth, shoemakers, confectioners, and street-vendors of spoons.

Already in the late seventeenth century a prose stylist expressed his contempt for the "modes and fashions" of such youth, whom he describes as "free-spirited and ruffianly" (*lawand o aubāsh*). It soon becomes clear that these were not the poorest of the poor, but uppity commoners: he expresses his disgust at their clothing, their vain and idle speech, and their cries of "Hui!" Their dishonor was expressed in the characteristic disorder of their head and feet: it is clear from the way they tied their turbans that they had a "twist" (*pechishī*) in their heads, while their high-heeled shoes evidenced

143 Hatim, *Dīwān-zāda*, 389.
144 Hatim, *Dīwān-zāda*, 392.

their snooty refusal to let their feet touch the ground. They slayed a thousand savage lions, but only with the swords of their tongue. They considered it bravery to frighten shopkeepers (*baqqālān*); and when they were processed through town on a donkey, they considered themselves honored as Jesus. During the procession, they thought the drum of announcement to be the king's kettledrum; they regarded children's sticks (*tīrak*) to be their royal long pipes (*qarranai*), and the crowds of cursing folk to be their own army. These youths did not refrain from their assertions of independence and their misguided fights (*jang-i nā-haqq*) until the fetters fell on their feet, and the pillory around their necks: for the scourge on their backs was their refuge, and the prison their schoolhouse.[145] Such men were not the city's poor; but, as Hatim's words make clear, they seemed to disregard the customs of gentility, were quick to fight in the markets, and had no fear of the king's authority. And perhaps beneath even them were the unemployed, the idle, the vagabonds called *luccha* or *shuhda*, who were found "sitting on the steps of the congregational mosque, and in fact in every market and square of the city."[146] Together they comprised the spectators (*tamāshā-bīnān*) who observed the processions of the great noblemen, the "event-seekers" (*wāqiʿa-talibān*) who stirred up unrest, and it is they would finally come together as a popular gathering (*hujūm-i ʿāmm*), the mob (*aubāsh*) in riot (*balwā*).

Yet this underclass was as much produced by the workings of imperial power as the city's enormous wealth. This is apparent in the case of the community of the Turani Mughals, who were prominent among the city's potentially disorderly and fractious folk. The precise referents of the term "Turani Mughal" are ambiguous, but it seems to have denoted those who claimed origins in the Iranian plateau or Central Asia and were called Irani or Turani Mughal respectively.[147] We are not here concerned with the stream of learned doctors, poets, theologians, divines, painters, astronomers, mathematicians, and administrators from Turan who entered imperial service from the late sixteenth to the mid-eighteenth century, but rather their less respectable

[145] Hatim, "Abr-i Faiz," fols. 57b–59a.

[146] Ashob, "Tārīkh-i Shahādat [A]," fol. 285b.

[147] Irvine's caution in this regard is apposite: "In using this term Mughal, I vouch in no way for its accurate application, ethnographically or otherwise. It must be understood to be an unquestioning acceptance of the term as employed by Indian writers of the period." Irvine and Sarkar, *Later Mughals*, I:272. The problems with such a schematic division between Irani and Turani are well-explicated in Péri, "A Turkic Clan in Mughal India"; Davis, "Tūrān." For the eighteenth century, see Gommans, *The Rise of the Indo-Afghan Empire, c.1710–1780*, 61–66; Kia, "Contours of Persianate Community, 1722–1835," 174–82.

countrymen, in particular soldiers.[148] An imperial perspective on these people emerges from the collections of correspondence attributed to the emperor Aurangzeb, circulated after his death in 1707. Aurangzeb poses the challenge of rulership as that of the management of the empire's main ethnic communities, the dispositions of each being governed by astrological conjunctions. Thus for instance, Hindustanis, governed by Saturn, were "accustomed to toil" but also influenced by the planet's slight "natural inferiority and meanness." Iranis, on the other hand, derived their "intellectual keenness" ("four times as great as that of the Hindustanis") from the Sun, though its conjunction with Venus had made them "ease-loving."[149] In this schema, the Turanis appear as excellent soldiers, unafflicted by the "crass stupidity" of Hindustanis, "who would part with their heads but not leave their positions [in battle]." By contrast, the Turanis are praised for their skill in making tactical retreats on the battlefield, and described as "very expert in making charges, raids, night-attacks and arrests."[150] Aurangzeb's words of praise are perhaps attributable to the fact that, as a descendant of Amir Timur, he considered himself a Turani; more pragmatically, however, they indicate the importance attached to employing Turani warriors for specialized purposes within a longstanding market for military servicemen.[151]

While many communities were valued for their martial prowess, Mughal troops were particularly connected to imperial power and regarded as the sword-arm of the state. A letter by Aurangzeb's trusted confidante, the high-ranking eunuch Bakhtawar Khan, illustrates this point.[152] Praising the era as one of the "Justice of Chosroes and the fostering of Law," Bakhtawar Khan lauds Aurangzeb's signal achievement: the demolition of infidel places of worship. Among these was a pond near Thanesar, a hundred miles north of Delhi, favored by the "idol-worshippers" for their ritual ablutions. Aurangzeb, we learn, had the pond filled up and a large inn established on it. Around it were settled several hundred "Turani Mughals zealous in the faith" (*mughūl-i tūrānī-yi muta'assub [o] dīndār*), with the surrounding lands given to them as tax-exempt grants for Muslims (*madad-i ma'āsh-i Islāmiyān*).[153]

148 On which, see Foltz, "Central Asians in the Administration of Mughal India"; Foltz, "Cultural Contacts Between Central Asia and Mughal India."

149 Khan, *Anecdotes of Aurangzeb*, 117–18; Khan, *Ahkām-i 'Ālamgīrī*, 64–65.

150 Khan, *Anecdotes of Aurangzeb*, 53–54; Khan, *Ahkām-i 'Ālamgīrī*, 15.

151 See the discussion in Gommans, *Mughal Warfare*, 69–72; Kolff, *Naukar, Rajput, and Sepoy*.

152 Ansari, "Bakhtāwar Khān."

153 Khan, "Sāqī-nāma," fol. 140a-b.

The Turani Mughals who were settled around the desecrated place of worship may have been immigrants from central Asia, but not all those who claimed Mughal ethnicity were recent arrivals in the land of India. Nor indeed were the Turani Mughals (or their counterparts, the "Irani" Mughals) anything like a cohesive "faction," as they have been sometimes treated by modern historians.[154] Claims to membership in such "ethnic" communities were derived from clan and patrilineage, origin from a homeland (*ʿasl-i watan*), and to a lesser degree, language, and devotional affiliation. Thus the early-eighteenth-century chronicler Nur al-Din Faruqi could describe himself as animated by a sense of love for his homeland (*habb al-watan*) of Multan, while simultaneously recalling his ancestral homeland of Balkh ("in the clime of Turan") and his family connection to a certain Baba Qashqa Mughal, comrade of the first emperor Babar on his conquest of India almost two centuries previously.[155] In much the same way, the chronicler Warid saw himself as having been transplanted from his true origin (*ʿasl*) of "the garden of Tehran" to the rather more obscure locale of Nagina, in Hindustan.[156]

Born in India or abroad, the Mughal soldiery appear to have frequently served together under noblemen who were regarded as their community heads. In the early eighteenth century, the family of the great nobleman Muhammad Amin Khan, his son the vizier Iʿtimad al-Daula, and his nephew Nizam al-Mulk were all seen as the leaders of the Turani Mughal soldiery and employed them in their contingents. While they were integrated vertically with the nobility through structures of patronage and military service, the Turani were not always the most disciplined of soldiers. An early eighteenth century chronicler includes unusually detailed descriptions of the enormities inflicted by Turani soldiers on residents of Patna during the nobleman Mir Jumla's presence there in 1715: internecine warfare, drunken rape and plunder, summary execution of innocent peasants, and the kidnapping and enslavement of children are all attributed to these men.[157] Led by Bahadur Dil Khan, notorious as the executioner of the overthrown emperor Jahandar Shah, the same soldiers then seriously disrupted city life in demanding their back pay from Mir Jumla in Delhi early in the next year.[158]

[154] A point made forcefully in Malik, *A Mughal Statesman*, 57, fn. 271.
[155] Multani, "Jahāndār Nāmā," fols. 2b–4a, 61a–b.
[156] Warid, "Mīrāt-i Wāridāt," fol. 9a–b.
[157] Lakhnavi, *Shāhnāma*, 9–11.
[158] Muhammad, "Tārīkh-i Muhammadi," fols. 145b–146b.

Figure 2.7. Muhammad Shah and the people on Moonlight Avenue. (Courtesy Rampur Raza Library, Rampur.)

Though it is not at all obvious whether such behavior was unusual by the standards of the time, by the early eighteenth century Turani Mughals were widely regarded as a disorderly presence in the city of Delhi. Their everyday disruptiveness can be gleaned from a minor disturbance in the city in 1743, occasioned by the arrest of a man of Mughal descent (*mughalbaccha*) who had stolen the courtier Mukhlis' horse from an inattentive groom, claiming it as his own. Though the victim's high status at court ensured the culprit was swiftly apprehended, Mukhlis felt it politic to release and in fact employ the thief "in order to stop the tongues of idle prattlers."[159] Mukhlis' diplomatic handling of the situation was undoubtedly motivated by fear of the potential turbulence of the city's Turani Mughals, a theme to which we will return again in subsequent chapters.

Indeed, the proverbial refractoriness of the Turani Mughals appears in a strange way to have become integral to the urban experience and identity of the city. No other explanation can suffice to explain a practice of the Baijal Seths, a subcaste of the Delhi Khatris, which was recorded by a colonial ethnographer in the late nineteenth century. The tonsure ceremony of a boy of this clan required the presence of two persons "disguised as Mughals," one bearing a bow and arrow, and another a shoe. After the conclusion of the ceremony, the women of the family beat their breasts and cried "Woe! Woe! Who shaved my son, who shaved the son of a Seth?," and observed a day of funerary mourning. The custom commemorated an incident in the past, when two Mughals forcibly shaved a poor lice-infested boy of the clan and overcame the barber's protestations of caste restrictions with threats and blows.[160]

Conclusion

The turbulent Turani Mughal soldiers, who swaggered through Delhi's streets tonsuring little boys as they pleased, were a far cry from the urbane vision of the city celebrated by poets such as ʿAqil. Yet, as this chapter has argued, lowly communities such as these were very much the product, however unanticipated, of the city and the conditions of imperial power more generally. It was after all through the city and its architecture that the people

[159] Mukhlis, *Chamanistan*, 39–40.
[160] Rose, *Glossary*, II.516.

received the values of the discourse of sovereignty that Shah Jahan enunciated. And it was the success of Shah Jahan's ideal of *faiz* which produced the wealth for which the city was justly famed. Yet Shah Jahan's confident actions had unanticipated effects. The commercial vitality of Delhi also produced an underclass, shaped but by no means dominated by the imperial vision of urban prosperity, order and docility.

In the years after Farrukh Siyar's regicide, a new perspective on the sovereign, the city, and the people becomes evident in another remarkable painting of an imperial procession: that of the emperor Muhammad Shah (r. 1719–1748) (Fig. 2.7).[161] While we cannot speculate on its provenance, this painting's scope suggests that it may not have been produced for the imperial court. We are again greeted with the spectacle of the king's parade, replete with all the integuments of his rule. But the emperor's figure, hardly central, appears lost within the city's teeming crowds, in whom the painter is more interested. Though the poor state of preservation obscures many of the painting's details, the painter's obsessive attention to the urban spectacle produces a visual catalog of the city's denizens and their activities and pleasures in the commercial heart of the city. We see that while the servants of the king are absorbed in their tasks, the people of the city appear to give the king little heed (save perhaps for the group of poor women who receive his charity by the pool). Like the urbanites who are the true subjects of this painting, our gaze is also led to wander aimlessly through the square. We observe well-to-do buyers and sellers in fancy colonnaded shops. More humble shopkeepers sit in makeshift thatched huts, chatting as they inhale from water-pipes. Hawkers peddle their wares from baskets. Orange-robed mendicants cross the square on foot. Gentlemen about town strut around on horses led by retainers. A water carrier serves a thirsty customer. Gaily dressed groups of women are urged on by their children. Cows and goats are tended by their owners. Palanquins and carts crisscross the street. A play or mock combat, performed to the sound of drums, is observed by a curious

[161] This painting is briefly described in Schmitz and Desai, *Mughal and Persian Paintings*, 72. While the learned catalogers date the work date to the early nineteenth century, there is no internal evidence that secures it to the nineteenth century. The title of the painting, inscribed in the lower right-hand corner, names it "a painting in Shahjahanabad of the procession of Muhammad Shah Badshah Ghazi," suggesting a contemporary rather than antiquarian representation. More generally, the treatment of the subject, which is reminiscent of some of the urban topographies of Rajasthan of the eighteenth century, indicates the work may have been produced in the eighteenth century. The name of the painter, inscribed below the title, is too damaged to decipher. I am grateful to Dipti Khera for discussing these points with me.

crowd, three rows deep. Another smaller crowd watches an entertainment with a monkey and a goat nearby, while gentlemen curiously peer over from horseback. And everywhere, singly or in groups, men wearing humble *dhotī*-s or *shalwār*-s wander through the square, taking in its sights, sounds, and smells. Their numbers more than balance the king's procession, which no longer dominates the square but is now subsumed within its buzzing commercial life.

Most intriguingly, the painting conveys an air of ambivalence in the popular throng, whose gazes are not humbly lowered or fixed in rapture upon the ruler. Their indifference suggests they are as capable of approaching the king's procession with outstretched hands as with raised fists. To explore this air of political possibility on the pulsing streets of the city of Delhi is the chief objective of the pages that follow. As we shall see in coming chapters, the lowly people who marched in Delhi's streets in the eighteenth century were activated by their own interpretations of the values of imperial rule; and it was in relation to the expression of imperial power to which they responded with symbolic acts outside the fort or in the city's congregatory mosque. But before we turn to the practices of their politics and the conditions of their activation, we must first examine how the people found their voice.

3

Poetry and the Public in Aurangzeb's Delhi

One day in 1688 or 1689, the emperor Aurangzeb received a petition from his chamberlain (*khān-i sāmān*) Kamgar Khan, which would have stood out among the great torrents of the routine correspondence of state that daily reached him. The khan had written:

> Mirza Muhammad Niʿmat Khan, whose malignant nature is accustomed to satirizing, has published certain verses on my marriage, saying, "The object of it (i.e., marriage) is lawful movement, but in this case, there is a coupling of two quiescents." And he has besides introduced into them other disgraceful remarks about me, so that I have been put to shame before high and low (*ruswā-yi khāss o ʿāmm shuda*). I hope that your Majesty will so punish him that he may not again venture to compose such idle tales. What was appropriate has been related.[1]

We can be sure the emperor read this epistle with his customary attention, because the collator of this anecdote reports that Aurangzeb crossed out the standard bureaucratic phrase "what was appropriate" and instead scribbled "what was inappropriate." The imperial pen then reached for the upper margin of the petition, where it wrote:

> Punishing him will cause greater disgrace [to you than before]. This naïve (*sādah-lauh*) hereditary servant wishes to make me his sharer in this humiliation, so that Niʿmat Khan may say and write about me whatever he likes, and fame it through the world (*shuhrat-i ʿālam sāzad*). Formerly, too, he had not spared me [in his satires]; in return, I had increased his reward, that he might not do it again; yet in spite of this [favor] he had not on his part been less [satirical]. It is not possible to cut out his tongue and sever his neck. One must burn and accept it

[1] Khan, *Anecdotes of Aurangzeb*, 127 (translation slightly amended to match current style).

The King and The People. Abhishek Kaicker, Oxford University Press (2020). © Oxford University Press.
DOI: 10.1093/oso/9780190070670.001.0001

> (*bāyad sūkht o bāyad sākht*). *He is a friend, who neither clings to thee nor separates himself from thee.*[2]

Who was Niʿmat Khan (hereafter referred to by his poetic penname ʿAli, "the sublime"), and why did his words cause such gnashing of teeth in the imperial court? Though we will shortly return to the substance of his "disgraceful remarks," we note at the outset the cause of such chagrin in the highest stratum of the empire: not the admittedly offensive verses in themselves, but rather their circulation "among high and low." It was in response to this that Kamgar Khan rashly demanded punishment for the poet. But the wiser emperor's forbearance signals his recognition of the existence of a realm outside the control of the Shadow of God and the Ruler of Land and Sea. This site of potential infamy—the "world"—had to be managed with particular and politic care: to advocate violence in attempting to control the fickle opinions of the "high and low" was the course of the simple-minded. Much though he wished to behead and mutilate his courtier, Aurangzeb could only dissuade ʿAli through his kindness; and when it failed, the silently seething emperor could do nothing but grin and bear it. To outline the development of this uncontrollable realm of hurtful words and its political importance is the objective of the pages that follow.

The controversy around ʿAli's satire reminds us that behind the intricate façade of Persian poetry, forever concerned with the Rose and the Nightingale, and ruled by "metaphorical" allusions to ruby-red wine and the handsome cupbearer, lies a somewhat seamier reality: that of the fighting words of satire, invective, and mockery (*hajw, hazl*). Given its frequently astounding rudeness and obscenity, it is understandable that the tradition of satire in poetry has attracted little scholarly attention, particularly among historians. Nevertheless, satire and invective have been an integral feature of Persianate poetic practice from its emergence as a recognizable form in the eleventh century. This is the tradition defensively invoked in the *oeuvre* of a late-seventeenth-century poet named Ghalib, which appears to consist mostly of poems in praise of pederasty. The names paraded as evidence of the permissibility of satire are in fact those of the greatest luminaries of the tradition: Firdausi (d. 1020), Azraqi (d. ca. eleventh c.), Sanaʾi (d. ca. 1141), Sozani (d. 1173/74), Anwari (d. ca. 1191), Saʿdi (d. 1292), ʿUbaid-i Zakani

[2] Khan, *Anecdotes of Aurangzeb*, 127 (Qurʾanic quotations in italics). I have amended the translation according to the Persian text provided.

(d. 1371), Amir Khusrau (d. 1325), Mulla Jami (d. 1492), as well as sixteenth- and seventeenth-century poets Mulla Shafa'i, Fauqi, Sozani, and Rustam Mirza.[3] Ghalib might also have listed the poets Muhammad Quli Salim (d. 1647) and Mulla Shaida (d. 1669), who were similarly known for their biting satires. The robustness of the culture of satirical poetry in the seventeenth century can be judged from Salim's oeuvre, which satirizes not only such expected themes as the avarice of the kings of his era, and his contemporaries and acquaintances, but also more everyday matters: the negligence of his scribe, a porcelain cup the poet disliked, and even a river near Gilan whose waters he found unacceptably turbid.[4]

The satire of the seventeenth century appears to have adhered to well-established conventions of transgression. The object of criticism, usually a man, is formulaically mocked for sexual passivity; respectable women, if mentioned, are not named. Yet such familiar rules could never limit the power of mockery to wound, or contain its danger to the utterer. This caused a fundamental ambiguity about the place of satire within the poetic tradition. On the one hand, it was seen as unbefitting of the practitioners of the serious arts of "fresh speech" (*tāza-gū'ī*), who were supposed to spend their days excavating new "meaning" (*ma'nī*) in ever deeper intricacies. On the other hand, the pleasures of observing palpable hits, particularly against the powerful, were widely shared and difficult to renounce. The poet and anthologist Muhammad Afzal Sarkhwush frankly admits to this contradiction after recording the verses he wrote in criticism of a neighbor:

> Although to utter satires is not [worthy] of the poet, and to soil the tongue by mocking these unworthies is an error, it is true of poetry that he who is worthy of being praised is worthy of being satirized. And since those with *daulat* in this era are neither worthy of praise nor satire, it is appropriate to satirize them.[5]

In defending himself, Sarkhwush points to an essential feature of the culture of poetry which makes satire inevitable: he who is worthy of praise is also liable to censure. That this was most true of kings was already established by the famous satire against Mahmud of Ghazna (d. 1030) by his own panegyrist

[3] Ghalib, "Sharh-i Dīwān-i Ghālib," fol. 3a.
[4] Tihrani, *Dīwān*, 514–23, 506.
[5] Sarkhwush, *Kalimāt al-Shu'arā'*, 68.

Firdausi.[6] Half a millennium later, what was particularly disturbing about the satires of ʿAli for Aurangzeb and Kamgar Khan was not their content, which, though brilliant, did not leap from the well-worn grooves of custom; it was rather the remarkable speed with which the poet's mockeries were transmitted through a realm that Aurangzeb, for all his horses and all his men, could not control.

While it is hardly the job of the historian to defend long-dead emperors, it is impossible to not feel some sympathy for Aurangzeb's predicament with regard to his satirical courtier, which the king had himself caused. For Niʿmat Khan's earlier offense, to which the emperor alludes, was a biting mockery of his enunciation of sovereignty. Aurangzeb, as we shall see, fashioned himself less a mystical king and more a pious one, who ruled according to the dictates of God's Law. In doing so, he diminished the personal compact of justice with the people established by his ancestors in favor of a more bureaucratic and legalistic vision of justice, delivered by the establishment of the supremacy of law. Such a shift in imperial ideology produced complicated effects. On the one hand, Aurangzeb's heavy-handed imposition of his interpretation of God's law privileged certain forms of Sunni piety and contributed to their development. On the other hand, the denizens of the increasingly commercialized realm responded not just with disobedience but with audible derision; both were intensified by the development of new circuits of social interchange that were themselves produced by the flow of silver. To trace the development of this public arena, in which the poetry of praise and satire percolated through Delhi and other cities of the realm, we must first examine the shift of emphasis in Aurangzeb's enunciation of sovereignty from the mystical fortune of *daulat* to conformance with the law of *sharīʿa*.

Aurangzeb's Discourse of Sovereignty

Despite his troubled ascension to the throne, Aurangzeb did not abandon the aspects of sovereignty enunciated by his predecessors. He visibly maintained the established commitments to personal justice and generosity.[7]

[6] The controversy on whether Firdausi actually composed the satire attributed to him remains unresolved. See Huart and Massé, "Firdawsī"; Feuillebois, "Firdawsī, Abū l-Qāsim, and the Shāhnāma."

[7] See, for instance, Aurangzeb's bizarre generosity to a humble gardener while visiting Hasan Abdal, in Khan, *Maʾasir-i ʿAlamgiri [EN]*, 82–84.

Yet, as both his contemporaries and later scholars have noted, sovereignty under Aurangzeb acquired an increasingly Islamic tint, with a concomitant lessening of emphasis on the more mystical aspects of kingship. While the stress on conformance with Sunni Islam was not absent in Shah Jahan's reign, Aurangzeb's turn toward one vision of orthodoxy has been explained by the need to consolidate his authority in the aftermath of a brutal war of succession, which required the execution of his brothers and the imprisonment of his aged father Shah Jahan. In considering Aurangzeb's actions motivated by his piety, some historians have emphasized his religious zeal in persecuting Hindus, which marked the reversion of the Islamic state to its true type.[8] Others have been at pains to defend his actions as political gestures against upstarts and rebels that were cloaked in the language of the faith.[9]

Whether apologetic or condemnatory, such judgments rely on a particular kind of distinction between the categories of "religion" and "politics," which reduce the emperor either to an unthinking bigot driven by religious zeal or a cynical instrumentalist motivated by purely political considerations. In this light, a comparison with the Ottoman Sultan Mehmet IV, Aurangzeb's younger contemporary, is instructive. It has been recently argued that Mehmet IV should be seen as converting from a lesser to a greater piety *within* Islam. In the context of an unsettled succession, the king's demonstration of his internal transformation in turn required that of others, motivating not only the conversion of the king's Jewish and Christian subjects, but also the conduct of righteous war (*ghazā*) against infidel enemies.[10] This model may also apply to Aurangzeb; although his initial position was stronger than that of Mehmet IV, Aurangzeb too came to the throne in a moment of crisis, and his legitimacy remained open to question until the death of his imprisoned father in 1666. It is unclear whether Aurangzeb's piety increased steadily from his youth, or whether it was given a fillip by his relationship with the judge ʿAbd al-Wahhab, who was instrumental in giving legal sanction to his disputed accession in 1658. In either case, Aurangzeb's changing private practices, the increasing incentives toward conversion at court and the sharpened rhetoric of "righteous war" against "infidels" should be located

[8] Sarkar, *Aurangzib*, vol. 2; Sharma, *The Religious Policy of the Mughal Emperors*.

[9] Chandra, "Some Considerations on the Religious Policy of Aurangzeb during the Latter Part of His Reign"; but see also Azizuddin Husain, "Religious Policy of Aurangzeb during the Later Part of His Reign—An Examination"; Azizuddin Husain, *Structure of Politics under Aurangzeb, 1658–1707*.

[10] Baer, *Honored by the Glory of Islam*.

in the context of an increasing personal piety during a period of profound instability. Likewise, we should regard Aurangzeb's actions as rational and strategic given deeply held beliefs and faith.

Such piety did not preclude the pragmatism required of rulers by the ethical traditions in which Aurangzeb, like other princes, was steeped. Nor did it stifle his curiosity and willingness to engage with Hindu mendicants (if he found them accomplished enough to merit his attention).[11] Yet the demonstrated adherence to the precepts of Islam and the proclamation of the theoretical supremacy of the 'Community of Muslims,' though not absent from the reign of Shah Jahan, is more strikingly apparent in Aurangzeb's courtly milieu (a matter to which we shall return shortly). The dramatic lessening of emphasis on the "semi-divine" character of the ruler is visible in Aurangzeb's architecture, as Catherine Asher has shown.[12] It is also palpable in the texts produced at or around his court. Though probably no more than an authorial quirk regarding style, it is nevertheless intriguing that the courtly encomiast Mulla Tughra appears to exclude the term *daulat* completely from his panegyric text celebrating Aurangzeb's accession.[13] Writing early in the reign of Aurangzeb, the high nobleman Zafar Khan Ahsan evokes the familiar vision of sovereignty:

> By these four things is *daulat* set aright:
> By Faith, justice, and liberality, and by the sword to fight[14]
> . . .
> From *daulat* gains a ruler success
> Just as a particle becomes from *faiz* the sun[15]

But Aurangzeb's accession is greeted as a time of the revivification of law and the suppression of infidelity:

> I bring glad tidings to the people of the *sharīʿa*
> The coming of an emperor with faith and justice
> Gives vitality to the law (*sharʿ*) in this era

[11] See, for instance, his considerable grant to the Bairagi Shri Mangaldas Maharaj in 1700/01: Bhatt, "Two Persian Documents Relating to the Religious Policy of the Mughals."
[12] Asher, *Architecture of Mughal India*, chap. 6.
[13] Mashhadi, "Julūsiyya-Yi Tughrā."
[14] Ahsan, "Masnawīyyāt," fol. 56b.
[15] Ahsan, "Masnawīyyāt," fol. 58a.

For he brings the law to a fresh spring[16]
. . .
A shah who the *sharīʿa's* ambit transgresses
Quickly hurls his *daulat* to the breezes
For a king, the poll tax (*jizya*) is lawful gain
Why does the king wittingly forbear from tax?
Hurl out from India's lands the temple
And populate the wilderness with the mosque
So if you accept my petition
Like Mahmud, your name will be "iconoclast."[17]

Zafar Khan was an imperial nobleman of high rank, and his casual exhortations here perhaps reflect the ruminations of an elite who suffered an honorable but forcible retirement in the reign of Aurangzeb, whose rise he had opposed.[18] On the other end of the courtly spectrum, consider an obscure ornate treatise on the composition of chronograms named the *Central Pearl* (1699), by a certain Mir Muhammad Fazil.[19] Not otherwise concerned with kingly affairs, the text appears to have nevertheless harmonized with the tenor of the court. After various prolegomena, the author begins with a section on the "sprouting of the tree of the king's *daulat*": we are informed that there is no more ubiquitous gift of God than his appointing a king to protect creation (*khalāʾiq*) from the oppressive hands of tyrants. But before we learn of his legendary justice and other laudable features, it is mentioned that Aurangzeb, the current occupant of the "throne of the *daulat* of the sultanate," is an iconoclast (*but-shikan*). From the very beginning of his reign, he has desiccated many false gods (*lāt o manāt*) through the scorching wind of his support of the faith (*dīndārī*) and toppled them into the dust of oblivion by the fire of his rage. Not a trace of idol-worshippers now remains.[20] That such sentiments reflect the reigning discourse of sovereignty, and not the personal predilections of the author, is evident in his casual reference elsewhere to the "Way of the Hindus" (*mazhab-i hindūʾān*), which he

[16] Ahsan, "Jalwa-yi Nāz/Wasf-i Kashmīr," fol. 55a. It is intriguing that these verses are prefixed by a long and defiant poetic screed against the figure of the preacher (*wāʿiz*) who vainly attempts to restrain the author's tippling.

[17] Ahsan, "Masnawīyyāt," fol. 57b.

[18] Aurangabadi, *Maʾāsir al-Umarāʾ [En]*, 2:1014–20; for a broader discussion of this work and its author, see Sharma, *Mughal Arcadia*, 147–51.

[19] Fazil, "Wisātat al-ʿIqd."

[20] Fazil, "Wisātat al-ʿIqd," fol. 3a–b.

finds symmetrical with (and thus implicitly not inferior to) the "Way of the Muslims" (*mazhab-i Islāmī'ān*).[21]

Such verbiage was undoubtedly derived from the atmosphere at Aurangzeb's court, where even the tiniest conquests were rendered in the language of the supremacy of Islam. Take the "incorporation" of Tibet into the empire in 1665; according to the official chronicle, Tibet was a land enveloped in the "darkness of infidelity" and unwarmed by the "light of belief." Aurangzeb sent a missive to the "landholder" of Tibet, one "Daldan Namjal," to the effect that if he were to become submissive to Islam (*mutīʿ al-Islām*); propagate its practices through his lands; recite the Friday sermon (*khutba*) and distribute coins bearing the king's name; then he would be permitted to continue in his tenure. According to the chronicle, Daldan Namjal obeyed these orders. Having had the sermon recited before the teeming masses of Tibet, he promised everlasting obedience to Islam and Aurangzeb.[22]

The incorporation of Tibet into the Mughal realm and the spread of Islam there was no more than a polite fiction, as the chronicler well knew, but it reflected the ideological orientation of Aurangzeb and his circle. Such aggressive if stylized claims to the domination of the 'Community of Muslims' have led some to regard Aurangzeb's reign as a period in which Islamic orthodoxy was imposed willy-nilly on an unwilling population, provoking their rebellion and the empire's ultimate demise.[23] But these views derive from an inability to distinguish between the literary hyperboles of courtly writers and the actual reality of Mughal society. The 'Community of Muslims' as it emerges in Aurangzeb's enunciation of sovereignty was an idealized population that conformed to Aurangzeb's idea of orthopraxy and was submissive to his rule. This courtly vision of a unified 'Community of Muslims,' denoted with a capital C, to which we shall return repeatedly over the course of this book, must be contrasted with the actually existing *communities* of Muslims, disparate and heterogeneous, which had been scattered across the subcontinent for centuries before Mughal rule and would long outlive it. Again, this imperial impetus toward "confession-building" might be profitably compared with similar processes in the Ottoman empire of the seventeenth century.[24] As

[21] Fazil, fol. 7b. Nor, it should be added, is there any trace evident in the manuscript of offence taken by the Hindu scribe Rup Ram, who copied the text on April 23, 1703.

[22] Kazim, *Álamgír námah*, 920–23.

[23] The classic statement of this view remains Sarkar, *Aurangzib*, essentially reproduced in later standard treatments such as Richards, *The Mughal Empire*.

[24] Cf. Terzioğlu, "How to Conceptualize Ottoman Sunnitization: A Historiographical Discussion." I thank Nir Shafir for the reference.

Samira Sheikh has persuasively argued, a key concern for Aurangzeb was to discipline variegated local communities of Muslims into conformance with his ideals, often with disastrous results.[25] It is in this light that we must see the fond reminiscences of the observer, who, having experienced the turbulence of the 1710s, recalled that although Aurangzeb had (rightly) broken the precedent of his forefathers in imposing the poll tax (*jizya*) on the Hindus, it was the "wicked innovators and dissimulators" within the Islamic fold on whom his sword fell wherever they arose.[26] The question of making non-Muslims "submissive to Islam" was thus a secondary objective, important only insofar as it contributed to the former goal of regulating the 'Community of Muslims.'

Aurangzeb's primary means of disciplining a 'Community of Muslims' into existence was his unprecedented establishment of the supremacy of law over his subjects. In practice this was to be achieved by the bureaucratic systemization of the delivery of justice, which would now supersede the previous commitments to personal justice among his predecessors. He did not go so far as to cancel the practice of personal audiences for justice, as is sometimes claimed.[27] But a raft of measures evidence this objective, including the appointment of public censors (*muhtasib*-s), who were tasked with not only preventing vice but also more generally regulating markets and maintaining public spaces; the granting of greater powers to local judges (*qāzī*-s); the imposition of the poll tax; the investment in creating a theological infrastructure, with the construction and endowment of seminaries; the appointment of scholars and the granting of stipends to students; and, most notably, the commissioning of a vast legal digest titled *'Alamgir's Judgements* (*fatāwá-yi 'Ālamgīrī*), which remains a standard work on Hanafi jurisprudence to the present day.[28] Through these systemic transformations, Aurangzeb can be seen as making justice, the core value of the discourse of imperial sovereignty, less dependent on his mystical nature and more on the law, broadening its sweep and intensifying its reach across the empire.[29]

[25] Sheikh, "Aurangzeb as Seen from Gujarat."

[26] Anonymous, "Mihakk al-Sulūk," fol. 445b.

[27] Thus see the specific orders in 1671 to allow petitions at the window of presentation: Musta'idd Khan, *Ma'asir-i 'Alamgiri [EN]*, 60.

[28] Munis D. Faruqui, "Awrangzīb"; Anooshahr, "Muslims among Non-Muslims: Creating Islamic Identity through Law."

[29] For a view of this development treated as a broader social process, see Smith, "The 'Ulamā' in Indian Politics," 204–05; for an Ottoman parallel, see Burak, *The Second Formation of Islamic Law*, 212–13; on Aurangzeb's deep personal involvement in shaping the canon, and in the controversies this produced, see Dihlawi, *Anfās al-'Arifīn*, 24–25.

Such actions undoubtedly empowered new groups of people throughout the city and the realm. They also produced a chorus of criticism that is particularly audible in the satire of the era. And the spread of such satire through an expanding arena of popular intercourse in the city was accelerated by the same forces of commerce that were exercising their effect on so many other features of urban life in our period. For, as we shall see, it is in the popularization of the long-established poetic ambivalence between praise and censure of the king that the voice of the city's people becomes audible in the historical record.

In making this case, this chapter focuses particularly on the works of two poets of the late seventeenth century: the aforementioned Niʿmat Khan-i ʿAli ("The Sublime"), and the rather more refined Mir Jaʿfar Zatalli ("The Prattler"). The reception of their works can be traced through a world of poetic appreciation that, by the late seventeenth century, had expanded beyond the imperial court and into the gatherings of elites (*mahfil, majlis*) and into the streets and bazars beyond. This process of *décloisonnement*, to borrow the term Shirine Hamadeh has used to describe a similar expansion in Ottoman Istanbul, was neither seamless nor unidirectional.[30] It is apparent in a variety of domains, from the loosening of the strictures which regulated the elite assembly and the emergence of lowly entertainers as celebrities, to the marketization of poetic forms such as chronograms, and odes of praise and blame. Under these conditions, poetry, and particularly political satire, came to circulate more intensely within the city's coffeehouses and squares, and coagulated the political solidarities that appeared on its streets in the eighteenth century.

Niᶜmat Khan-i ᶜAli and Mir Jaᶜfar Zatalli

Niʿmat Khan, with the poetic nom de plume of "The Sublime" (*ʿĀlī*) occupies a contested place in the Mughal archive. While his works are invariably to be found in almost every collection of Persian manuscripts from India, most late-Mughal commentators speak of him with a barely disguised hostility. This contradiction throws into sharp relief the dangerous pleasure of satire, as loved for its humor as feared by its potential victims. In his anthology of poets, Muhammad Afzal Sarkhwush cautiously praises his contemporary

[30] See Hamadeh, *The City's Pleasures: Istanbul in the Eighteenth Century*, particularly 11–14.

ʿAli's poetry and refrains altogether from mentioning his satirical bent.[31] Sarkhwush's disciple Bindraban Das Khwushgu was more forthright in his own anthology, no doubt because ʿAli was safely dead. While he praised the poet for his learning, and his verses in the then-fashionable "fresh speech" (*tāza-gūʾī*) style, he also noted that the vice of satire was as if "leavened" in ʿAli's temperament.[32]

From the account of Khwushgu and others it is possible to reconstruct something of ʿAli's life and career as a courtier and poet. Though it is unclear where or when ʿAli was born, most commentators believed his family originated in Shiraz. His father was a doctor at the imperial court and was established in India by the mid seventeenth century. ʿAli may have entered imperial service through the princess Zeb al-Nisa, who, despite her father's disfavor and her confinement in Delhi, appears to have been a key source of patronage for artists and intellectuals in Delhi during the second half of the seventeenth century.[33] Such service, in ʿAli's case, did not involve military, commercial, or administrative affairs. He appears to have spent most of his career in assignments within the king's establishment. According to one mid-eighteenth-century commentator, ʿAli became the superintendent of the imperial kitchen in 1692 and received the title of Niʿmat Khan ("the gracious"); by the end of Aurangzeb's reign he had received the title of Muqarrab Khan ("the intimate") and the superintendence of the imperial jewel-house and the imperial seal (*nagīn-i daulat*). In the reign of Bahadur Shah he received the prestigious title of Danishmand Khan ("the learned") and was assigned to write the official imperial chronicle, a task that remained incomplete at his death in 1710.[34]

While he has received more scholarly attention than ʿAli, Zatalli is much the obscurer figure.[35] It is impossible to establish the dates of Zatalli's life and death with any certainty. From evidence internal to his works, it appears that he lived until the first decade of the eighteenth century, though there is no corroboration for the oft-repeated claim that he was executed for a satire by

[31] Sarkhwush, *Kalimāt al-Shuʿarāʾ*, 137–38.

[32] Khwushgu, *Safina-yi Khwushgu*, 59–61.

[33] The earliest anecdote of ʿAli's life recounts a tiff with the princess over a jeweled headpiece he prepared for her. Bilgrami, *Khazāna-yi ʿĀmira*, 333.

[34] This account is included in Arzu, *Majmaʿ al-Nafāʾis*, 189–94. For Arzu's own distinctly less celebratory telling, see 99–101. See also Menon, "ʿĀlī, Neʿmat Khan"; Berthels, "Niʿmat Khān, Called ʿĀlī."

[35] Faruqi, "A Long History of Urdu Literary Culture, Part I"; Ataullah, "Jafar Zatalli and the Historical Context"; Oesterheld, "Humor and Satire: Precolonial, Colonial, and Postcolonial"; Oesterheld, "Satirizing the Late Mughals."

Farrukh Siyar. It appears he belonged to a provincial but technically highborn family of the Sayyids of the small town of Narnaul, near Delhi, and that he served for a while in the retinue of the prince Kam Bakhsh (d. 1708). Unlike ʿAli, Zatalli does not appear to have produced a formal collection of poems (*dīwān*); the very high degree of textual variation among the manuscripts that record his writings suggest that his works circulated in snippets and fragments that were only collated after his death.

ʿAli and Zatalli make for a series of instructive comparisons. ʿAli typifies the courtly elite of the period. His poetry and prose are ornate, complicated, and embellished with rhetorical flourishes and allusions to the wider body of Perso-Arabic learning with almost no specific reference to India. Zatalli, by contrast, offers vulgar satire and biting invective in language that mixes in the local vernaculars called "Hindi" with his Persian verses. ʿAli's works did not remain limited to elites; his prose quickly became a model of style for aspiring writers. Likewise, Zatalli was by no means a representative of the masses; that he depended for his sustenance on the condescension of princely and noble elites for whose entertainment he produced his works is clearly visible in his writings. ʿAli has little concern for the world beyond the courtly arena. Zatalli, by contrast, gazes up at the edifice of the empire, betraying the concerns not of the rulers but those of the ruled. Though they were contemporaries, ʿAli and Zatalli reveal no awareness of each other. Yet their satires mirror each other in intriguing ways. Both played with the bureaucratic genres of the imperial administration to voice critical responses to the discourse of sovereignty as it was enunciated in the reign of Aurangzeb. And, designed as they were to circulate widely, the words of both came to have a life in the urban arena which was larger than their authors could have ever expected.

Poetry and Courtly Politics

A key form of courtly poetic practice for ʿAli and others was the production of chronograms, poems in the genre named "*tārīkh*," a term representing both "date" and "history." The chronogram poem was defined by its final hemistich, in which the numerical value assigned to each letter by the *abjad* scheme would yield the date of an event being commemorated. Though the chronogram achieved the status of a "distinctive and independent genre" by the end of the fourteenth century, it appears to have only become truly widespread at the Mughal court at the turn of the seventeenth century.[36] The chronogram became popular at court because it could both encode the date of an event in metrical verse more securely than a number, and tied a meaning or sentiment to the memory of an event. "Court-poets," Hadi Hasan has aptly noted, "were essentially court-historians."[37] ʿAli's first prominence at Aurangzeb's court, then engaged in the conquest of the Deccan frontier, was likewise almost certainly due to his ability in this regard. The favor in which he was held can be judged by the fact that Aurangzeb ordered his poetic chronogram recording the capture of the enormous cannon called the "Lord of the Battlefield" (*malik-i maidān*) be inscribed on its barrel, and on which it can still be read in Bijapur today.[38] By comparison, it is surely a mark of Zatalli's lowly place that only two chronograms are attributed to him.

But it is not for such polite poetry that ʿAli was notorious among his contemporaries, for his vicious satires served as even more powerful weapons in courtly intrigues. The innocuously named "Verses on the Wedding of Kamgar Khan," which provoked the wounded nobleman to complain to Aurangzeb, were perhaps the most famous—but by no means sole—instance of such satirical assault.[39] The poem was written after Kamgar Khan somehow failed to adequately honor ʿAli's chronogram celebrating Kamgar Khan's second marriage to a much younger noblewoman. In response, ʿAli produced a satirical poem designed to humiliate Kamgar Khan, a figure already notorious in his day for his simple-mindedness and his aristocratic aloofness.[40] Incorporating a variety of technical terms and dense allusions to the branches of knowledge, the poem is a work of exquisite literary craftsmanship that serves above all to establish ʿAli's virtuosic excellence as a poet and scholar. As a work of satire, it serves to illuminate both the values and the realities of courtly elites in the late seventeenth century.

ʿAli's poem strikes at the khan by attacking his manhood, which is the basis of his honor and demonstrated by virility and sexual activeness. Accordingly,

[36] Losensky, "Mādda Tārik̲"; Losensky, "Coordinates in Time and Space"; Schimmel and Waghmar, *The empire of the great Mughals*, 246.

[37] Hasan, *Mughal poetry*, 36.

[38] ʿAli, *Dīwān-i ʿĀlī*, 229; Ahmad, *Waqiʿāt-i Mamlakat-i Bījāpūr*, 2:46.

[39] Given the absence of a critical edition of this poem, I base my analysis on a preliminary reconciliation in Kaicker, "Unquiet City," 316–19; this is based on ʿAli, *Dīwān-i ʿĀlī*; Bilgrami, *Sharh*; and Anonymous, "BL Commentary." I have given precedence to the lattermost version because it appears to be the oldest and offers the most helpful commentary on this otherwise abstruse work.

[40] Aurangabadi, *Maʾāsir al-Umarāʾ [En]*, 1:760–61.

ʿAli stages the bulk of the poem in the bridal bedchamber on the night of the marriage, when the passionate young bride demands consummation, but the aged Kamgar Khan is unable to perform. The khan feebly prevaricates with obscure allusions to the various branches of knowledge; his wife responds with humiliating insults and cutting repartees. Thus, Kamgar Khan alludes to the "ten categories" of philosophy in seeking to delay with promises of "quality" and "quantity"; his wife asks specific questions of "identity" and" location," referring to the whereabouts and condition of the Khan's male organ. When the khan begins to speak loftily of predestination, his wife pointedly takes the position of supporting free will. He begs off again by claiming adverse astrological conditions. He must wait until the moon has moved to the second of ten possible stages, which is considered propitious; Venus, which signifies strength, has returned to its former auspicious position; and the sun has arisen. Rightly skeptical of such foolish mumbo-jumbo, his wife retorts that her new husband might as well await the day of resurrection. Now seizing the offensive, she asks the khan whether he thinks he's in a bridal bedchamber or a seminary. Her throat aches from such ridiculous wrangling over obscure trivialities. Such pathetic erudition and silly pomposity, she avers, is the work of the offspring of theologians (*mullāzāda*). The phrase offered is euphemistic: Kamgar Khan needs to be reminded that "hair-splitting," (sexual intercourse) is the work of the "Little Mulla" (*mullāzāda*). But such labors are well beyond Kamgar Khan, for even at this late hour of the night he remains unable to achieve congress. ʿAli finally ends the argument between the spouses, with the observation that since only a "firm argument" could resolve this endless dispute, and may God dispatch a merchant from the "Eastern Oceans" (*Zīrbād*) to provide one to the couple. A contemporary commentary, which sheds light on this otherwise incomprehensible allusion, is worth quoting at length on this issue:

> By "the firm argument" (*hujjat-i muhkam*) the author refers to a thing that is made in the lands of the Eastern Oceans, which is called a *Kīrkāsh*; and traders have taken it to other countries. In the palaces of emperors and noblemen where there are many singing and dancing girls, and since besides the master of the house no one else is permitted within, those women buy this merchandise at great prices. And one woman ties it around her waist and has intercourse with another and in this way they satiate their lust. Because the argument between husband and wife had gone beyond the limit, and proceeded for too long, the poet says that may God will that

> a merchant from the eastern regions bring a *Kīrkāsh* and with it settle the affair of the bride.[41]

ʿAli then alludes to his own difficulties in maintaining the rhyme scheme: his rhymes end with—*ayn*, which signifies a plural (in Arabic), and the author is running out such plurals to use; these troubles are in contrast to the Kamgar Khan, whose problems with conjugation lie in the realm of the dual. In the same way, the "short vowel" of the Khan has to be enlengthened, and a wise old man—no doubt the author himself—remarked that in this case grammar had to go against its own rules; two "passive" or "quiescent" consonants cannot normally be joined, but in this marriage they were of necessity yoked together. With this final stab at Kamgar Khan's manliness, ʿAli returns to his own affairs: he had graciously offered a poetic chronogram to Kamgar Khan and sought his customary reward. But the Khan had refused: not on account of a miserly nature, but because of his own freely acknowledged illiteracy and mental incapacity. Luxuriating in his dazzling literary sophistication, ʿAli concludes with a request to all his broader community of readers: may they reward him according to their own appreciation of the poem.

While, by his own account, ʿAli's poem was primarily directed against a courtly enemy, it is possible to discern a vein of social commentary within it. The poem invites its listeners to laugh at the aged dandies and fops who purchase aphrodisiacs and trust the stars to solve their problems in the bedroom. Likewise, it amusedly presents the reality of powerful, desiring, agentive, and querulous women who dominate domestic space—far indeed from the idealized vision of the patriarchal household with its silently immured wives and daughters. There is besides an underlying sense of piety that expects of the aged to tame (if not renounce) their carnal desires, and is developed at length by the poet elsewhere.[42]

While the poem's complexity, frequently verging on abstruseness, would have limited its audience to a select group of cognoscente, both Kamgar Khan's petulant cry of dishonor before high and low, and Aurangzeb's act of forbearance deserve to be taken seriously. If Kamgar Khan's fear of dishonor was grounded in his awareness of the viral propagation of satire, the king's restraint was surely motivated by his knowledge that ʿAli was just as capable

[41] Anonymous, "BL Commentary," fols. 194b–195a.
[42] ʿAli, *Ruqqāt o Muzhikāt*, 19–25.

of turning his poison pen against him. Aurangzeb's allusion to having been mocked previously undoubtedly refers to ʿAli's attack on the policies of the king's war in the South, which expertly undermined Aurangzeb's assertion of sovereignty in the very terms of its enunciation. This act of political criticism was occasioned by Aurangzeb's war against the Qutb Shahi dynasty, which culminated in the bitter siege and pyrrhic victory over the fort of Golconda in 1687. ʿAli's text, titled *Report of the Siege of the Fort of Golconda*, suggests a laconic and precise account conforming to the genre of the bureaucratic intelligence reports produced for the court. The *Report* is precisely the opposite: a work of numbing prolixity, littered with the author's trademark obscure allusions and Arabic quotations. The text consists of eight chapters, each reporting the events of a single day in an extensive and digressive essay. On the report of the eighth and final day, ʿAli turns to describing the events of Friday, July 11, 1687 in the camp of the imperial army. It is not without significance that the scene is the key site of the expression of the king's claims to sovereignty before the people at large: the Friday sermon. After reciting the appointed first part, the sermonizer (*khatīb*) sets about reciting a novel second part, which is included in the report for reason of its "madness" (*saudāʾī*).

The sermonizer begins in the expected fashion, with a long Arabic invocation warning all men to know well that God has granted them incomparable bounties, and to thank him for the appointment of a just ruler who is their leader in all rectitude.[43] He assures them that the king, in accordance with the dictates of the Qurʾan, is busily engaged in improving the condition of his people:

> In this bountiful era, many commentaries and analyses (*taʾwīlāt o tamsīlāt*) have explicated the difficult and intricate verses of the Qurʾan (*ayāt-i mutashābih*) and many divine injunctions have been interpreted by royal strength and power. Among these, due to the limitless favors of his excellency the Caliph of the Age [Aurangzeb], infinite happiness and abundant mercy have been the lot of the servants of the threshold: they have been excluded from the love of God, because He has decreed that "*God does not love those who rejoice*."[44]

[43] The following extract is translated from ʿAli, *Waqʿiʿ-yi Niʿmat Khān-i ʿĀlī*, 136–46; I have also consulted ʿAli, *Chronicles of the Siege of Golkonda Fort*.
[44] Qurʾan 28:76.

ʿAli's line of attack is immediately clear. The sermonizer reminds his audience of the perfect congruence between the intentions of the ruler and the wishes of God. We learn that this is a "bountiful era" because the emperor has taken it upon himself to interpret divine injunctions, a task that is ordinarily the work of the scholars of religion, not rulers. Aurangzeb's self-serving and indeed cockamamie interpretations have yielded God's favor in a way that can only be described by a Qurʾanic quotation used fantastically out of context: God is happy, we are told, insofar as Aurangzeb's soldiers are "far from homelands, deprived of families, despairing of the birth of sons, subsisting on bread and water, continually in mortal fear." The slightest attenuation of this suffering thus brings them in opposition to the "Beloved of God," Aurangzeb, who believes the Qurʾan demands of him to inflict unending misery on his subjects.

The audience is thus not to regard its tribulations as accidents of fate, but the infliction of "God's mercy" by Aurangzeb on them. The sermonizer yearningly recalls the halcyon days of life in the reign of Shah Jahan, "when we were at perfect ease and in repose in the harems and mansions of Shahjahanabad [Delhi], rejoicing in its canals and gardens, feasting on viands and quaffing cups." But, like the people of Sheba, the inhabitants of Delhi had become arrogant and ungrateful in their joy: Aurangzeb was heaven's retribution upon them, "making them a bulls-eye for the arrow of recompense, and impaling them on the spear-head of retribution."

From the pleasant gardens of Delhi to the cactus-strewn wastelands of the Southern frontier, it was indeed a punishment of Qurʾanic proportions for Delhi's nobility. Yet whenever it seemed that these tortures might abate, Aurangzeb prolonged them. In this he acted not out of malice, but out of piety and far-sightedness. "By the grace of God—and God is great!—what stewardship of the faith has the emperor! Hail the Renunciant!," exults the sermonizer, describing how Aurangzeb repeatedly snatches defeat out of the jaws of victory by deliberately appointing bunglers for generals. All this to give Muslims the gift of dying for their faith: "For let it not be that the battle (*jihād*) draw to a close and the residue of one's life pass without righteous war (*ghazā*)." But Aurangzeb's stubborn refusal to let advisors more competent than himself win the war was not due to obstinacy or mulishness. Such apparent vices were in fact the virtues borne of the monarch's great piety, illustrated and supported by another stream of cherry-picked Qurʾanic quotations, interpreted as absurdly as possible (as Aurangzeb, it was implied, did himself):

> Of course one is aware that *the greatest works are the hardest*,[45] so surely the turning of the rein of intention from the easy and appropriate path, towards the direction of the most difficult of ways, is solely for the purpose of increasing beneficences. God be thanked that he [Aurangzeb] is constantly engaged in securing beneficences by pursuing impossibilities, so as to atone for the past victories that were achieved with such ease. In relation to these virtues of his prayer, the great achievements of war have demonstrated many times that *the good deeds of the pious are the evils of the saints*.[46] *"Verily, Good deeds drive away evil deeds."*[47]

Aurangzeb's gratitude for former victories is now expressed in deliberately inflicting defeat on his forces: indeed, he is pious, and these are good deeds, though they may appear to the common eye as the "evils of the saints."

Taken together, ʿAli's sarcasms produce a lacerating and comprehensive critique of the emperor's image in precisely the terms in which he articulated his sovereignty. His sense of piety and for his faith in his exegetical abilities is mocked in the cutting implication that he cannot understand the Qurʾan. His pretensions to fighting as a holy warrior of Islam and as a successful leader in wartime are equally ridiculed, and he is compared unfavorably to his deposed father Shah Jahan.

In light of ʿAli's bracing criticisms, it is perhaps easier to sympathize with Aurangzeb's desire to "cut out his tongue and sever his neck." But Aurangzeb was surely restrained by the fact that such an intemperate action would only add to the chorus of criticism he had come to face by the late seventeenth century. Dissatisfaction with Aurangzeb's expression of sovereignty is evident across the archive. Consider a letter supposedly written by the high-ranking nobleman Mahabat Khan to Aurangzeb, and recorded in an anonymous commonplace book of the late seventeenth century.[48] Because of its remarkable frankness of language, the letter is probably not authentic. It is perhaps better regarded a general articulation of discontent with the king's actions among his servants. Here too we see a direct critique of Aurangzeb's enunciation of sovereignty. At the outset the king is tartly reminded that it is "advisable for kings and generals to conform to established administrative

[45] Hadith, Maqāsid al-Hasanah, No. 135.

[46] On this Sufi saying, see Schimmel and Ernst, *Mystical Dimensions of Islam*, 204.

[47] Qurʾan 11:114.

[48] Anonymous, "Copies of Persian Letters, accounts, etc.," fols. 8a–11b; this manuscript is discussed in Chandra, "Jizyah and the State," 338.

precedents (*dastūr-i peshagān*)." The author laments that under Aurangzeb affairs have come to rest in the hands of "hypocritical Shaikhs and unsound theologians," whose employment is "neither the way of God, nor the means of worldly management (*intizām-i dunya*)." The increased power which Aurangzeb granted to judges is criticized, for now upright financial officers (*madār-i kār-i dīwānī*) could be challenged by judges who were susceptible to bribes.[49] Another letter in the same collection, ostensibly from Aurangzeb's rebellious son prince Muhammad Akbar, elaborates these criticisms in terms of the rise of lowly weavers (*julāha o bāfinda*) and hypocritical Shaikhs to offices of state, and twists the knife:

> In the reign of the Emperor Aurangzeb the holy warrior
> The soap-sellers have become judge and almoner[50]

As its language suggests, such criticism of imperial policy represented the perspective of the imperial nobility. By the late seventeenth century, however, words of criticism were becoming increasingly audible from beyond the walls of the Red Fort. A specimen of the disaffection of one such group—the disgruntled women of Delhi—is recorded in a line of Hindi verse from the period, which laments the departure of their menfolk to the Deccan War:

> A city lovely is Delhi, bright rains more pleasure give,
> But ʿAlamgir hath taken our husbands, how are we to live?
> *Response*:
> Wait patiently all ye and summon fortitude, nor burn,
> And prayers offer up that ʿAlamgir may yet return[51]

The most extensive articulation of such criticism from a popular perspective, however, is recorded in the works of the poet Zatalli. Unlike ʿAli, Zatalli's criticisms are subtle and indirect. This is no doubt because he appears to have directly depended on the patronage of the great for his livelihood. Like ʿAli, Zatalli expresses his sentiments through the inversion of a bureaucratic genre, the news report. But where ʿAli's parody made the news reports prolix and literary, Zatalli deflates them with ridicule. A typical example is:

49 Isfahani, "Shāhid-i Sādiq," fol. 106a.
50 Anonymous, "Copies of Persian Letters, accounts, etc.," fol. 15b.
51 Fallon, *A New English-Hindustani Dictionary*, 224. Translation in original, slightly amended and updated for style.

> At one kiss (*chumma*) and half a gasp (*siskī*) of the day, [the emperor] emerged and held an audience in the imperial washroom (*ghusl khāna*). It was submitted that although Zu'l-faqar Khan had participated in the rebellion with Prince Kam Bakhsh, he nevertheless was ready to sacrifice his life and property in the name of the emperor.
>
> The emperor responded: "Friendship with the arse, but picking a fight with the tail!" ("*gāndh sē dostī, dum sē bair*").[52]

The humor in this formulation, perhaps not immediately apparent to the modern reader, lies in Zatalli's mocking take on the staid protocols of court reportage. One imagines the practiced eye of a middling bureaucrat, accustomed to precise and dry officialese, stumbling over the playfully erotic words that have replaced the precise and routine times at which the emperor gave audience—as if Zatalli imagined days at court were to be measured in kisses and gasps rather than hours and minutes. The matter presented regards the usual machinations of high politics, though here taken to absurdity. To this, the emperor retorts not in the chaste literary Persian for which he was renowned, but in the rustic idiom of Hindi. The use of Hindi is significant, for Zatalli appears to be one of the earliest exponents of the practice of employing colloquial language within a literary register to produce what Walter Hakala has described as "proximal irony."[53] In Zatalli's case, however, the introduction of such "low" language into privileged literary genres also served as a means of criticism. Many of the rustic proverbs Zatalli introduces into his anecdotes serve to reflect in general terms on the inequity and iniquity of social relations, a topic in which 'Ali had no interest.[54]

The subversive power of Zatalli's court anecdotes derives from the fact that they rarely take aim at a single target. Varying linguistic registers serve to veil the objects of his political critique. Consider, for instance, a complaint against a specific individual:

> It was reported that 'Abd Allah Khan, the fort-commander of Akbarabad [Agra], dispensed alms to daily stipendiaries and pensioners after much toil and trouble.

52 Zatalli, *Zatal Namah*, 59.
53 Hakala, "A Sultan in the Realm of Passion," 374.
54 For instance Zatalli, *Zatal Namah*, 72.

> The emperor responded: "The *dom*, the footman, the opium-eater—all three are faithless" ("*dom, piyāda, pūstī, tīnon bī-īmān*").[55]

The complaint that serves Zatalli the humorous pretext to liken the administrator of the fort of Agra to an untouchable and menial is, from the perspective of the administration, a triviality. Its very mention, however, represents the articulation of the concerns of the lowly who depend on the king's largesse; and, importantly, the king is made to resignedly acknowledge his ineffectuality.

But the lowly perspective does not restrict Zatalli to commenting on minor matters. Take, for instance, another (self-implicating) report, from the nobleman Khan-i Jahan to the emperor:

> The essence of the affair is that: due to the enterprise of this old servant, besides jackals and foxes and mongooses and scorpions and venomous serpents, there remains not even a trace of man in the city of Lahore. The price of grain equals that of ornamental jewels. Pleasure-increasing parks and gardens in the surrounding regions and environs have been incinerated, and the populousness on both sides of the roads and paths has been entirely cleansed (*safā safā wa dakkā dakkā namūda*) for a hundred *kuroh*-s. The interior of the city has been rendered a specimen of the desert of Karbala, and every brick of the fort has been flung to the skies with grief. Commoners and nobility (*ra'āyā wa barāyā*), drunken and intoxicated on the dregs of their own wishes, have been sent to hell. And of the city's group of the itinerant and the settled, the pious and the saintly have chosen to flee to the grave (*rāh-i taht al-sarā*). But despite all this toil, his highness withholds his favor from this old servant.
>
> The emperor responded: "Spit on your beard, fye on your face!" ("*Thūkī dārhī, phittē mū*").[56]

As we have come to expect, Khan-i Jahan is not the only target of this generalized critique of misgovernance, which is softened somewhat by comic exaggeration. It is significant that Zatalli makes Khan-i Jahan utter the precise inversion of the discourse of sovereignty as it manifests in the space of the city. For just as elevated prices, destroyed gardens, and eradicated population

[55] Zatalli, *Zatal Namah*, 63.
[56] Zatalli, *Zatal Namah*, 67.

mark the failure of the king to bestow prosperity and comfort on his subjects, so the destruction of the fort signals the uprooting of imperial authority. But while Khan-i Jahan is made to play the part of the fool, it is Aurangzeb on whom the blame must rest for the violation of the compact of sovereignty.

The implication that Aurangzeb is unable to exercise proper control over his nobility is elaborated in other instances:

> Nafs-Parwar ("Egotistical") Khan reported that the nobility are consuming the *daulat* of His Highness, and not doing their work in accordance with His Highness' wishes.
>
> The emperor responded: "The donkey grazes the crops; neither sin nor boon."[57]

Such failures of imperial governance are attributed to Aurangzeb's single-minded desire for conquest on the Deccan frontier. Though the emperor's nobility remind him that the affairs of the heartland of empire (*hindūstān*) are in disarray and require his personal attention, the king is shown to persist (albeit with regret) in his folly. To one such complaint he ruefully asks, "When one's placed one's head in the mortar, why fear the pestle's pound"?[58] To another nobleman's warning about the danger of leaving Delhi unattended, he comments, "The king's left the city; let him take it, who wants it."[59]

Zatalli also takes more direct aim at the king's vision of himself. Like ʿAli, he mocks Aurangzeb's noted love for Arabic as the language of faith and piety. But where ʿAli had lampooned the king's self-regard by invoking the Qurʾan in purposefully ridiculous contexts, Zatalli simply places rude faux-Arabic phrases in his mouth:

> It was offered that in the reign of his Sublime Highness [Shah Jahan], vaginas were scarce and penises plentiful; but in the present reign penises are few and vaginas many.
>
> The emperor responded: "The shortage of dicks and plenitude of pussies is a sign of doomsday" ("*qillat al-lodāt wa kasrat al-chūt min āsār al-qiyāmat*").[60]

57 Zatalli, *Zatal Namah*, 60.
58 Zatalli, *Zatal Namah*, 61.
59 Zatalli, *Zatal Namah*, 64.
60 Zatalli, *Zatal Namah*, 63; for another instance, see 66–67.

Finally, Zatalli's lowly perspective permits him to cast a jaundiced eye on the everyday workings of the imperial administration in a manner quite unknown to ʿAli. Perhaps the most brilliant instance of this is his recreation of the bureaucratic correspondence regarding a generic dispute in the countryside that ultimately involves the forces of the central state.[61] In Zatalli's parody, however, the dizzying array of actors—landholders, officials, soldiers, noblemen—are all replaced by personified fruits and vegetables. What is lost in terms of the narrative's coherence and comprehensibility by this parodic shift, we shall see, is more than recouped in terms of critical effect.

The matter begins with a report of a village official ("Pumpkin Pandit"), describing the misdemeanors of a presumable clansman, Bitter Gourd Pandit, who behaved dishonorably with the daughter of Colocasia. Killing Ginger and Onion, Bitter Gourd fled the scene, but not before having ruined Mint, Lettuce, and all other herbs. Though Bitter Gourd appears to have been of some local stature, this misshapen and quintessentially Indic vegetable was acting at the behest of two plump imports from the Mughal homelands: Mirza Melon Baig and Shaikh Watermelon, who have now falsely implicated the innocent Colocasia Root Rajput in the murder. The writer thus requests the intercession of the chief judge, Mir Tangerine (another luscious elite), who might dispatch local officials (the commissioner Turnip Baig and Eggplant Nath the accountant, among others) to present themselves for investigation before Hill Cucumber Khan, the local garrison commander. The news reporter should be told that the matter is under hand so that authorities outside the province are not involved.

The next report, dispatched from the provincial governor Pudding Khan to the Apricot Court of the Pineapple Emperor, describes a more refined realm. A parade of fruity noblemen (Mirza Apple Quli Samarqandi, grandson of Lady Pear, and foster son of Guava, the foster father of Prince Mango) and astringent officers (Mirza Ginger Baig the Superintendent of Police and Agha Garlic Khan the superintendent of the law court)—descend upon the locality to investigate matters. When Melon Baig, who was identified as the culprit in the first report, is questioned, he brings two local pious worthies to his

[61] The following is derived from Zatalli, *Zatal Namah*, 79–81.

defense. Shaikh Water Chestnut, ("who is a man of prayer and spends his day and night by the water"), and the refuge of rights Shaikh Nutgrass (*kaserū*) the dervish ("who is a black-robed renunciant"), both testify to Melon's innocence. Instead blame is cast upon the two rebellious village chiefs, who are falsely accusing Melon: Eggplant and Pomelo. The actions of Bitter Gourd, the dishonor of the daughter of Colocasia, the killing of Ginger and Onion, and the machinations of Melon—all these matters have now fallen by the wayside. Instead it is decided to make an example of Eggplant and Pomelo, and the matter is cast in terms of ensuring the dominance of the 'Community of Muslims' over the countryside. The report concludes with the punishment meted out:

> It was therefore established that the right lay with Melon Baig. For this reason, Date Quli Baig the censor (*muhtasib*) was instructed to punish this calumny so that it would serve as a warning to others. The aforementioned police chief uprooted Eggplant from his place and killed him with a variety of tortures (*anwāh-i ʿuqūbat*), cut him into four pieces, boiled him in a cauldron and having made a delicious meal of him, sent it to the houses of the 'Community of Muslims' (*jamīʿ-yi musalmānān*) to eat with wheat bread and boiled rice. This became the cause of peace and tranquility (*aman o āmān*) in the whole district.
>
> May the favor of the State remain resplendent.

Peace is thus re-established not by the punishment of the guilty, but by the public and sanguinary execution and post-mortem somatic defilement of Eggplant. The state demonstrates its ideological obligations have been fulfilled by dispatching the executed wretch or delicious meal to its primary constituents in the countryside: the 'Community of Muslims.' Yet, as we see, Zatalli heaps scorn on every aspect of the administrative process. Important figures, puffed up on their own nectar, grandly enact their tasks and in so doing they are made to seem ridiculous. The state routinely enacts its procedures, but the mechanical process of justice is worthy of derision. Perhaps most subversively, Zatalli undermines the category of Hindu and Muslim, on which the justice of the state operates, by drawing instead a primary distinction between earthy indigenes and the exotic transplants who rule them. Despite its reveling in the land's cornucopia, it is hard to miss Zatalli's opinion of the practical workings of imperial rule in the countryside.

Sites of Circulation: The Elite Gathering

How did satirical texts such as those of ʿAli and Zatalli circulate? Complicated poems or imitation news reports would primarily have been passed around on paper. The innumerable copies of ʿAli's *Reports*, which are to be encountered in every collection of manuscripts from the period, testify not only to the runaway popularity of his works, but to the vibrant networks of the late seventeenth century, through which books traveled from city to city, were copied and recopied with ever greater frequency, and in turn inspired new authors to take up the pen.[62] The highly variant collections of Zatalli's works, by contrast, suggest that they originally circulated in more obscure ways, perhaps recited among smaller circles and recorded on disconnected sheaves of paper. In either case, however, the primary site of such circulation was the institution of the elite assembly (*majlis, mahfil*). Though precise boundaries are impossible to establish, it is evident that there were qualitatively different kinds of gatherings, from the pious meeting or theological dispute in the hospice (*takya*) to the formal readings attended by serious poets. But that with which we are concerned is the general form of the elite assembly, integral to the sociability of the courtiers and noblemen, and conducted in their mansions and gardens.

The assembly of the seventeenth century was a restrained and formal affair according to the manuals of gentlemanly conduct from that era. As Rosalind O'Hanlon has shown, such gatherings produced a refined domestic space, demarcated from "the culture of servants, menials, and the bazaar" within the context of an "expanded and more accessible world of commodities."[63] Discerned by restraint in all affairs, at these events the gentleman was to cease eating before satiation; and to refrain from daily tippling, "as it is the habit of the rabble of the marketplace." He was to speak sparingly, and never on matters of faith: at dinner, to avoid jurists and "argumentative people." Likewise his dress was to be unostentatious, never involving "brocade or cloth of gold . . . a golden or embroidered turban . . . trousers of cloth of gold or satin."[64] Most importantly, the gentleman did not suffer the company of an uncouth man (*pājī*), and was earnestly enjoined to not even cast his gaze

[62] Thus the eighteenth-century chronicler Nur al-Din Multani Faruqi reports being inspired to write his own history on reading the Book of War of ʿAli, despite the fact that "whatever befell him is not hidden." Multani, "Jahāndār Nāmā," fols. 2b–3a, 4b.

[63] O'Hanlon, "Manliness and Imperial Service in Mughal North India," 68.

[64] Ahmad, "British Museum Mīrzānāma," 101, 105, 107–8.

at such a one if standing before him. A person of refinement did not speak to his servants: "he [the gentleman] should try to communicate with him [only] by signs or gesture. If such a person does not understand his gestures, he should not retain him in his service."[65]

The musicians, singers, dancers, and jesters who entertained elites at their gatherings all fell into this category of unspeakables. It is the unsophisticated local elites who were unaware of these strictures that ʿAli mocks in a line of verse:

> I've never heard a fitting word from the people of India
> except when they say [in Hindi] to the musician, "Play! Play!"[66]

The gentleman was to appreciate music but never to sing, which might lead involuntarily to the ignominy of dancing and worse disgraces.[67] The status of ordinary musicians can be judged from the Delhi nobleman Faʾiz's message to a friend, in which he lavishly praises the "promised tambur-player" who has now been sent along to him, automaton-like, presumably bearing the letter: "he will be willing to play in every way that you might fancy, for he is capable." The musician, of course, is not named.[68]

Despite these rigid conventions, the assembly was not without mirth. Its highest pleasure was surely poetry. In injunctions against admiring "obscure verses which take time to understand" and butting in to recite the second hemistich when another recites the first, we sense that rules of conduct did not inhibit a relatively freewheeling culture in which poetry was exchanged and discussed.[69] In the same way, the barbs of satirists and mimics invariably present at such gatherings were to be taken with good humor: thus, while the gentleman is advised to shun jesters, he is to "enjoy the performances of the *bhūya* who realistically satirize all sorts of people. If one wants to learn about one's own faults, one should once in a while sit in one's own ambush."[70]

In the poetic anthologies of the era, assemblies appear to be relatively informal and even intimate affairs. In the reminiscences of the elite nobleman Sarkhwush, we see the obligations of piety and decency routinely flouted, wine copiously consumed, calls to prayer ignored, attractive men and women

65 Ahmad, "British Museum Mīrzānāma," 106.
66 Khwushgu, *Safina-yi Khwushgu*, 62.
67 Ahmad, "British Museum Mīrzānāma," 101.
68 Faʾiz, "Kulliyāt-i Fāʾiz," fol. 161a.
69 Ahmad, "British Museum Mīrzānāma," 107, 108.
70 Ahmad, "British Museum Mīrzānāma," 101.

"seduced," etiquette constantly breached, and slights and cutting verses the norm.[71] One of his anecdotes suggests that such elite sociability was more common among émigrés than among native-born Indians: the nobleman Himmat Khan is recorded remarking to a poet that the practice of friends eating in one another's house is "a good tradition" among "us Mughals," while Indians are of coarse temperament (*rakīk taba*ʿ), for they eat meanly, crouching in the solitude of their own homes.[72] It is also the case that the conduct manuals discussed above bear the perspective of recent immigrants who are somewhat less than familiar with the land's music, food, and customs. Nevertheless such gatherings became firmly established as the hub of sociality in the increasingly integrated culture of late-seventeenth-century imperial elites.

It is by such assemblies that works of poetry and satire percolated through the fabric of imperial society, as also the jests and witticisms that are recorded in the joke books of the era. It should come as no surprise that ʿAli himself had produced a small work of jokes and humorous essays, though their dense allusiveness placed them beyond the comprehension of all but the learned.[73] But most collections of jokes from the period are not ascribed to individual authors and contain humorous anecdotes in the simplest of language. They involve long-standing figures of fun such as the theologian Mulla Dopiyaza ("Meat and Onion Stew") and the dervish Shaikh Chilli, the emperor Akbar and his minister Birbal, the musicians (*kalāwantān*) Lad and Kapur.[74] Their pages are populated by the stock figures of narrow-minded judges, foolish husbands, loose women and prostitutes; blind men, opium addicts and dumb thieves; cunning Mughals, stupid Turks, and bigoted Afghans. Collections from the eighteenth-century collection are particularly remarkable, for they include jokes involving contemporary kings and ministers: Aurangzeb, Haidar Quli Khan, Amir Khan, Ali Vardi Khan, Sar Buland Khan, and Delhi's chief of police Faulad Khan now begin to make an appearance.[75]

The critical or political charge of such humor is evident in works such as a short "dictionary" of terms from the late seventeenth century (in some recensions attributed to the Mulla Dopiyaza, and frankly inspired by the work of Ubaid-i Zakani), which casts a jaundiced eye over the land and

[71] Sarkhwush, *Kalimāt al-Shuʿarāʾ*.
[72] Sarkhwush, *Kalimāt al-Shuʿarāʾ*, 136.
[73] ʿAli, *Ruqqāt o Muzhikāt*.
[74] Naim, "Popular Jokes and Political History."
[75] Anonymous, "Collection of Essays in Verse and Prose," fols. 354–64; Anonymous, "Hikāyat-i Latīf"; Rai, "Malāhat-i Maqal"; Mir, *Zikr-i Mir*, 130–43.

systematically mocks the categories through which empire was articulated. In this vision, which forms a neat contrast with the writing of imperial ideologues on the beauties of the city, only God and the prophet are spared criticism. The king is a "lazy-bones," whose sonorous titles are a "potion of sleep," whose trumpets are "the fart of *daulat*" and drums "the crushing of *daulat*." The judge is an "enemy of all," and the jurisprudent "writes whatever anyone says." The censor is the "*penis et testes* of the judge," the police chief is "an instance of the Lord of Death," and a tax collector is "a stupid little man." A nobleman is "a blood-drinker of the poor," and a noble scion is "unconscious." The faith of Islam, so valued by Aurangzeb, is extensively ridiculed. The mosque is simply "a farting-ground for travelers," the prayer leader has "the face of a heron," the mosque keeper is a "shameless fly." The recluse is someone who "eats for free," a pious mendicant is a "rare wonder," and a pilgrim is "a seller of the faith"; so a truly prayerful man is no more than "the entertainer's monkey." The land of India is "a pot of honey, full of flies," and its various inhabitants are no better. The Hindu is "abstrusity-loving," the Muslim "eats after eating." A Khorasani "copulates with man and woman alike," an Afghan is a "heap of barbarism," and the Mughal is expectedly criticized for "a killing a day"; his chief pleasure is "joy in pederasty," perhaps because the Mughal wife "beats her husband with shoes." In this world, where marriage is "a pillory on the neck" and alcohol is "prohibited—but only for the lowly," a man's only joys are cannabis paste ("a mine of fancies") and opium ("visions in sleep").[76] Sophomoric though such jokes may seem, their presence in the archive is akin to little fossils from the great sea of conversation that resounded among the salons and parlors of the turn of the century. Their existence reminds us that the highfalutin literary articulations of imperial ideology we have encountered did not escape the derision of their rather cynical audience.

The Expansion of Poetic Practice

The increasing visibility of such sentiments in elite culture is matched by their diffusion beyond the rarified circles of the imperial court. It is indexed by the widening ambit of poems of praise, celebration, and condolence, and

[76] Anonymous, "Copies of Persian Letters, accounts, etc," fols. 3a–7b; Anonymous, "Lughat-i Mullā Do-piyāza."

above all chronograms, which were increasingly designed for broader circulation over the course of the seventeenth century. Until the beginning of that century, extant chronograms appear confined to courtly contexts, recording significant events in the life of the king.[77] Chronograms inscribed on early-seventeenth-century buildings on the high road running through the imperial heartland between Delhi and Agra invariably begin by praising the king before naming the donor.[78] By the end of the century, however, a poet like ʿAli wrote chronograms recording not only Aurangzeb's doings, but also those of others, including his own. Thus he records the construction of a female residence in 1681; a garden in 1688; a new pavilion (*dīwān-khāna*) in 1689, which marked his return from the Deccan frontier "like one who emerges from darkness into light"; and a private residence (*khilwat-khāna*) in 1691.[79] His published *Collection* (*Dīwān*) also contains poems commemorating the birth of sons to princes and noblemen, their accession to office, and their receiving of honors. ʿAli's assaults against Kamgar Khan, we recall, were provoked by the latter's failure to properly appreciate (or reward) such one such poem. ʿAli also penned chronograms recording the death of those he disliked, such as the high nobleman Mahabat Khan:

> I said, who's this coward who died?
> An unseen voice cried out, "Mahabat Khan"![80]

Such rude chronograms were not ʿAli's invention, for the historian Badaʾuni was already composing them to celebrate the demise of his enemies one hundred years previously.[81] But, by the turn of the century, chronograms like those of ʿAli were circulated more widely among the salons of imperial society. Even the most vocal exponents of mystic quietism, such as Delhi's foremost poet Mirza Bedil, leave us a large corpus of chronograms praising the emperor and his noble patrons, and celebrating the building of gardens, mosques, and schools.[82]

[77] Hasan, *Mughal poetry*, 21–23.
[78] E.g., Parihar, *Land Transport in Mughal India*, 149, 155.
[79] ʿAli, *Dīwān-i ʿĀlī*, 234–35.
[80] ʿAli, *Dīwān-i ʿĀlī*, 239.
[81] As, for instance, the chronogram "You are dead, you great hog" to commemorate the death of Shaikh Gadaʾi Kamboʾi. Badaʾuni, *Muntak͟hab Ut-Tawārik͟h*, II:119. I am grateful to Hasan Siddiqui for this reference.
[82] See, for instance, Umar, *Urban Culture*, 173; Bedil, *Kullīyāt-i Bedil*, 2:124–32, 150–56.

A similar expansion can be discerned in the use of the poetry of praise and criticism for purposes of patronage. The model, again, was set by the imperial court, where an elegant poem of praise could win a fortune. The poet Saʿida, it is said, was weighed against silver by both Jahangir and Shah Jahan for two odes he composed. Similarly, the poet Kalim supposedly received 5,500 rupees—about 137 pounds of silver—for his 63 couplets on Shah Jahan's second coronation.[83] By the late seventeenth century, however, the imperial court was no longer the only site of poetic patronage. The practice of poetry, more broadly, had become a means by which the lowly could secure the favor and patronage of their betters in an explicitly financial form. This is why Sarkhwush, who expended great energy in producing chronograms and poems of praise for the nobility of the day, bitterly records when he received no more than "verbal favor" (*maharbānī-yi zabānī*) from his patrons.[84] And if the purpose of penning a poem of praise was frequently to garner money, then the lack of generosity exposed the subject of the poem to the threat of satire. The transactional nature of this relationship is captured in the joke about the frustrated poet who appeared yet again after several rejections at a nobleman's gate: When asked what he wanted, he said, "I wrote an encomium (*madh*) and he gave me nothing; I wrote a satire (*hajw*) and he gave me nothing; so now I've come to write his requiem (*marsīya*)."[85]

By the late seventeenth century, the culture of praiseful and satirical poetry had become so entrenched that even gentlemen with no particular claim to poetic excellence could satirize their betters if provoked. Sarkhwush relates the tale of a minor cavalry officer (*mansabdār*) who wrote a satirical poem against the high nobleman Ruh Allah Khan out of professional frustration. The poem eventually reached its target (presumably having been recited from one to another in the meantime), and the terrified officer apologized abjectly when summoned before the nobleman. Instead of dismissing him from service, however, the nobleman rewarded him handsomely and had his stipend increased. His generosity stood in contrast to those miserly noblemen who had failed, in Sarkhwush's estimation, to reward his brilliance, and whom he accordingly satirized.[86]

[83] Hasan, *Mughal Poetry*, 55–56.
[84] Sarkhwush, *Kalimāt al-Shuʿarā*ʾ, 65.
[85] Anonymous, "Collection of Essays in Verse and Prose," fol. 352b; Sarkhwush relates essentially the same tale, making its object the nobleman Bakhtawar Khan. Sarkhwush, *Kalimāt al-Shuʿarā*ʾ, 65.
[86] Sarkhwush, *Kalimāt al-Shuʿarā*ʾ, 65–66.

The Gathering in the Eighteenth Century

On May 26, 1718, as the clouds of conflict between Farrukh Siyar and his Barha noblemen gathered over the city, the visiting minor nobleman I'timad 'Ali Khan arrived at the house of an acquaintance named Mirza Jalil Beg. What transpired there he does not record in his diary, save for the phrase: "the whole night was made to pass in frolic and pleasure (*'aish o 'ishrat*)." Two days later he attended a party (*ziyāfat*) thrown by the "wife of Khuda Bakhsh Khan, the mother of Muhammad Khizr." On June 1, Zafar Quli Khan, the steward of Aurangzeb's daughter, invited him for a party to his residence in Mughalpura; because of a dust-storm he spent the night there. On the next day he encountered Har Dayal, the son of the agent (*wakīl*) of the nobleman Najabat Khan, in the house of Shaikh Abu Bakr, a compatriot of the author. The next few days were windy and dusty, but on June 6, the administrator Ghiyas al-Din Khan sent a formal invitation to the author.[87] While some of these encounters may have been family visits, I'timad 'Ali Khan's packed social calendar vividly illustrates the central and everyday importance of the institution of the gathering in the culture of these middling urban elites who served in the offices of princes and high nobility.

That the courtly practices of poetry now diffused widely through the city in the gatherings of quite humble urbanites is evident in the chronograms of the obscure émigré poet Husaini (fl. 1713–1760). A resident of Delhi, Husaini wrote the usual poems addressed to the king and the highest nobility: over the years he produced chronograms celebrating the accession of Farrukh Siyar and quotidian events from the life of Muhammad Shah—including the king's birthdays, his recoveries from illness, the birth of his son, the birthday of the princess Qutbi Begam, greetings to him on the Eid festival, and finally, his death. He also composed chronograms praising the achievements of the great nobles, such as the construction of the massive palatial complex by Burhan al-Mulk in 1737/38, and the gardens and wells built by his successors. But many of Husaini's chronograms celebrate the everyday achievements of the minor or middling bureaucrats and officers who served with him in the imperial artillery: the building of houses, births, weddings, and deaths, of not only Sa'd al-Din Khan, the commander of the artillery, but also men like Shafi' Beg Khan, a captain (*jamā'a-dār*) of the vizier's troops, and Lala Kripa Rao, the accountant (*daftar-band*) of the artillery. They record the

[87] Khan, "Majma' al-Fawā'id / Masdar-i Akhbār," fols. 133b–34a.

wedding of Muhammad Amanat Khan, a captain (*mink-bāshī*) of artillery, and of Shadman Beg, a servant (*chelā*) of the commander; the attainment of Ganga Bishan to the office of the manager (*peshkār*) of artillery; the birth of a son him, and to Idris Khan, the son-in-law of ʿArab ʿAli Khan the artillery-commander, among others.[88] Though their increased number is undoubtedly the product of their sale and purchase—a facet of the commercialization so evident in other aspects of urban culture—the chronograms of poets such as Husaini did not move through an open market.[89] Most were probably read and circulated within—and between—groups of acquaintances. Some, as we shall see, were almost certainly recited on the streets. But the somewhat restricted circle to which Husaini's poems are addressed emphasizes the limited porosity of such urban assemblies.

By this time, Delhi's elite gatherings also appear to have a much less formal character than was suggested by the seventeenth century conduct manuals. One aspect of this *décloisonnement* was in the domain of language. Delhi's literary elites of the seventeenth century resolutely refused to sully their Persian prose with words from the vernacular they called "Hindi." For the courtier and poet Iradat Khan, it was a sign of the emperor Jahandar Shah's unfitness for kingship that he conversed familiarly with the uncultured daughter of a nobleman in her own idiom of the "coarse Hindi speech."[90] But the next generation of noblemen, who rose to the top in the churn of the violent successions of the early eighteenth century, were not much hampered by their taste for the local vernacular. In the 1710s, Mirza Muhammad, a highly literate but unsuccessful scion of an established family, was horrified that a person like Shaikh Muhammad Amin of Sambhal rose to high station even though "he could not speak Persian properly, and was illiterate, uncouth (*pājī-tabʿīyat*), and betrayed an utterly pedestrian nature (*suflagī-yi tamām*)."[91] Three decades later, the courtly litterateur Anand Ram Mukhlis warmly remembered the colorful Raja Hari Singh, who could only speak Persian "after a fashion" but nevertheless recited memorized poems, and composed verses in Hindi.[92] And why not, given that already by the turn of the century Aurangzeb's own sons and grandsons were not merely patronizing Hindi poets but themselves composing in the language?[93] In this

[88] Husaini, "Kulliyāt-i Husainī," fols. 85a–140a.
[89] For a parallel process in Iran, see Losensky, "Coordinates in Time and Space."
[90] Wazih, *Tārīkh-i Irādat Khān*, 144.
[91] Muhammad, "ʿIbratnāma," fol. 171a.
[92] Mukhlis, *Chamanistan*, 30–31.
[93] Busch, *Poetry of Kings*, 159.

context, Zatalli's free use of Hindi words and phrases marks an important if precocious move toward the greater embrace of the local vernacular, which would result in the development of the literary register of the "mixed language" (*rekhta*) over the course of the century: a process spurred as much by the interest of established elites in pastoral vernaculars as the rise of new men from the provinces.

This literary indigenization was paralleled by a perceptible shift in the relations between elites and those who served them. The paradigmatic instance of this shift was again embodied in the emperor Jahandar Shah, whose love for a lowly dancing girl, claimed his critics, led to the dominance of her musician brethren (*kalāwantān*) over the court, with the resulting destruction of the king's *daulat*. But Jahandar Shah's overthrow did nothing to check the rise of the lowly in the life of the city. In this context, a striking feature of Dargah Quli Khan's experience of the elite gatherings in Delhi in the late 1730s is the prominence of non-elites among them. Whereas in previous epochs, singers and musicians were barely mentioned, Dargah Quli Khan writes rapturously of the experience of listening to Baqir the tambur player, or Ghulam Muhammad who performed on the sarangi. While Dargah Quli Khan adjudged their music as a connoisseur, he also noted the independent celebrity of men such as the hand-drum (*dholak*) maestro Husain Khan, which derived from the popular approbation of the "people of India," and not nameless service to the king or nobility.[94]

Behind such celebrity lay the hidden hand of the market that had come to exercise such a profound influence over so many other aspects of city life. In his account of the parties of the aristocrat Mirza Mannu, whom he regarded as the finest procurer of beautiful young men in the city, Dargah Quli Khan betrays his recognition of this fact through a telling metaphor:

> Every downy-cheeked lad who is not connected to this assembly is a false document (*fard-i bātil*), and every dark-complected beloved unconnected to this gathering is missing from the description-roll of Trust (*az hulya-yi iʿtibār ʿātil*). His gathering is the assay (*dār al-ʿiyār*) of spectators, and his party the touchstone of the test (*mihakk-i imtihān*) of the flower-faced. Until the defaced currency of beauty (*naqd-i qurāza-i husn*) is not returned to the mint (*dār al-zarb*) of his party, it is not of full measure, no matter if

[94] Dargah Quli Khan, *Muraqqaʿ-yi Dihlī*, 92, 96.

> it is the purest gold; and until the silver of grace is not melted down in the pitcher of his assembly it is not sterling, even if it be utterly unalloyed.[95]

Mirza Mannu's assemblies, in other words, are like the administrative office that verifies the authenticity of claim, or an imperial mint in which the bodies of young men had to be stamped with the insignia of elite approval before they were fit to circulate in the urban economy of desire. Their circulation did not merely resemble the flow of silver that animated Delhi's economy of exchange, but was in fact driven by the impersonal forces of the marketplace. And this was a public market: elsewhere he describes the lowly fellow Miran, who conducted a sort of monthly talent audition to bring the newest fresh face or sweet voice before his master, the vizier. This assembly, filled with musicians, devotional singers, dancers, and mimics, welcomed not only elites but served as a "public gift" (*salā-yi ʿāmm*) to the city's folk, who were also allowed to watch.[96]

Yet this was not simply a world in which people could be bought and sold (though they were): It was also one in which it was possible to marketize oneself as a commodity. It is this combination of skill and a talent for marketing which produced the many celebrities of low status who jostled on the city's stage in the 1730s. Among them the greatest was undoubtedly the courtesan Nur Bai. Though Nur Bai belonged to the low-born class of entertainers (*domnī*), Dargah Quli Khan describes her as akin to a member of the nobility: she inhabited a sumptuously furnished house and rode an elephant accompanied by heralds and mace-bearers (*chāwūsh o chobdār*). Her power can be judged by the fact that she penned "letters of recommendation in patronage of whosoever: because she is beloved everywhere, whatever she says is immediately accepted."[97] In 1749/50, some ten years later, when Nasir al-Mulk, the financial administrator of Bengal, requested Nur Bai to hasten to the provincial capital to entertain the governor Ali Vardi Khan, he offered her the enormous sum of 50,000 rupees, and promised to employ her son Ghulam-i Imam Khan at the head of fifty horse and one hundred footmen "with all distinction."[98] A book of witty tales written in the same decade mentions Nur Bai as a fixture in Delhi's politics, hobnobbing with the

[95] Khan, *Muraqqaʿ-yi Dihlī*, 79–80.
[96] Khan, *Muraqqaʿ-yi Dihlī*, 73–74.
[97] Khan, *Muraqqaʿ-yi Dihlī*, 104.
[98] Qalandar, *Dastūr al-Inshā*, 105.

city's nobility, and many anecdotes were related to the hypnotic charm she exercised on Nadir Shah, who almost carried her away to Iran.[99]

For Dargah Quli Khan, Nur Bai's status depended not merely on her beauty, but rather on her expertise in the subtle art of conversation and the fact that her colloquial speech (*rozmarra*) was as entrancing as her polite idiom (*muhāwara*). Nur Bai's charms, in other words, lay in her synthesis of elite manners with her common origins. A similar figure was the courtesan Bihna'i, who also rode an elephant and was accompanied by mace-bearers. Dargah Quli Khan observed that the vizier I'timad al-Daula had gifted her a set of bejeweled utensils for serving and consuming alcohol, which was worth 70,000 rupees—an indication of how the abstraction of favor could be measured precisely in the currency of the realm. The courtesan made no effort to hide her lowly origins, for the name "Bihna'i" refers to a cotton carder.[100] Yet here was a cotton-carder who rode an elephant, and who maintained "relations of perfect equality" with the nobility, and who again "pulled at the ropes of the imperial offices" by writing letters of recommendation, which, like Nur Bai's, were "accepted."[101]

Though women like Nur Bai and Bihna'i were exceptional in a world where a slave-girl (or boy) could be easily purchased for a few rupees to satisfy the sexual desires of men, their celebrity demonstrated how the commerce in conviviality opened new opportunities for commoners savvy enough to use them. This success did not mean erasing the marks of one's non-elite origins (which were in any case ineradicable), but rather parlaying them into a desirable commodity in Delhi's market for conviviality. Nur Bai, for one, never lost sight of the primacy of market relations in determining her success: for, as Dargah Quli Khan observed, "her conversation is available so long as the purse is full, and her companionship is available only until ready money remains."[102]

This was also true of individuals much less exalted than the city's reigning courtesans. An intriguing example of such a person was Shah Daniyal. Shah Daniyal thought himself respectable as the descendant of a line of pious worthies, but he entered the soiree as a *naqqāl*: an entertainer who could both recite witty stories and produce satirical impressions. Dargah Quli Khan regarded Shah Daniyal with a horrid fascination, describing him as of the

[99] Rai, "Malāhat-i Maqal," fol. 37a.
[100] Platts, *A Dictionary of Urdu, Classical Hindi, and English*, 192.
[101] Khan, *Muraqqa'-yi Dihlī*, 105.
[102] Khan, *Muraqqa'-yi Dihlī*, 104.

tribe of hangers-on who appeared wherever the slightest profit was to be found. At the meal, the spectacle of the Shah's "uninhibited voracity" induced nausea among his more genteel companions: just as his mode of sleeping "was not without its appalling aspects," so his expectorations on awaking were "not without [their] terrors." These were precisely the attributes that had rendered someone unfit for polite company in the eyes of the seventeenth-century commentators. But Shah Daniyal's exceptional abilities made him, in the final estimate, "capable of the assembly and worthy of the party."[103] Another such figure was the Mughal Shah Maʿsum, whose name betrays a pretension to some pious status. A contemporary noted his proficiency in singing devotional songs praising the prophet's family and also the martyred Shiʿi Imam Husain; besides entertaining songs in Hindi and fresh "anecdotes and stories." Shah Maʿsum was of an insouciant (*bī-parwā*) bent: he freely accepted all gifts by noblemen, and immediately wasted them on his seedy companions. Indeed there was something extortionary about these "gifts," because those who appeared ungenerous were liable to his satirical assaults. But Shah Maʿsum's extractions were driven at least in part by the market in which he thrived, for he was generally neck-deep in debt and chased by his creditors. In this way, he exemplifies the multifold manner in which the market had made the satirical voices of non-elites a staple feature of the elite assembly in the eighteenth century.[104]

The Marketplace of Praise and Censure

In his account of Zatalli, the mid-eighteenth-century poet Mir relates that the poet was in the habit of carrying both an encomium and a satire with him on his visits to people's homes. If treated with courtesy, Zatalli read out the encomium; if not, he gave the "wing of circulation" (*bāl-i shuhrat*) to the satire.[105] Mir's account is significant because it passingly illustrates three key aspects of the place of poetry in the eighteenth-century city. Firstly, the poetry of praise and satire had become an object of commerce, that could be bought and sold. Secondly, poetry enjoyed a public presence beyond the

103 Khan, *Muraqqaʿ-yi Dihlī*, 98.
104 Jaunpuri, "Sūrat-i Hāl," fols. 19b–20a.
105 Mir, *Tazkīra-yi Nikāt al-Shuʿarā*, 31.

polite assembly; and finally, as we shall see, poetry could be put to the service of carrying an opinion and to circulate through the city.

Like everything else, poetry did not escape the forces of commercialization that were transforming life in the city at the turn of the century. As their ubiquity suggests, poems of praise and censure had become an everyday object of sale in the marketplace, as a useful means of securing favor or threatening dishonor. Mir's story may not be as apocryphal as it sounds, because traces of the operation of these market relations are already visible within Zatalli's works of the late seventeenth century. Take, for instance, the satire Zatalli composed against a certain Mirza Khuda Yar Baig, which describes how the Mirza was ignominiously tied to a tree and beaten by his enemies at Kishan Das' Pond, some miles south of the city. To ameliorate his shame, the Mirza promised Zatalli five gold coins for an encomium, but refused to give him the sum after it was recited. In response, Zatalli composed a satire, which mocks him for his foppishness and cowardliness, and expresses regret for writing the encomium in the first place.[106] In much the same way, when Fath ʿAli Khan, the financial administrator of the lady Qamar al-Nisa, gave Zatalli only five of the thirty rupees she had promised him, Zatalli promptly produced a satire on the official and sent it to the lady.[107] Such sums, which were hardly enormous for someone with pretensions to status, are suggestive of the everyday value of the poetry of praise and satire in the city at the turn of the century.[108]

The imbrication of poetic production and matters of money is evidenced in another way in the works of the minor poet and artillery officer Husaini, wherein we find his ode of gratitude to his commander Saʿd al-Din Khan, thanking him lavishly for having his military stipend (*mansab*) increased.[109] Next follows a satire against the same man, who is now described as his "enemy." In it, Husaini relates how his reward for the encomium was not a bag of silver, but, as is typical of the financialized world of the eighteenth century, a pay slip: "an increase of twenty cavalry rank at the five-month pay scale, paid in cash." But when the paperwork reached the disburser Sabha Chand, son of Jagjiwan, that wily "cur" began to prevaricate. Worse still, Saʿd al-Din Khan himself began to make a fuss (*nakhra*) about disbursing the grant. When Husaini stopped presenting himself before the Khan in a huff,

[106] Zatalli, *Zatal Namah*, 171–73.
[107] Zatalli, *Zatal Namah*, 166–67.
[108] Cf. the remarks in Habib, "Persian Book Writing," 517.
[109] Husaini, "Kulliyāt-i Husainī," fols. 74b–75a.

the Khan had him marked "absent." In response Husaini now launches a barrage of invective: he accuses Saʿd al-Din Khan of lying about his descent and describes his mother as one of the "man-destroying" whores of Kabul. He charges Saʿd al-Din Khan with cowardice before Nadir Shah, to whom he also turned over all his wealth and possessions, even all his cloth: pashminas, dushalas and shawls. This was not all that he handed over, however: for Husaini goes on to call the khan a "sodomite" (*muʿtī*), declares his love of "giving his rear" to all and sundry, and asks, finally, to also be given the favor.[110] In another poem, Husaini goes on to add the gravest imprecations against Saʿd al-Din's Khan's faith.[111] Yet there is almost an element of the conventional and routine to these accusations. It is apparent that Husaini expected his slurs to be tolerated, for he went to produce chronograms celebrating the appointment of Saʿd al-Din Khan's son to the command of the artillery in 1743.[112]

Poetry and the Spaces of Popular Politics

The power of such satires evidently derived from their ability to circulate rapidly through the public realm of the city. The constraints on the circulation of the complex poetry of a nobleman like ʿAli did not apply to his chronograms, which could be committed to memory and repeated easily. Even more, Zatalli's brutally simple rhymes and sharp images lend themselves to immediate memorization. Within Zatalli's satires there are also traces of a context of public recitation, which suggests how they might have disseminated among the people at large. Zatalli's invective against Mirza Khuda Yar Baig is explicitly directed toward the city as a whole:

> I now inform the city and the market
> Let my sigh wound Khuda Yar[113]

And his attack on the financial administrator Sabha Chand appears to be composed for recital in a courtyard where administrative disputes are resolved:

[110] Husaini, "Kulliyāt-i Husainī," fols. 75a–76b.
[111] Husaini, "Kulliyāt-i Husainī," fol. 103a–b.
[112] Husaini, "Kulliyāt-i Husainī," fols. 127b–128a.
[113] Zatalli, *Zatal Namah*, 170.

Just you keep hopping about this square like a toad
And keep pecking at bugs and insects
. . .
Beat the drum of truth in this court
And don't hasten to light a haystack.[114]

As such references to context indicate, the life of such poetry was primarily lived publicly: outside the space of the assembly and in the teeming marketplaces and squares of the city. That Zatalli's poems addressing the elites who had angered him were designed to be read or heard by an amorphous but larger public in the city suggests how the commercialization of poetry also drove it to circulate among non-elites. For, just as the private gathering was a center of elite sociability, so too new spaces became associated with the percolation of poetry and political opinion through the fabric of urban society.

An important site of poetic intercourse in the city was its coffeehouse, which stood both metaphorically and literally at its center. Coffee appears to have started arriving in large quantities in the imperial port of Surat in the early seventeenth century, where it fetched higher prices for the East India Company than it did in Iran.[115] The sparseness of evidence for Delhi's coffeehouses, and the passing terms in which they are invariably mentioned, suggest that such places were neither ubiquitous nor particularly exotic in the city. Yet the coffeehouse was a significant place of assembly for the city's intellectuals, particularly poets. Visiting in the late 1730s, Dargah Quli Khan remarks on the coffeehouses in the central expanse of the Moonlight Avenue, which perhaps indicates that they had an outdoor element; he observes that poets gathered here every day, giving proof of both their poetic ability (*sukhan*) and "humorous abilities" (*bazla sanjī*), indicating that jests and satires were very much part of this place of public performance.[116]

Writing a few years later, Anand Ram Mukhlis compared the "two or three" coffee shops of Moonlight Avenue to those of Iran, which he had heard were famed for their ceremonious air (*latāfat o takalluf*). In Delhi too, gentlefolk ducked into the coffee shops in the evenings to converse and recite poetry over many cups of coffee. Mukhlis mentions visiting these coffeehouses in

[114] Zatalli, *Zatal Namah*, 164–65.
[115] Wild, *Coffee*, 81; See also Hattox, *Coffee and Coffeehouses*; Matthee, "Coffee in Safavid Iran"; Hakala, "A Sultan in the Realm of Passion"; Kafadar, "How Dark Is the History of the Night."
[116] Dargah Quli Khan, *Muraqqa'-yi Dihlī*, 62.

his youth, though as an elite, he refrained from drinking their brew: instead, his servants prepared his coffee at home and carried it along for him. Now, in his old age, he remembered nostalgically promenading along the avenue and gazing at its wares, and the pleasures of good poetry and the company of witty friends.[117] By then, the café had been a feature of Delhi's poetic life for almost a century, for the poet Sarkhwush recalled seeing the poet Munʿim Hakkak Shirazi at one before his death early in the reign of Aurangzeb.[118] And the fact that he describes a certain Mir Ziyaʾ al-Din Dihlawi as frequenting the coffee-house in old Delhi suggests that the institution of the café preceded the construction of Shahjahanabad in the mid seventeenth century.[119] Yet though the coffeehouse was a recognized destination for poets, it does not appear to have been dominated by a regular clientele, but was a potentially somewhat anonymous clearinghouse of poetry. Thus, while some poets such as the eighteenth-century Shah Yaqin were to be seen "at most times" in the coffeehouses at Moonlight Avenue, Sarkhwush mentions others he encountered only once or twice there.[120] And not only coffee was consumed, for jokes from the period also mock opium addicts engaging in banter and uttering wild rumors at the coffeehouse or the confectioner's shop.[121]

Given these qualities, it seems inevitable that the café and its surrounding spaces also became a site for the exchange of political information. Poetry again served as the means of transmission. To see this aspect of urban life, let us return to Shah Yaqin, who, as we have seen, was frequently to be encountered lingering in the cafes of the square, exchanging poetry with his friends. Shah Yaqin, of Turani Mughal extraction, described himself as a mendicant and related his descent from a companion of the dynastic founder Babur. In the 1720s, onlookers and passersby might have paused to listen to him recite a long poem on the history of India, commissioned by the nobleman Sabit Qadam Khan. Of course, we cannot be sure if the poem was ever heard on Moonlight Avenue. But the patron's wish that it be derived from accurate histories and composed in simple language, so that it might be easily memorized (*hifz*) by high and low, suggests that it was crafted for a public context. The frequent exhortations in the poem to "listen now" (*bashanū*) to

[117] Mukhlis, *Chamanistan*, 42.

[118] Sarkhwush, *Kalimāt al-Shuʿarāʾ*, 179.

[119] Sarkhwush, "Kalimāt al-Shuʿarāʾ," fol. 40a; cf. Sarkhwush, *Kalimāt al-Shuʿarāʾ*, 124, which omits this detail.

[120] Khwushgu, *Safina-yi Khwushgu*, 259; for an instance of the latter, see the entry on the "Mad Qasim," in Sarkhwush, *Kalimāt al-Shuʿarāʾ*, 86.

[121] Anonymous, "Collection of Essays in Verse and Prose," fol. 359a.

the tale (*qissa*) of this or that event indicates the presence of an audience that may have found the privileging of facticity over literary quality somewhat tedious. In this way, the poem suggests how even those who had never held a book might encounter the contents of literary chronicles diffusing through the streets of the city.

Yaqin's poem began with a rapid history of Delhi itself, which had been built, abandoned, and repopulated in antiquity before the coming of Islam. Our poet then described the righteous war (*jihād*) against India, blending in popular legends with dated historic battles. Thus, in his account of the early conquest of India, we are told that the (fictional) Salar Masʿud, the nephew of Mahmud the Ghazi, captured Delhi and then crossed the Ganges to be famously martyred at the hands of the infidels.[122] At a brisk canter, the poet describes the defeat of the Raja Pithaura by Muʿizz al-Din and his conquest of Delhi, and the travails of subsequent dynasties until the eventual establishment of the Mughals. The Mughal emperors are lauded for their achievements: Akbar, for setting up the empire, and Shah Jahan, for building the new city of Shahjahanabad and its canals. Aurangzeb was warmly commended for being both pious and politic, cunning and brave, his signal achievement being the compilation of his legal digest and the founding of Aurangabad in the Deccan. His successor Shah ʿAlam was pointedly praised for his Sunni faith, and his knowledge of the reports of the prophet (*hadīs*)—a matter of controversy in the years after his death, as we shall see in Chapter 4.[123] We learn that Jahandar Shah succeeded him, but was overthrown by the prince Farrukh Siyar, who was supported by the two Sayyid brothers, to whom is ascribed a *daulat* that had crossed all limits.[124] While initially sympathetic to the Sayyids, the poet describes how they treacherously imprisoned their own king; he describes the coronation of Neku Siyar, which was conducted by an "artful Hindu Brahmin" named Mitr Sen. Finally, after the deaths of the briefly-lived kings Rafiʿ al-Shan and Rafiʿ al-Daula, Muhammad Shah ascended the throne. Displeased with the "outrageous innovation" (*bidʿat*) of the power of the Sayyids, and, for the welfare of God's creation (*khalq-i Allāh*), Muhammad Shah then set about reclaiming his power, the convolutions of which our poet describes in some detail, while gently lamenting the violence of the process.[125]

122 Yaqin, "Tārīkh al-Sābit / Khilsī-yi Zubda," fol. 3b; Amin, *Conquest and Community*.
123 Yaqin, "Tārīkh al-Sābit / Khilsī-yi Zubda," fols. 10b–11a.
124 Yaqin, "Tārīkh al-Sābit / Khilsī-yi Zubda," fol. 12a.
125 Yaqin, "Tārīkh al-Sābit / Khilsī-yi Zubda," fols. 10a–14a.

Shah Yaqin then launches into an account of the history of the Chaghatai dynasty of which the present emperor was the scion. He next describes the local histories of the regions of India—the Deccan Sultanates, Berar, Khandesh, Bengal, the Sharqi dynasties, Malwa, Ajmer, Sindh, Multan, Kashmir—many of which terminate with their incorporation into the Mughal empire. He ends with a statement of the revenues (*jamʿ-i mahsūl*) of the empire and its territorial extent: the income of twenty-one provinces, excluding Sindh, are individually added up to produce 180,640,000 rupees.[126] Finally come the boundaries of this great domain: from the extremities of Bengal in the east to Kandahar, Ghaur, Kij and Jam in the west; from Tibet in the north to the Sea of Sarandip (Sri Lanka) in the south. The poet concludes with an account of his own genealogy, and with prayers to God that may elites and commoners alike benefit from reading this work.[127]

While we have no evidence to prove that Shah Yaqin ever uttered these verses in the square, we have seen that aspects of the poem suggest it was meant to be heard, recited and memorized by ordinary people. The poem therefore further demarcates an oral sphere of public communication, in which the audience of ordinary people were expected to have a deep historical sensibility, a sense of pride in the extent and richness of the realm in the capital of which they lived, and, most importantly, a fine-grained understanding of the machinations in the Red Fort. Shah Yaqin's diplomatic handling of the controversial overthrow of the king Farrukh Siyar in 1719 (on which see Chapter 5) is important in this regard, for the turmoil around the king's dethronement and execution would have been fresh in the memories of his listeners. As in Robert Darnton's description of Paris in the same period, we can thus observe the poem transmitting political information among ordinary people through a network of urban communication in which spaces such as the coffeehouse were central nodes.[128]

The coffeehouse may have been open to a wide range of people, but was probably still dominated by the well-to-do. The place of the city's lowly inhabitants—its artisans and craftsmen, and below them menials, hawkers, peddlers, itinerant sellers, mendicants, beggars, and ruffians—was surely in its streets and the markets. From Dargah Quli Khan's account of the city it is apparent that by

[126] Yaqin, "Tārīkh al-Sābit / khilsī-yi Zubda," fols. 30a–31a; on fol. 30b, the total is given as "Haft arab o bīst o do [karor] o panja o shash lak [dām]." I have converted at the rate of 40 dām to the rupee. Intriguingly, this is a significantly lower number than that reported in administrative manuals since 1667. Cf. Habib, *The Agrarian System of Mughal India, 1556–1707*, 454–55.

[127] Yaqin, "Tārīkh al-Sābit / Khilsī-yi Zubda," fols. 31b–32a.

[128] Darnton, *Poetry and the Police*.

the eighteenth century, such common folk had a vast number of entertainments to behold in the city's public places. There were devotional singers (*qawwāl*-s), who hung about the city's pious men and tombs and shrines, reciting poems and songs and pestering gentlefolk for small sums in recompense.[129] The jesters (*hazzālān*) who were encountered in elite gatherings were also to be seen in the streets. Their mimicry of elites surely had a sharper edge when conducted in the square before crowds of jeering commoners. That jesters conducted precisely such mockeries is evident from a poetic description of the public performances occasioned by the wedding of Farrukh Siyar in 1715. The poet ʿAbd al-Jalil begins his description of these men by dwelling on the comic inversions of their dress, which signal their lack of honor and thus harmlessness:

> Turbans on their waists, pants on their heads
> Come and see, what's on top is on bottom

Yet it is important that one of their primary acts is to recite poetry:

> Of imitative appearance in the marriage party
> They recite poetry with all forms of wit
> . . .
> They have the temerity in uttering follies
> To bring such verses into rhyme

It is also made clear that such rhymes are directed against the high and mighty:

> Such metaphors take flight from them
> That from a picture of faults, the eagle is discerned

Recognizing that such biting words have the power to wound the elites against whom they are directed, ʿAbd al-Jalil offers only a muted defense:

> Greatness is praised for all length of time
> [But] prominence is marked by the relating of flaws
> . . .
> For spring's first blush makes the garden brighter
> And hearing the nightingale makes the jasmine whiter[130]

[129] Khan, *Muraqqaʿ-yi Dihlī*, 54–55, 63, 66–67.
[130] Bilgrami, *Maṣnawī*, 59–60. I thank Sunil Sharma for discussing these verses with me.

ʿAbd al-Jalil's claim, that faces rendered red with rage or white with shame by the hearing of satire makes the victim even more attractive, can barely contain the dangerous and subversive power of such public acts of recitation. In this context, the jester's silly costume, which signals a controlled and ritualized parodic inversion, masks the truly subversive power of his words.

The same tendency is even more apparent in the case of the *naqqāl*, whose abilities lay in the realm of reciting stories or making satirical impressions. The origins of the *naqqāl* and his work in the square remain shrouded in mystery. According to a nineteenth-century colonial ethnographer, it appears that the "caste" of the *naqqāl*, which was merely the Muslim equivalent of the Hindu caste of the *bhānd*, was subdivided by castes of origination, suggesting that what had congealed into a "caste" in the late nineteenth century was in fact an occupational group a hundred years previously. *Naqqāl*-s such as Shah Daniyal and Shah Maʿsum, previously encountered in the elite assembly, were liminal figures. While they attended noble gatherings, they were not retainers or employees, and claimed a kind of respectable status. They also had a life and existence beyond the lordly mansion, for Dargah Quli Khan describes *naqqāl*-s as performing at squares and other sites of public interchange. The nineteenth-century observer described them as "impudent fellows who make wry faces, squeak like pigs, bark like dogs, and perform many other ludicrous feats. They also dance and sign, mimicking and turning into ridicule the dancing boys and girls, on whom they likewise pass many jokes." It is easy to imagine the *naqqāl* doing precisely the same a century and a half before, but mocking the nobility and articulating political criticisms before the crowds in the square.[131]

A rare and unusually detailed account of the punishment of one *naqqāl* in 1735 offers a sense of their importance in generating public opinion in precisely this manner in the city. According to the chronicler Yahya Khan, when news of the nobleman Samsam al-Daula's abortive campaign against the increasingly-threatening Marathas reached Delhi and Agra in that year, the people began to speak publicly (*mutaʾaiyina*) and eloquently, in Persian and Hindi poetry, on the matter. They praised the "bravery of the Islamic faith of the vizier," who had opposed Samsam al-Daula's policy, and equally "recited Farsi and Hindi verses in the same rhyme and meter mocking

[131] Crooke, *The Tribes and Castes of the North-Western Provinces and Oudh*, I:256–58; Pamment, *Comic Performance in Pakistan*, 52.

Samsam al-Daula." Muhammad Shah was informed that satires of Samsam al-Daula had become so widespread among the people, that in the markets, *naqqāl-s* were reciting "malignant" (*wazh-kār*) satires against him in places of intercourse.

Muhammad Shah responded in a measured fashion: he ordered that one of the *naqqāl-s* be seized, have his face blackened, seated backwards on an ass, and processed through the city. One such fellow was duly arrested and produced before the Abyssinian police chief Faulad Khan. When the police chief gave the order to have his face blackened, the *naqqāl* begged for this not be done, "lest people imagine that he too was an Abyssinian." The police chief laughed it off. When the *naqqāl* was processed, as the crier announced, "Anyone who mocks the Khan-i Dauran [Samsam al-Daula] will be reduced to this condition," the *naqqāl* also yelled out, "Anyone who pays the Marathas their 'one-fourth' tax [*chauth*] and claims to have honor will be reduced to the same condition!"[132]

The *naqqāl*'s brazen responses—and his humiliation—were anticipated in Muhammad Hatim's criticism from 1692 of the lowly youth of his day, who had already become impervious to such forms of punishment. No doubt the *naqqāl*'s courage derived from the support of the onlooking crowds, who appreciatively recited his poems to each other. For elites, the disturbing power of these sentiments derived from their combination of personal invective against an individual nobleman—not an unknown feature—with a perhaps newer critical tone addressing matters of imperial policy toward the rising power in the South. It is also significant that the elite author was not sure where these political criticisms originated: while a *naqqāl* was punished, it was the people who were first noticed speaking publicly.

Though the "Persian and Hindi poems" that the *naqqāl* recited were not recorded, we can approximate their tone and tenor from a satire composed some decades earlier by Zatalli on Delhi's chief of police Mirza Zu'l-Faqar Baig.[133] Even among Zatalli's remarkable works, the poem stands out. For one, it uses a markedly more Persian register than many of his poems, as if to indicate that the author is not merely clowning about. For another, the poem combines the expected personal attack with a professional critique of the Baig, accusing him of failing to perform his duties toward Delhi's citizens. Mirza Zu'l-Faqar Baig has sullied his robes of office with his shameful

[132] Khan, "Tazkīrāt al-Mulūk," fol. 139a–b; for a discussion, see Malik, *A Mughal Statesman*, 68.
[133] Zatalli, *Zatal Namah*, 168–70.

performance, which is worse than the vilest of hounds: for even such a lowly creature gives thieves momentary pause with his barking in the way that the chief cannot. As is to be expected, Zatalli attacks the Mirza's high-born status (accusing him of descent from a *bhānd*), attributes homosexual passivity to him, and compares him to the filthy pig whose mindless rootling has ruined the garden of civic order. Aside from these rather formulaic criticisms, Zatalli also accuses him of stupidity and senility, which have prevented him from acting on good counsel. The result is widespread disorder, rendered in standard tropes of crimes against property. Significantly, Zatalli also appears to allude to specific instances, which perhaps occasioned this critique: the theft of horses from the provisioning market (*nakkhās*), and the murder of a certain Chunni Das.

While Zatalli elsewhere attacks Mirza Zu'l-Faqar Baig by heaping abuse on the name of his daughter (suggesting the possibility of a personal conflict), here the poet's outrage appears to have been evinced by a decline in urban order.[134] In this light, it is important that Zatalli's criticisms are directed against the mirza's incompetence and "unconsciousness," and that he does not impute either malice or venality to the official. Nor does Zatalli petition for the khan's replacement or for imperial intervention. What he offers is a narrow and limited form of criticism, directed against an official's performance that does not hold up to the standards of his constituency—the people of the city, whose lives and property he is to safeguard. This critique is voiced from a position that considers the responsibilities of this official to lie not above—in maintaining peace for the emperor—but below, to the city's residents. We cannot say if Zatalli's poem was sung in the streets by the *naqqāl*-s who performed daily in Sa'd Allah Khan Square, in front of the Red Fort, or recited in the cafés in Moonlight Avenue, within earshot of the police station. What the poem suggests, however, is that a robust culture of political criticism was part of the life of the city by the early eighteenth century.

Conclusion

The emergence of such a culture of public criticism rested upon practices of poetry that had been driven out of the king's court and the elite assembly

[134] Zatalli, *Zatal Namah*, 101–3.

and into the city's streets. Yet the criticisms of satire remained the flip-side of the obsequies of the encomium. Even the most ruthless satirist was happy to return to uttering praises when his wounded ego had been appropriately salved by silver's soothing balm. ʿAli, for instance, was only briefly dismissed from service before returning to the court, thereafter rising to ever higher office. He resumed his usual encomiums of the king: in 1698/99, twelve years after the events of Golconda, on the execution of the Deccani leader Santa, ʿAli composed a praiseful chronogram that is in perfect consonance with Aurangzeb's own assertions of sovereignty:

> With God's grace, on leaving for this holy war did ride
> fortune and *daulat* by the reigns, and victory sit by side
> The head was lopped off the infidel and
> "The Faith restored by its protector ʿAlamgir"
> Victory's date did decide.[135]

Zatalli, whose place appears to have been rather more tenuous than ʿAli's, records an apologetic poem for his satire against the prince Kam Bakhsh.[136] Whatever his opinions of Aurangzeb, he composed a perfectly sincere elegy on the king's death, lamenting his loss and expressing some anxiety for the future.[137]

The forked tongue of poetry, equally capable of sweetness as of poison, mirrors the dual nature of the politics of the people who recited it in the city: as capable of launching to the king's defense as challenging his right to rule. The circulation of political chronograms and poetry in the political crises of the early eighteenth century is symptomatic of the rise of the city's ordinary people as political actors. Yet this process, which depended on the *décloisonnement* of poetic practice, was spurred by the very forces of commercial circulation that were enabled by the making of Moonlight Avenue. As we will shortly see, words of poetry, whether satirical or praiseful, whether whispered in the alleys or shouted out on Moonlight Avenue, would undergird the massive popular assertions of the period. If Shah Jahan's remaking of Delhi, and the commercial vitality of his *faiz* that animated it, produced a Mughal people, then truly it is Aurangzeb's

135 ʿAli, *Dīwān-i ʿĀlī*, 230.
136 Zatalli, *Zatal Namah*, 140–46.
137 Zatalli, *Zatal Namah*, 137–39.

enunciation of sovereignty that gave them their tongue, as liable to launch into humble supplication as scornful insult. But before we turn to the emergence of the political action such speech enabled, we must first establish the constitutive relationship between Aurangzeb's enunciation of sovereignty and its objects, the people.

4
Aurangzeb's Law and Popular Politics

The discourse of sovereignty as it was enunciated by Shah Jahan and Aurangzeb had no place for the participation of imperial subjects in politics other than as passive subjects. But by the early eighteenth century, urbanites had begun to respond to the king and his servants with more than words alone. Indeed, Mughal writers recorded accounts of a range of urban riots and tumults in Delhi and other imperial metropolises from the late seventeenth century onwards. Some of these disorders were instances of the everyday social conflict that routinely erupted over questions of home and honor, clashes at festivals, and other urban struggles and antagonisms. But other instances of popular violence marked new developments. In coming together over questions of "justice," and in gesturing to invoke the aid—or challenge the power—of imperial administrators and the king, the people of the city began to exhibit a previously unrevealed political sensibility.

What generated the capacity in ordinary people to come together and engage in such political action? In his study of the Mughal province of Gujarat, Farhat Hasan has argued that the steady penetration of imperial authority into the fabric of social life over two centuries integrated sub-elite strata of merchants and local gentry into the system of rule. Popular protest, in his conception, operated within the "shared normative context of the *Shariʿa*" and served to "incorporate subordinate social groups in the political system."[1] Hasan's analysis of this process in the commercial hub of Gujarat is also applicable to the imperial center in Delhi. Yet popular politics did not spring autochthonously from beneath the carapace of the imperial state. As Muzaffar Alam and Sanjay Subrahmanyam have speculated, Aurangzeb's efforts at "*qānūn*ization"—the imposition of a canonical legal system on the provinces of the empire—may have provoked the numerous rebellions that marked his reign.[2] In a related vein, the following pages suggest that Aurangzeb's enunciation of sovereignty—central to which was

[1] Hasan, *State and Locality*, 126, 128.
[2] Alam and Subrahmanyam, "Introduction," 31.

The King and The People. Abhishek Kaicker, Oxford University Press (2020). © Oxford University Press.
DOI: 10.1093/oso/9780190070670.001.0001

the application of the juridical aspects of *sharīʿa*—had much to do with the increasing incidences of disorder of his era: indeed, we know of many minor disturbances only because they merited a disciplinary response from the king's judicial apparatus in the first place. Aurangzeb's more bureaucratized imposition of the law in questions of justice can thus be seen as stimulating the development of a popular politics in Delhi (and elsewhere) by empowering even humble folk to act upon their interpretation of justice according to the law, which was not infrequently at variance with the opinions of the learned doctors who served the imperial establishment.

To make this case, the following pages explore in greater detail the relationship between the king and his people, in theory and practice, during the reign of Aurangzeb and after. While the imperial perspective on the people was depicted as one of the paternal stewardship of "God's creation," with no possibility of popular assertion (much less participation) in matters of government, the realities which confronted administrators were far more complex. Plagued by conflict over honor and home, the ever-more teeming cities of the seventeenth century became increasingly subject to sudden tumult. No doubt to quell these everyday forms of social disorder, whether the intestine wars that periodically flared up in the city or the clashes that routinely erupted at festivals, Aurangzeb made dramatic and unprecedented efforts to bring the administration of justice into accordance with the law. To do so, the emperor reconfigured the discourse of sovereignty he inherited from Shah Jahan, with greater emphasis on conformance with the strictures of a Hanafi Sunni piety supported by the expansion of a theological-legal infrastructure. The disciplinary intrusions this enabled—the restriction of feud and private war, the banning of vice, intoxicants, heterodox, or "infidel" practices of piety—all provoked resistance from his subjects. But such interventions also brought these very subjects into greater contact with imperial sovereignty, stimulated the activation of community, opened new channels of negotiation with the state, and created new possibilities to invoke its resources to their own ends.

These developments, in which ordinary people invoked and manipulated the discourse of sovereignty in the pursuit of local ends, are most evident in Delhi and other metropolises of the early eighteenth century. In them we shall see the central promise of imperial justice was used by subordinate groups to win struggles against their betters. Because the imperial discourse of sovereignty promised abundance, shortages of food led the people to challenge the authority of the state and forced it into action. Merchants combined appeals to patrimonial care with economic pressure to have the hated poll tax (*jizya*) rescinded. And finally, since Aurangzeb sought to mold diverse Muslim groups into his vision of an obedient 'Community of Muslims,' even the lowest strata of society began to invoke its theoretically privileged stature, not only in conflicts within the city but even against the king himself.

The People in the King's Eyes

From the perspective of the ideologues of the Mughal dynasty, the relationship between the king and his subjects was essentially one of pastoral care. The people were the passive objects of governance, merely a segment of the Circle of Justice that animated the world, and generally lumped together with all creatures as part of "God's creation" (*khalq-i Allāh*).[3] The Ryots over whose prospects colonial authority endlessly agonized were the lineal and genealogical descendants of a Mughal "flock" (*ra'iyat*), to be overseen by the ruling elite (*ra'is, amīr*). Attendant on this view of the world, Mughal thinkers did not recognize any forms of authority in the realm as independent of the king. When confronted by the inevitable conflict (*fitna*) and corruption (*fasād*) of rebels (*mufsidān*), Mughal bureaucrats and literati refused to recognize their claims to legitimate authority. While the Mughal state has been regarded as a "patchwork quilt" of variegated arrangements with local forces across its length and breadth, there was a hard limit to its accommodativeness. As evident in the mangled bodies displayed in the city's police station as by the towers of heads assembled in the countryside, the ruling power's primary impulse in responding to those who "raised their heads" (*sar-kashī*) in rebellion was to detach them from their bodies.[4]

Yet rule demanded more than the practice of unrelenting violence. It was necessary to be gentle with the weak while chastising the refractory, all the more so because imperial ideologues recognized that tyranny (*zulm*) and oppression (*ta'addī*)—the very opposite of justice—delegitimized the ruler. A measure of the ubiquity of this ideology is its frequent appearance in routine bureaucratic documents of the sort that Zatalli mocked in his satire on the disorderly actions of vegetables (cf. Chapter 3). Thus a sample appointment

[3] Darling, "Do Justice, Do Justice, for That Is Paradise."
[4] For a persuasive assertion of the former case, see Hasan, "Zamindars under the Mughals."

contract for the post of regional garrison commander (*faujdār*) counsels persuasion over violence unless necessitated by the "inherent deceitful villainy" of the incorrigibly rebellious. Even so, the "smaller cultivators" are not to be harmed.[5] But such a conception of administration had no place for popular representation, no formal ability to take into consideration the opinion of the governed. While petitions were accepted and indeed expected, the state did not accept the possibility that its subjects might express their legitimate grievances outside the established framework of appeal, most certainly not through violent protest. Justice was to be given by the law, though, as Wael Hallaq has noted, the "expediency of political rule" was always a priority in societies where the *sharīʿa* was considered the ruling law.[6] This was particularly the case in the Mughal realm, where the majority of the population would not identify themselves as Muslim: a fact that had perhaps required *daulat* to be cast in mystical terms in the first place. That the administrative work of justice was therefore something more than the simple enforcement of law is evident in the writings of an eighteenth-century chronicler, whose description of "legal injunctions and the investigation of disputes" (*ahkām-i sharʿī wa tanqīh-i qazāyā*) was sensitively rendered by a contemporary translator as "distributive justice."[7] In this context, the regularization of justice under Aurangzeb would begin to produce new effects and new responses across the spectrum of imperial society.

The King and the 'Community of Muslims'

Despite his bureaucratization of imperial justice, Aurangzeb cultivated an image of a "renunciate king" in the mold of a "living saint" (*zinda pīr*) and continued to personally administer justice to supplicants.[8] It is in this light that we discern the significance of the many portraits of Aurangzeb, which show him stooped in old age over the Qurʾan—the king deriving his sanctity not from the light of the other world but rather the words of God as they were available in this one. The object of these carefully staged representations was not only his courtly nobility, but also the people at large. The people appear in the imperial vision as the 'Community of Muslims,' an idealization

[5] Richards, *Document Forms*, 35–36.
[6] Hallaq, *Sharīʿa*, 198–99.
[7] Khan and Mustepha, *Seïr Mutaqherin*, 173; Khan, *Siyar al-Mutaʾakhkhirīn*, 49.
[8] Faruqui, "Awrangzīb"; Sangar, "Procedure of Work."

that is captured in literary and administrative writing in variations of the common formula "The Firm Faith and the Exalted Community" (*dīn-i hanīf wa millat-i munīf*). Though their terms were different from those of preceding emperors, such enunciations of sovereignty maintained a personal link between the body of the king and the body populace that was expressed in the language of shared commitments to Islam. These commitments were not wholly abandoned by Aurangzeb's successors, and would survive in the discourse of sovereignty long after his death.

Such commitments to the 'Community of Muslims' had never been absent from Mughal conceptions of sovereignty even before Aurangzeb's reign. It was the king's task, in theory, to ensure the well-being of all Muslims, particularly privileged lineages such as Sayyids and Shaikhs. In its material form, this involved the giving of "aid of sustenance" (*madad-i maʿāsh*) tax-free land grants to pious worthies, who were required to pray for the king and so enlisted in what the emperor Jahangir had memorably conceived as an "army of prayer."[9] Theory dictated that, as the leader of Muslims, the king was supposed to punish the enemies of Islam and encourage conversion to the faith. Yet these aspects of rulership acquired a much greater significance in the reign of Aurangzeb than any preceding, and seems to have exercised a hold on his subjects, the chorus of critical satires notwithstanding.

Why, despite his fruitless long wars, are the echoes of Aurangzeb's popularity audible in the uniformly laudatory biographies of the king produced by eighteenth-century writers? Consider the sentiments of the chronicler Khwush Hal, who, even forty years after the event, vividly recalled the unforgettable sounds of wailing that wafted across the city when news of Aurangzeb's death reached Delhi. Khwush Hal typically describes the calamity as being accompanied by the portentous appearance of a comet. The reason for the people's terror at the king's death, he adds, was twofold: first, Aurangzeb had maintained an incredible discipline, so that even at the distance of a thousand *kuroh*-s, neither high nor low dared to misbehave. Second, an entire world of people had been born, matured, and grown old under this half-century reign, and had known no other. After extolling the deceased king's incredible commitment to justice (which required him to listen patiently to the broken and imperfect speech of the people), the chronicler

[9] Habib, *The Agrarian System of Mughal India, 1556–1707*, 355; Eaton, *Sufis of Bijapur, 1300–1700: Social Roles of Sufis in Medieval India*, 219; the army of prayer was not restricted to Muslims, however. For speciments of land-grants to Hindus, see Goswamy and Grewal, *The Mughals and the Jogis of Jakhbar; Some Madad-i-Ma`ash and Other Documents*.

added that the “firm faith and the exalted community” (of which he does not appear to have been a member) had spread far and wide across the vast realms of Hindustan in these years. As the administration spent huge sums on erecting mosques and disbursing stipends to prayer leaders, sermonizers, theologians, teachers, and students, 100,000 Hindus converted to Islam and became firmly established in Delhi and other cities.[10] Though Khwush Hal surely exaggerated, his words represent his sense—and approval—of the expanding infrastructure of piety and legality in the empire.

Aurangzeb's saintly air exercised a powerful effect on the popular imagination. When, in 1690, the king mockingly gave a hundred rupees and some gold-dust to be handed over to a man who claimed he had come “from the far-off land of Bengal to become your majesty's disciple,” the person cast the money away and hurled himself into the nearby river at the prospect of being seen as insincere.[11] After Aurangzeb's death, this aura continued to radiate from his resting place: on September 22, 1711, a Hindu woman deposited a small child at Aurangzeb's grave, claiming that she had been childless for a long time and vowed her firstborn to service the pious king's grave if she were granted a son.[12] Was this an act of guile, produced by the desperation of a woman with an unwanted child, or one of sincere faith in the powers of the departed emperor? Whatever the case, this halo of divinity also clung to his descendants. Thus the gesture of the “Musalman person” who approached the imperial procession at the congregational mosque and brought a child before Farrukh Siyar, claiming a vow to present his son before the king if one were born to him. Farrukh Siyar understood well his part in this pantomime of sacrality: he granted a gold coin and a rupee to the man while saying, “I have granted you a son.”[13]

Besides these personal forms of relation, a number of more-or-less mundane tasks associated with the leadership of the 'Community of Muslims' also bound the king to his subjects at large: pilgrimages, festivals, and charity. Again, these forms of relation endured after Aurangzeb's death. When, for instance, the deputy judge Shariʿat Khan represented that the heavy clouds had parted and that he had espied the new moon on September 20, 1713, Farrukh Siyar ordered it be proclaimed in Delhi that Ramazan would begin on Friday; the censor (*muhtasib*) was tasked to ensure that bakers and others did not

[10] Khwush Hal, “Nādir al-Zamānī [B],” fols. 25b–26a; 5b–6a.
[11] Khan, *Maʾasir-i ʿAlamgiri [EN]*, 201.
[12] “Akhbārāt, Bahādur Shāh, RY 5-6/II,” 344.
[13] “Akhbārāt, Farrukh Siyar, RY 6-7/II,” 29.

open their shops before the evening as was customary.[14] Farrukh Siyar commissioned special prayers against natural disasters, such as drought and earthquake, which were led by judges, jurisprudents, censors, and almoners at the congregational mosque or the new festival grounds west of the city. Likewise he policed the boundaries of the community, personally interrogating and confirming the sentence of death against heretics such as a certain Nasir Allah, who was arrested and executed in 1718 near Delhi for making wild claims to prophethood.[15]

Conversion to Islam was a central means by which the king's status as the head of the 'Community of Muslims' was affirmed.[16] The news reports of Aurangzeb's reign are studded with accounts of Hindus who converted to Islam and were rewarded for doing so.[17] The increasing ranks of the 'Community of Muslims' opened a promising avenue of negotiation between the ruler and his subjects, with potential gains for both.[18] Consider the business of a single day at Aurangzeb's court on February 4, 1670. First the king heard a petition from the out-of-favor Gond landholder of the locality of Chaukh Garh, who, begging for "mistakes" to be forgiven, asked the holding be transferred to his brother Murar Das. Aurangzeb, assenting, offered rank, cavalry assignment, and landholding to Murar Das—but if only he converted to Islam. Murar Das must have wavered at the rider, but others did not, for, ten months later, it was reported that two other Gond notables had become Muslims "for the reason of the land-holding of Chauk Garh." Aurangzeb ordered they be given rank at court and the papers to the coveted landholding, but only after they had been circumcised.[19]

Incorporation into the 'Community of Muslims,' here, was not inflicted from above; it was an opportunity with benefits for both the king and the convert. From the imperial perspective, it integrated local elites into the

[14] "Akhbārāt, Farrukh Siyar, RY 1-2," 91.

[15] Lakhnavi, *Shāhnāma*, 140; Mirza Muhammad, "'Ibratnāma," fol. 173b; "Akhbārāt, Farrukh Siyar, RY 6-7," 145.

[16] I am thus not here concerned with the well-studied historical dynamics of conversion to Islam in South Asia, on which see Hardy, "Modern European and Muslim Explanations of Conversion to Islam in South Asia"; Eaton, "Approaches to the Study of Conversion to Islam in India"; Eaton, "Shrines, Cultivators, and Muslim 'Conversion' in Punjab and Bengal, 1300–1700."

[17] A typical instance is that of the seven nameless men who embraced Islam in March 1667 and were granted robes of honor at court. Anonymous, "Akhbārāt of the Reign of Aurangzeb and Bahadur Shah (Transcripts)," fol. 127b.

[18] A phenomenon explored in Eaton, *The Rise of Islam and the Bengal Frontier, 1204–1760*, 116; such imperatives, though intensified under Aurangzeb, were not new to the subcontinent, nor indeed without their consequences for those who converted to Islam. Talbot, "Becoming Turk the Rajput Way," 13–14 passim.

[19] "Akhbārāt of the Reign of Aurangzeb and Bahadur Shah (Transcripts)," fols. 158b, 160a.

king's vision of a network of shared identity that would join disparate groups throughout the empire in obedience to him. Likewise, given their competitive eagerness to convert to Islam, the Gonds regarded the advantages of local power and imperial incorporation as greater than any injury occasioned by conversion, psychic or penile. And Aurangzeb's desire to expand the 'Community of Muslims' was always tempered by practical exigencies. Right after he had finished dealing with the affair of Murar Das, he heard another petition from one Chanda, who offered to become a Muslim if the landholdership of his agnatic "brother" Budh Prakash was given to him instead. Chanda's petition sparked a discussion at court, where both Aurangzeb and his minister Raʿd Andaz Khan felt that Budh Prakash was a loyal officer, and replacement by an agnatic "brother" would set a bad precedent in the locality. The emperor reserved his judgment.[20]

The attractions of such integration would continue to lead communities and individuals to convert to Islam long after Aurangzeb's passing.[21] Quite aside from the advantages of joining the 'Community of Muslims' for local elites, the imperial imperative of conversion to Islam continued to serve as an opportunity for humble individuals. Take the case of the Hindu man who approached Jahandar Shah's procession in 1712/13 and said that he would become a Muslim if he would be given "one woman, who is widowed and without heirs." The king, greatly amused, declared that if the man became a Muslim, one was to be turned over to him (what the woman's opinion was in all of this is not recorded).[22] In much the same way, in February 1718, when Farrukh Siyar's palanquin reached the entryway to the Special Council, an officer produced one Khwush Hal, saying that he wanted to become a Muslim. Farrukh Siyar stopped the palanquin, asked him to recite the *kalima*, and granted him a Muslim name before continuing on.[23]

In approaching the imperial procession to convert to Islam, even the most inconsequential of individuals established a personal connection to the highest power in the land. But if Aurangzeb's enunciation of sovereignty had created new possibilities of invoking imperial power at the level of the

[20] "Akhbārāt of the Reign of Aurangzeb and Bahadur Shah (Transcripts)," fol. 159a.

[21] See, for instance, the case of Sabit Khan, the eighteenth-century governor of Kol, near Delhi. Sabit Khan enjoined conversion within the resident *badgūjar* community, which subsequently took on the appellation of "Sabit Khani" and remained locally important until the early nineteenth century. Atkinson, *Descriptive and Historical Account of the Aligarh District*, 489; Nevill, *Meerut: A Gazetteer, Being Volume IV of the District Gazetteers of the United Provinces of Agra and Oudh*, 92; Siddiqi, *Aligarh District*, 99–107.

[22] Anonymous, "Akhbārāt, Jahāndār Shāh," 128.

[23] Anonymous, "Akhbārāt, Farrukh Siyar, RY 7," 68.

individual, it also generated new channels of resistance, which became increasingly evident in his reign. Despite—or perhaps because—of his aura, the king was expected to respond to gestures of opposition with magnanimity. Because of their proximity to his person, our court chronicles are generally dismissive of any signs of resistance, usually ascribing them to mental derangement. But there is much evidence to show that individuals expressed their discontent with the king through harsh speech and more. Their actions illustrate a popular conception of the relationship between ruler and subject as personal and unmediated, which was a refraction of the emphasis in imperial discourse on the accessibility of the king's justice.

It is therefore precisely because of his disciplinary impositions that even the great Aurangzeb was sometimes not treated with the awe he strove to project. The traveler Manuzzi reports of a mendicant (*faqīr*), who, in 1669, was arrested for defacing the steps of the congregational mosque with a hammer. When confronted with the king and the judge, he took the opportunity to criticize Aurangzeb's mistreatment of his family and railed against his misgovernance.[24] In March 1673, as the king returned from Eid-prayers at the congregational mosque, "a mad man coming up the equipage flung a stick," which struck the imperial knee. The person was quickly arrested by imperial mace-bearers, but released on the king's order.[25] An "ill-fated disciple" of Tegh Bahadur, the Sikh leader who had been executed in 1675, received less mercy. As the emperor returned from the mosque in October 1676, the disciple flung two bricks, "one of which reached the [sedan] chair." For this crime, he was handed over to the police chief.[26] A "complainant," who hurled a stick at Aurangzeb as he mounted his horse a few months later, suffered the same fate. In October, the king was yet again accosted by a "wretch . . . with an uplifted sword" as he mounted his horse outside the mosque; the mace-bearers wished to execute him then and there, but the emperor instead gave him a daily allowance of half a rupee and dispatched him to the prison in Ranthambor.[27]

Again, such everyday resistance was not confined to Aurangzeb; early in the reign of Muhammad Shah, a flag (*bairāq*) was discovered fastened to the railing of the police station on Moonlight Avenue, saying (in Persian) "When the king comes out of the fort, let him beware." After the ruler was informed,

[24] Manucci, *Storia Do Mogor*, III:268.
[25] Mustaʿidd Khan, *Maʾasir-i ʿAlamgiri [EN]*, 78.
[26] Mustaʿidd Khan, *Maʾasir-i ʿAlamgiri [EN]*, 94.
[27] Mustaʿidd Khan, *Maʾasir-i ʿAlamgiri [EN]*, 94–95.

a public proclamation was made to uncover the perpetrator. A Muslim mendicant named Niranjan, of the "Free" (*āzād*) sect, bare of head and wearing a loin-cloth (*lung*), took responsibility. Such behavior was not shocking, because mendicants described as "Free" were famed for their social deviance and challenging attitude toward elites.[28] According to one report, Niranjan was taken before the emperor and then given over to a nobleman's custody, who tortured him severely before releasing him. Another chronicle offers an account more in accordance with kingly comportment: Muhammad Shah gave the man four gold coins and set him free.[29]

Although the motivations of such individuals remain obscure, it is possible to glimpse political intention in even the smallest of such acts of resistance. Consider the case of the humble water carrier, who, also in November 1676, approached Aurangzeb and cried out the usual greeting of "*salām ʿalaikum*."[30] Why was this simple act treated as an offense by the court? It was just around this time that the king had issued an order "that when Musalmans met with each other, they were to greet each other by the *salām* prescribed by the law and not to raise their hands to their heads like infidels."[31] Yet such rules only applied to ordinary Muslims, for, even after this proclamation, the privilege to greet the king with only a simple "*salām ʿalik*" was noted as a special mark of distinction for a particularly learned and pious theologian.[32] In this light the significance of the water carrier's greeting becomes manifest. Unmarked by deference, it challengingly asserted the equality of the 'Community of Muslims,' which Aurangzeb claimed in theory to espouse. On the other hand, it intended an intolerable subversion of hierarchy: it is for this reason that a contemporary manual of comportment advises the aspiring gentleman to take debt only from properly submissive Hindu moneylenders, and not the Muslim ones "who make their claims . . . saying *salām ʿalayka* like equals and lord over the debtor."[33] In using the greeting of *salam*, the water carrier thus asserted a radical equality with the king, exposing the hypocrisy of his dictum: were all Muslims to greet each other as equal members of a single community, or were some Muslims in fact more Muslim than others?

[28] See, for instance, the anecdote of the mendicant who challengingly begged from an aristocrat's son by calling out, "*Ai* crow of the sky, do you see the earth at all or not?" Anonymous, "Hikāyat-i Latīf," fol. 3a–b.

[29] Khan, *Tazkirat us-Salatin*, 232; Lakhnavi, *Shāhnāma*, 115.

[30] Mustaʿidd Khan, *Maʾasir-i ʿAlamgiri [EN]*, 95.

[31] Syed, *Aurangzeb in Muntakhab-Al Lubab*, 271; Mustaʿidd Khan however dates this proclamation to 1670, and limits its scope to courtiers. Khan, *Maʾasir-i ʿAlamgir [EN]*, 62.

[32] Khan, *Maʾasir-i ʿAlamgiri [EN]*, 62.

[33] Ahmad, "British Museum Mīrzānāma," 102.

His cleverness unappreciated, the water carrier was dispatched to the police station like the rest.

Disciplining Social Violence: Honor, Home, Women

One day in 1694, two friends, an imperial officer and the servant of a prince, were walking together to a place. In the course of their walk, the chronicler informs us, "they had words, their friendship was broken up, and a quarrel followed."[34] Aman Allah, the prince's servant, unsheathed his dagger and stabbed his companion, who was a Sayyid of Barha. Shocking though this act may seem to us, the author was unmoved. In his experience, such sanguinary violence was neither rare nor random. While imperial ideologues spoke loftily of the repose and contentment of the king's subjects, the chronicles and news reports of the late seventeenth century reveal a landscape brimming with fractious peoples who joyfully drew blood at what might today seem slight quarrels. So routine and scripted was such violence that commentators described its outbreak in purely formulaic terms: a dispute on the street would begin with a verbal exchange, escalate to kicks and blows, until finally swords were unsheathed.[35] Whether the result of a spontaneous conflict or that of long-simmering animosities, such conflict was shaped by longstanding structures of family, kin, clan, and lineage, which together constituted society across the realm. Given that such routine and everyday forms of conflict over the ways of living in the city and sharing its space were integral and even definitive of urban sociality, I here collectively denote them under the rubric of social violence. It is this violent social landscape on which Aurangzeb sought to exert an unprecedented juridical discipline. To trace the unanticipated and unintended consequences of such an imposition—the growth of an increasingly politically articulate populace—is the object of the pages that follow.

The grounds of the social violence that confronted Aurangzeb and his successors was that of honor. Honor assumed many forms: the many words used to refer to it, though frequently used interchangeably, appear to demarcate its distinct aspects. The touchy mirza and the scarred general alike

[34] Khan, *Ma'asir-i 'Alamgiri [EN]*, 221.

[35] I take the notion of the scripted violence from Baker, "A Script for a French Revolution: The Political Consciousness of the Abbé Mably"; see also Baker and Edelstein, *Scripting Revolution*.

shared a sense of *ābrū*, which seems to express a bodily dimension; literally meaning the "water of face," one was dishonored when it was "poured out" (*ābrū rekhtan*).[36] *ʿIzzat* ("elevation") might represent one's "standing" that enabled recognition and participation in one's community; if *ghairat* referred to a sense of personal honor, *hurmat* and *ʿismat* indicated the protected or segregated status of *nāmūs*, a word which connoted the core bearers of a family's honor: its women.

Because honor defined the individual's standing in a community, it is no surprise that social violence was endemic among the most honorable, at the top of the Mughal order. The staid paintings of court ceremonial conceal the fact that, despite efforts at regulation, even so controlled a site as Aurangzeb's court was witness to conflicts of honor. No doubt a point of honor was involved when on September 18, 1669, Yaka Taz Khan and Girdharidas Sisodia fell into a quarrel during their ceremonial guard in front of the Lahori Gate; "the Hindu went to hell," reported the chronicler acerbically, while the Khan and some of his Mughal retainers were wounded.[37] Two weeks later, a young nobleman named Dildar suddenly stabbed a nobleman in the back with his sword in the midst of the imperial court, for reason of "previous enmity." Under a hail of blows, the assailant ran up toward the throne, but was killed by a bodyguard.[38] In 1673, when the nobleman Farjam Barlas broke off his daughter's engagement with his sister's son ("on account of his sister being the greatest shrew of the age"), the enraged matron provoked her child to either kill her brother Farjam in the imperial court, or to "don her veil" (which she removed and flung at his face) and "cower indoors." Thus compelled, the son slew his uncle in the hall of audience.[39]

If the locus of social violence was honor, its spatial site was the home, the restricted domains in which the family's women resided. The houses of individuals, particularly honorable ones, were not seen as subject to any external authority. While the king assigned or reassigned imperial mansions among his nobility, the privately owned homes of ordinary folk were considered inviolate. This is why the petitioners who appeared before Jahandar Shah in

[36] Steingass, Johnson, and Richardson, *A Comprehensive Persian-English Dictionary*, 7; the association of water with body and honor is evident also in the idea of *ʿirz*, defined as "[t]he body; the soul; a pore of the body; perspiration; effluvia of the body (good or bad); reputation (personal, ancestral, or relational, in a good or bad sense); honour, fame, estimation." Steingass, Johnson, and Richardson, *A Comprehensive Persian-English Dictionary*, 843.
[37] Khan, *Maʾasir-i ʿAlamgiri [EN]*, 55.
[38] Khan, *Maʾasir-i ʿAlamgiri [EN]*, 56.
[39] Khan, *Maʾasir-i ʿAlamgiri [EN]*, 78.

June 1712 complaining of soldiers forcibly occupying their houses in Delhi received immediate redress, with the king ordering that no one was to be so troubled.[40] That these individuals did not fight to protect their houses evidences their lowly status, for honorable folk would not have tolerated such violation. Likewise in Muhammad Shah's reign, when the new vizier Muhammad Amin Khan sought to enlarge the mansion assigned to him, the neighboring poor refused to relinquish their houses for the small sums they were offered, and a poor woman threw herself off her roof in objection. Such sharp protest was probably only the tip of the iceberg of popular discontent, for another relates that when the vizier died shortly thereafter, his son returned some 700 seized homes to their owners.[41] Those who considered themselves honorable, however, regarded it as proper to fight to the death against any violation of the home. Thus, for instance, no one was surprised, in April 1722, when the high-ranking officer Quraish Khan refused summons to the imperial court over a dispute about house-rent with his landlord, the senior palace eunuch Khwaja Almas, out of "an extreme regard for his honor" (*ghāyat-i ghairat-i khwud*); the khan was killed in the ensuing battle with the imperial artillery, routinely dispatched by the king to deal with such prickly noblemen.[42]

Warring Houses

The most common form of urban disorder revolved around conflicts of honor between homes and families, recognized by observers as a "war of houses" (*khāna-jangī*).[43] Perhaps because they signaled autonomous notions of elite honor, such instances of internecine warfare prominently drew imperial censure, which Aurangzeb pointedly enacted through terms of legal procedure rather than personal justice. Thus, it is significant that Aurangzeb did not personally decide the fate of the young nobleman who was compelled to murder by his mother. Instead, the case was pointedly transferred to a judge, and the man was executed on the basis of a legal judgment in the imperial forecourt.[44] Yet Aurangzeb's efforts to regulate elite disputes by legal means

[40] Anonymous, "Akhbārāt, Jahāndār Shāh," 135.

[41] Khwush Hal, "Nādir al-Zamānī [B]," fol. 118a; Khan and Mustepha, *Sëir Mutaqherin*, 222.

[42] Kamwar Khan, *Tazkirat us-Salatin*, 338; Lakhnavi, *Shāhnāma*, 153–54.

[43] Thus in some ways akin to the practice of feud in Europe of the same time, but without necessarily being driven by retribution. See Carroll, *Blood and Violence in Early Modern France*.

[44] Musta'idd Khan, *Ma'asir-i 'Alamgiri*, 78.

aroused great resistance, for his elite servants did not regard themselves as subject to the law. Take the matter of the princely servant Aman Allah, who had killed his friend the Sayyid of Barha in a sudden quarrel in Aurangzeb's camp. On hearing of the murder, a company of the Sayyids of Barha went to Aman Allah's tents, where they were met by the latter's men. The conflict between the long-standing values of honor that animated the feud and Aurangzeb's insistence on legal supremacy is evident in the chronicler's description of the ensuing disputes: an emissary from the king ordered both parties to stand down, but the Sayyids refused to relent. True to type, Aurangzeb sent Qur'anic injunctions and ordered the Sayyids to approach the chief judge. According to the chronicler, "These fools cried out, 'We won't go to the judge. We shall settle the matter with our enemies [ourselves].'" Enraged at this disobedience, Aurangzeb ordered expulsions and reductions in rank, and in the end the Sayyids were reinstated only after much "petitioning and mediation."[45] And such violence was not necessarily driven by elites. Clashes between retainers might spontaneously break out over perceived slights or insults to the honor of the house or its women, as notably transpired between the Mughal Turani troops of I'timad al-Daula and the contingent guarding the passing harem of Samsam al-Daula just outside Delhi in April 1716.[46]

Conflict between Communities

Another major axis of social violence was that of conflict between communities named by faith. Such violence derived its fundamental structure from the widely shared vision, which we have previously encountered, of India as a Hindu land that had come under Muslim sovereignty, and was now ruled with the peaceable consent of both communities. That the domination of Islam over Hinduism was guaranteed in theory by the Mughal emperor, whose title always included the sobriquet of "holy warrior" (*bādshāh-i ghāzī*), does not appear to have been a source of discomfort to his Hindu subjects (no matter how much it would disturb future generations). The fact that Islam was formally privileged by association with the state produced an axis of social conflict, through which communities were demarcated, differences asserted,

[45] Khan, *Ma'asir-i 'Alamgiri [EN]*, 221–22.
[46] Muhammad, "'Ibratnāma," fols. 148b–150a.

domination, subordination and defiance enacted. Yet it is difficult to dub such violence under the rubric of "religious conflict," for it resists easy classification and comparison with apparently similar violence elsewhere: the particularity of the Mughal empire, compared to the Ottoman empire or European states, was that Muslims, though in theory dominant, never constituted more than a small minority across the land, a fact of which rulers were hardly unaware. Intercommunal violence was not "interdependent" with tolerance; none of the ritualized and repetitive forms of integrative violence described by David Nirenberg for medieval Spain, for instance, find any obvious parallels in the Mughal case.[47] Mughal chroniclers seem to have taken for granted that meaningless disputes would arise between "Hindus and Muslims" by the simple fact of everyday proximity. When such violence did break out, it operated through a shared symbolic vocabulary, which betokened an intimate familiarity with the spaces, beliefs, and practices of other groups, and was predicated on expectations of continued coexistence.[48]

A classic instance of such conflict was occasioned by the spring festival of Holi. It is true that by the late seventeenth century (if not indeed from time immemorial), Holi was celebrated not only by Hindus but also by Muslim elites and commoners alike.[49] Traveling through Agra in 1718, the nobleman Iʿtimad ʿAli Khan noted without comment on joining in the Holi celebrations at the home of a certain Mirza Rukn, and in another feast at the deputy-governor's mansion.[50] The littérateur Muhammad Hatim, writing in the same city three decades before, praised the Holi celebrations at the house of his friend Lala Tej Rai by claiming that the spectacle of sprinkling colors "manifested the meaning of the Law of God (*sibghat Allāh*, lit. 'the color of God') in the gaze of those who perceive reality."[51] In this way he suggested that this non-Islamic festival in fact revealed the essence of the *sharīʿa*, which clearly for this author connoted something more than the strictures of the law.[52]

But aside from these genteel celebrations behind the walls of elite houses, Holi had a rougher aspect in popular culture. Over the course of its three

[47] Nirenberg, *Communities of Violence*.

[48] My thought here owes much to Davis, "The Rites of Violence"; Davis, "The Sacred and the Body Social in Sixteenth-Century Lyon."

[49] Alam, *The Languages of Political Islam: India, 1200–1800*, 186–88.

[50] Khan, "Majmaʿ al-Fawāʾid/Masdar-i Akhbār," fol. 132a.

[51] Hatim, "Abr-i Faiz," fol. 65b.

[52] The argument of the many meanings of the *sharīʿa* is centrally made in Alam, *The Languages of Political Islam: India, 1200–1800*.

days, revelers enacted a series of ritualized confrontations and inversions of hierarchy. A late-eighteenth-century commentator was unable to discern what it celebrated, but declared it "the Carnaval of India, where the populace, extremely modest and reserved at all times, becomes licentious in those three days, and do and say what they please."[53] The standard excesses involved the spraying of water and colored powder and dust on all those who were encountered, without heed to their willingness. Then there was the bonfire. The early-twentieth-century colonial ethnographer William Crooke tells us the fuel for the Holi bonfire was in many places customarily taken by force. In Bengal, after community leaders had contributed their share of the kindling, "the rest collect whatever they can lay their hands on—fences, doorposts and even furniture . . . If these things be once added to the pile, the owner cannot reclaim them . . . any measures, however, are allowable to prevent their being carried off."[54] Gender roles were similarly reversed, as in the villages near Mathura, southeast of Delhi, where women gathered to collectively beat their menfolk with staves.[55] The festival climaxed in a rowdy procession. Thus, in central India, a colonial official observed "a fat merchant . . . fully intoxicated . . . bestriding a small donkey, his face smeared with ochre; and behind him came the travesty of a royal parasol, made of the bottom of an old basket fastened on to a cane. His cortege consisted of a drunken and vociferous crowd of half-naked men and women, who howled and rolled themselves on the ground . . . ."[56] Such parades obviously inverted the conventional expressions of sovereignty embodied in imperial processions.

Associated with excess, inversion, and transgression, it is perhaps unsurprising that Holi routinely occasioned intercommunal violence, which was taken as inevitable when it coincided with a festival of the Islamic calendar.[57] And given his juridical orientation, it is not surprising that Aurangzeb attempted to regulate Holi celebrations, sending orders to restrict

[53] Khan and Mustepha, *Sëir Mutaqherin*, 78, fn. 69.
[54] Crooke, "The Holi," 57.
[55] Crooke, "The Holi," 70.
[56] Crooke, "The Holi," 72.
[57] In describing a particularly memorable Holi riot in Ahmadabad in 1714 (on which more in the next chapter), a later chronicler thought the spark of the conflict involved a Muslim objecting to the burning of the Holi bonfire in a shared courtyard, and retaliating by slaughtering a cow there on the next day in honor of the prophet's death-anniversary. In retaliation, the Hindus dragged the butcher's innocent son to the yard and slaughtered him then and there. This was a revealing misremembering on the part of the chronicler, for the prophet's death-anniversary did not fall anywhere near the Holi festival in 1714. See Haider, "A Holi Riot of 1714: Versions from Ahmadabad and Delhi," 131; Khan and Mustepha, *Sëir Mutaqherin*, 78.

the celebration of Holi in 1665.[58] Such commandments were not novel. A fracas near Surat two decades earlier had caused his father Shah Jahan to ban the celebration of Holi "in the marketplace or the streets."[59] Aurangzeb's commands, however, were not issued in response to a particular incident, but as a general statement of administrative principles. The disciplinary impetus to enforce the order of law on a moment of social inversion is evident in the order's specific injunctions:

> Hindus have given practice to false customs in the towns and subdistricts of Ahmedabad: lighting lamps on the evening of Diwali; and in the days of Holi, they wag their tongues in uttering obscenities and burn the Holi [bonfire] in the markets and districts; they take whoever's wood they can, and throw it into the bonfire by force or theft. [Administrators] must establish that they [the Hindus] do not light lamps for Diwali; do not take anyone's wood by theft or force and throw it into the bonfire; and do not utter obscenities.[60]

Of course commandments against obscene words, brazen theft, and assertive rituals were utterly unenforceable: reports of pitched battles on Holi between participants and those sent to stop them routinely reached the imperial court.[61] In his stylized account of a day in Aurangzeb's court in 1699, the bureaucrat-poet ʿAbd al-Jalil Bilgrami described news being relayed of Holi celebrations in Bengal and elsewhere, in which the censors (*muhtasib*-s) who arrived to curtail the celebrations were beaten with sticks, had their palanquins destroyed, and were treated with "derision and contempt."[62] The king is not recorded as issuing any major sanctions in any of these cases.

Holi was only one instance that demonstrated the limits of the professedly pious Aurangzeb's efforts to improve the lamentable state of orthopraxy in his empire. Similar restrictions issued against Shiʿi practices of mourning were disregarded in precisely the same way. The king's abilities in this regard were constrained by the meager capacity of his state, the indifference or disinclination of his officials to enforce his dicta, his deep reliance upon Hindu and Shiʿa officials, and, not least of all, the general recalcitrance of his subjects.

58 Sarkar, *History of Aurangzib, Based on Original Sources*, III:318.
59 Hasan, *State and Locality*, 69–70.
60 Khan, *Mirat [Fa]*, I:276; Khan, *Mirat [En]*, 233.
61 As for instance in 1693: Anonymous, "Akhbārāt, Aurangzeb, RY 36-40," 9.
62 Bilgrami, *Inshāʾ-yi Jalīl*, 8.

Aurangzeb's record of grand symbolic acts, such as ordering the destruction of temples, is well known. More prosaically, however, he maintained a canny and politic restraint in the face of opposition to his legalistic urges. In 1669, for instance, Aurangzeb learned that a wandering Hindu mendicant named Uddhav Bairagi had been confined to the police station "for his seducing men to false beliefs." When his two Rajput disciples failed to secure the mendicant's release from the judge Abu al-Mukaram, they stabbed the judge to death on a road. Because the victim was the son of the chief imperial judge ʿAbd al-Wahhab, it was not surprising that both the Bairagi and his disciples were executed.[63] Aurangzeb's reaction to a very similar occurrence was more subdued twenty-five years later, when he learned from a secret reporter that a community of Bairagi religious mendicants had been worshiping idols in Delhi. In accordance with his mandate, the censor (*muhtasib*) of the city had arrested the Bairagis and seized their idols, which he transported to his own residence. At this, "the people of the Rajputs" gathered at the house of the superintendent and attacked him. Overwhelmed and helpless, the desperate official released his prisoners and moved the idols to the custody of the administrator ʿInayat Khan. The emperor's only recorded response to this outrage was to ask of ʿInayat Khan why he had not aided the superintendent at the time of battle.[64] This restraint was undoubtedly the product of the ferocious resistance his meddling in the practices of faith of local communities caused. For Aurangzeb would remember how his attempt to curtail the heterodox practices of the Matiyas and Mominas (who, it was noted "outwardly live as Hindus . . . but inwardly follow the Sayyid") only a few years previously had resulted in a revolt which wracked the province of Gujarat, and required much bloodshed to quell.[65]

Invoking Community for Justice

By the early eighteenth century, if not already earlier, urban groups had begun to invoke the supremacy of the king's justice in disputes that could not be resolved by the systems of administration that Aurangzeb had built up over his reign. In such situations, groups of the otherwise disadvantaged

[63] Khan, *Maʾasir-i ʿAlamgiri [EN]*, 53–54.
[64] Anonymous, "Transcripts from Jaipur State Archives, Years 36–40 of Aurangzeb's Reign," 125.
[65] Khan, *Mirat [En]*, 286–89.

were sometimes able to appropriate the discourse of imperial sovereignty toward their own ends by activating forms of community and demanding justice as an established right. This phenomenon was particularly apparent in Delhi, where ready access to supreme authority (in the person of the king) was available after 1712.[66] A striking instance of such manipulation is visible in a public dispute that flared up in the city in 1718 regarding the disappearance of a young jeweler's-boy (*jauharī-baccha*) during his errands. As a result, the jewelers of the city came together to search for him, and it was finally determined that he was last seen entering the mansion of a certain Khwaja Khalil.

The chronicler Mirza Muhammad knew Khwaja Khalil as the nephew of Khwaja Husain Khan, who had briefly held the stratospheric title of "Khan of the Ages" (*Khān-i Daurān*) in the brief reign of Jahandar Shah and was assigned as the tutor (*ataliq*) of Jahandar Shah's son.[67] In this capacity, Khwaja Husain had led the army to oppose the budding rebellion of the Sayyids of Barha and Farrukh Siyar, but shamefully fled on the eve of battle. His abrupt departure left the spoils of his vast army to the Sayyids, thus arguably handing them the empire.[68] Despite his ignominy, Khwaja Husain survived the death of Jahandar Shah, and his family seemed to have retained its importance. In the mansion resided the disgraced Khwaja Husain's brother, Khwaja Nizam al-Din and his two sons, Khwaja Khalil and Khwaja Sadiq. Khwaja Sadiq was married to his first cousin, Saliha Banu, the daughter of Khwaja Husain, while Khwaja Khalil had a son by the name of Muhammad Nasir.

Outside the gate of this elite mansion now assembled a crowd (*hujūm namūdand*) of jewelers who came together as a community of artisans, recognizably engaged in the longstanding practice of "coercive demonstration," *dharna*.[69] In taking advantage of the constraints of unplanned urban space to obstruct the everyday workings of public space, such an act of gathering was perhaps the most elementary microtechnique of everyday collective action in the city. Yet no response emerged from behind Khwaja Khalil's door.

[66] Yet such popular forms of action were hardly confined to Delhi. For the case of Agra in a slightly later period, see Khan, "Glimpses of the Administration"; Khan, "Local Administration in Agra."

[67] Khwaja Husain was the husband of the sister of Kokaltash Khan, and honored at Bahadur Shah's court. Khan, *Tazkirat us-Salatin*, 138.

[68] "His cowardice was such," remarks the biographer coldly, "that without drawing his sword from its scabbard, or a drop of blood having fallen from a soldier's nose, he, at night, left the camp with the said prince [son of Jahandar Shah] and took the road to Agra." See Aurangabadi, *Ma'āsir al-Umarā' [En]*, 1:197.

[69] Fink, "The Hindu Custom of 'Sitting Dharna' "; for a translation of the term, see Sarkar, *Fall of the Mughal Empire*, IV:323. The chronicler does not use the term "dharna."

After several days of fruitless assembly, the jewelers escalated their dispute and approached the king. Farrukh Siyar's involvement changed the affair's trajectory, for the king dispatched his personal force of the imperial artillery (*topkhāna-yi bādshāhī*) to summon Khwaja Khalil. In response, the nobleman fortified himself in his house and made apparent his intention to die fighting if necessary.[70]

Such behavior, as we recall from the death of Quraish Khan, was perfectly in accord with elite conceptions of the home as the primary site of honor. Unlike Quraish Khan, Khwaja Khalil did not fight to the death, but proved to be amenable to persuasion by "the many" (*jamʿī*) who materialized to intercede at this impasse. Who comprised this community our author does not say, but the place of the king and the ideal of imperial justice is encapsulated in the advice it "made understood" to the resistant nobleman: "it is not possible to wage war against emperors; it is better that you obey the order and enact whatever the king wishes." Khwaja Khalil consented to stand down, but on condition that "no harm come to his honor" (*ābrū*). And it was the community (*jamāʿat*), again, which led now him to the mansion of the chief of imperial artillery for investigation, where he was detained overnight with all courtesy. On the next morning, however, the officer's servants "picked up the Khwaja's dagger in front of him."[71] Apprehending the loss of his honor, Khwaja Khalil managed to secretly send a message to one of his people, who slipped him the vial of poison "with which he ended his toils."[72] About the fate of the jeweler's boy, however, there were only rumors. Mirza Muhammad had heard that the boy tended to tarry overlong at Saliha Banu's door during his frequent visits to the mansion's harem, where he bought and sold jewelry to the ladies of the house. Eventually Khwaja Khalil's son Muhammad Nasir, and his father Khwaja Nizam al-Din grew suspicious, and so one night they killed the boy and buried him within it. Others said that Khwaja Khalil's son Muhammad Nasir's jealousy was aroused because he was himself involved in improper relations with his aunt Saliha Banu.[73]

This unusual tale provides us with significant insights into the workings of justice in the city. As in other instances, the conflict operated on the question of the honor of the family, here encoded both literally and figuratively in the

[70] Muhammad, "ʿIbratnāma," fol. 184b.

[71] The text is not entirely clear here: ". . . *jamdhar rā az pesh rū bar-dashtānd*." Mirzā Muhammad, "ʿIbratnāma," fol. 185a.

[72] Muhammad, "ʿIbratnāma," fols. 184b–185a.

[73] Muhammad, "ʿIbratnāma," fol. 185b.

name of the lady Saliha Banu ("Chaste Beauty"). Just as Saliha Banu's chastity was worth killing for, so Khwaja Khalil's suicide was not motivated by a fear of the outcome of the process of justice, which, according to an eighteenth-century legal digest, commanded simply that "if someone kills another with malice aforethought; [and] if his killing is not for other reasons impermissible; he is also to be killed with iron weapons, or with an iron-tipped stave, or a large rock, or by fire."[74] More than this legally permissible right of retribution (*qisās*), which, under Hanafi jurisprudence was theoretically available to the Hindus, Khwaja Khalil feared the loss of honor (*ābrū*) that came from contact with the judicial process, which existed, after all, to discipline the common masses.[75]

Such a conflict does not fit the usual model of the War of Houses, because the bereaved jeweler whose son disappeared into Khwaja Khalil's house had no faction. As a member of a powerful and well-connected community of jewelers, he was formally subordinate to those who were honorable because they did not toil. While we cannot say whether the bereaved jeweler regarded himself as honorable, the fact that Mirza Muhammad did not deign to record even his name is a telling indication of how even rich artisans were regarded by the city's wellborn. Yet the jewelers were far from helpless. Their clout as a community can be discerned from a previous instance of protest, when, in the summer of 1713, they intercepted Farrukh Siyar's procession to complain that a certain Nar Singh Rao had taken jewels worth 80,000 rupees from one of their number and slain him. The jewelers had refused to conduct funerary rituals for the body, but the chief of police was prevaricating, and the murderer had fled. The king immediately ordered the chief of police to produce the murderer and his accomplice.[76] Then as now, the community of jewelers were able to transcend the limitations of the systems of urban administration by invoking the supreme power of imperial justice. Once the emperor was involved, events acquired a momentum outside the limited dynamic of the city's judicial organs. Like Nar Singh Rao, Khwaja Khalil may have been above the law of the police chief and the judge, but he was not above the emperor's justice.

What made the jewelers approach the king? The act of petitioning the king suggests that the disciplinary institutions of the city, embodied in its judge

[74] Khān, "Mirʾāt al-Masāʾil-i Muhammad Shāhī," 157.

[75] On Hanafi views regarding the availability of retaliation to non-Muslims, see Friedmann, *Tolerance and Coercion in Islam*, 42–44.

[76] Anonymous, "Akhbārāt, Farrukh Siyar, RY 1-2," 87.

and police chief, had failed to intervene against the scion of a noble family on the behalf of a group of mere artisans, even if as jewelers they claimed a certain status in the city. But the king's justice was not restricted by these social distinctions. In petitioning the king, the aggrieved jewelers took advantage of a contingent circumstance, which was his proximity. A similar event far from Delhi might well have resulted in the story ending with their defeat. But more than that, the jewelers were able to mobilize as a community, and, in compelling the king to side with his humbler subjects against a member of the nobility, demonstrated a facile appropriation of the discourse of imperial sovereignty.

The Price of Food

Popular invocations of imperial justice were not limited to such extraordinary criminal disputes. A question of key importance for both rulers and ruled was that of the price and availability of food. Again, control over the fluctuations of the prices of essential commodities had been a concern of kings already in the fourteenth century.[77] But by the late seventeenth century, a prominent domain of popular political action emerged around the idea, enshrined in the discourse of sovereignty, which made the king responsible for ensuring abundance and prosperity for all his subjects. In everyday terms, the ideal of ensuring abundance was manifested in the deep importance imperial administrators attached to the price of food in the empire's markets. The gazetteer of Gujarat regarded it as an ancient tradition that "when the pan of balance of dearness of corn and high price of cereals rose high, the people began to moan and lament."[78] Market prices were also directly associated with political stability, since at moments of crisis the prices of grain shot up.

It is surely to improve the regulation of urban markets (as well as the behavior of urbanites) that Aurangzeb instituted the appointment of censors (*muhtasib*-s) across the empire.[79] By the eighteenth century, this office was frequently combined with that of the price-reporter (*nirkh-nawīs*), who was tasked with regular dispatches of market prices to the imperial center. The sensitivity of this issue can be gauged from Aurangzeb's reaction upon

[77] Pathak, "Ziyauddin Barani's Theory of Price Control—A Critical Estimate"; Zafarul Islam, *Fatāwā Literature*, 60–63.

[78] Khan, *Mirat [En]*, 268.

[79] Siddiqi, "The Muhtasib under Aurangzeb."

learning in 1696 that the people were "crying out" (*nālish mīnumāyand*) against the "oppression" (*taʿaddī*) of an officer connected with provisioning in the province of Berar. The offender was immediately fired, and another appointed in his stead.[80]

Aurangzeb's alacrity might have been shaped by his memory of the famine in Gujarat eleven years previously. In 1685, though the king had waived taxes on grain when news of the famine reached him, Shaikh Muhyi al-Din, the son of the supreme judge Shaikh ʿAbd al-Wahhab, was nevertheless accosted by an angry crowd of men and women while on his way to the Friday prayer at the mosque. Because Muhyi al-Din held the offices of judge, revenue-assessor (*amīn*), poll tax (*jizya*) collector and price-reporter he was believed, rightly or wrongly, to be in the pocket of the city's grain merchants and therefore fixing an unfair price for grain. The crowd destroyed the Shaikh's palanquin by pelting it with stones and clods of earth, and it was only with the greatest difficulty that the worthy retreated to his home. Muhyi al-Din thought this affray was a conspiracy against him, provoked by his rival, the judge of the city of Ahmedabad.[81]

By the eighteenth century, however, imperial administrators had come to understand that the people would act of their own accord if prices were seen as too high. The political dynamic between the king and the people over questions of the price of food was markedly visible during the famine which gripped the region of Delhi in the second decade of the eighteenth century.[82] Consider the extensive measures the court took to alleviate famine, and its responsiveness to protest. In May 1712, Jahandar Shah learnt that supply to Delhi's King's Quarter grain market was declining because some people had set up barriers and were taking away grain for themselves. In response, the king ordered the police chief to remove these hindrances and ensure the uninterrupted supply of grain so that prices might fall.[83]

Administrators could exhibit a distinct and pointed disregard for the life and property of the rich when matters of distributive justice became pressing. In December 1712, when it was reported to Jahandar Shah that food prices had risen again, he ordered a nobleman to plunder the grain sellers so that prices fell.[84] Some years later, when food prices rose in Ahmadabad, the local

[80] Anonymous, "Akhbārāt, Aurangzeb, RY 36-40," 187.
[81] Khan, *Mirat [En]*, 275–76; Hasan, *State and Locality*, 55.
[82] Alam, *Crisis of Empire*, 31–35.
[83] Anonymous, "Akhbārāt, Jahāndār Shāh," 169.
[84] Anonymous, "Akhbārāt, Jahāndār Shāh," 318.

administrator "tore open [the] stomachs of two chief grain-dealers," whose bodies were then paraded on camels through the city. The warning had its intended effect: "prices of food-stuff fell."[85]

The conditions of the famine, which intensified after Jahandar Shah's overthrow in 1713, were described by a contemporary observer in terms that are all the more chilling for their insouciance:

> Prayer-leaders of mosques, teachers of schools, and professors of academies, stupefied by the violence of hunger, gave up their calls to prayer and academic disputations, and considered "Oh Belly! Oh Belly!" to be their call and recitation. And the Brahmins of the monasteries and the idols of the temples erased the ways of their faiths and their distinctions among sects out of hunger: not only longing for cow-meat: but in fact ingesting their intestines and bowels without washing or cleaning them.[86]

But the people were not so abject in their hunger, nor were administrators simply stirred by sympathy for their plight. In December 1713, soon after Farrukh Siyar went to offer *ʿId* prayers at the congregational mosque, urbanites complained directly to him that not even four units of wheat could be had for a rupee. A later chronicler remembered a preacher (*waʿiz*) at the mosque who threw a sheaf of "Questions from God's Creation" (*fardiyyāt-i suwwalāt-i khalq-i Allāh*) before Farrukh Siyar, saying, "the kings of the day are the Givers of Daily Bread (i.e., God, *qāsim al-arzāq*). If you want your portion of heaven, don't be parsimonious with their portion (*qismat*)." The king immediately signed in approval of all these petitions.[87]

Confronted by the assertive voices of putatively-quiescent "God's creation" at the site of the public enunciation of sovereignty, Farrukh Siyar acted rapidly. On December 27, he ordered that the headmen of the grain market be turned over to Bahadur Dil Khan, a fearsome figure otherwise known for having strangled the deposed king Jahandar Shah. This was a serious threat, but the king must have been exasperated: he had initially asked the grain dealers of the city to lower prices two days after he first marched into Delhi in the preceding February. Neither pleas nor imprecations had any impact on prices: less than a week after the headman's punishment, the

85 Khan, *Mirat [En]*, 388.
86 Aurangabadi, "Ahwāl al-Khawāqīn," fol. 63a.
87 Shahabadi, "Tārīkh-i Hindī," fols. 307b–308a.

king's personal artillerymen reported arresting some traders who had been detected selling grain three units for a rupee. Faced with the failure of his supply-side intervention, Farrukh Siyar ordered that the vast sum of 8,000 rupees be distributed daily among the poor.[88] Like his ancestor Aurangzeb some four decades before, the king's responsiveness underscores his sensitivity to demonstrations of public disaffection at the congregational mosque that emblemized the imperial commitment to the 'Community of Muslims.'

Because the price of food grains hurt the weakest the most, high prices represented an obvious if only periodic impetus for political action among the poor. Even if politically disenfranchised, the richer had greater means of exerting political pressure on the administration. As Farhat Hasan has shown, forms of merchant protest were well-organized already by the early seventeenth century.[89] A straightforward tactic, as Irfan Habib has noted, was emigration: faced with an oppressive administrator to whom no recourse was available, traders might flee, thus attracting the attention of the king who would coax them back.[90] That this was a well-worn dynamic is evident from proceedings at Farrukh Siyar's court in June 1717, when news arrived that the money-changers and traders of Multan were emigrating with their families because of the "tyranny and oppression" (*zulm wa taʿaddī*) of the local garrison commander; the king ordered his vizier to see to the matter.[91]

But members of trading communities could also act in far less passive ways. The chronicler Khwush Hal reports that in 1713, when the trader (*baqqāl*) Uddhav Das decided to avenge the execution of his son by Delhi's police chief Faulad Khan, he gathered 200,000 rupees by collecting "ten or twelve rupees" from every shop in the city's peri-urban grain markets (*shāh ganj o shāh dara*). With this bribe given to the nobleman Mir Jumla, the trader could ensure the blameless police chief's execution along with the others who were put to death at the beginning of Farrukh Siyar's reign.[92] Even if this figure is an exaggeration, it is suggestive of the financial ability and power that the city's merchants were seen to have.

[88] Farrukh Siyar warns grain traders: Anonymous, "Akhbārāt, Farrukh Siyar, RY 1-2," 55; artillerymen arrest grain traders: Anonymous, "Akhbārāt, Farrukh Siyar, RY 1-2/II," 265. It was another matter, of course, that those tasked with distributing this imperial largesse channeled it toward their own dependents and followers, so that only a fraction reached its intended recipients. Khan, *Tazkirat us-Salatin*, 193–94.

[89] Hasan, *State and Locality*, 60–65.

[90] Habib, "Peasant and Artisan Resistance in Mughal India."

[91] Anonymous, "Akhbārāt, Farrukh Siyar, RY 6-7," 19.

[92] Khwush Hal, "Nādir al-Zamānī [B]," fol. 65a.

Protests against the Poll Tax

A prime example of traders' ability to mobilize was the struggle around Aurangzeb's re-imposition of the poll tax (*jizya*) on the non-Muslims of the empire in 1679, a tax that had been abolished by the emperor Akbar in the previous century. In his study of the poll tax, Satish Chandra has suggested that its reimposition had both a "political" and a "religious" motive: it marked both an attempt to staunch a "deepening political crisis" caused by setbacks in the Deccan war, and its considerable proceeds were essentially used as a "huge bribe" to rally "orthodox clerical elements."[93] Rather than attempting to decode Aurangzeb's actions through this distinction, we might instead recognize that in Hanafi jurisprudential thought, the poll tax served as a legal obligation that gave formal status to a non-Muslim group. In this sense, the imposition of the tax could simply be regarded as part and parcel of Aurangzeb's other attempts to discipline and mold the many communities under his care by way of the law.[94]

The people who were expected to pay a new tax, however, did not react to this privilege with gratitude. From the perspective of an encomiast of Seth Rustamji Manikji, a Zoroastrian merchant and broker of Surat, the poll tax was only an instance of "tyranny" which fell disproportionately on the poor. The seth was accordingly praised for ameliorating their burden, and even liberating the men "of other communities", who were imprisoned for failure to pay, on hearing the pleas of their wives.[95] For the same reasons, a little wave of resistance appears to have washed over Delhi in 1679. All notice of popular protest is absent from the official chronicler's declaration of the tax.[96] But according to contemporary accounts, "all of the Hindus" of Delhi gathered beneath the window of presentation—which, as we have seen, was the key symbolic site where subjects might demand justice—"in their hundreds of thousands" to protest the tax: Aurangzeb clearly did not share their vision of what was just, for he did not heed their plaints.

This did not quell the protest. When, on a Friday, the king proceeded to the congregational mosque, "Hindus" gathered in throngs (*izdihām*) to complain. These crowds of "money-changers, clothiers, and all the artisans of the Urdu Bazar" continued to increase in number and obstructed the movement

[93] Chandra, "Jizyah and the State," 336, 337.
[94] Friedmann, *Tolerance and Coercion in Islam*, 78: Hindus as Zimmis; 51: Jizya as integrative.
[95] Modi, *Asiatic Papers*, IV:286–89; Subrahmanyam, "The Hidden Face of Surat," 237–38.
[96] Khan, *Ma'asir-i 'Alamgiri [EN]*, 108.

of the procession toward the mosque; after repeated warnings, the emperor ordered the procession forward, and several were trampled and killed by the elephants and horses. The public protests nevertheless continued for several days before the population at last acquiesced to the tax.[97] It was true, in one sense, that the people approached the king in the only places they might—at the window of presentation and on his way to the mosque for Friday prayers. But the people's cries for justice surely derived some their power by their location in sites that were infused with the symbols of the discourse of sovereignty. Such protests serve as precocious instances of a trend that would only intensify in coming decades: a popular engagement with the ideals of kingship, which provided the grounds to challenge the king for deviating from his assigned role as guarantor of justice.

How effectively the poll tax was collected is unclear, but local opposition to the tax continued intermittently throughout Aurangzeb's reign.[98] Jahandar Shah abolished the tax in 1712; it was reabolished by Farrukh Siyar, briefly revived in his reign, and abolished yet again by Muhammad Shah. This process of abolition is conventionally attributed to the efforts of Raja Jai Singh, who counted as among the greatest Hindu grandees of the empire. But, as Chandra notes, such efforts were fueled by the protest of Delhi's "bankers, merchants and artisans," who, in the words of a contemporary, "assembled together of their own accord, and with full agreement of all, lodged a complaint and closed their shops in the metropolis" in 1722.[99]

The argument against the poll tax that is attributed to Raja Jai Singh's petition to the king is essentially the familiar historic one, and draws deeply from the fount of Mughal sovereignty. In the chronicler Shiv Das's rendition, it is pointed out that India was a land of two communities: originally populated by Hindus and conquered by Muslim warriors (*mujāhidīn*). To Khwush Hal's mind, the Mughal dynasty had ruled the land for 400 years, fostering their subjects like their own sons. The land's Hindu inhabitants had thus been rendered "submissive to Islam" (*mutīʿ al-islām*) and loyally prayed for the king. Since Muhammad Shah was the emperor of India, both communities prayed for his well-being; and Jai Singh himself had marshalled a Hindu "army of prayer" to support Muhammad Shah, promising them not only the

[97] Khwafi Khan, *The Muntakhab Al-Lubáb [Fa]*, 1874, 3:255.

[98] The tax was at least sometimes strictly collected. Eaton, *The Rise of Islam and the Bengal Frontier, 1204–1760*, 178, fn. 58. Chandra however suggests that the indigent may have been frequently exempt from the tax, and that remittances were frequently granted by officials, despite Aurangzeb's opposition. See Chandra, "Jizyah and the State," 338–39; for instances of local opposition, see fn. 6.

[99] Chandra, "Jizyah in the Post-Aurangzeb Period."

revocation of the poll tax but the granting of tax-free charitable endowments in return. In response Muhammad Shah graciously remitted the poll tax, and the people were contented as a result. Though such chroniclers elided the traders' protest into an attractive narrative of the Hindu Raja successfully negotiating with his sovereign and the merciful release of a vexed populace from a heavy tax, the brief description of the mobilization is indicative, again, of the tremendous power that had come to rest in the hands of Delhi's merchants and financiers, and their skill in using the discourse of sovereignty to remind the king of his duties.[100]

This pleasing appeal for the equal distribution of the patrimonial care of the emperor for both his Muslim and Hindu subjects purposefully circumvented the belief, vehemently asserted by some, that the collection of the poll tax was an integral legal requirement of state policy because it marked the subordination of Hindus to the 'Community of Muslims.' The hagiographer Muhammad Ihsan, for instance, attributed Farrukh Siyar's loss of the throne to the heavenly disfavor occasioned by his shameful abandonment of the poll tax.[101] Such strident opinions appear to be associated with the firebrand piety of humble preachers, whose constituents included Turani Mughal subalterns and others who had no claim to honor but membership in the 'Community of Muslims.'

Conclusion

In emphasizing the supremacy of law, in creating new cadres of officials such as the censor (*muhtasib*), in empowering judges to an unprecedented degree, and in imposing the poll tax, the emperor Aurangzeb made unprecedented interventions in the fabric of imperial society. It is these very intrusions, however, that opened new avenues of negotiation between the imperial administration and those whom it governed. From the late seventeenth century onwards, humble urbanites began to invoke forms of community in order to

[100] Lakhnavi, *Shāhnāma*, 112–15; Khwush Hal, "Nādir al-Zamānī [B]," fol. 119a–b. The author reproduces the verses of his colleague in the revenue office bearing the poetic nom de plume of ʿAjib, which praise the Rajas Jai Singh and Girdhar Bahadur. The administrative order which arrived in Gujarat bearing news of the cancelation of the tax offered no such pleasing homilies of inter-religious harmony. It merely noted that the tax was canceled on behalf of the Raja Ajit Singh (not Jai Singh), and ordered the closing of the tax-office in Ahmadabad. Khan, *Mirat [En]*, 388.

[101] Muhmmad Ihsan, *Rauzat-i Qaiyūmiyya*, 2002, IV:131; Muhmmad Ihsan, "Rauzat-i Qaiyūmiyya," fols. 334b–335a.

engage the ruler in the terms of his formulation of sovereignty in the pursuit of justice. There was a fundamental agonism in such forms of protest, which tended to exceed and overflow the norms that the imperial court sought to impose on them. Nor did the court always respond with forbearance. Thus, when on July 14, 1713, Sibghat Allah Khan, the superintendent of the "Second Court of Justice" captured four men wearing clothes adorned with words of protest (*kāghazī libās*), the king did not react with kindness: the men were jailed, and the superintendent was given robes of honor for his action.[102] While the motivations of this protest remain unknown, it appears in the historical record as a symptom of a popular engagement with kingship that had begun to bubble up in response to Aurangzeb's impositions and only seemed to accelerate in the tumultuous years after his death in 1707. In the three decades that followed, the people of Delhi would increasingly demonstrate the capacity both to rise in defense of the king at moments of crisis (as against Nadir Shah in 1739) and to challengingly invoke his authority in everyday urban struggles. Both of these modes of political action were galvanized by events in the second decade of the eighteenth century, and will be considered in turn. To trace, first, the emergence of the popular capacity for extraordinary action in defense of the king, we must turn to the greatest political crisis yet witnessed in the Mughal empire: the unprecedented regicide of the Mughal emperor Farrukh Siyar at the hands of his nobility in 1719.

[102] Anonymous, "Akhbārāt, Farrukh Siyar, RY 1-2," 337. I thank Prashant Keshavmurthy for explaining the significance of term denoting robes of protest to me.

5

Daulat's Flight

Regicide and the Popular Intervention, 1719

On February 28, 1719, a group of soldiers and minor noblemen broke open the doors of the Harem in the Red Fort in Delhi. On the command of a cabal led by the vizier ʿAbd Allah Khan and his brother Husain ʿAli Khan of the clan of the Sayyids of Barha, the soldiers brushed aside the resistance of the Harem guards and roughly dragged the emperor Farrukh Siyar to a prison cell. As the young prince Rafiʿ al-Darajat was taken from captivity and placed on the throne, a darker custom awaited the deposed king: his eyes were blinded, and, some weeks later his discolored and mutilated corpse was flung out in the fort for all to behold.

The story of Farrukh Siyar's execution is familiar to historians, as part of the general upheaval of the decades after the death of Aurangzeb, which saw a parade of emperors rise and fall from the throne in rapid succession.[1] Farrukh Siyar had himself come to power after he overthrew and executed the reigning emperor Jahandar Shah in 1713. Yet while Jahandar Shah's removal could be imagined as a normal succession—and justified by criticizing his foibles—Farrukh Siyar was the first to be unambiguously overthrown by his own ministers.

Farrukh Siyar's dethronement also marked another, less well-known moment of novelty in the empire: for the first time in its history, the common folk of the city rose up in defense of their ruler. They attacked the Sayyid-led army that had come from the Deccan to overthrow the king, and they vigorously protested against his killers in the days and weeks to come. Their expressions of dissent marked an intervention in a realm of imperial politics seen as restricted to elites alone. The popular agitation thus marked an important moment of inflection in the emergence of ordinary people as political subjects in late-Mughal Delhi.

[1] The classic accounts are Irvine and Sarkar, *Later Mughals*; Chandra, *Parties and Politics*.

The King and The People. Abhishek Kaicker, Oxford University Press (2020). © Oxford University Press.
DOI: 10.1093/oso/9780190070670.001.0001

For present-day historians, the death of Farrukh Siyar, and Jahandar Shah before him, have only demonstrated their incapacity to reign. Already in Aurangzeb's reign, for Athar Ali, the "factionalism" of the nobility represented their "grievous lack of confidence in the Emperor and the Imperial policy."[2] Similarly, Satish Chandra described the contest between Farrukh Siyar and his ministers as one over the meaning of the viziership. In this interpretation, the Sayyids were the agents of a progressive historical force "conducive to the growth of a national state and monarchy," while the Emperor and his advisors obstinately "sought to preserve the privileges of a comparatively narrow group, and took their stand upon the apparently orthodox and uncompromising principles of Aurangzeb."[3] Such interpretation may be contrasted with the horrified observation of a diarist who understood the significance of the coup against Farrukh Siyar in rather different terms: "It is a strange affair of the rule of Hindustan," wrote he, "that the choosing of emperors has fallen in the hands his servants! They are making emperor whoever they know and want."[4]

As such sentiments remind us, Farrukh Siyar's execution was a shocking event that irreparably damaged the Mughal ideal of sovereignty. The Sayyid ministers who killed Farrukh Siyar were unable to create a stable dispensation of power: both were themselves killed within a few years of Farrukh Siyar's execution, while Muhammad Shah's long tenure on the throne marked a greatly circumscribed reconsolidation of imperial authority.[5] More recently, Muzaffar Alam has suggested that the question was not one of the relative strength of the emperor or the vizier, but the systemic shift of power from the absolute ruler to the nobility as a class, which accompanied the nobility's hold over the empire's provinces.[6] As we shall see, this was a shift marked not by a change in the concept of viziership but kingship itself.

The uprising of Delhi's humble city-dwellers in defense of Farrukh Siyar, by contrast, has been broadly overlooked by modern historians. This is in part because the Mughal observers who have left us their memoirs and histories of the turmoil of the 1710s kept their eyes tightly focused upwards, at the king and his nobility. They did not condescend to describe the actions of the lowly—let alone their motivations and intentions—unless in service of a

[2] Ali, *The Mughal Nobility under Aurangzeb*, 111.

[3] Chandra, *Parties and Politics*, 142, 167.

[4] Khan, "Majmaʿ al-Fawāʾid/Masdar-i Akhbār," fol. 161a.

[5] In this context, S. A. A. Rizvi's observation that "saving the Mughal empire from the process of disintegration was no concern of the Sayyids" is apt. Rizvi, *Shah Wali-Allah and His Times*, 131.

[6] See Alam, *Crisis of Empire*, particularly chap. 2.

direct narrative purpose. Reproducing the prejudices of their sources, later historians too have not turned their gazes below.

Accordingly, it is the objective of this chapter to reconstruct, even if by necessity in outline, the uprising and protest of Delhi's urbanites in March 1719. But before we can begin to reconstruct what the people were acting *for*, we must gain a sense of what they were protesting *against*: namely, the execution of Farrukh Siyar by his servants. What did it mean for the imperial nobility to decapitate the body politic, and to put the broken body of the Shadow of God on public display? The coup of 1719 was a dramatic blow by an increasingly autonomous nobility against the claims of the imperial discourse of sovereignty. It demonstrated that the king was no longer the primary or only repository of *daulat*, and that the nobility could claim a *daulat* all of their own. Such assertions are not to be found in the courtly texts that enunciated the discourse of sovereignty. As the first part of this chapter demonstrates, they are expressed in the new histories and memoirs written by middling peri-courtly service elites and styled as "Books of Admonition" (*ʿibratnāma*). In narrating these events, observers struggled to explain how *daulat*, once imagined as heaven's gift to the ruler, could now be violently wrested away by his servants, their claims made manifest on the figure of the king's body.

But if the violence to Farrukh Siyar's corpse constituted a naked challenge to the established form of sovereignty, it also catalyzed a response from an unexpected quarter: the people, who were linked to the body of the king through the bonds of justice, and who had their own distinct views on the imperial order. As the second part of this chapter shows, by rising up in riot to preserve the king, and by conducting the rites of his funeral, Delhi's urbanites expressed their opposition to the Sayyid coup and what it signified. In this way, the people asserted their commitment to the older discourse of sovereignty, which guaranteed them justice, against the claims of the nobility. Delhi's denizens played an overlooked but important role in the rearticulation of sovereignty that undergirded Muhammad Shah's long and mostly uneventful tenure on the throne.

The Discourse of Sovereignty after Aurangzeb

While the discourse of sovereignty continued to be articulated along familiar lines in textual forms at the courts of the kings who followed Aurangzeb, there were important changes. Aurangzeb had ceased the practice of courtly chronicling in the tenth year of his reign. But his successor Bahadur Shah resumed the practice on his accession, asking none other than Niʿmat Khan-i ʿAli, whose satires of Aurangzeb were by now famous, to write the history of his reign. Niʿmat Khan's vision of the emperor and the nobility he ruled betrays significant changes from the era of Shah Jahan and Aurangzeb. That the empire was now much more a bureaucratic state than ever before is apparent in its author's slightly sardonic introductory description of God as the perfect administrator of the empire of creation.[7] The idea of *daulat* similarly appears in a somewhat different form. Though he describes his chronicle as a "book of the supreme *daulat*," the concept is encountered comparatively rarely. Used in conventional ways, the term appears to have been reduced in meaning to simple "fortune," both in the sense of "luck" and "wealth." It still seems to describe something of the king's substance. Thus we learn how on one occasion the great nobility have, in being given gifts of jewels and perfume, profited from the smell and color of *daulat*. But when the nobility are now described as the Grandees (lit. "eyes") of *daulat* (*aʿyān-i daulat*), it is not clear whether it is the king's or their own.[8]

It is a testament to the unsettled nature of the next emperor Jahandar Shah's brief reign that no official chronicle is known to survive. Perhaps because of the difficult circumstances of his overthrow and Farrukh Siyar's shaky claim to power, the latter ruler patronized the production of a courtly chronicle by Mir Muhammad Ihsan "Ijad," a poet of some repute. Farrukh Siyar's direct interest in this project, evident from his extensive marginal emendations in his own hand on a gorgeous manuscript, indicates the continuing importance of the imperial chronicle as a site of the articulation of claims to absolute authority.[9] The work describes kingship in a language that hearkens back to Aurangzeb's court; indeed the king is given the name "The second ʿAlamgir" (*ʿĀlamgīr-i Sānī*) as part of his titles at the outset of the text.[10] But though the king's commitments to Islam are explicitly stated, the model of kingship evokes the classical ecumenicism of a previous era. Thus we learn of constellations which link Farrukh Siyar to his ancient Mughal ancestors (such as Qachuli Bahadur, the progenitor of the Barlas tribe). And again we encounter the "divine light" (*nūr-i ilāhī*), which had passed through Amir

7 ʿAli, "Bahādur Shāh-Nāma," fols. 1b–3a.
8 ʿAli, "Bahādur Shāh-Nāma," fols. 200a, 71a, 244a.
9 Ijad, "Farrukh Siyar-nāma [A]."
10 Ijad, "Farrukh Siyar-Nāma [B]," fol. 7a.

Timur to the Emperor Akbar, was thus transmitted to the present king's (unnamed) mother, and now provided the "radiance of his rising *daulat*" (*sha'sha'a-yi tulū'-yi daulat*). Yet, though the king's *daulat* is described as God-given, and though he is called the "Khedive of Faith and *daulat*," the term does not seem to have the overbearing significance it carried in the courtly rhapsodies of Shah Jahan. Instead the author emphasizes the standard virtues, of bravery, justice, and disciplining authority.[11] This evocation of the classical past of Timur and Akbar perhaps represents a reassertion of the more distant mystical and millenarian attributes of kingship and a hearkening to the glamor of origins during what was, even by the flexible standards of the dynasty, an unorthodox accession to the throne. By the reign of Farrukh Siyar, it seems, the discourse of sovereignty had come full circle.

Books of Admonition

It was of course natural for the star of *daulat* to grow dimmer in the constellation of imperial discourse, given the highly personal literary styles of the individuals associated with the court, the changing fashions of prose and poetry over the period, and the simple requirements of producing rhymed prose. But what the official chronicles obscure is a broader shift in the way that *daulat* was imagined and conceived during the late seventeenth century. This change is visible, however, in the remarkable flurry of historical writing in the aftermath of the deposition of Farrukh Siyar in 1719. The significance of these works, which circulated equally if not more widely than the court chronicles of the period, lies in the fact that they were not commissioned by the king. Instead, they were produced by individuals who appear to have been only loosely if at all associated with the imperial court: minor noblemen, educated soldiers, scribes, and bureaucrats. Such middling officials had been increasingly writing and circulating diaries, first-person narratives and versified descriptions in the second half of the seventeenth century, perhaps because imperial patronage of chronicling appears to have ceased after the tenth year of Aurangzeb's reign.[12] But the troubled years of the early eighteenth century saw a veritable explosion in such literary

[11] Ijad, "Farrukh Siyar-Nāma [B]," fols. 2b–14a; quote at f. 10a-b.

[12] Sarkar, *Studies in Mughal India*, 231–50; Alvi, "The Historians of Awrangzeb: A Comparative Study of Three Primary Sources." For the study of one such writer, see Alam and Subrahmanyam, "The Making of a Munshi."

production. Primarily concerned with the political turmoil that roiled the empire, such peri-courtly histories debate and justify why kings rose and fell so rapidly from the throne. They reveal a changing conception of imperial sovereignty, wherein *daulat* is no longer the sole possession of the king, but is now claimed—with increasing assertiveness—by his putative servants, the nobility.

A defining feature of such works is their evocation of *'ibrat*, a word that contains within it both a sense of "weeping, being sad and melancholy . . . silent grief" and of "miracle, prodigy, mystery, example, or warning."[13] *'Ibrat* was a sensation akin to the experience of awe at the witnessing of the passage of historical time, particularly evoked by architectural ruin: it is powerfully articulated by the Persian poet Khaqani (d. 1190) on seeing the destroyed palaces of Ctesiphon:

> Know, O heart, to draw a lesson, regard with your eyes
> The ruins of Ctesiphon to be the mirror of admonition[14]

It is likewise this sentiment that the Mughal connoisseur Dargah Quli Khan experienced on observing the "obliterated graves and crumbling edifices" of the half-inhabited ruins of the Old City of Delhi while on his way to Shahjahanabad in 1739:

> This imaginary abode is not the resting-place of attachments
> Draw admonition from the nature of your self's roof and gates[15]

'Ibrat thus also had a spiritual and instructive dimension: It warned the discerning individual of the folly of pride, the inscrutability of fate, and the power of God, who casually destroyed the fragile works of man.

This sense of *'ibrat* was evoked in the contemporary histories of the early eighteenth century. Indeed, the period saw the composition of at least three works titled *Books of Admonition* (*'Ibrat nāma*-s): one by Mirza Muhammad, the learned scion of a famous noble family, who was an uncle of the chronicler Ashob; and others by the more obscure Sayyid Muhammad Qasim

[13] Steingass, Johnson, and Richardson, *A Comprehensive Persian-English Dictionary*, 882.

[14] Thackston, *A Millennium of Classical Persian Poetry*, 29; I have based my translation of this verse on the one in Meisami, "Khāqānī, Elegy on Madā'in," 162–63; see also Mottahedeh, "Some Islamic Views of the Pre-Islamic Past."

[15] Khan, *Muraqqa'-yi Dihlī*, 75.

Lahori and Kam Raj, both of whom appear to have served the Sayyids of Barha and wrote in their defense.[16] Other books of the period, even if they were not given the title, nevertheless frequently invoked the sense of admonition in describing events. The meaning of *ʿibrat* in the context of the period is apparent in Mirza Muhammad's account of Farrukh Siyar's deposal, which culminates with the Qurʾanic verse: "Learn a lesson, then, O you who are endowed with insight!"[17] Another chronicler wrongly—but tellingly—believed that same verse itself was a chronogram for the date of Farrukh Siyar's death.[18]

What admonishing lessons were to be drawn from Farrukh Siyar's death at the hands of his own nobility is rather less clear. Books of admonition rarely offered direct analysis of the events they described, because perhaps as elsewhere in the early modern world, history was still seen as the teacher of life, and the varied stories of old tomes all illustrated the same lessons of the deceptive jugglery of the heavens and the imperfections of man.[19] How the figures of Farrukh Siyar, his allies and his opponents were cast, and how their actions were described, therefore determined the lesson of the past; and on these matters the histories did not speak in unison. The tart prefatory words of one historian convey the sense of a multitude of contradictory perspectives which constituted the public discussion of Farrukh Siyar's end, and their audience, which, significantly, was now seen as the populace at large:

> A few points from the events of the oppressed king Farrukh Siyar are being jotted down on paper in order to provide admonition (*ʿibrat*) to the common people (*jamhūr ānām*). If found appropriate, they [the audience], they should listen after examining and investigating them; and if the opposite is perceived by the discerning and observant, they should not foul their tongues by uttering criticisms; for every one considers themselves to be an Avicenna, and fancies their mental powers to equal Aristotle's. And so the author should not be considered at fault.
>
> Hemistich: Everyone has their own ideas.[20]

[16] Muhammad, "ʿIbratnāma"; Lahori, *ʿIbratnāma*; Kam Raj, "ʿIbratnāma."
[17] Qurʾan 59:2; Muhammad, "ʿIbratnāma," fol. 223b.
[18] Khan, *Tazkirat us-Salatin*, 261.
[19] Cf. Koselleck, *Futures Past: On the Semantics of Historical Time*, chap. 2.
[20] Aurangabadi, "Ahwāl al-Khawāqīn," fol. 147a.

Modern historians have held an ambivalent view of such disputatious histories. For William Irvine and Jadunath Sarkar, the discrepancies and contradictions of the "fanciful" anecdotes that appeared in such narratives made them suspect as sources for the positivist history of Mughal decline they sought to establish. Yet their own method was hardly as scientific as they claimed: when it served his narrative purposes, for instance, Irvine sometimes simply treated the most fantastic tales as true accounts of events at court.[21] At other times, such anecdotes were rejected outright as "bazar gossip" which was "worthy only . . . of opium-eaters," as in the acid judgment of Jadunath Sarkar.[22] Even the sober-minded historians who have produced the most sophisticated accounts of the politics of the period occasionally reproduce such anecdotes while cautiously refraining from comment or analysis.[23]

In extracting a few grains of truth from the chaff of falsehood that littered such unreliable accounts, Irvine and Sarkar set the precedent of paving a smooth, artificial narrative of positivist history over the vitality and complexity of a landscape of ideological contestation. But it is of the utmost significance that, despite their claims to sober veracity, the historians of the eighteenth century rarely claimed to be eyewitnesses to the events they described, and subtly demarcated the realm of personal experience from hearsay. Such histories were thus not—or not merely—plain statements of "how it actually was." They were rather amalgamations of news reports, official documents, "public knowledge," gossip and rumor—and, frequently, the recombinations of extracts from other histories. Though in their prefaces historians often claimed their writings were simply journals (*roznāmcha*), left "as a memento on the folio of time," the frontispieces and colophons of their manuscripts betray the marks of the circulation of political knowledge and ideas, news and gossip within a pulsating Mughal economy of information centered not at the court but within a broader public realm. This is why we must see such non-courtly histories as not only recordings of a traumatic past, but also as expressive of ongoing concerns; as purposeful, pointed, and persuasive representations of recent events; and as ways of shaping memory

[21] See, for instance, the verbatim inclusion of the wild excesses of the son of Shah ʿAbd al-Ghafur. Irvine and Sarkar, *Later Mughals*, I:269–70.

[22] Sarkar, *A History of Jaipur*, 87.

[23] Cf. the treatment of the emperor Jahandar Shah's consort Lal Kunwar in Chandra, *Parties and Politics*, 110–13. The dynamics of the Mughal harem in the eighteenth century remain inadequately explored. But for the preceding period see Lal, *Domesticity and Power*.

and intervening in debates regarding the disorder of empire after the death of Aurangzeb in 1707. And it is in such *ʿibrat*-inflected writings that we see a new, non-courtly conception of *daulat* as a gift from God that no longer solely inheres in the king alone. To the mind of the service elites of this vast, bureaucratic empire of the eighteenth century, the king could now forfeit that which granted him the right to rule. Even more: it could be robbed of the king by a nobility who increasingly imagined possessing a *daulat* of their own. This changing meaning of *daulat* provided the ideological basis and justifications for the coup against Farrukh Siyar, and against which the people would most forcefully assert themselves.

The Transfer of *Daulat*

The central problem with which the authors of the admonitory histories grappled was that of the proper succession of kingly power. God-given though *daulat* might be, its recipients enjoyed only a definite mortality. How should the mantle of kingship be passed from one to another? What, other than death, were the conditions under which a Muslim king might depart the throne? The intellectual tradition presented no definite answer. The eleventh-century Sunni jurist al-Juwaini believed that it was possible for the leaders of the pious community (*ahl al-hall wa'l-ʿaqd*), which in theory appointed the caliph, to declare him deposed; his student al-Ghazali extended the argument to the case of oppressive Sultans. Pointedly, no mechanism for enacting a deposition was ever specified.[24] As an aside, it was unquestionable that the people had absolutely no role to play in the overthrowing of kings.[25] Mughal courtly intellectuals likewise offered vague statements of principle regarding succession: Jahangir's courtier Muhammad Baqir typically listed a very general series of causes, any one of which might endanger a king's rule: the removal of prudent advisors; indulgence in sensual pleasures of women, hunting, drinking, or other amusements; harshness against subordinates; and foolishness in behavior and disposition.[26]

[24] Crone, *God's Rule*, 231–32. The notion of appointing Caliphs was itself a "pious fiction" driven by the political exigencies of the period. See Andrew March, "Representation"; Böwering and Crone, *The Princeton Encyclopedia of Islamic Political Thought*, 460.

[25] Crone, *God's Rule*, 156; Lambton, *State and Government in Medieval Islam*, 116.

[26] Najm-Sani, *Advice on the Art of Governance*, 69–70.

In practice, succession was an "open-ended" system, grew ever more unrestrainedly violent over the course of the dynasty's history.[27] The fact that no routinized form of transition had emerged by the emperor Aurangzeb's death in 1707 indicates that the idea of *daulat* remained a broadly personal feature of the ruler, the acquisition and retaining of which now required the bodily elimination of all contenders.

These unresolvable tensions, inherent in the open-ended institutions of succession, precipitated around the question of partition. Because *daulat* resided in the body of all imperial descendants equally, Aurangzeb's death in 1707 opened the field of contest to no fewer than three adult sons and nine adult great-grandsons.[28] Though the dynastic founder Babur had favored partition over internecine warfare among his successors, the latter tendency had increasingly won out in the seventeenth century—as observers noted with dismay.[29] That his brother Aurangzeb's offer to divide the realm during the war of succession was a ploy was something the prince Murad Bakhsh only learnt on the chopping block.[30] Some contemporary historians thought that Aurangzeb himself left a deathbed will requesting the empire be partitioned (one tells us that such a document was found beneath his bolster).[31] His successor Bahadur Shah is related as having magnanimously offered to partition the empire with Kam Bakhsh before the latter's defeat and death; Kam Bakhsh is said to have refused the offer with scorn.[32]

During the unanticipated war of succession in 1712, the powerful nobleman Zuʾl-Faqar Khan is described as recommending the partition of the empire between three of the princely contenders while he himself would serve as the sole vizier for the collective. This scheme, which like the others came to naught, has been regarded as his recognition of the fact that the empire had become "unwieldy" and required "decentralization."[33] But that Zuʾl-Faqar Khan wished to create three sovereigns all dependent on his

[27] Faruqui, *Princes*, chap. 1.

[28] Faruqui, *Princes*, 42.

[29] Tripathi, *Muslim Administration*, 108. An eighteenth-century observer thought the unfortunate innovation (*bidʿat*) of killing contenders in the family, never practiced by Amir Timur and his descendants, was begun by Shah Jahan and only intensified thereafter. Ram, "Tuhfat al-Hind," Add. 6584: fols. 22b–23a.

[30] Faruqui, *Princes*, 40–41; see also Aurangzeb, "ʿAhdnāma-yi ʿĀlamgīr wa Murād Bakhsh."

[31] Fraser, *History of Nadir Shah*, 36–37; but cf. the version of the will which makes no mention of partition, preserved in Khan, *Anecdotes of Aurangzeb*.

[32] Warid, "Mīrāt-i Wāridāt," fols. 108b–109a; see also the account in Wazih, *Tārīkh-i Irādat Khān*, 43, 85–86.

[33] Chandra, *Parties and Politics*, 105.

administrative abilities in fact indicates the contrary: the problem was not of increasing administrative efficiency but rather of curbing the competition to attain *daulat*. That the idea was never resuscitated suggests that discursive centrality and tenacity of the idea of unitary kingship.

To go further, it is entirely possible that the recurring accounts of intended partition were fictions crafted by historians for narrative purposes: depending on one's perspective, such stories could connote either filial virtue or ruthless amorality. In both cases, such accounts serve to make the behavior of the highest political actors in the empire intelligible to the distant reader. That these stories came to be told and retold around the wars of succession after Aurangzeb's death in 1707 indicates that the empire continued to be seen as an indivisible entity to be ruled under unitary control: as a chronicler remarked, in the hunting grounds of heavenly favor (*iqbāl*), only one prince could succeed in the pursuit of the gazelles of *daulat*.[34]

The Changing Imagination of the King-Noble Relationship

While Shah Jahan's courtly ideologue had proclaimed that the nobility were no more than stars in the firmament of his *daulat*, a more restricted vision of a king with correspondingly greater powers for his servants begins to appear in the admonitory histories of our period. There were surely structural reasons for this. Observers universally condemned the executions of noblemen that accompanied the accessions of both Jahandar Shah in 1712 and Farrukh Siyar in 1713. The cause of such violence against the nobility, however, was their increasing unwillingness to die for the sake of a princely contender in repeated wars of succession. The diary of ʿAbd al-Rasul, a minor nobleman who participated in these wars, illustrates how each such contest offered opportunity for those with aspirations to higher station, but at the cost of substantial financial investment and the risk of death.[35] In the war that followed Aurangzeb's death, no fewer than fifty-two noblemen (to say nothing of the five or six thousand cavalrymen and an "uncountable" number of infantry) were believed to have perished.[36] A nobleman who survived it similarly

[34] Warid, "Mīrāt-i Wāridāt," fol. 110a.
[35] see ʿAbd al-Rasul, *Nairang-i Zamāna*, particularly 3–4.
[36] Warid, "Mīrāt-i Wāridāt," fol. 109a.

estimated 100,000 soldiers and 25 elephants were killed.[37] Khwush Hal, amazed by the unprecedented scale of the violence, described how people searched for their wounded and dead in the battlefield for days afterwards, while mass graves had to be prepared for the piles of the unclaimed dead.[38] The two wars that followed in the next six years could only have encouraged the desire for self-preservation among princely retinues.

Perhaps this is why Khwush Hal's frame of reference for the wars of succession is not the Ramayana, with its morally clear victory of righteousness over evil, but the Mahabharata, which describes an internecine war conducted without regard to morality. And it is surely the experience of amoral, catastrophic violence that caused noblemen to defect freely from one princely contender to another in the succession struggles after 1707, in flagrant violation of much-vaunted commitments to loyalty. In fact, the vehement reassertions of loyalty by noble authors in themselves suggest that the ideal was becoming somewhat incoherent. Thus, in describing the war of succession of 1712, the elite observer Khwaja Khalil recalled with distaste the many who took money to fight for a prince and then decamped; some took money from all sides and joined with none. "God's curse!" he fulminated, "neither fear of their beards being shorn, nor upholding the honor of Hindustani origin."[39] That Khwaja Khalil cared deeply about his honor was made evident in his suicide while in judicial custody in Delhi in 1718 (examined in the previous chapter). It was another matter, of course, that Khwaja Khalil had himself nimbly jumped from the service of one prince to another in the same years. By his own account, and that of many other observers of the period, the battleground of succession was rife with conspiracies and plots. Turncoats on the battlefield, not the capabilities of any individual prince, now determined the course of the day. This was particularly evident in Farrukh Siyar's defeat of Jahandar Shah in 1712, in which the timely defection of the noblemen Lutf Allah Khan (the father of Shakir Khan) and Muhammad Amin Khan arguably turned the tide of battle against the incumbent.[40]

Unsurprisingly, the king who won was rarely kindly disposed to those who had abandoned him on the battlefield, nor able to fully trust those who seemed to support him. Yet the admonitory histories tend to censure kings

[37] Khan and Yar, "Inshā-yi Dilkushā," fol. 74b.
[38] Khwush Hal, "Nādir al-Zamānī [B]," fols. 34b–35a.
[39] Khalil, "Tārīkh-i Shāhanshāhī," 11.
[40] Khalil, "Tārīkh-i Shāhanshāhī," 33–35.

and princes for their severity rather than the nobility for their transgressions. Thus Jahandar Shah was frequently criticized for the executions of men such as Rustam Dil Khan and Mukhlis Khan who had opposed him.[41] In emphasizing the king's unfitness to rule, chroniclers attributed only "little mistakes" common in time of war to these noblemen, glossing over the fact that they had gone so far as to yank the clothes and jewels of Jahandar Shah's harem ladies when they mistakenly imagined the prince had been defeated.[42] Similarly, when chroniclers blamed Jahandar Shah for murdering the prince Karim Bakhsh, they did not mention that the new ruler spared the life of his infant brother, who was adopted into the royal household.[43] The "unjustified" harshness of Jahandar Shah's regime was blamed for driving the nobility to side with Farrukh Siyar, rather than their brazen self-serving at this time of chaos.[44] In particular, observers were appalled by the imprisonments of noblemen, which were blamed on Jahandar Shah's vizier Zuʾl-Faqar Khan. Iradat Khan, who had served Zuʾl-Faqar Khan but defected to Farrukh Siyar after his victory, typically accused his former patron of eviscerating ancient noble families and establishing a regime of "imprisonments and enchainings and tortures and insults and outrages against the honor of noble ladies."[45] But these charges were composed after Jahandar Shah had been overthrown and the situation for Farrukh Siyar's enemies had become even more dangerous.

Jahandar Shah was also severely upbraided for giving undue and inappropriate preeminence to his consort, the courtesan Lal Kunwar. Indeed Khwaja Khalil identifies the people of Delhi as coming up with chronograms ridiculing the passing of the "parasol and throne and crown" to Lal Kunwar, which caused the desolation of the land.[46] Such verses criticizing the new king for his public embrace of a low-born woman surely represented the views of some urbanites. But their incorporation in elite histories more proximately reflects the position of elites who had first acknowledged Jahandar Shah as God's shadow on earth and then been forced to eat their words as Farrukh Siyar assumed the role.

41 Muhammad, "ʿIbratnāma," fol. 102a–b.
42 "Little mistakes": Khwush Hal, "Nādir al-Zamānī [B]," fol. 53b. For their crimes, see Wazih, *Tārīkh-i Irādat Khān*, 124; Multani, "Jahāndār Nāmā," fol. 36a.
43 Anonymous, "Akhbārāt, Jahāndār Shāh," 29.
44 Khan, *Tazkirat us-Salatin Chaghta*, 159–60.
45 Wazih, *Tārīkh-i Irādat Khān*, 131.
46 Khalil, "Tārīkh-i Shāhanshāhī," 23.

The self-interested nature of such accusations against Jahandar Shah, which have been uncritically repeated by historians, becomes obvious from the record of the transactions of his court. The new king's efforts were from the outset marked by attempts to impose a measure of fiscal prudence and to re-establish control over the nobility by the judicious application of rewards and punishments.[47] Jahandar Shah recognized the debilitating effects of succession struggles: he sought to streamline the process "in the Iranian fashion" by assigning a military stipend for his eldest son ʿAzz al-Din, and granting only yearly cash stipends to his two younger sons—effectively instituting a system of primogeniture.[48]

Another key goal was to bring order to the confused proliferation of ranks and titles that had apparently been widely promised by all contenders.[49] Thus, on April 1, 1712, after ordering the imprisonment of eighteen noblemen, he decreed that increases in ranks for imperial servants and the newly appointed were to be suspended.[50] Far from imposing indiscriminate punishments, Jahandar Shah prevented his vizier from executing prisoners such as Amin al-Din Khan.[51] Others such as Lutf Allah Khan had their "errors" forgiven, and protection given to their families (Lutf Allah Khan would nevertheless go on to defect to Farrukh Siyar soon thereafter).[52] And finally, on May 19, six weeks after Rustam Dil Khan had been executed for his heinous crimes, his brother Sultan ʿAli Khan was appointed to the (admittedly remote) Himalayan fort of Kangra.[53] Yet such efforts looked anything but moderate to the noblemen who felt wronged for having actively supported a losing contender in the struggle for succession, who complained about being sidelined, and who resented the re-establishment of order to their detriment.[54]

Farrukh Siyar's reign (Fig. 5.1) began with the same attempts to rein in the unruly mob of the nobility; again, improper promotions were canceled, which caused "heartbreak among elite and commoners alike."[55] Though the new king was not subject to the same kind of criticism, the blood-letting that marked his reign was, if anything, even greater. Bodies of strangled noblemen were hurled onto the riverside sand bank where the city's inhabitants

[47] Here I depart from the interpretation offered in Chandra, *Parties and Politics*, 116–22.
[48] Anonymous, "Akhbārāt, Jahāndār Shāh," 29.
[49] Cf. Alam, *Crisis of Empire*, 28–29.
[50] Anonymous, "Akhbārāt, Jahāndār Shāh," 9.
[51] Khan and Yar, "Inshā-yi Dilkushā," fol. 18b.
[52] Anonymous, "Akhbārāt, Jahāndār Shāh," 13, 30.
[53] Anonymous, "Akhbārāt, Jahāndār Shāh," 87.
[54] Multani, "Jahāndār Nāmā," fols. 36b–37a.
[55] Khan, *Tazkirat us-Salatin Chaghta*, 180.

Figure 5.1. The claim to the divine sanction of the king would be irrevocably damaged with Farrukh Siyar's overthrow. (Credit: Victoria and Albert Museum.)

promenaded in the evenings.[56] Such violence indicates the sense of insecurity with which the new emperor assumed the throne. Mutual resentment had come to characterize the relationship between the emperor and nobility well before Farrukh Siyar would be overthrown by his vizier in 1719.

How did the relationship between ruler and nobleman change in the eyes of the eighteenth-century nobility? For the mid-seventeenth century nobleman Zafar Khan, whose long poem of counsel to Aurangzeb was examined in Chapter 3, the vizier was no more than the guardian (*nigah-bān*) of *daulat*, whose job was to offer wise and calming counsel and administer the realm efficiently.[57] But a new ideal of the relationship between the emperor and his servants was most cogently conceptualized by Iradat Khan in his memoirs written during the reign of Farrukh Siyar. It appears in an imagined conversation between the king Bahadur Shah and his vizier Munʿim Khan just after their victory in the war of succession in 1707. Bahadur Shah asks his counselor what should be done with the noblemen who had supported other contenders for the throne. Should they be dismissed or punished? Munʿim Khan offers a long and thoughtful disquisition in response. He first acknowledges that all the noblemen who had sided with a rival were liable to be chastised for their words and deeds. Yet the vizier counsels forgiveness, for these men had done nothing other than support another contender. They could be expected to faithfully serve whoever inherited the throne, for they had sworn loyalty to the preceding ruler.

The vizier now offers a more expansive view of matters of state, and through it the author directly challenges the established discourse of Mughal sovereignty. The sublime empire (*saltanat-i ʿazīm al-shān*) of Hindustan, says Munʿim Khan, is a *daulat* that cannot be upheld by one body or two bodies alone. Instead it requires several tall pillars and strong ropes to keep the tent of state upright and erect. It is the nobility, who, from father to son, have inherited the etiquette of servitude over generations, and who are "the pillars of this Solomonic hall." Unless they are completely trusted and deputed great power, it will not be possible to bring order to the state, to enforce its laws, or to lead its armies. So all the king's slaves who now gather at his stirrup must be equipped with exalted *daulat* (*daulat-i ʿazīm*) and rank. At the same time, stresses Munʿim Khan, such favors are not to be extended to the minor servants of noblemen, who had held petty

[56] Khan, *Tazkirat us-Salatin Chaghta*, 181.
[57] Ahsan, "Masnawīyyāt," fol. 59a.

offices in the countryside, and who "by the grace of god" had been trickling into princely retinues. How could they know anything of the procedures of state, the administration of territory, the rules of etiquette, or the service of princes? Such qualities, of course, were the exclusive preserve of the scions of exalted families.[58]

Iradat Khan's words reflect the emergence of an established and hereditary nobility concerned with securing its place against the waves of new men from the provinces who were recruited into princely retinues with each iteration of the battles for succession. But they also show how profoundly the imperial discourse of sovereignty has been reshaped. We have already seen how Jahandar Shah is thought capable of shedding the sacral light of Alanquwa through his actions. Now it is asserted that the substance did not even belong to the king alone. Perhaps a trace of the shift this implies can be glimpsed in the verses of an obscure poet who produced a long encomium for the Barha nobleman ʿAbd Allah Khan in the years before he became the most important man in the empire and went on to depose Farrukh Siyar. The poem celebrates a central theme that is repeated in stanzas:

> The *daulat* of Lord ʿAbd Allah Khan is growing
> [Even] the entryway to his court becomes heavenly.[59]

Nor were such verses meant purely for the noble patron's private comfort: for, as the poet bragged of himself:

> His pen, in writing poems of praise, prances enchantingly
> The people (*khalq*) fall under its spell by the force of its sorcery.[60]

Such sentiments remind us that the poetry of praise was designed to be read in public contexts and served as a medium of propaganda directed at a world of listeners. What the people thought of the nobility's attribution of the substance of kingship to themselves, however, would not become apparent until Farrukh Siyar's overthrow. But first, how was such an act of naked violence to be justified?

[58] Wazih, *Tārīkh-i Irādat Khān*, 75–76; also see the discussion of the same passage in Faruqui, *Princes*, 257–58.
[59] Mutalliʿ, "Dīwān-Mutalliʿ," 74–77.
[60] Mutalliʿ, "Dīwān-Mutalliʿ," 62.

Engineering Succession

An implication of the claim that *daulat* was not the king's sole possession was that he might then be actively deprived of it. The customs of Mughal imperial succession that evolved over the seventeenth century indicated that once the king was established he could not be removed, except perhaps by an equal coparcenary of *daulat*. However, chroniclers began to raise the possibility of deposition during the unsettled years after the death of Aurangzeb in 1707. Again, the brief reign of Jahandar Shah was critical in letting this idea germinate. Consider, for instance, the anecdote related by Iradat Khan and repeated by others, in which Jahandar Shah accompanied his favored courtesan Lal Kunwar on a drunken ox-cart excursion in a bazaar, where they purchased pumpkins and cucumbers. The emperor of India, drunk out of his mind, became separated from his beloved and was driven by the carter into a cowshed. When a search was mounted for the king's whereabouts, he was discovered still in the ox-cart, supine and senseless. The ignominious vehicle bearing the unconscious emperor was taken to the fort, but only admitted to the palace once the administrator and garrison commander had investigated it carefully.[61] The story's import is obvious: Jahandar Shah literally snored in the "sleep of negligence," as the idiom had it, and the throne sat vacant. And yet the empire functioned headless, as is evident in the routine diligence of the palace administrators. What difference would it make if another came to occupy the throne?

Unconscious or not, how was the Shadow of God to be detached from his divinely appointed station? In his memoirs, Iradat Khan resolutely ruled out the use of force, even claiming that abstention from the assassination of royals was "a kind of oath and custom" in his family, a claim that only invites further questions. But he had already advocated violence against an imperial person in preceding pages. When his patron, the princeling Bedar Bakht, complained of the animosity of his father (the prince Aʿzam Shah) and fearfully asked for advice, Iradat Khan offered a courtly response. Summoning the rather shaky precedent of Aurangzeb's capture of Shah Jahan, he suggested a variety of schemes by which the prince might "imprison" his father.[62]

Such killing or imprisonment of one prince by another, though frowned upon, still fit the accepted model for the competition of *daulat*. A new

[61] Wazih, "Tārīkh-i Irādat Khānī," fols. 67b–68a.
[62] Wazih, *Tārīkh-i Irādat Khān*, 35–37.

possibility, however, emerged in Iradat Khan's claim, made elsewhere and in passing, that Jahandar Shah had developed a not-unfounded fear of being dethroned by his minister Zu'l-Faqar Khan.[63] A direct dethronement would not occur in Iradat Khan's lifetime, for he died some years before Farrukh Siyar was deposed and killed.[64] But the removal of a sitting emperor had already been presaged in the events following Jahandar Shah's shock defeat by Farrukh Siyar outside Agra. When the king fled to Delhi and sought refuge with Zu'l-Faqar Khan, the minister and his aged father Asad Khan (famed for his rectitude as Aurangzeb's vizier) immediately placed him in confinement. Asad Khan and Zu'l-Faqar Khan then handed Jahandar Shah over to Farrukh Siyar, thus sealing his fate in exchange for their own lives. In any event, their gambit was unsuccessful, for Zu'l-Faqar Khan was himself treacherously executed on Farrukh Siyar's order soon thereafter.

The key moment in this high drama, much represented in the chronicles of the period, was the exchange between Zu'l-Faqar Khan and Asad Khan as they debated what to do with the helpless Jahandar Shah in 1713. Because none of the chroniclers who describe this sensitive discussion between two of the most powerful noblemen in the empire could possibly have been privy to it, the many renditions of the exchange in the histories of the era cannot be regarded as a statement of historical reality. Rather, the conversation was a device that allowed Mughal observers to imagine a moment of crisis in the discourse of sovereignty, in which the right path was no longer obvious and had to be established anew (Fig. 5.2). All are unanimous in noting that Zu'l-Faqar Khan and his father disagreed over the proper course of action. Zu'l-Faqar Khan advocates continued resistance with Jahandar Shah against Farrukh Siyar and the Sayyids of Barha, but his father recommends that the old king be handed over to the new one. Zu'l-Faqar Khan reluctantly concedes, with fatal consequences for both himself and the former king.

The reflection of Iradat Khan's vision of the new relationship between the nobility and the king can be glimpsed in all these accounts. In the historian Warid's rendition, Asad Khan informs his son that it is best to surrender Jahandar Shah, whereas "our person, commingled with wisdom, is of the pillars of the rulership (*saltanat*), and our non-existence will be the cause of its collapse. Thus whoever comes to ascend the throne of this exalted *daulat*

[63] Wazih, *Tārīkh-i Irādat Khān*, 132, 144.
[64] Muhammad, *Tārīkh-i Muhammadī*, 32.

Figure 5.2. Asad Khan and Zu'l-Faqar Khan in debate: SMB Berlin 4596.

will place us on the seat of viziership." When Zu'l-Faqar Khan protests, Asad Khan remarkably blames the king for causing sedition and strife (*fasād, fitna*), points to the rising prices of grain as an index of the trouble Jahandar Shah has wreaked, and pleads with his son to not join the disloyal after "a hundred years of loyalty."[65] It is significant that the aged courtier's readiness to serve *whomever* sat on the throne in Delhi is here construed as "loyalty," while Zu'l-Faqar Khan's desire to fight for Jahandar Shah now serves as its opposite. That neither side of this debate regarded Jahandar Shah's *daulat* as substantial only indicates how much the ideal of kingship had changed since Babur's horror at the Bengali custom of rendering allegiance to a throne rather than a person.

This new position emerges clearly in Mirza Muhammad's account of the same debate. In this rendition, Asad Khan thought that Jahandar Shah's life could be used as ransom (*fidya*) for their own. He said, "*daulat* has turned away from this man. All his words and actions are repugnant to the temperament of God's creation. It is better that we turn him over to divine fate and cling fast to the hem of the emperor Muhammad Farrukh Siyar's *daulat* instead." Zu'l-Faqar Khan points out that all blame him for "demolishing the mansion of *daulat*" of Farrukh Siyar's father; he could expect no mercy. The ethical problem of handing over a person seeking protection is mentioned but only as an afterthought. The reply that Mirza Muhammad places in the aged father's mouth again mirrors the new vision of the relationship between emperor and nobleman: no nobleman can be blamed for choosing one side or another in the war of succession. Even though it goes against the "principles of humanity" to hand over someone seeking shelter to their enemy, there is no point in preserving Jahandar Shah, because the "common people" have a "perfect hatred" of him and no one will come to his support. Farrukh Siyar will be grateful to them, concludes Asad Khan, for he "has great use for noblemen like us, who are masters of both the sword and the pen; and so over time we shall gain control of his affairs."[66]

It is not a coincidence that elsewhere in his account Mirza Muhammad describes the nobility with the strikingly incongruous phrase "the people who fasten and bind" (*Ahl al-hall wa-l-ʿaqd*).[67] This is the very term used by the eleventh-century jurists al-Mawardi and al-Juwaini to denote the community of the pious who *in theory* were to appoint, counsel, and on occasion depose the leader of Muslims (*imām*).[68] The world of the late-Abbasid caliphate of Mawardi and Juwaini was far in time and space from the Delhi of the eighteenth century, and it is unlikely that Asad Khan and Zu'l-Faqar Khan

[65] Warid, "Mīrāt-i Wāridāt," fol. 145a.
[66] Muhammad, "ʿIbratnāma," fols. 109b–10a.
[67] Muhammad, "ʿIbratnāma," fol. 194a.
[68] Zaman, "Ahl al-ḥall wa-l-ʿaqd."

saw themselves in this way. But the fact that they traded Jahandar Shah's life for their own makes it clear that both the high nobility and those who wrote of their deeds had already come around to the view that one prince could be substituted for another on the throne, and that *daulat* was no longer held up by the pillars of state but resided within them.

Farrukh Siyar's End: From Fate to Reason of State

The tendency of the nobility to claim the *daulat* that had granted the king sovereignty for themselves could, in Jahandar Shah's dethronement, be hidden behind the veil of imperial custom; it was a polite fiction that Farrukh Siyar, and not the Sayyids of Barha, were responsible for Jahandar Shah's defeat. With Farrukh Siyar's deposal, however, the nakedness of noble assertion could no longer be concealed. Yet the Sayyids did not abandon the effort to maintain the veneer of imperial tradition. According to Mirza Muhammad, they forcibly selected the prince Rafiʿ al-Darajat before Farrukh Siyar was dragged to a dungeon. But, in claiming that Rafiʿ al-Darajat was seated on the Peacock Throne with his hands grasped by Raja Ajit Singh and Sayyid ʿAbd Allah Khan, Mirza Muhammad succinctly conveyed how the otherworldly significations of the king's *daulat* were rendered meaningless when the rituals of enthronement were reduced to an empty gesture, and the ruler became a pawn.[69]

In a letter to a powerful loyalist of Farrukh Siyar after the king had been deposed, the Sayyids offered the slimmest justification for their unprecedented action:

> Because, by reason of the madness which had been clouding his temperament, Muhammad Farrukh Siyar deviated from [established] customs and practices, and acted in ways outside [the traditions of] the exalted Timurid dynasty (*silsilā-yi ʿālīyya-yi tīmūrīyya*), he will receive God's punishment.[70]

But it was hardly as simple as that. Farrukh Siyar's deposal and execution, the first unambiguous occurrence of what was latent in Jahandar Shah's

[69] Muhammad, "ʿIbratnāma," fol. 223a.
[70] Anonymous, "Ajāʾib al-Āfāq," fol. 50a–b. Almost identical language appears in the text of a "proclamation" announcing the coronation of the new king Rafiʿ al-Darajat: Anonymous, "Mihakk al-Sulūk," fol. 654a.

dethronement, breached the imperial discourse of sovereignty that had asserted that the basis of earthly order was an inviolate ruler with absolute powers. Traces of the fissures this produced within the Mughal intelligentsia are evident in contemporary descriptions of the event; confronted with the starkness of the overthrow and the execution of a reigning king, historians offered a variety of confused and contradictory answers. In seeking to suture this unprecedented rupture in the discourse of sovereignty, some commentators began to offer explanations other than the usual attributions of heavenly disfavor: most significant among these, we shall see, was the emergence of something akin to the reason of state as grounds for Farrukh Siyar's removal.

The facts of the troubled relationship between the king and the Sayyids of Barha who had brought him to the throne are well established.[71] From the outset, Farrukh Siyar's alliance with ʿAbd Allah Khan and Husain ʿAli Khan, the brothers who led the Sayyids of Barha, was marked by distrust.[72] The Sayyid brothers claimed the chief imperial offices of the viziership and the Paymastership for themselves and sought to exercise absolute control over the affairs of the empire. Chafing under their overbearing attitude, Farrukh Siyar resorted to subterfuge to rid himself of them. Within a year of his enthronement, Farrukh Siyar and the Sayyids were openly making warlike preparations against each other. Tensions abated briefly but the court was thick with intrigues and conspiracies. In December 1718, on the pretext of bringing a captured pretender to Delhi, Husain ʿAli Khan marched north with an army of Deccani soldiers, including large contingents of the very Marathas he had ostensibly gone to quell. They reached the outskirts of Delhi on February 16, 1719. By this time, Satish Chandra has noted, the emperor was "almost completely isolated" since a "decisive section of the old nobility" had either defected to the Sayyids or "adopted a position of neutrality."[73] The abandonment of the imperial cause by the most powerful imperial noblemen, including Nizam al-Mulk, Muhammad Amin Khan, and Sar Buland Khan, thus created the conditions for his removal.

The authors of the admonitory histories who observed these events rarely analyzed them with such clinical precision. For these hostile

[71] Irvine and Sarkar, *Later Mughals*, vol. I, chap. 4.

[72] Chandra, *Parties and Politics*, chap. 4.

[73] Chandra, *Parties and Politics at the Mughal Court, 1707–1740*, 176.

commentators, heavenly retribution, rather than human agency, was the most convenient explanation for the act of regicide. Listing all those strangled on Farrukh Siyar's orders as the cause of divine revenge, the chronicler Kam Raj simply noted, "the heavens take back what they have given."[74] Lahori thought that whenever the king's "foot strayed beyond the carpet of justice, he suffered the consequences of his own actions."[75] So when Lahori described the blinding of Farrukh Siyar while in prison, it ironically required the author to find sympathy for Jahandar Shah; the king's torments were simply the recompense for "the knives and daggers which had been thrust into the livers and necks of Muhammad Muʿizz al-Din [Jahandar Shah] and other obedient servants."[76] Finally, in having the king disconsolately recite the following verse in prison, Lahori neatly extended the chain of causation from Farrukh Siyar's fate to that of his captors, the Sayyids:

> I've heard that a sheep said to the butcher
> At the moment when he cut its head off with his piercing cleaver
> "If this is the punishment for the grass on which I've nibbled
> What then will befall him, who eats my fatty side?"[77]

Heaven's vengeance here appears to obey the laws of karma as the impersonal and inevitable consequences of one's violent actions. Such invocations of fate are important, for they reveal attempts to rationalize what is otherwise inexplicable. In the same way, the chronicler Yahya Khan simply attributes to fate the fact that Muhammad Amin Khan did not kill his rival Husain ʿAli Khan on the day of the coup, but instead encouraged him to conduct it. Such fated utterances serve to exonerate Husain ʿAli Khan from originating the idea of the dethronement.[78]

Some strove for a more historicist explanation. One chronicler invoked the nobleman Mahabat Khan's temporary imprisonment of the emperor Jahangir as a (dubious) historical precedent.[79] The chronicler Kamwar Khan

[74] Kam Raj, "ʿIbratnāma," fol. 67b.
[75] Lahori, *ʿIbratnāma*, 187.
[76] Lahori, *ʿIbratnāma*, 218.
[77] Lahori, *ʿIbratnāma*, 218.
[78] Khan, "Tazkīrāt al-Mulūk," fol. 125a.
[79] Siddiqi, "Jauhar-i Samsām," fols. 112b–114a.

thought that, because "every event has been appointed a cause, every act an agent, and every action is indebted to a past moment" what befell the king was the result of "inexperienced and thoughtless advisors." This was a theme extensively elaborated in the ethical treatises which commanded kings to prefer wise enemies to foolish friends. As Kamwar himself pointed out: "In books open [before one] it is also written of how many dynasties have been ruined by unworthy companions."[80] Lahori likewise thought the king had succumbed to the poor advice of mischief-makers, whose unworthiness is evident in their being "new to *daulat*" (*nau-daulatān*).[81] In the same vein, another said that "if the martyred king had not rejected all the old nobility, and not given power to strangers, his *daulat* would not have departed; for the departure of *daulat* begins at the elevation of the lowly."[82] Mirza Muhammad discerned a foundational tension between Farrukh Siyar's old retainers and the upstart Sayyids who brought him to power, which the king did not have the character to manage.[83] Iradat Khan had pointed to the same kind of conflict between Jahandar Shah's family retainer Kokaltash Khan and the nobleman Zu'l-Faqar Khan.[84] Such explanations, again, directed blame toward the king and away from his murderers. The Sayyid partisan Kam Raj sought to distance the brothers from the "unpleasant event," claiming that the brothers were instigated by others, and "were not in actuality" disloyal and seditious.[85] Similarly, the authors of the worshipful biographies of the Sayyids offered a tortured exculpation of their evidently unprincipled actions by blaming the victim: "in the first place he should not have conferred on the Sayyids the great office of vizier to which the Sayyids of Barha had no claim," and so, "what happened [to the king] was the result of his own doing."[86]

Besides these traditional explanations, some commentators began to offer new reasons for the disorder in the realm, where again blame fell on the king. The chronicler Kam Raj, for instance, offered a systemic and historic perspective, in which kingly laxity in the enforcement of administrative regulations led to rebellion, the influx of unworthy provincials into imperial service, and the progressive decline of empire. According to Kam Raj, Shah

[80] Khan, *Tazkirat us-Salatin*, 257.
[81] Lahori, *'Ibratnāma*, 188.
[82] Hasan, "Guldasta," 131.
[83] Muhammad, "'Ibratnāma," fols. 122a–23a. On the importance of a prince's retinue, cultivated from his early youth, see Faruqui, *Princes*, chap. 3, particularly 103–12.
[84] Wazih, *Tārīkh-i Irādat Khān*, 131–32.
[85] Kam Raj, "'Ibratnāma," fol. 67a.
[86] Aurangabadi, *Ma'āsir al-Umarā' [En]*, 1:713.

Jahan's era, which had ended some seven decades before, was one of prosperity and tranquility. But in Aurangzeb's rule, "the thought of equaling the King of Kings became widespread" and the empire was troubled by "the malignant infidels of the Deccan, and the uprisings of worthless Rajputs." The king made matters worse by assigning ranks without regard to the availability of land grants. In Bahadur Shah's reign, all rules were abandoned and "no means of disciplining the rebellious remained effective." Jahandar Shah destroyed the *daulat* of his ancestors with his "abominable practices," so that the "bride of the God-given empire pulled herself away from the embrace of desire." Finally, by Farrukh Siyar's time, "lowly vagrants from small towns in the provinces of Bangla [Bengal] and Bihar joined the Victorious Stirrup" and the ruler was led astray by evil seekers of strife.[87]

The implicit critique of Jahandar Shah as the slumbering king is in Kam Raj's account of Farrukh Siyar sharpened into something akin to an argument of reason of state: it was necessary to depose the emperor to check the disorder of empire. Though not sharing Kam Raj's bleak vision of increasing rebellion, the historian Lahori also casts doubt on Farrukh Siyar's administrative acumen, describing him as "by nature insensible of the principles of rulership (*bīgāna-yi riyāsat*) established by law or custom, and having no restraint on his unnecessary expenditures or the keeping of unworthy company."[88] This framing suggests that the sovereignty granted by the light of Alanquwa may be displaced if its bearer displays financial imprudence. Later, in relating the secret counsel offered by "a Deccani" to Husain ʿAli Khan, Lahori recasts this argument of reason of state in a medical form. According to this advisor, there were two kinds of cure for a disease: either it was assuaged with medicine, or removed by "tearing out at the root." In the present situation, when "the disorder in the world's condition" was beyond medication, the "health of the domain" (*sihhat-i mizāj-i mamlakat*) could not be restored without resort to radical surgery. Such a vision of the body politic was not unprecedented; Shah Jahan's court poet Haji Muhammad Jan "Qudsi" (d. 1646) had presented the following lines in a history of the king's glories:[89]

> The head of the rebel is better below ground
> The body's better cleansed of disorderly interminglings

[87] Kam Raj, "ʿIbratnāma," fols. 54a–55a.
[88] Lahori, *ʿIbratnāma*, 210.
[89] Losensky, "Qodsi Mashadi."

> Not everything that grows from the body should remain in place
> Nails are worthy of being cut off the hands and legs.[90]

But Qudsi was offering a justification for Shah Jahan's execution of five distant imperial contenders after his enthronement: two nephews, two cousins, and a half-brother. Somewhat less than a century later, Lahori could now suggest that in order to save the body politic, sometimes it might be necessary to cut off its head.

Sovereignty Remade

In February 1738, the imperial court commissioned the Delhi litterateur and philologist Siraj al-Din ʿAli Khan Arzu to pen a reply to a letter that had recently arrived from the neighboring Safavid realm.[91] After the usual prolegomena, the letter presents the official narrative of the events of Muhammad Shah's accession. It recounts how the "martyred emperor" Farrukh Siyar was killed by the disloyalty of the Barha nobility, ("ʿAbd Allah and Husain ʿAli"), who had responded with ingratitude to the "great gift and *daulat* of imperial servitude (as is the wont of those newly reached to *daulat*)." The two went on to behave in unfortunate ways, "which became the cause of *ʿibrat* for the short-sighted." Husain ʿAli was killed by a certain Mir Haidar (lavishly praised for this action) in October 1720. ʿAbd Allah, who had promptly placed another Mughal prince on the throne in Delhi, was captured within a month and poisoned in captivity two years later. Having recounted this history, the letter ends with support for the Iranian program of suppressing Afghan rebels, and has words of praise of Tahmasp Quli Khan's efforts in this regard.[92]

It is not clear whether Arzu's letter was ever dispatched or received, for Tahmasp Quli Khan—or Nadir Shah, as he had now styled himself—was

[90] Hasan, *Mughal Poetry*, 41. I have consulted the author's translation but provided my own.

[91] Arzu, "Tārīkh-i Istīsāl-i Sādāt-i Bārhā." It is unclear why the letter is addressed to the Safawid ruler Tahmasp Mirza, who had been deposed by Nadir Shah two years previously. Had the preceding letter been sent under Tahmasp Mirza's name, or in referring to him was the Delhi court pointedly denying the validity of Nadir Shah's takeover in the same way that the Ottoman court had slightingly ignored Farrukh Siyar's claims? In any case, this letter confirms the claim of the famed émigré Shaikh ʿAli Hazin to the effect that the Mughal court was "confused and perplexed" as to what "titles or forms of address" were to be used for Nadir Shah. See Malik, *A Mughal Statesman*, 77 fn. 329.

[92] Arzu, "Tārīkh-i Istīsāl-i Sādāt-i Bārhā." The dates of these events are derived from Irvine and Sarkar, *Later Mughals*, I:1, 56, 96.

already making preparations to cross the Mughal frontier.[93] In tone and style, however, Muhammad Shah's letter is written in the classic language of Mughal kingship, as if sovereignty had suffered no interruption in preceding decades. Yet, the very fact that the Mughal court felt compelled to dwell on the distasteful events of two decades earlier that had preceded Muhammad Shah's ascension indicates that his reign did not mark the seamless resumption of the older discourse of kingship.

For the Sayyid coup against Farrukh Siyar had produced not some reconfiguration of power but a catastrophic destabilization of the entire imperial order: as an observer sympathetic to the Sayyids put it, "oceans of rebellions lapped from all sides."[94] On the one hand, in exchange for their support against Farrukh Siyar, the Sayyids made substantial concessions to the Deccani groups who had long resisted Mughal suzerainty, going so far as to cede them a quarter of revenues collected in the Deccan provinces. Even those who sympathized with the Sayyids attributed this capitulation as the cause of the Deccani enemy's ultimate victory over the hard-fought frontier.[95] On the other hand, no less than five princes were crowned by various parties in the year after Farrukh Siyar's dethronement. Among these, a serious challenge was posed by the accession of the prince Neku Siyar in Agra in May 1719, some five weeks after Farrukh Siyar was buried. The chronicler Khwafi Khan relates rumors that Mitr Sen, who orchestrated the coronation of Neku Siyar, was propped up by powerful Hindu nobles who had supported Farrukh Siyar, such as Raja Jai Singh and Raja Chhabela Ram.[96] Finally, and most intriguingly, a minor administrator who was no friend of the Sayyids regarded the populace (*ʿawāmm*) as responsible for enthroning Neku Siyar, while noting that he was not supported by any of the established nobility.[97]

Whether or not he was popularly appointed, Neku Siyar's abortive enthronement was the logical consequence of the fissure in the Mughal discourse of sovereignty: it signaled that any one—even a mere "Hindu physician" such as Mitr Sen—could prop up an imperial contender. Mitr Sen's backing never materialized; but the effort to crush the uprising cost the

[93] Lockhart, *Nadir Shah*, 122–25.
[94] Bilgrami, *Maʾāṣir al-Kirām*, II:160.
[95] Bilgrami, *Maʾāṣir al-Kirām*, II:167.
[96] Khwafi Khan, *The Muntakhab Al-Lubáb [Fa]*, 3:825–26; Malik, *The Reign of Muhammad Shah, 1717–1748*, 33; Irvine and Sarkar, *Later Mughals*, I:408–13.
[97] Singh, "Masnawī," fol. 19a.

Sayyids time, energy, resources, and attention.[98] Nor did the suppression of Neku Siyar solve the Sayyids' problems: while facing a series of rebellions, the king Rafiʿ al-Darajat and his successor Rafiʿ al-Daula died with disconcerting swiftness before Muhammad Shah was placed on the throne in September 1719.

Muhammad Shah's era began the reassertion of sovereignty along classic lines, especially after the power of the Sayyids was broken. The old language of *daulat* is resurrected in a courtly chronicle of his era, written by an unnamed but literate confidante of the queen mother. Thus the king's accession is described as the dawn of *daulat* and his nobility are again described as the pillars of the perpetual *daulat*.[99] Early in his reign, the king ordered that a chain of justice be fastened to the window of his residence in the Red Fort and petitions accepted at the window of presentation. In the celebrations of his coronation, Muhammad Shah not only accepted precious gifts from his nobility but also "five baskets of vegetables" from a "vegetable seller."[100] More generally throughout his rule, the king fashioned himself as solicitous of the people's welfare.[101] New legal compendia were assembled to guide the ruler, and new ethical treatises written to re-establish the relationship between the king and his nobility on the traditional basis.[102] Literary works extolled Muhammad Shah's conformance to the traditional ideals of kingship and his justice, generosity and munificence.[103] And his chancellery continued to dispatch orders appointing judges and administrators, granting rewards and honors, and gifting land grants to deserving folk.[104]

Though Muhammad Shah's practices recalled those of his venerable ancestors, his reconstitution of kingship was markedly fragile. The young king's fears can be discerned from the fact that on the day after he heard that Mahmud Khan the Afghan had overthrown Sultan Husain, the ruler of Iran, Muhammad Shah ordered that the room in which his ancestor Jahandar Shah had been executed was to be demolished.[105] And there is a noticeable

[98] The precarious position of the Sayyids after the deposal of Farrukh Siyar is evident in their correspondence from the period. See Balmukund, *Letters of a King-Maker of the Eighteenth Century (Balmukund Nama)*.

[99] Anonymous, "Sahīfa-yi Iqbāl [A]," fols. 4a, 8a, passim.

[100] Lakhnavi, *Shāhnāma*, 120.

[101] Lakhnavi, *Shāhnāma*, 126; Khan and Mustepha, *Sëir Mutaqherin*, 249; Khwush Hal, "Nādir al-Zamānī [B]," fol. 226b.

[102] Khan, "Akhlāq"; Khān, "Mirʾāt al-Masāʾil-i Muhammad Shāhī."

[103] Anonymous, "Sahīfa-yi Iqbāl [A]."

[104] See, for instance, the examples preserved in Ahmad, *Farāmīn-i salātīn*.

[105] Khan, *Tazkirat us-Salatin*, 351.

change in the tenor of two ethical treatises written to guide the king in the period. The *Guidance of Regulations*, a simple and prosaic work from the reign of Farrukh Siyar, sees the king as "God's shadow" and prescribes an activist agenda of personal rule for him.[106] By contrast, the *Ethics for Muhammad Shah*, commissioned for the new king by the rising nobleman Amin al-Daula, offers a very different view of kingship.[107] Remarkably, the text does not begin with the divine origins of kingship, but rather its "conditions." The ruler is enjoined to a series of duties and advised on deportment and behavior. An equal amount of attention is devoted to those who are described as "masters of *daulat*" (*sāhib-daulat*): the nobility.[108] Browsing the pages that inform the reader of how the nobleman is to conduct and comport himself, it becomes quickly apparent that the audience of this text, despite its title, is not the king, but his servants: thus also, the long section on how the "companions" of the nobility should be chosen, and how they should behave. It is hard to escape the impression that administrative power has, in the conception of the author, shifted decisively to the ranks of the new masters of *daulat* who now require counsel. Indeed, the stamp of the recent events can be sensed in the author's quiet but significant rearrangement of the old paradigm: for now we learn he who receives the king's favor (*iqbāl*) gains *daulat* by virtue of the king's awe and sanctity (*haibat wa hurmat*). But this bearer of *daulat* inevitably attracts the increasing jealousy of his enemies, who eventually overthrow him. The problem is the management of these tensions, and in this light the vizier is enjoined to not intrude upon the perquisites of kingship.[109]

Such theorization reconstituted the older understanding of *daulat* from the mystical substance of the king to the general fortune to exercise authority, which no longer reposed solely in his body. Authors thus emphasized new aspects of the ideal of *daulat* itself. Consider the view of the mystically inclined author of a curious work that interspersed pious and philosophical reflections with historical narratives of the early eighteenth century. The author chooses to demarcate two kinds of *daulat* just before he describes the war of succession of 1712. One kind of *daulat* was attained by falling under the shadow of Hazrat Khizr, the mystical figure of lore.[110] Those indigents

[106] The text is dated to 1708 but dedicated to the Farrukh Siyar (r. 1713–1719). Hidayat Allah, "Hidāyat al-Qawā'id," fols. 1b–2a; 4b–6a.

[107] Khan, "Akhlāq"; Aurangabadi, *Ma'āsir al-Umarā' [En]*, 1:240–41.

[108] Khan, "Akhlāq," fols. 20a–30b.

[109] Khan, "Akhlāq," 18a–b.

[110] On whom, see Dames, "K̲h̲wād̲ja K̲h̲iḍr."

who received it fell to counting their fortune (*daulat-shumārī*) and became insensible of their obligations to God. This sort of *daulat* was named "rejected" (*mardūd*). The recipients of "true" (*khalīlī*) *daulat* by God, however, kept it concealed and gave themselves up to His commandments.[111] In one sense, the author's ideas resemble the sufi claims to a separate and higher *daulat*, which were also expressed elsewhere in these years.[112] But the distinction here is between something like a transient financial wealth that leads one astray, and the secret divine approbation concealed by seemingly poor pious men. The struggle of princely contenders was surely for the former debased variety. Both, again, were far indeed from the visions of the courtly ideologues of the previous century who claimed absolute power for the king.

And so, as theorists theorized, panegyrists eulogized, courtiers fawned, and musicians performed, the empire's great nobility began to slip away, carving principalities out of provinces. There was no question now of fighting for power in Delhi and its central bureaucracy, since the experience of the Sayyids had shown that even the semblance of unitary authority could not transfer to any nobleman or clan without provoking powerful responses from other groups.[113] An enervated ideal of paramountcy would therefore continue to linger in the king's body, for, as Muzaffar Alam has argued, the devolution of power paradoxically required the revitalization of the "myth of Mughal imperial authority."[114] Yet the king's power was radically limited, literally manifesting in his immobility. Where Mughal rulers had once constantly toured their realms, Muhammad Shah (like Farrukh Siyar) was essentially confined to Delhi's environs.

But by tacitly ceding authority beyond Delhi's walls, Muhammad Shah regained a measure of control within them. In this he was aided by an administrative restructuring that reduced the power of the vizier. In pointed contrast to the overweening Sayyid ʿAbd Allah Khan, Muhammad Shah's new vizier Iʿtimad al-Daula claimed no administrative prerogative. Serving mostly as a fiscal manager in his capacity as the "Exalted Administrator" (*dīwān-i ʿālā*),

[111] Anonymous, "Mihakk al-Sulūk," fol. 497b.

[112] See, for instance, the casually expressed wish for the expansion of the "Daulat-i Muhammadī" in Shahjahanabadi Chishti, *Maktūbāt-i Kalīmī*, 98.

[113] In this context, Satish Chandra has offered the intriguing suggestion that Nizam al-Mulk's choice to not overthrow Muhammad Shah and instead depart for the Deccan was "to some extent influenced by the attitudes of the citizens of Delhi." Chandra, "Cultural and Political Role of Delhi, 1675–1725," 115. I have however been unable to locate the evidence for his claim, which is not included in his discussion of Nizam al-Mulk in Delhi. See Chandra, *Parties and Politics*, 212–13.

[114] Alam, *Crisis of Empire*, 55.

the vizier ceded many of his practical powers to the imperial paymaster (*mīr bakhshī*).[115] Doubtless occasioned by the very real fear of a coup prompted by the regicide of Farrukh Siyar, such administrative rebalancing permitted the king to forge a limited and less expansive rulership, one which still preserved a measure of freedom of action for himself.[116] And while Muhammad Shah overlooked a certain measure of intrigue at court, this autonomy permitted him to assert himself against presumptious courtiers at critical moments. In 1732, the king managed to overthrow a cabal including the mystic Shah ʿAbd al-Ghafur, the harem servant Koki Jiu, the palace eunuch Hafiz Khidmatgar Khan, and the powerful nobleman Raushan al-Daula.[117] The same year also occasioned the rise of Lutf Allah Khan, who, if we are to believe his son Shakir Khan, consolidated finances, revalued treasures, and greatly augmented the treasury at the king's command.[118] Yet Lutf Allah Khan's service could not save him from dismissal in the aftermath of Nadir Shah's invasion (for having too readily handed over control of the imperial princes to the conqueror).[119] But such events were rare in Muhammad Shah's era; for the most part, the king's reign was unmarked by the aristocratic strife that had bedeviled his predecessors.

Though much of the story outlined above is well known to historians, there was one other factor which shaped the dispensation of power in Muhammad Shah's reign: the people of the city of Delhi. For, in 1719, as Sayyid Husain ʿAli Khan arrived with a Deccani army to overthrow Farrukh Siyar, the fiercest resistance he encountered was not from the courtiers who were sworn to protect the king with their lives, but the humble folk of the imperial capital. As we shall see in coming pages, the people's action, though it failed to save Farrukh Siyar, nevertheless marked a novel intervention in the business of imperial politics. In this way, the tumult of 1719 did not only mark a violent struggle to rearrange the disposition of power between the king and his nobility. It also provoked a massive response from an unexpected quarter: the people of the city. Though elite observers were reluctant to ascribe such importance to lowly folk, Farrukh Siyar's removal catalyzed the emergence of the urban masses as political actors in the heart of the empire, and marked an important precedent for the uprising in 1739 against Nadir Shah.

[115] Malik, *The Reign of Muhammad Shah, 1717–1748*, 265.
[116] Malik, *The Reign of Muhammad Shah, 1717–1748*, 373–74.
[117] Malik, *The Reign of Muhammad Shah, 1717–1748*, 90–91.
[118] Khan, "Hadīqa," fols. 144a–146a.
[119] Aurangabadi, *Maʾāsir al-Umarāʾ [En]*, 2:840.

The King's Body

Central to the popular uprising in defense of Farrukh Siyar was the fate of his body. Because *daulat* was by nature embodied, the claim to its removal was publicly inscribed on the king's person, in 1712 and again in 1719. These violent assertions were deeply significant for the city's spectators, who were used to deciphering the workings of imperial power on bodies, such as the abject corpses of rebels routinely encountered in the city's police station or the gates of the fort.

The symbolism of such violence depended on the conception of the body as a heterogeneous ensemble. Honor, as a condition of sociality and political participation, was unequally distributed within the body from top to bottom. The head, as a site of identity, was most honorable, and the feet the least. Heads were adorned by turbans as repositories of honor, while the dishonor of feet was mitigated and enclosed by shoes. In matters of punishment, heads, faces, and genitals were regarded as inviolable by the classical jurists because they marked the individuality of the self.[120] This discursive constitution of the body coded the practice of the sovereign's rule and rendered it legible for his subjects; the disfigurement of the heads of opponents was, unsurprisingly, a hallmark of imperial power made evident in the towers of heads gathered from the bodies of rebels and opponents.[121]

The intensification of the struggle for the throne over the seventeenth century corresponded with an escalation of the violence done to the bodies of those who lost the battle for *daulat*. Where princes had been blinded in Jahangir's reign, they were killed in Shah Jahan's. Aurangzeb imprisoned his father, executed his brother Dara Shukoh, and publicly paraded his head and body in Delhi: an action, we will shortly see, that was met with popular outrage. Bahadur Shah slew his siblings in open battle. As a similarly legitimate victor of the next war of succession, Jahandar Shah renamed the battlefield "Victory of *Daulat* Field"; the corpses of his three defeated brothers, now decanted of their *daulat*, lay for three days for all to see on the river's sandy bank outside Lahore before being dispatched for burial in Delhi at their father's side.[122]

[120] See the introduction in Fierro and Lange, *Public Violence in Islamic Societies*.

[121] Asher, *Architecture of Mughal India*, 97–98; Minissale, *Images of Thought Visuality in Islamic India, 1550–1750*, 172–74.

[122] Anonymous, "Akhbārāt, Jahāndār Shāh," 31; Khan, *Tazkirat us-Salatin*, 154.

Those who welcomed Farrukh Siyar's accession represented Jahandar Shah's crimes as manifestations of his bodily inability to retain *daulat*, an incapacity represented by his abjection and senselessness in love with the courtesan Lal Kunwar. When Farrukh Siyar made his triumphant procession into Delhi, casting flowers of gold and silver into the assembled crowds, he was followed by an elephant on which a youth held aloft Jahandar Shah's head on a pike. The next elephant bore his body. The third elephant had Zu'l-Faqar Khan's corpse ("uncovered of head and foot") attached feet-first to its tail. Khwush Hal, in those days a young man, had just managed to catch one of the silver flowers ("weighing seven *māsha*-s")[123] thrown by the new king into the crowds when he saw Jahandar Shah's pitiable state. He observed how the people were not rendered joyous at this grisly spectacle. Instead everyone was reduced to "grief and astonishment." Left lying at the gate of the fort "in great abjection and humiliation" for some days, both bodies signaled the gaining of *daulat* by Farrukh Siyar.[124]

Farrukh Siyar's parade of Jahandar Shah's body evoked the memory of Aurangzeb's parade of Dara Shukoh on the same street half a century before. In doing so, Farrukh Siyar strove to shape the narrative of his enthronement not as a forceful coup against a legitimate ruler but as merely an iteration of the accepted and customary contest for *daulat* between members of the same family. The inversion of Zu'l-Faqar Khan's remains represented the reversal of his fortune and the subordination in death of this upstart nobleman to the majesty of Farrukh Siyar's *daulat*. But the parade of bodies marked not Farrukh Siyar's strength, but only the tenuousness of his claim to the throne.[125]

Accounts of Farrukh Siyar's dethronement likewise linger on his bodily humiliation to illustrate the extent of the violation of sovereignty it indicated. The king's health fared little better than that of the body politic over the course of his reign. He was frequently indisposed and absent from public view. In his third year, the king received surgical treatment from a doctor named William Hamilton who had accompanied an English embassy desperately petitioning

[123] Approximately 6.3 grams, therefore containing about half a rupee's worth of silver.

[124] Khwush Hal, "Nādir al-Zamānī [B]," fols. 61b–62a.

[125] In a letter to the Ottoman emperor in 1713, Farrukh Siyar claimed Jahandar Shah revolted after refusing the appointment of a provincial governorship; he was only defeated after Farrukh Siyar took the Delhi citadel by force. The wild variance of these statements from the facts provoked a response from a displeased Sublime Porte, which coolly ignored Farrukh Siyar's claims. Farooqi, *Mughal-Ottoman Relations*, 70–72.

for trading rights.[126] Khwush Hal's version of this story emphasizes the link between bodily and political efficacy: Farrukh Siyar's doctors had warned him that he would be rendered impotent by the surgical procedure. In the popular imagination, the Englishman's knife turned the king from a sexual agent into a passive receiver. By choosing life over potency, Farrukh Siyar was "defamed by elites and commoners alike," his impotence paralleling his political incapacity.[127]

The link between the king's body and the possession of *daulat* indicates why observers dwelt so greatly on the humiliations of Farrukh Siyar's body as he was removed from the throne. It also suggests why, despite the emergence of a variety of retroactive explanations for the overthrow of Farrukh Siyar, the desacralization of the king's power was a traumatic experience for those who witnessed it. Even his detractors acknowledged that the king's *daulat* was not seamlessly transferred to his successor. Lahori, by no means warmly inclined toward Farrukh Siyar, describes how the skies lurched, the very doors and walls cried out, and how *daulat* and pomp "shed blood" as the king was taken prisoner.[128] Mirza Muhammad emphasized Farrukh Siyar's valiant but doomed resistance, and lingered mournfully on the violation of the imperial person: in dragging him by the hand and collar, and in violently knocking off his turban, Farrukh Siyar's captors destroyed the centuries-old "rights of loyalty" established by their ancestors. "They handled a scion of the throne and the crown and a memorizer of the Qur'an," he lamented, "in the way that no infidel combatant (*kāfir-i harbī*) would ever be treated." He and others described how Farrukh Siyar's daughter was stripped of her jewels in the affray, and how the king was blinded and imprisoned. Mirza Muhammad was moved to invoke the line from the Qur'an which encapsulated the sentiment of *'ibrat*: "Learn a lesson, then, O you who are endowed with insight!"[129]

Mirza Muhammad made apparent this admonition in describing the fate of the king's body. His hands, which had once conveyed a sacral beneficence to the heads of orphans, were transgressively grasped by his captors. His garments, once given as "robes of honor" to individuals, were now rent. The

[126] Hamilton, lavished with gifts by the grateful emperor, himself died soon thereafter. His gravestone recorded that he cured the "KING of INDOSTAN" of a "malignant distemper" to the credit of the English at court. A copy of the text of the gravestone is preserved in Smith, *Physician and Friend*, 6.

[127] Khwush Hal, "Nādir al-Zamānī [B]," fol. 78b.

[128] Lahori, *'Ibratnāma*, 211.

[129] Khwush Hal, "Nādir al-Zamānī [B]," fol. 82b; Khan, *Tazkirat us-Salatin*, 261; Muhammad, "'Ibratnāma," fol. 223a–b.

falling of his turban signified the displacement of his autonomy and honor. The act of blinding, customarily performed on competitors by the winner of an imperial succession, now ensured that the king could not hold the throne again. All of these gestures marked the violation of what had once been an inviolate receptacle of *daulat*. As this description makes plain, the coup asserted that *daulat* was no longer the exclusive property of the king's body. Not only could a ruler be deprived of it, but *daulat* itself could be wrested away by persons other than those of "exalted lineage of Timur." If Jahandar Shah's death had opened a rupture in the discourse of Mughal sovereignty, the conceptual transformation of *daulat* marked by Farrukh Siyar's fate revealed its widest breach. By the Sayyids' assertion, it was no longer the nobility or rival princes who perished at moments of imperial succession but the king. The body which would next adorn the Peacock Throne, if it held *daulat* at all, did so only provisionally, and at the mercy of a nobility who now enjoyed a *daulat* of their own.

The Popular Intervention

Whether seen as an unprecedented act of disloyalty or a necessary amputation in the body politic, the officials, gentry, and literati who recorded the events of 1719 regarded them as an internal convulsion of elite politics. So it is with a sense of something akin to wonder that our chroniclers recorded, in passing, the discontentment of the urban mob at the sight of the king's abject corpse. Because such unrest was purely incidental to the proper subject of historical reflection (the doings of the king and his nobility), the people's actions, to say nothing of their sentiments or motivations, barely warranted comment. Whether due to a generic feature of historical writing or a pointed act of elision, the multitude, always aggregate, speak nothing on the rare occasions they appear in the backdrop of history. "The people, who are like cattle" (*ʿawāmm-i kālā-nʿām*), as the phrase went, were generally capable of uttering only animal sighs or bellows of pain or discontent. And although William Irvine recorded the activities of urbanites during the unrest of 1719, the historians who have followed him have generally excluded or minimized the acts of the city's fractious folk. But, by teasing out the traces of their presence from elite writings, we will see that the uprising of 1719 was in fact an act of popular assertion regarding the highest question of elite politics: who would sit on the Peacock Throne? By rising in defense of Farrukh Siyar,

Delhi's urbanites staged an unwelcome intervention against the reformulation of sovereignty being engineered by the empire's elites.

While the popular action of 1719 thus offered a precedent for the uprising against Nadir Shah in 1739, it was not the first time that the people had intervened in the workings of an imperial succession. Though evidence is tantalizingly slender, it appears that the city's people had already risen in 1659 to express their disapproval of the newly crowned Aurangzeb's treatment of his defeated rival, the prince Dara Shukoh. A stridently celebratory early-eighteenth-century chronicle of Aurangzeb's reign simply tells us that it was "necessary for various reasons" to kill Dara Shukoh.[130] But Aurangzeb's official chronicle, from which this bland description was derived, offers a rather more elaborate explanation. According to its author, it was decided that the defeated prince and his son would be publicly promenaded on the back of an elephant through Moonlight Avenue and Sa'd Allah Khan Square so that:

> the people, great and small, elites and commoners, might witness his fate without doubt or suspicion; and heedless chatterboxes (*zhāzh-khāyān*) and tumultuous provocateurs would not dare to utter falsehoods or bear false thoughts; and the mob would not have the excuse to cause sedition and strife in the borderlands.[131]

The fear, for the seventeenth-century chronicler, was not (yet) of the city's people, but of the threat of pretenders, as much a nuisance for new emperors as an object of hope for the fevered imaginations of those who entertained hopes of the empire's collapse (such as the Portuguese).[132] This was why it was necessary to publicly show that the *daulat* in Dara Shukoh and his branch was being pruned, though an impostor Dara appeared anyway and collected "a number of misguided desert-people" near Ahmadabad before his ultimate suppression there.[133]

But while Dara Shukoh was in prison, "an ember of tumult" arose from his mischievous person and sparked a fire in the city. The mob (*aubāshān*) and idlers (*harza-kārān*) of Delhi's alleys and markets coalesced in a popular multitude (*hujūm-i 'āmm*), and attacked the retinue of the minor landholder

[130] Khan, *Ma'asir-i 'Alamgiri [EN]*, 15–16.

[131] Kazim, *Álamgír námah*, 431.

[132] On Mughal pretenders, and their place in Portuguese plans, see Flores, " 'I Will Do as My Father Did' "; Flores and Subrahmanyam, "The Shadow Sultan."

[133] Syed, *Aurangzeb in Muntakhab-Al Lubab*, 212.

Malik Jiwan, who had arrived to receive his reward from Aurangzeb for betraying Dara Shukoh. The official history therefore claimed that Aurangzeb was *compelled* to execute his brother because the city was poised on the verge of a grand revolt (*fitūr-i ʿazīmī*). The history also invoked the king's adherence to religion and law and the exigencies of "*daulat* and leadership" as justification. Soon thereafter, a cavalryman named Haibat was identified as the leader of the uprising and put to death for "causing the ruin of Muslims."[134] While it was standard administrative practice to identify and punish "a leader," the unfortunate Haibat was not alone responsible for the uprising. The traveler Manuzzi recorded that in the days after, "the common people composed a song about Fortune and the little durability of its glories," which so offended Aurangzeb that he proclaimed no one was to sing it "under penalty of losing his tongue." That "almost everybody [nevertheless] sang it under concealment" only indicates Aurangzeb's tenuous hold on the urban populace, and his caution in punishing the satirist ʿAli decades later.[135]

In attacking Malik Jiwan, who had been granted the title of Bakhtyar ("the fortunate") Khan for turning in the "heretic" Dara Shukoh, and in singing satirical songs under their breaths, the denizens of Delhi made a political gesture. They indicated their disapproval of Aurangzeb, their preference for Dara Shukoh, and their indifference to the elite rhetoric which cast the defeated prince as a heretic and infidel. Who were the people who comprised the mob? Were they the long-time residents of the Old City, or some of the vast numbers who had already swarmed to the new city within a decade of its construction? It is difficult to say, but according to the eighteenth-century historian Khwafi Khan, the mob that attacked Malik Jiwan comprised "idlers, well-wishers of Dara Shukoh, all kinds of artisans . . . and sight-seers from every group." He particularly noted the role of the city's women, who hurled pots of urine and excrement from rooftops, injuring innocent bystanders and sullying the streets. And finally, after Dara Shukoh was beheaded for having "stepped beyond the circle of the law, brought ill-fame to spiritual practice, [and] become a heretic (*mulhid*) and an infidel (*kāfir*)," grieving spectators met his corpse as it was again paraded through the city on an elephant.[136] Whether Khwafi Khan, writing in the eighteenth century, relayed

[134] Kazim, *Álamgír námah*, 431–32, 434.

[135] Manucci, *Storia Do Mogor*, 1:362.

[136] Khwafi Khan, *Muntakhab al-lubāb*, 93–94; Syed, *Aurangzeb in Muntakhab-Al Lubab*, 139–41; on the relationship between the chronicles of Aurangzeb, see the exemplary study in Alvi, "The Historians of Awrangzeb: A Comparative Study of Three Primary Sources."

the recorded particulars of past insurgency, or whether he simply interpolated the Delhi crowd of his day onto the memory of a protest, by 1719 urban popular protest was not a novel phenomenon. A chronicler's stray claim that Zu'l-Faqar Khan toyed with the idea of employing the mob (*aubāsh-i bad maʿāsh*) to protect Jahandar Shah in Delhi after the defeat by Farrukh Siyar indicates that Mughal elites were not unaware of the possibilities of popular mobilization by this time.[137]

A View from the Ground Up

Despite their representation in the sources, the people who rose up to protect Farrukh Siyar were not a mindless mob. Although they may have acted spontaneously, they did so in a miasma of fear and anxiety which built up over many months before the deposition. While a lot of politicking was conducted in the private chambers of the mansions of the elite, the people composed an urban audience that observed every move and parsed every gesture. It is surely for their benefit as much as anyone else's that the first public flaring of tensions between the Sayyid ministers and their king in 1715 was contained by having Farrukh Siyar join the assembled nobility in Friday prayer at the congregational mosque, before the eyes of the assembled.[138]

The slow accumulation of tension among the people of the city can be gleaned from the journal of a minor nobleman named Iʿtimad ʿAli Khan, who was present in Delhi until the very eve of Farrukh Siyar's overthrow.[139] While the author's laconic jottings adhere to the scribal conventions of bureaucratic documents such as court news-reports, he fills them with rumor, gossip, and hearsay about the private words and deeds of the king and his nobility. His diary bears the traces of the network of unofficial information exchange in the city, and suggests how the convulsions of elite politics were popularly understood. If the vision of this nobleman may not be representative of the views of the urban masses, his diary nevertheless offers a general sense of the mounting fear of a coup against the king and the dislike for those who conspired against him.

137 Warid, "Mīrāt-i Wāridāt," fol. 144b.
138 Khwaja Khalil, "Tārīkh-i Shāhanshāhī," 59.
139 Khan, "Majmaʿ al-Fawāʾid/Masdar-i Akhbār."

The sense of a watchful urban populace that constantly discussed every occurrence is indicated by the hyperbole and anxiety that begin to appear in the diary six months before the coup. Thus the diarist related how, in September 1718, Sayyid ʿAbd Allah Khan refused to attend court. When, after hectic machinations, ʿAbd Allah Khan was persuaded to go to court, he laid his sword aside and asked the king to "kill his slave if he so desired": an exaggeration that doubtless reflects a popular understanding of reconciliation more than a factual record of statements made.[140] In November, when it became apparent that Sayyid Husain ʿAli Khan was holding a pretender prince in the Deccan, the diarist noted his dismay with a single terse Hindi idiom translated into Persian: "now we must see what form matters will assume."[141] After ʿAbd Allah Khan refused a visit from the king to condole him on the death of his wife, the diarist jotted down a line in the margin that perhaps captured the popular perception of this shocking rudeness: "I'm not a servant, to wait on you." The very next day, it became known that Husain ʿAli Khan was marching on Delhi with an army and the pretender prince, without the king's permission. "What will happen when he reaches Shahjahanabad?" wondered the diarist fearfully.[142] On December 26, the diarist noted how the distracted king sent a message to his upstart minister renouncing the empire, while claiming, "I have no work other than serving as the fort-commander of Shahjahanabad."[143] Then, on February 13, while at a friend's house just outside the city walls, Iʿtimad ʿAli Khan heard news that the king and his entourage were bombarded by a sudden hailstorm while out hunting, which shattered the limbs of men and beasts alike; the imperial cortege crawled back to the fort with the greatest trouble. So clear and unmistakable was the omen that no comment was necessary. Another chronicler simply noted: "A strange condition befell the king and his troops."[144]

The anxiety of the court and the city evident in these gossip-inflected records heightened to a fever pitch with the arrival of Husain ʿAli Khan's Deccani army, the ominous beating of its drums an insolent and public infringement of the royal perquisite. As the danger to the king became obvious, the diarist's sympathies for the ruler emerged sharply: from here on he begins to style the Sayyids "traitors." The diarist now departed the city, but

140 Khan, "Majmaʿ al-Fawāʾid/Masdar-i Akhbār," fol. 139a–b.
141 Khan, "Majmaʿ al-Fawāʾid/Masdar-i Akhbār," fol. 140a.
142 Khan, "Majmaʿ al-Fawāʾid/Masdar-i Akhbār," fol. 140b.
143 Khan, "Majmaʿ al-Fawāʾid/Masdar-i Akhbār," fol. 142a.
144 Khan, "Majmaʿ al-Fawāʾid/Masdar-i Akhbār," fol. 145b; Khan, *Tazkirat us-Salatin*, 254.

continued to record the news that reached him, as if in real time; on the 27th, he wrote that the Deccani army, which had been pillaging the surrounding countryside for the past few days, fell into "great turmoil" in Delhi. "A different course of events is coming into view," he wrote, before adding his devout wish: "May God the Victorious bring about well-being." But heaven wished otherwise: a long entry for the 28th recounts the news of the Sayyid "traitors" who violated the emperor's "sanctity," "knocked off his turban," and brought him "with hands fastened" before ʿAbd Allah Khan. Later that day, after Rafiʿ al-Shan had been seated on the throne, public proclamations were made to settle down the "tumult and strife" (*fitna o fasād*). Almost parenthetically, Iʿtimad ʿAli Khan noted that many Deccanis died in the unrest.[145]

Though he offers invaluable insight into the long-simmering tension in the city, Iʿtimad ʿAli Khan alluded only briefly to the "tumult and strife" in which Deccani soldiers lost their lives. Another sense of the disorder is preserved in the pious reminiscences of a minor nobleman named Kamgar Khan, who arrived in Delhi with the army led by Husain ʿAli Khan to overthrow Farrukh Siyar.[146] In a slim volume, Kamgar Khan recorded the discussions he attended over the course of several weeks at the Sufi hospice of Shaikh Kalim Allah, then the most eminent Sufi of the Chishti Way in the city. Kamgar Khan's account reveals that the Sufi gathering of the eighteenth century was just as much a site of political interchange as the salon, the coffeehouse, or the square. So he records how, a week before Farrukh Siyar's dethronement, conversation in the pious assembly was filled with criticism of the king, who was described as "negligent, foolish . . . [and] ignorant." Kalim Allah himself chimed in with a long anecdote about Aurangzeb's administrative acumen, in implicit but unfavorable contrast to that of the present king.[147] Two days later, all talk was on the "revolution of the era and the transience of the visible world"; Kalim Allah took the opportunity to mention how only Sufi acolytes understood the subtleties of transience and permanence, while the common people were "negligent and foolish."[148]

But if this were a criticism of the common folk, who opposed the "realities of worldly transience" implied by the king's dethronement, opinions shifted in the days that followed. At first, there was some confusion about which prince had ascended to the throne. After leading prayers for "the tranquility

[145] Khan, "Majmaʿ al-Fawāʾid/Masdar-i Akhbār," fols. 147b–48a.
[146] Kamgar, *Majālis-i Kalīmī*.
[147] Kamgar, *Majālis-i Kalīmī*, 25–29.
[148] Kamgar, *Majālis-i Kalīmī*, 29.

of the people and the independence of the ruler," Kalim Allah declared that although a mass uprising (*balwāʾī-yi ʿāmm*) appeared to be underway, it would lead to the common people (*ʿawāmm al-nās*) defeating the enemy; in other words, the common people were now seen as the object by which the hated foreigners from the Deccan would be humbled.[149] At another gathering some days later, when the coup had been accomplished, attendees remarked on how the common people routed the "infidel army" (*fauj-i kuffār*), whose dead lay in heaps around the city. While some criticized the Sayyids for their lack of "loyalty and humanity," others related tales about the reconciliation between the Sayyids and the new king, who had foreseen his elevation to the throne in a prophetic dream six months previously.[150]

As the accounts of Iʿtimad ʿAli Khan and Kamgar Khan reveal, for the city's elites, "the common people" appear as a scourge of nature, as impersonally administered by heaven as a hailstorm or a plague; while they defeat the hated outsiders, the people's own motivations are irrelevant. Yet it was not the case that Delhi's lowly denizens were without aspiration. Ordinary people have left us no record of what compelled them to take on the Deccani soldiers who entered their city to overthrow their king. Luckily for us, the people's actions, as ever, spoke louder than words. We must therefore reconstruct the popular action and the intentions that drove it from the stray references of observers who only permitted the crowds to appear in their accounts when it served their narrative purposes. But before that, we must first distinguish between mass and elite reactions to the coup of March 1, 1719.

The Popular Uprising

Despite widely diverging perspectives on who was to blame for the coup, most chroniclers agree that only a small group of noblemen, led by Ghazi al-Din Khan and Sadat Khan, rode out to resist the Sayyids on that fateful day.[151] Sadat Khan rode down the Moonlight Avenue toward the fort, but

149 Kamgar, *Majālis-i Kalīmī*, 30.
150 Kamgar, *Majālis-i Kalīmī*, 33–34.
151 There is no agreement in the sources about who besides these two fought against the coup. For instance, the chroniclers variously suggest that Muhammad Amin Khan, the most important of the noblemen of the Mughal ethne, encouraged the coup: Kam Raj, "ʿIbratnāma," fol. 66a; that he was proceeding with his force on the summons of the Sayyids when his retainers clashed with

was struck by a bullet near the police station and forced to fall back. One of his sons was killed; another was captured by the Sayyids but treated with kindness and released. Ghazi al-Din Khan proceeded in a more disciplined fashion. Though he was noted as fighting with the utmost bravery while mounted on his elephant, his personal contingent was outnumbered by the Deccani Army and so forced to retreat.[152]

The resistance of these noblemen was driven more by personal concerns than by any principles of loyalty. For one, Sadat Khan's daughter was married to Farrukh Siyar. Similarly, Ghazi al-Din Khan was a foster brother of Jahandar Shah who had defected to Farrukh Siyar. Because of his fervent loyalty, the king had given him command of the all-important imperial artillery *(top-khāna)* six months before his execution.[153] But after Farrukh Siyar's death, both Sadat Khan's son and Ghazi al-Din Khan put aside their disgust to join the Sayyids. When the Sayyids were in turn defeated, both noblemen deftly maneuvered to prime perches in Muhammad Shah's court.[154] In this way, both defenders of Farrukh Siyar in fact exhibited a moral flexibility characteristic of the eighteenth-century nobility.

The people had a very different understanding of the king's place. The palpable tension in I'timad 'Ali Khan's account was, by the eve of the coup, widespread throughout Delhi. Even "empty-brained fools," says the chronicler Aurangabadi, understood the implications of the arrival of the Deccani army better than the king's advisors, who "stuffed their ears with cotton" and wasted their days swapping "witticisms."[155] In fact, he says, the collectivity of the people *(jamī'-yi khalq-i Allāh)* were loudly proclaiming:

> What is coming to befall the ruler? Even we, who are of imperfect understanding, can nevertheless distinguish between good acts and bad. Given all this strength and the crowd of exalted advisors, why is the long veil of error (*jilbāb-i ghaflat*) pulled over the rose-colored face?[156]

the Marathas on the street: Mirza Muhammad, "'Ibratnāma," fol. 220b; Or that he urged Qamar al-Din Khan and Zakarya Khan, the two scions of the Mughal ethne, to remain aloof from the fighting: Lahori, *'Ibratnāma*, 211–12.

---

152 Muhammad, "'Ibratnāma," fol. 221a–b; Lahori, *'Ibratnāma*, 213–14.
153 Muhammad, "'Ibratnāma," fol. 197a.
154 Aurangabadi, *Ma'āsir al-Umarā' [En]*, 2:652–54; 1070–72.
155 Aurangabadi, "Ahwāl al-Khawāqīn," fols. 139b, 141a.
156 Aurangabadi, "Ahwāl al-Khawāqīn," fol. 141a.

The arrival of the Deccanis produced immediate conflict with the residents of the city.[157] By the night of February 28, when news ceased to flow from the fort and it became obvious that a coup was underway, "heart-rending cries" began to rise up from the city's people (*jamhūr-anām*).[158] "No creature touched bread or water, and no man lay to rest in his bed," wrote Kamwar, "and all living things spent the night in a state of hope and fear." We can only imagine the conversations that animated the city's squares and alleys during the night, but by dawn there were people dispersed throughout the sandy riverbank near the fort. These were not the city's noblemen with their armed retainers, who largely did not bestir themselves from their mansions, but "commoners and urbanites and people of the markets," who had arrived to protect the king "by whose favors they were fostered."[159]

Though their importance was understated in the chronicles, it is evident that three distinct categories of the city's lowly folk were involved in attacking the Deccanis: soldiers, artisans and shopkeepers, and the urban poor. The violence was seen to originate in an inadvertent clash between the military contingents that were massing in the city. According to Mirza Muhammad, Muhammad Amin Khan's Turani Mughal troops, requested by the Sayyids, encountered a mass of "infidel" Deccanis as they marched down Moonlight Avenue toward the fort and roughly pushed them aside. The Deccanis, whom our author contemptuously describes as "accursed ones, long accustomed to tasting blows from Mughal fists," turned to flight. It is after this initial clash, says Aurangabadi, that "the people of the streets" began to rain down stones on the Deccanis. They were joined by "the people of the shops," and a group which Aurangabadi names the "free-spirited" (*lawand-mashribān*): those driven "by the desire to seek fights without reason," who "in fact will give their lives at a single call of 'Hu!'," and who were "incredibly pleased" by the disorder.[160] The Deccanis wilted under the combined onslaught of masses (*hujūm-i ʿāmm*) of the city's artisans and malcontents who made their "loathing" perfectly clear.[161]

157 Lakhnavi, *Shāhnāma*, 40.

158 Aurangabadi, "Ahwāl al-Khawāqīn," fol. 143b.

159 Khan, *Tazkirat us-Salatin*, 259.

160 Aurangabadi, "Ahwāl al-Khawāqīn," fol. 144a–b; the term denotes someone who is "an adventurer; without a fixed residence; a libertine who fears not God nor regards man . . . a frequenter of taverns and stews; a prostitute, a strumpet . . . a servant or labourer; a naughty boy." Steingass, Johnson, and Richardson, *A Comprehensive Persian-English Dictionary*, 1133.

161 Lahori, *ʿIbratnāma*, 211–12.

While some downplayed the people's role and attributed the Deccani rout to the "unseen world" (*ʿālam-i gha'ib*), the chroniclers' joy in the popular violence against the Deccanis reveals not only its unsparing intensity, but also the animosity of Delhi's Mughals toward those perceived as outsiders.[162] One writes how "idle spectators and unemployed Mughals" dishonored the Deccanis by "stealing turban from head, and head from body"; even butchers, fullers of cloth (*gāzurān*), and sweepers, he goes on, liberated the Deccanis of their marks of honor (particularly their much-prized parasols) with swords or sticks or even just by curses and reproachful glares.[163] Mirza Muhammad likewise noted the ease with which the Deccanis were made to relinquish their horses and large lances by the riffraff of the streets (*luccha wa shuhda-hā*). Eventually, he claimed, even the victualer-women of the Mughalpura suburb grabbed their horses' bridles, each knocking down five or ten of these lancers with brickbats and staffs before stripping and killing them.[164] Kam Raj, otherwise a fervid partisan of the Sayyids, likewise reveled in the plight of the "infidel" (*kuffār*) Deccanis, describing how their calls for mercy in their alien dialect ("nakko, nakko") went unheeded. Many found particular pleasure in how the vanquished foes signaled their submission by placing pieces of hay in their mouths and crawling on all fours like cattle.[165] Such abject gestures did not arouse the people's compassion. The Deccanis, gloated observers, "scurried like mice into every street and doorway" but were "killed like dogs and cats" or had "their filthy heads crushed like those of snakes."[166] Even innocent dark-skinned people of other communities, mistaken for Deccanis, were killed in the affray.[167] Deccani corpses were to be encountered for miles around the city; Mirza Muhammad contentedly estimated that "more than three or four thousand infidels were dispatched to hell."[168]

The pleasure in such representations of the Deccani army's abjection doubtless marked the fear and insecurity of an imperial elite who regarded a frontier enemy that, far from being subjugated, was growing in strength every day. For one, the Deccanis' rout was an act of God, because otherwise their

[162] Khan, "Tazkīrāt al-Mulūk," fol. 125a.
[163] Khwafi Khan, *The Muntakhab Al-Lubáb [Fa]*, 3:810–11.
[164] Muhammad, "ʿIbratnāma," fols. 220b–221a.
[165] Aurangabadi, "Ahwāl al-Khawāqīn," 144a; Khan, "Tazkīrāt al-Mulūk," fol. 125a; Kam Raj, "ʿIbratnāma," fol. 67a.
[166] Muhammad, "ʿIbratnāma," fols. 220b–21a; Aurangabadi, "Ahwāl al-Khawāqīn," fol. 144a.
[167] Khwafi Khan, *The Muntakhab Al-Lubáb [Fa]*, 3:810–11.
[168] Muhammad, "ʿIbratnāma," fol. 221a.

children might have boasted that "we went to the imperial capital of Delhi, and it was by the help and the forearms of the Marathas that the emperor of India was imprisoned, and we appointed another one in his place!"[169] In such visions, the people of the city played no greater a role than that of serving as the means of a hated enemy's defeat: the more menial the people, the greater the dishonor inflicted.

But the city's butchers and fullers, sweepers and vegetable-sellers did not attack the Deccanis because they wished to render them unclean or because they were agents of the unseen. Their desire, above all, was to protect the king from his rebellious nobility. Again, as in the case of the uprising that would break out against Nadir Shah two decades later, rumors offer us the best insight into their motivations. It was said, for instance, that ʿAbd Allah Khan had been assassinated in the fort.[170] Others claimed that that Nizam al-Mulk was coming with his army to free the king. Such news increased the consternation of the Deccanis and heartened the nobility who "favored the king's *daulat*."[171] The unrest and rumors did not cease even after news of Farrukh Siyar's dethronement spread through the city: Delhi fell into a "severe mourning," and the "strange tumult and rare disorder" went on through the night.[172] It was only the loud playing of the ceremonial music which marked the ascension of a new king, and his subsequent appearance at the window of presentation, that would have reassured the people that the dynasty had not ended, and curbed the fighting in the streets.[173]

Even after the new king was firmly established, stories of Farrukh Siyar continued to circulate through the city for the three weeks he lived in confinement. On March 27, 1719, Iʿtimad Ali Khan noted how Farrukh Siyar was refused his demand for a little butter to accompany his meager daily portion of rice and lentils, prisoners being given no better than this. The diarist was by now in a familiar state of philosophical resignation: Farrukh Siyar was only receiving the recompense of his own harsh actions, and the disloyal Sayyids would get theirs.[174] Another recalled that the prisoner's poor diet caused him diarrhea, but he was not given water to clean himself.[175] In the same vein it was alleged that the Sayyids had helped themselves to

[169] Khwafi Khan, *The Muntakhab Al-Lubáb [Fa]*, 3:811.
[170] Warid, "Mīrāt-i Wāridāt," fol. 157b.
[171] Khan, *Tazkirat us-Salatin*, 260.
[172] Lahori, *ʿIbratnāma*, 214.
[173] Khwafi Khan, *The Muntakhab Al-Lubáb [Fa]*, 3:813.
[174] Khan, "Majmaʿ al-Fawāʾid/Masdar-i Akhbār," fol. 150b.
[175] Warid, "Mīrāt-i Wāridāt," fol. 159a.

the imperial treasury, and, even more damningly, taken "seventy or eighty" women from the king's harem for their own pleasure.[176]

The circulation of stories of the king's humiliation, whether true or false, fueled continuing unrest in the city. Some of these tales were doubtless recited by performers on the streets. The verses with which one author ends a poem detailing the events of Farrukh Siyar's capture and blinding (and the "incidental" death of some Deccanis) suggest this recitative context:

> These few lines are a kind of guide for every listener
> So that by hearing them there's admonition (*ʿibrat*) and wonder and also the tale.[177]

Such sentiments illuminate the context for the chronicler Lahori's comments on Delhi's "event-seekers" (*waqiʿa-talbān*) who sat about with their heads on their knees, scraping "the phantom poppy of news of the situation," their tongues wagging fearlessly in "fanciful chatter and streetcorner narration." At least some lived in the hope that "this or that army" would come to free him. Others believed that the Sayyids had become ashamed of their actions and, after restoring the king, would return to Barha as mendicants or perhaps depart for the pilgrimage to Arabia.[178]

Such mutterings surely influenced the Sayyids' decision to execute Farrukh Siyar. The chronicler Lahori justified his killing by sententiously claiming that, since the laws of imperial administration were a refraction of God's law in nature, "the plurality of rule, or even the name of such equivalence (*shirk*)," was impermissible. He also added that the Sayyids sought "rash and incautious" legists, such as those employed by Aurangzeb against his brother, to give legal sanction for their treatment of Farrukh Siyar.[179] Both the fact that none were apparently forthcoming, and the gap of several weeks between Farrukh Siyar's blinding (which made him incapable of rule) and his killing (which made it impossible) indicate that the fear of continuing popular disapproval may have been a factor in the Sayyids' actions. Indeed, some claimed that Farrukh Siyar's mutilated body was thrown on a coarse

176 Khwafi Khan, *The Muntakhab Al-Lubáb [Fa]*, 3:821.
177 Anonymous, "Mihakk al-Sulūk," fol. 655a.
178 Lahori, *ʿIbratnāma*, 218–19.
179 Lahori, *ʿIbratnāma*, 219.

mat outside the entryway to the Public Council precisely so that the city's "event-seekers" might regard it with the "eye of admonishment" (*ʿibrat*).[180]

But instead of casting the people into philosophical quietude, this spectacle only sharpened their resistance. A prime site of protest was the king's bier. Given his royal stature, Farrukh Siyar's funeral cortege on April 2 was accompanied by imperial eunuchs and minor officials. "But because the good qualities of that innocent emperor . . . remained in the people's memory," writes Lahori, "a world" of people also joined in the funeral procession. The sober-minded Kamwar Khan estimated that no less than 15,000 people of the imperial market assembled at the Akbarabadi mosque when Farrukh Siyar's bier was brought there. Not only did "the doorways and walls of the capital redound with the sounds of weeping and wailing," said Kamwar, "but men and women, great and small, young and old . . . cursed the tyrannical." The depth of their mourning lent the packed procession a distinctly "tumultuous" aspect. Women wailed loudly from the rooftops, and poured down a hail of brickbats on the servants of the Sayyids. Likewise "uncountable numbers of mendicants," uttered words of abuse against "their enemies" and flung stones at the accompanying noblemen's palanquins.[181]

The common people's mourning incorporated pointedly political gestures of criticism against the implications of the Sayyids' coup. The poor refused to accept the customary offerings of bread and pudding (*nān o halwā*) or small money (*pūl-i siyāh*) from the nobility who had been tasked with distributing them. Instead, the city's lowly folk enacted their own theater of funerary ritual. Albeit some decades later, Khwush Hal recalled that, since the king was inordinately fond of cloth trimmed with gold and embroidered silk and lace (*zarī, kinārī*), Delhi's drapers forced their way into the fort on the third day after his death. Despite great efforts to prevent them, they insisted on praying at the three-arched gateway, beneath the room in which Farrukh Siyar had been killed.[182] Others said that the "beggarly riff-raff" assembled at the platform where the king's body had been readied for burial, where they prepared and distributed among themselves the funeral repast for the ceremonies of the third day. The poor even held a day-long wake which, again,

[180] Khan, "Majmaʿ al-Fawāʾid/Masdar-i Akhbār," fol. 150b; Lahori, *ʿIbratnāma*, 219–20. Another chronicler however denies reports of Farrukh Siyar being stabbed. Khwafi Khan, *The Muntakhab Al-Lubáb [Fa]*, 3:820.

[181] Lahori, *ʿIbratnāma*, 220; Khwafi Khan, *The Muntakhab Al-Lubáb [Fa]*, 3:820; Khan, *Tazkirat us-Salatin*, 270–71.

[182] Khwush Hal, "Nādir al-Zamānī [B]," fol. 84a.

involved the public recitation of poetic laments (*majlis-i maulūd*). Such gestures served as public reproof of the Sayyids' regime as tyrannical and unjust. In gathering and performing symbolic acts at sites associated with the king's dead body, the people did not merely express a personal attachment to the martyred ruler but also re-asserted the direct compact between king and populace, so rejecting the Sayyid attempt to reshape the terms of Mughal kingship.[183]

Nor did the city's poor stop at these gestures. According to Lahori, the "wandering poor" (*ibn al-sabīl*) not only ceased to approach and beg at the palanquins of the city's elites, but began to actively confront their betters. Whenever the masses (*mardum-i ahad al-nās*) saw a person of rank in the city's marketplace or at the gate of the fort, they fearlessly and loudly uttered calumnies, without care for the consequences. Something of their background can be discerned from the fact that the most vocal protesters were "young Kashmiri spoon-sellers" and "itinerant peddlers." It is possible that the city's Kashmiri population may have felt particularly affronted because the king's mother herself hailed from that province. The particular object of their ire was Raja Ajit Singh, whose daughter had been married to Farrukh Siyar with great pomp in Delhi only a few years before. As the Raja's procession marched to and from the fort, they were met with ugly curses, taunts and reproaches: the city's *luccha*-s cried out, "do you want revenge (*khūn-bahā'ī*) for your son-in-law, or dishonor (*rū-siyāhī*)"? With chilling casualness, Lahori tells us that Ajit Singh's Rajput troops were ordered to cut down a few insolent people at the head of his procession, but the unrest nevertheless continued. The city's administration resorted to the classic gesture of public humiliation to warn the refractory: "some Kashmiris were arrested for this error and . . . processed on donkeys." It is claimed that they were put to death for the crime of "speaking too freely" and that their bodies were put on degrading display. But even as their procession wended its way through the city's streets, among the hubbub and clamor of the drums, Kashmiri children could be heard crying in unison "this is the very punishment for malevolent bastards!" The object of the phrase was ambiguous, but the people knew exactly to whom it referred.[184]

[183] Lahori, *'Ibratnāma*, 221; Lakhnavi, *Shāhnāma*, 53; Khwafi Khan, *The Muntakhab Al-Lubáb [Fa]*, 3:820.

[184] Khwafi Khan, *The Muntakhab Al-Lubáb [Fa]*, 3:823; Lahori, *'Ibratnāma*, 221.

Conclusion

Even decades later, a commentator recalled vividly the lacerating partisanship that ensued after the execution of Farrukh Siyar, which he likened to the proverbial antagonism between the Shiʿi sects of the Haidaris and Niʿmat Allahis.[185] The polarization it produced is captured in the two famous chronograms of Farrukh Siyar's death which were said to have circulated in the city after his death.[186] The first ran:

> Did you see what they did to that weighty king?
> They erred in inflicting a hundred tortures on him
> When I sought the date from Wisdom, it replied:
> "The Sayyids were disloyal to him."[187]

Though some said the lines were uttered by the great poet Bedil, the minor poet Mir ʿAzmat Allah Bilgrami "Bikhabar," who was moved to pen a rejoinder, simply attributed them to "an acquaintance" (*ʿazīzī*) unaware of the situation's "true reality" (*ʿasl-i haqīqat*).[188] Bikhabar's response recoursed to the same medical language of healing the body politic that others had used in justifying the king's removal in the same form as the earlier chronogram:

> They did what was right for a mad king
> They simply did whatever the Doctor commanded
> One wise as Hippocrates wrote the date's prescription:
> "The Sayyids gave him the necessary dose."[189]

Chronograms such as this marked the broadening of a politically aware audience in the city. Once inscribed on the doorways of the gardens and mansions and other tangible achievements of the great, such circulating poems now etched opinions among a wider urban populace, in which formal literacy was not required as a condition of political participation. We cannot say whether Delhi's itinerant spoon-sellers and vagabonds sang out these verses at the processions of the Sayyid nobility in the city after Farrukh Siyar's death; but

185 Aurangabadi, *Maʾāsir al-Umarāʾ [En]*, 1:712.
186 Aurangabadi, *Maʾāsir al-Umarāʾ [En]*, 1:712–13; Irvine and Sarkar, *Later Mughals*, I:395.
187 Bilgrami, "Safīna-yi Bīkhabar," 53–54.
188 No such chronogram appears to be recorded in Bedil's collected works.
189 Bilgrami, "Safīna-yi Bīkhabar," 53–54.

the established forms through which poetry circulated through the city's streets was crucial to shaping, clarifying, and expressing their sentiments.

In the political wrangling after the assassination of the Sayyid minister Husain ʿAli Khan, a courtly writer warned the high nobleman Burhan al-Mulk from daring to support the Sayyids with the admonition that "when the favor (*iqbāl*) of kings and princes is lifted [from a person], it is an ancient custom (*rasm-i qadīm*) that loyalists and the collectivity of residents (*jumhūr-i sakana*) combine to prevent their entry into the fort."[190] By draping the garment of ancient legitimacy on a most recent development, the author acknowledged the importance of the people's action. In picking up stones to hurl at the Maratha army, in conducting their own funeral ceremonies for the "martyred king," in disdaining the charity of noblemen, and in jeering them in the streets, Delhi's urbanites rose up in defense of the ideal of sovereignty that had ordered their world. Through all these little actions the city's people asserted themselves against the centuries of tradition, the wordy proclamations and the fat tomes that all demanded their silent obedience. Though it would not be the last regicide of a ruling Mughal monarch, Farrukh Siyar's overthrow was an exceptional event. More generally, however, the people only became more contestatory in their everyday relations with authority in the years after Farrukh Siyar's discolored corpse rendered all kingly claims to divinely granted *daulat* hollow. How the city's people forged a language by which to make themselves heard by their rulers is the question to which we must now turn.

[190] Rasa, "Bayāz-i Īzid Bakhsh 'Rasa,'" fol. 4b.

6

Islam as a Language of Popular Politics

The popular uprising in support of Farrukh Siyar in 1719 marked an extraordinary moment in the history of the empire. Delhi's denizens would not have cause to mobilize in defense of their king again for two decades, until Nadir Shah's occupation of the city in 1739. Such interventions were animated by the fear that the entire political order, from which the virtue of justice derived, was in danger of collapse. But these exceptional moments of mass mobilization are only the visible peaks of an evolving everyday practice of politics. The uprising of 1719 sharply inflected a trajectory of popular assertiveness that had been steadily growing in capacity since the late seventeenth century. Such an everyday practice of popular politics became particularly plain after the regicide of Farrukh Siyar in 1719.

To make this case, this chapter offers a new interpretation of a series of disorderly gatherings, rioting, and urban warfare—some well-known, others less so—from the late seventeenth to the mid eighteenth century, which have generally been understood as "economic" disturbances or outbreaks of "religious" violence. Unveiling the political significance of such events will require us to question these categories and distinctions, which reflect our contemporary experience more than historical realities.[1] Economistic explanations for precolonial social violence, for instance, serve to preempt accounts that might instead emphasize the determinative role of religion. Thus the pioneering scholar of religion Wilfred Cantwell Smith argued in a seminal essay that the rebellions that disordered the empire (all rural), were in every case instances of class struggle, albeit "fought with religious ideologies."[2] In this context, Christopher Bayly's seemingly mild suggestion that "the widespread Hindu-Muslim symbiosis of the pre-colonial and early colonial periods did not totally exclude the possibility of riot and disturbance along communal lines" was received with a measure of outrage by his peers.[3]

[1] For a similar critique of explanations of such violence in the modern period see Brass, *Production of Hindu-Muslim Violence*, chap. 1.

[2] Smith, "Lower-Class Uprisings in the Mughal Empire," 328.

[3] Bayly, "The Pre-History of 'Communalism'?," 180; Bayly's application of the term communalism to such riots has been critiqued by Gyanendra Pandey, who sees it as a modern and specifically

The King and The People. Abhishek Kaicker, Oxford University Press (2020). © Oxford University Press.
DOI: 10.1093/oso/9780190070670.001.0001

While the most reasoned critiques of Bayly have come from scholars of modern South Asia, the response of historians of the premodern period has generally been to place redoubled emphasis on precolonial India's much-vaunted "composite culture."[4] Thus, Muhammad Umar, while allowing the use of the term "communalism" in reference to the precolonial period, is nevertheless at pains to insist that the "dimension and scale" of Hindu-Muslim conflict was small and localized. "The two communities had long learned to live together," writes Umar, "and this mutual tolerance was easily reflected in their mode of life, customs and festivals."[5] In another vein, S. A. A. Rizvi simply declares urban conflicts under the rubric of "Hindu-Muslim riots" as communal and sectarian in nature.[6] Whether they ascribe acts of violence to economic tensions or regard them as outbreaks of blind religious passion, such analyses are predicated on reified notions of "Hindu" and "Muslim" as describing preexisting, distinct, uniform, permanent, and changeless communities.[7] By contrast, a growing body of scholarship has demonstrated the intermingled, co-constituted, and contingent development of identities of faith in South Asia in the premodern period.[8]

Perhaps the most sophisticated explanation of premodern urban violence yet has been offered by Farhat Hasan. In considering a 1644 riot in Surat, Hasan sees it as a case of "lower-class defiance against local power holders and the state." He regards events such as these as "religious conflicts," emphasizing the importance of economic status of participants, while cautioning against reducing them to "class context." Hasan rightly suggests such

colonial discourse of knowledge. Pandey, *Construction of Communalism*, 15–17. Yet, as David Lorenzen points out, the inapplicability of the term does not negate Bayly's observations regarding the incidences of "religious" conflict in the eighteenth century. Lorenzen, *Bhakti Religion in North India*, 5–6; see also the remarks in Subrahmanyam, "Before the Leviathan."

[4] See, for instance, the impassioned pleas in Malik, "The Core and the Periphery," 21–26; Jha, "Against Communalising History." Such positions are however already critiqued in Kumar, "Left Secularists and Communalism"; see also Subrahmanyam, "Violence, Grievance and Memory in Early Modern South Asia," 81–83. An excellent critique of the category of communalism in describing South Asian Muslim political thought is Jalal, "Exploding Communalism: The Politics of Muslim Identity in South Asia."

[5] Umar, *Islam in Northern India*, 394, 395.

[6] Rizvi, *Shah Wali-Allah and His Times*, 197–202.

[7] Cf. Umar, *Islam in Northern India*, 370–71; similarly reified notions of community are however to be encountered in scholarship that searches for inter-religious conflict: Kruijtzer, *Xenophobia in Seventeenth-Century India*. Scholars of the precolonial period have not yet engaged with the more sophisticated notions of community deployed by historians of modern South Asia. See Freitag, *Culture and Power in Banaras*; Prior, "Making History."

[8] To mention only some highlights of this vast literature, see Digby, "Encounters with Jogis in Sufi Hagiography"; Talbot, "Inscribing the Other, Inscribing the Self"; Stewart, "In Search of Equivalence"; Ernst, "Muslim Studies of Hinduism?"; Flood, *Objects of Translation*.

conflicts (specifically over "religious places") were "political in nature, a part of the wider political process of identity formation."[9] Yet his assessment still raises the question of how to conceive of the relationship between "religion" and "politics" in such instances, particularly because the categories were not demarcated in these ways for either the rioters or those who governed them. Indeed, those who witnessed or joined in the many riots and tumults, large and small, of the eighteenth century, would not have recognized explanations of either "fixed" religious oppositions or "underlying" economic causes.

My own claim in this regard is that neither explanation suffices to account for the disorders under consideration in this chapter. While the economic status of participants may have patterned persistent antagonisms, they do not explain the structure, intensity, and symbolism of popular violence. Similarly, it is true that sectarian affiliation and sentiment animated and shaped the everyday urban disorders that we shall examine. But the general absence of theological or doctrinal wrangling, the frequent lack of discernible leadership, and the fact that violence was precisely targeted against particular offenders and agents of state, and not the "other community" at large, all suggest that such disorders cannot be described as the "communal violence" that would become a staple of Indian life in later centuries.

Accordingly, this chapter argues that only by dispensing with both blind religious passions and simple economic resentment as determinative categories, can we begin to recognize the political nature and significance of everyday urban disorders of the period. In doing so, we begin to see how ordinary people appropriated the discourse of sovereignty for their own ends. This they did by using the gestures and practices of faith to evoke community, build solidarities, and pressure imperial authority into action over local struggles. Specifically, by casting their actions as demands for "justice" in the face of "oppression," or as the "defense of Islam" against overweening "infidels," as well as by loaded gestures in symbolic sites such as the mosque, urbanites invoked the theoretical privileges of the 'Community of Muslims' to force the king and his agents to act according to the terms of the imperial discourse of sovereignty. And when agents of state inevitably resisted such mobilization from below, the agitating people took it upon themselves to challenge the very right of the king to rule. In such ways, ordinary people fashioned the gestures and practices of Islam into a language of popular politics.

[9] Hasan, *State and Locality*, 66–67.

This argument requires some specification. I use the term "language" here to not only indicate the vocabulary employed in written texts, but the repertoire of words and actions useful in making, sharing, and contesting meaning regarding the distribution of power in the city. Although it may be that Islam took this role because, in the words of Joachim Matthes, its "*Sitz im Leben* is more pronounced in everyday life, in the social and cultural bonds which connect people, in their ways of communicating with one another," there was nothing timeless or unhistorical about this process, which was given direction and impetus by Aurangzeb. Already in his lifetime and increasingly thereafter, the ideal of the 'Community of Muslims' that was given a privileged status in his discourse of sovereignty would be most enthusiastically appropriated, and its rights most forcefully asserted, by precisely those lowly individuals and groups who had few other privileges to claim.

It is not my contention, however, that Islam served as the only possible language of politics in the empire. Indeed, the traditions that constituted the broad category of "Hindu" were equally robustly capable of generating political meaning and were interjoined in key sites and symbols with the political language of Islam.[10] Nor, again, do I imply that the 'Community of Muslims' convened in the imagination of Aurangzeb and his jurists represented anything like reified social reality. As the next chapter will demonstrate in depth, its coagulation in the matrix of the social was at best episodic, and occurred primarily in demands for "justice," which reflected not the considered opinions of imperial jurisprudents, but popular perceptions of what was right and true.

In this vein, the following pages examine a range of conflicts that played out in the streets and bazars of imperial cities from the late seventeenth century onwards. This chapter begins by exploring the elite use of the language of Islam and shows how it increasingly became a tool for non-elites in local conflicts within the city. Visions of righteous Muslims marching for justice or to protect the faith were only appealing to chroniclers when the community arose at the call of their betters. But, in our period, members of the 'Community of Muslims' seemed ever more often to break off from the script assigned to them, and to turn against their own rightly appointed leaders, as in the case of the famous Holi riot of 1714. Events such as this proved that the 'Community of Muslims' could now challenge the powers that be, and even the Shadow of God himself.

[10] See, for instance, the essays in Lorenzen, *Bhakti Religion in North India*.

The second part of this chapter offers a close study of the making of the key political microtechnique that in the language of Islam symbolized a direct challenge to the ruler: the interruption of the Friday sermon (*khutba*) by its audience. Such interruptions were first occasioned in 1711 by an alteration in the sermon by the emperor Bahadur Shah (r. 1707–1712) which was remembered by Mughal chroniclers to hold pro-Shiʿi implications. While chroniclers recalled opposition to this innovation as spearheaded by a righteous community of theologians, the court records of the reign suggest that the confrontation of the people of Lahore forced the king to retreat. This resistance, moreover, was not so much occasioned by sectarian sentiment as a sense of popular opposition to any change in the enunciation of sovereignty represented by the sermon. This was why the theological origins of the gesture became quickly forgotten, and interruptions of the Friday sermon became the primary means for popular assertions of opposition to the king. The development of this gesture thus illustrates the arrogation and elaboration of Islam as a language of politics by those it was meant to govern.

Islam as a Language of Elite Politics

As we have seen in previous chapters, Aurangzeb increased the emphasis in his enunciation of sovereignty on the textual and gestural repertoire provided by Islamic learning and piety, which percolated through his court and beyond. To the great range of the many "languages of Islam" spoken by early modern kings, jurists, theologians, and Sufis that Muzaffar Alam has explicated, we should add the casual fluency of seventeenth- and eighteenth-century imperial elites in the language of Islam toward local ends.[11]

A typical example of such use is evident in an instance, sometime in the 1740s, of the "war of houses" in which the nobleman and chronicler Shakir Khan was personally involved, and which he describes in his self-serving way. The object of the dispute was one Anup, a revenue collector of Shakir Khan's family who came under suspicion of embezzlement. Evading interrogation, Anup first took shelter at the house of Raja Lacchmi Narayan, a friend of Shakir Khan's, and then at that of the Raja Jugal Kishor. When Shakir Khan arrived with a small retinue to seize Anup from Jugal Kishor's great mansion on Moonlight Avenue, he was rudely rebuffed. The author

[11] Alam, *The Languages of Political Islam: India, 1200–1800.*

sought reinforcements from the city's nobility, and a large crowd gathered to surround the mansion. After a series of protracted negotiations, Anup was taken from Jugal Kishor and produced before Shakir Khan's father, who settled matters amicably with him.[12]

As Shakir Khan describes those who rushed to his aid, abandoning their half-eaten lunches and clutching swords and shields in unwashed hands, the language of his recollection suddenly acquires a distinctly Islamic hue. A dispute that until now has been described as a financial conflict between master and servant is now recast in rich excess. No longer a high-ranking nobleman, Jugal Kishor now appears as an "infidel" (*kāfir*). Firoz Jang, the son of Nizam al-Mulk, instructs his soldiers to be prepared to "ruin that infidel's house." The vizier Iʿtimad al-Daula and his son tell their followers to be ready to "send the infidels to hell." When vagabonds (*luccha-hā*) ("who were patronized by Raushan al-Daula") espy these aristocratic scions prepared for battle, they too begin to swarm around "the infidel's mansion like so many ants and locusts." Yet this crowd (so tightly packed that "not even a mustard-seed could fall to the ground") is not the mob of the Mughal nobleman's nightmares, but appears garbed in the virtuous cloth of "Allah's army" (*junūd-i Allāh*).[13]

Why, in Shakir Khan's telling, did the description of an everyday conflict slide into the reductive language of Muslim versus Infidel? In the heat of the moment, his belief in the rectitude of his cause appears fused into a starker vision: he belongs to the community of believers, arrayed against those who reject God. Such aggressiveness is perhaps necessitated by the countervailing clamor of the palace eunuchs who complain to the king that Shakir Khan, "drunk on alcohol," is brazenly besieging the house of a loyal servant at the very door of the imperial palace. But the servant of the chief of artillery who arrives to summon the author for his disorderly violation of imperial discipline is beset by noblemen who utter the most extravagant threats:

> Greet your master, and tell him, you practice a strange kind of Islam! The infidels have united to defend infidelity; while we and you are Muslim, and make ourselves be called noblemen, he [Jugal Kishor] is a servant, and merely an agent (*wakīl*)—what a contradiction! [Now] his highness the king has sent such a message; and your master [the chief of artillery] cannot combine bravery and honor, or else he would quickly send a message to

[12] Khan, "Hadīqa," fols. 209a–213a.
[13] Khan, "Hadīqa," fols. 210b–211a.

> Faulad Khan [the police chief] to hand over that wretch [Anup]. If not, the walls of the exalted fort will be tinged with the blood of martyrs, and we will resign the imperial service.[14]

When the all-too-familiar news of tumultuous mobs reaches the king, he orders Anup be locked up. Sycophants protest this decision, but Shakir Khan remembers Muhammad Shah cutting them off: "[W]hy should I disgrace my aged white beard on behalf of an infidel?"[15]

This polarized language—of the faith in danger, enemies united and Muslims divided, uppity servants who need to be put in their place—all serves to defend Shakir Khan's actions, which, from the perspective of the court and the law, might justifiably seem undisciplined and high-handed. Such polarization also enables blood-curdling threats against imperial officials. Shakir Khan has already warned Jugal Kishor of "great strife" and even "a general massacre" (*qatl-i ʿāmm*) if Anup is not made over to him. The angry noblemen who imprecate the messenger go even further and obliquely threaten the king himself.

It might seem that that Shakir Khan's immoderate language was an artifact of his memory, an embellished retrospection that cast his actions in righteous hue. Yet his account suggests that such language was not confined to the pages of literary texts, but also used by elites to mobilize popular support in urban struggles such as this one. Thus, in the heat of the conflict, the nobleman Khan-i Zaman tells his mace-bearer to proclaim amongst the Afghans of the city that any youth who remains in his house is no kin to him: "All are to come prepared for battle! For since we oppose infidels, martyrdom is being granted for free." Such words activate the community of noble retainers, common folk, and vagabonds (*ʿawāmm o luccha-hā*), who comprise the huge crowd which is crying in unison: "The Faith, The Faith, Muhammad!"[16]

Yet this language of Islam was not spoken by elites alone. While Shakir Khan would like to believe the crowds had been at his beck and call, it is apparent from his own testimony that many of the people who swarmed Jugal Kishor's house—and particularly the city's vagabonds—were acting of their own accord. After Shakir Khan's victory had been achieved, the nobility could

[14] Khan, "Hadīqa," fol. 211b.
[15] Khan, "Hadīqa," fol. 212b.
[16] Khan, "Hadīqa," fol. 212a.

send their soldiers back and return to their leisurely lunches. But the crowds would not disperse docilely, and their management was a challenge for everyone. It is fear of them that drives the police chief Faulad Khan bowing and scraping before our author. When he conveys the defeated enemy's willingness to kiss Shakir Khan's feet in abject submission, he points to the real danger: "[T]he people of the Armies of God are striving to preserve the honor of Islam (*mardum-i junūd-i Allāh rā hamīyyat-i Islām dar yāfta ast*); they will fall upon him [Anup] on sight; he will not survive, and your words and mine will be lost in the din." Shakir Khan offers a diplomatic solution, by declaring that in calling Anup an infidel (*kāfir*), he had only meant him to be a "*kāfir-i niʿmat*" ("one unthankful for benefits received"), and was not in fact commenting on his "appearance and origins and manner." Overcome with emotion at his tact, the police chief kisses Shakir Khan's hand and entreats him to go home so that the tumult (*fitna*) may finally subside.[17]

After Shakir Khan rides home with his "God-given victory," matters return rapidly to keel. When the captive Anup is conveyed to Shakir Khan's father, he hands over promissory notes (*tamasukkāt*) worth 12,000 rupees. Though Shakir Khan (rightly) suspects these are forgeries, his father and elder brother prefer to conciliate there and then. Not only does Lutf Allah Khan accept the worthless notes, he also gifts a shawl to the sometime-infidel before sending him on his way.[18] And, just like the "ants and locusts" to which they are routinely compared, the people yet again vanish from the text.

One might read Shakir Khan's account as representing a bigoted self, subject to barely concealed passions that periodically erupt in hatred of "the other community." But such an explanation would be insensitive to the contingency of the conflict: for if Shakir Khan had intercepted Anup at the house of his friend Raja Lacchmi Narayan, the transcendental question of the honor of Islam would never have risen. The faith fell in mortal peril only when Anup fled to the house of Jugal Kishor, with whom Shakir Khan did not happen to enjoy cordial relations.

Another reading of the unfolding conflict would be to see words like "Muslim" and "infidel" cynically cast about by elites to mobilize an unthinking mass in the service of their own objectives. Yet the people who swarmed around Jugal Kishor's house would not have known of the precise nature of the dispute between the parties, and could hardly have cared about

[17] Khan, "Hadīqa," fol. 212a.
[18] Khan, "Hadīqa," fol. 212a–b.

a financial conflict between master and servant. No such instrumental explanation is sufficient to explain why the crowd gathered, and, why it only dissipated after Shakir Khan marched away.

What, then, was the nature of the Islam being defended by the multitudes, who rallied to the slogan of "The Faith! The Faith! Muhammad!"? While for Shakir Khan, the language of Islam clarified a boundary and evoked a solidarity in a moment of urban conflict, what the people defended was not so much a relation to the divine as much as relations to each other: to allies and adversaries, friends and foes. Perhaps the attractiveness of this language to the nameless multitudes who thronged the streets was that it produced, however momentarily, a community of equals in a world otherwise defined by inequality.

The Language of Islam and the Politics of Justice

Brief though such moments of solidarity and equality may have been, by the early eighteenth century they were not rare. Already in the late seventeenth century, chroniclers had begun to note how ordinary folk began to veer from the script assigned to them in the empire's theater by appropriating the language of Islam for their own political ends. Sometimes pious worthies were seen as leading these protests, for instance, during the 1681 famine in the province of Gujarat. Here, as the governor Muhammad Amin Khan returned from ʿId prayers, the people "small and great, young and old, men and women . . . loosened [their] tongues in complaints and lamentation." They went on to throw "stones, clods of earth, and rubbish" on the governor's palanquin, who, perceiving a "public revolt," prevented his soldiers from retaliating and retreated to the fort. On Aurangzeb's order, a "mischief-monger" named Abu Bakr, regarded by the people as a pious worthy, was identified as the chief instigator. The governor dealt with him in the most politic fashion, by personally feeding him slices of a poisoned melon at a public feast.[19]

It is significant that Abu Bakr was determined to be the leader only after the tumult—in which he did not play a visible role—subsided. In part leaders like him had to be found because the administrative imagination could not conceive of ordinary people acting of their own accord. It is also true that the popular preachers who appear with increasing frequency in the

[19] Khan, *Mirat [En]*, 268–69.

empire's cities from the late seventeenth century onwards were associated with uprisings and disorders. Thus a preacher named Sayyid ʿAli ("in whose nature mischief and revolt were kneaded [together]"), gathered the people ("who are like animals") through his shouts of "The Faith! The Faith!," and led them in tumult sometime in 1722/23 in the port of Surat for reasons unrecorded. The port commander Rustam ʿAli Khan arrested and imprisoned the preacher; his disciples, who included Arabs, Ottomans, and Indians then went on a rampage, which ended in a day-long battle in the city streets.[20]

But popular preachers or other leaders were not always identifiable in popular protests articulated in the language of Islam. Take, for instance, the dramatic disturbances that rocked the imperial metropolis of Lahore four years before the poisoning of Abu Bakr. In 1677, a new governor by the name of Mirza Qawam al-Din entered Lahore.[21] His "aristocratic self-regard" quickly led him into conflict with the city's judge ʿAli Akbar, who was famed for his "rectitude, sharpness and severity." What precipitated open warfare between the two was less clear. Some attributed it to Qawam al-Din, who instructed the city's police chief to arrest the judge on the basis of a (nonexistent) royal order; others thought that ʿAli Akbar's nephew provoked the police chief. Whatever the cause, the judge ʿAli Akbar fortified himself in his mansion and prepared to fight to the death rather than be arrested, which, as we have seen, was the standard response of the noble to the potential breach of honor. After pitched fighting, the police chief was victorious, and the judge and some of his family were slain.

Thus far events had been entirely in accord with the familiar practice of the "war of houses" by which the honorable preferred to adjudicate their disputes. Now, however, matters took a turn. "Because in such affairs the people of Lahore seek excuses [to misbehave] under the pretense of following the Law of Muhammad," commented a contemporary chronicler, "at the judge's death several thousand of the learned and the barbarous, and weavers, and all the artisans, came together and massed on the governor and the police chief."[22] The later biographer of Qawam al-Din amplified these

[20] Khan, *Mirat [En]*, 414–15.

[21] Khan, *The Maásir i ʿÁlamgírí [FA]*, 188; Khwafi Khan, *The Muntakhab Al-Lubáb [Fa]*, 1:256. Anees Jan Syed notes this incident has been lifted from the chronicle of Abu al-Fazl Ma'muri, and notes the discrepancy in the date, variously attributed to either the twenty-first or the twenty-third year of Aurangzeb's reign. Syed, *Aurangzeb in Muntakhab-Al Lubab*, 276–78; see also 278, fn. 51; Khan, *Maʾasir-i ʿAlamgiri [EN]*, 116; Aurangabadi, *Maʾāsir al-Umarāʾ [En]*, 2:518–20.

[22] Khwafi Khan, *The Muntakhab Al-Lubáb [Fa]*, 1:257.

criticisms in rephrasing them: the people of Lahore who "pretended" to defend the law were mere artisans, "who, having read only a few words styled themselves as the learned (*ʿulamāʾ*), but are [in fact] less than savages."[23] The denizens of Lahore had already acquired a certain notoriety for their juridical pretensions: a mid-seventeenth-century commentator, for instance, had slightingly commented on their propensity to "stretch their lips" on legal matters far above their station.[24] Learned or otherwise, Lahore's weavers and artisans confined the governor and police chief to their houses, to the extent that officials were unable to traverse the streets of the town safely. On hearing of the turmoil, Aurangzeb removed both officials from their offices and sent reinforcements to the city. The police chief was turned over to the judge's family and executed. The governor Qawam al-Din, secretly spirited to Aurangzeb's court for trial to shield him from the people's wrath, died of the indignity of awaiting a judicial sentence.[25] No leader is known to have been found or punished.

An eighteenth-century chronicler attributed the disequilibrium between aristocratic nobleman and upstart judge to Aurangzeb's juridical interventions, for his favor (*iʿānat*) had encouraged judges to exercise a "greater autonomy" in matters of the law.[26] While such imperial intrusions were recognized as altering the workings of local power, what observers found unaccountable was the ferocity of the popular uprising, which confined the city's resident governor and police chief to their houses and ultimately led to their end. The scathing condemnation of the "unlettered barbarians" who "pretended" to defend Islam does more than betray the fear and hatred with which elites regarded those commoners who dared to act against their betters. It also indicates that the much-reviled common people did not passively receive the "law of Muhammad" as it was handed to them from above, but fashioned it to their own ends: in this instance, by intervening in an elite conflict to impose their vision of justice in favor of a popular judge against the governor and police officer.

23 Aurangabadi, *Maʾāsir al-Umarāʾ [En]*, 2:519; Aurangabadi, *Maʾāsir al-Umarāʾ [Fa]*, 3:113.

24 Various, "Historical and Geographical Extracts," fols. 181b–182a.

25 Aurangabadi, *Maʾāsir al-Umarāʾ [Fa]*, 3:114; Aurangabadi, *Maʾāsir al-Umarāʾ [En]*, 2:520.

26 Khwafi Khan, *The Muntakhab Al-Lubáb [Fa]*, 1:256.

The Holi Riot of 1714

While imperial elites were not averse to the vision of crowds mobilized in service of the faith, the popular appropriation and manipulation of the language of Islam gave them pause. Popular mobilizations behind the banner of Islam could thus evince contradictory responses in the observers who recorded their unfolding. A paradigmatic case was the Holi affray of 1714, again recorded from the city of Ahmedabad in Gujarat, which resulted in several days of pitched urban warfare and was disruptive enough to require Delhi's intervention.[27] Here again we see how ordinary people could assemble, stimulate leaders, and lead protests in service of a local political struggle articulated through the language of Islam.

Holi, as we have already seen, was a festival of inversion and transgression which frequently occasioned violence. According to the gazetteer, the events of 1714 began with a certain Hari Ram, an agent (*gumāshta*) of the wealthy and influential money-changer (*sarrāf*) Madan Gopal. Hari Ram and his friends were engaged in sprinkling colored powder on passersby in front of his employer's house, and generally behaving with the typical insolence (*badmastī*) against which the emperor Aurangzeb had issued fruitless injunctions half a century before. According to the gazetteer, the revelers accosted a passing Muslim and aggressively showered him with both color and contumely. Upon escaping, the offended person gathered some friends of his own and proceeded to complain to the preacher (*wāʾiz*) Muhammad ʿAli. Like the unfortunate Abu Bakr who had been killed by a poisoned melon, Muhammad ʿAli was a popular and influential divine who however did not hold any office of state. "Gathering Muslims high and low," he sent a message to Mulla ʿAbd al-ʿAziz, the leader of the Sunni Bohra community. Accompanied by "common Muslims" (*sāʾir al-nāss-i muslimīn*), consisting of soldiers and artisans who lived in and around the city, both figures headed to the congregational mosque to the cries of "The Faith! The Faith!" (*dīn dīn*). This mass gathering (*hujūm-i ʿāmm*) resolved to plunder and kill Hindus, and proceeded first to the house of the judge Khair Allah Khan, calling for his support of the "law and the defense of Islam."[28]

Until this point, the gazetteer appears to support the mass action, which is described as the collectivity of Muslims rightfully demanding justice. But

[27] This event has been extensively analyzed in Haider, "A Holi Riot of 1714: Versions from Ahmadabad and Delhi"; in the following pages I supplement his translation of the relevant sources and with my reading of the Persian text presented in Khan, *Mirat (Supplement)*, 405–10.

[28] Khan, *Mirat (Supplement)*, 406.

the crowd's behavior veered off-script, and the "collectivity of the people of Islam" (*ijmāʾ-i ahl-i islām*) mutated into something else entirely. As the frightened judge Khair Allah Khan refused to come out in support of the angry mob, the "barbarous" (*jahhāl*) among the common people "lost hope of success": without the judge's approval, after all, the forces of state could not be leveraged against the "oppressive Hindu." The mood turned against the judge. Those present began to imprecate him, and some among them set fire to his door. The people, now cast as "turbulent fellows," manifested "arrogance and self-assertiveness." They plundered and set fire to the shops of the marketplace and the residences of the money-changers, "which were brimming with goods and cash."[29] Next they proceeded to the house of Madan Gopal, which was in the neighborhood of the richer jewelers. They also encircled the house of Kapur Chand Bhansali, who was titled the "city chief" (*nagar seth*) and treated as the leader of the "Hindu community."[30] These notables and their kin defended themselves by throwing stones and clods of earth from their terraces. As an official of state, Kapur Chand rallied his (presumably Hindu) Gujarati retainers, and other Muslim soldiers. On this, the author's opinion swerved again, for he criticized Muslim "unemployed warlike event-seekers" (*sipāh-pesha bī-rozgar wāqiʿa-talb*) for fighting on the side of the Hindu money-changers and traders, thus exchanging their "faith" (*dīn*) for the "world" (*dunya*). It was only after two days of pitched street battles, when the provincial governor's soldiers arrived to secure the town, that the fighting finally subsided.[31]

Najaf Haider has placed the Holi disturbances of 1714 in the context of economic difficulties, wherein the shortage of specie had led to the substitution of instruments of credit for ready cash—an arrangement that would have had a disproportionate impact on the region's artisans and manufacturers.[32] Likewise, the gazetteer opens the account of the Holi riot by noting that Madan Gopal, one of the two main targets of the uprising, had only recently arrived in Ahmadabad, built a "very lofty" house, established an "extremely profitable" money-changing establishment, and was deeply connected to the financial establishment of the city.[33] As a showy arriviste associated with the financial troubles of the province—which would imminently result in

[29] Haider, "A Holi Riot of 1714: Versions from Ahmadabad and Delhi," 129; Khan, *Mirat (Supplement)*, 405–06.

[30] On the position of the Nagarseth see Tripathi and Mehta, "The Nagarsheth of Ahmedabad."

[31] Khan, *Mirat [En]*, 358–59; Khan, *Mirat (Supplement)*, 406–07.

[32] Haider, "A Holi Riot of 1714: Versions from Ahmadabad and Delhi," 138.

[33] Khan, *Mirat (Supplement)*, 405; Khan, *Mirat [En]*, 358.

open conflict between his agent Hari Ram and the city chief—Madan Gopal and his establishment were the obvious targets of local resentment.[34] Then, as Haider suggests, there was the fact that Sunni Bohras and Banias competed with each other in markets, in trades, and in businesses for imperial appointments in the port of Surat, the provincial capital of Ahmadabad, and indeed all the way to Delhi.[35] This is why the crowd proceeded not only to the financier Madan Gopal's house, but also to that of Kapur Chand, the city chief: for, the gazetteer explains, Mulla ʿAbd al-ʿAziz, the "head" (*seth*) of the Bohra community, was as motivated by "fanaticism" (*taʿassub-i dīn*) as by his desire to "equal" (*ham chashmī*) his Hindu rival.

But while Mulla ʿAbd al-ʿAziz's competitiveness is thus explained, the question of his "fanaticism" remains. Though the Mulla's own subjective disposition must remain obscure, the language of our gazetteer reveals how the conflict was expected to play out, and what happened when events did not conform to the script in our author's mind. As usual, the complex social order of castes, groups, and communities shrank to the primal categories of Hindu and Muslim for the author as he recalled the conflict.[36] In this narrowed vision, the festival of Holi was only an occasion of general misbehavior, and the gesture of Hindu assertion demanded retribution. Collective action by the "community of the people of Islam" under the guidance and leadership of established leaders was therefore justified. But the author's sympathy halted where violence against established elites began. In attacking the judge's house, and in plundering the richly packed shops of the city, the righteous community turned into a barbarous mob. Then again, while the author disapproved of attacking the houses of the city's Hindu elite, he had equally cutting comments for the Muslims who so callously betrayed their co-religionists by serving the Hindus.

Such an account does not tell us anything of the views of the members of the disorderly mob, who have left us with no explanation of their actions. But they evidently had their own sense of their place in the 'Community of Muslims,' their own understanding of the conflict, and the rectitude of their actions—none of which were determined by either their supposed leaders or related by later commentators. In coming together as the 'Community of Muslims,' and in marching to the judge's house demanding action, the people invoked a communal identity that had been authorized by the

[34] Khan, *Mirat [En]*, 363.

[35] Haider, "A Holi Riot of 1714: Versions from Ahmadabad and Delhi," 139.

[36] Haider, "A Holi Riot of 1714: Versions from Ahmadabad and Delhi," 135–36.

state. The burning of the judge's door and the looting of the marketplace expressed the people's rage at the state's agents in failing to provide the justice that was their due as Muslims. The subsequent attack on the houses of the rich Hindu merchants was not merely motivated by class envy, but by a sense that the proper relation between the 'Community of Muslims' and the category of "Hindus" needed to be re-established by force. Yet this was not a vision shared by all those who identified themselves as Muslims: most prominently the soldiers who fought to protect their Hindu employers. Finally, the stated leaders of the crowds were not its movers. While chroniclers focused on the preacher Muhammad ʿAli and Mulla ʿAbd al-Aziz, it was the people who first approached them and instigated them to action. And the practices of solidarity in faith within the shared space of the mosque enabled the people to assemble in joined purposes, and to distribute in common the risks of participation. In these ways, Islam provided the language by means of which a local political struggle was imagined, articulated, and waged.

The Emergence of a Political Gesture: Interrupting the Friday Sermon

Though public expressions of discontent, rowdy processions and gatherings, attacks on homes, shutting down shops, hurling stones and refuse from rooftops, and other such gestures may appear with increasing frequency in the historical record from the late seventeenth century onwards, they surely drew on a time-honored history of protest. But a marker of the powerful ferment of Mughal urban society by the early eighteenth century is the emergence of a new gesture of popular resistance to imperial power, which was framed directly in response to the imperial discourse of sovereignty and drew on the language of Islam. This was the act of hindering the recital of the Friday sermon (*khutba*), an essential feature of the obligatory Friday prayers at the city's congregational mosque. Such interruptions were neither a timeless gesture, nor one apparently widespread in other parts of the Islamic world: they certainly constituted a novelty in the Mughal empire.[37] In an important essay, Farhat Hasan has

[37] No instances of such disorders are recorded in a recent and comprehensive study of sermons in the medieval Islamic world (which does not however include South Asia). See Jones, *The Power of Oratory in the Medieval Muslim World*, particularly chap. 6.

rightly recognized the Friday sermon as a "political act," and describes audience interruptions as "acts of ritualistic communication" that "injured sovereignty."[38] My objective in the following pages is to trace the emergence of this act in a moment of Shiʿi-Sunni conflict and its rapid development into a political gesture of challenge to the enunciation of sovereignty, in order to demonstrate precisely how the practices of Islam came to serve as techniques in a popular politics.

Interruptions of the sermon appear to have begun in Lahore in 1711, during the reign of the emperor Bahadur Shah (1707–1712), in opposition to his introduction of the word "heir" (*wasī*) as an epithet for ʿAli during the invocation of prayers for the family of the prophet. Such an intervention in the Friday prayer was seen by some as an unacceptable turn toward Shiʿi doctrine, and provoked resistance in cities across the empire. Basing their analyses on the chronicles of the period, historians have regarded the ensuing "Khutba riots" as instances of sectarian controversy.[39] This picture must now be revised. Since we are unusually fortunate in having available the news reports of Bahadur Shah's court during the disturbances, it is possible to compare the retrospective vision of chroniclers with the immediate perspectives of reporters, who were seeking not to shape future memory, but only to inform their masters of present events. This comparison shows how elite chroniclers created a neat narrative of sectarian challenge and victory to contain the ambiguity and messiness of an act of popular assertion. This act not only forced the king to reverse his policy, but also originated a new practice of general opposition to imperial rule through the appropriation and refashioning of its language.

For commentators of the early eighteenth century, Bahadur Shah was a divisive and controversial figure. On the one hand, his harsh quelling of the Sikh uprising in the region of Punjab was welcomed by the ideologues of empire.[40] One recalled him as a king whose discipline and justice caused even high noblemen to micturate involuntarily, a fitting successor

[38] Hasan, "Forms of Civility and Publicness in Pre-British India," 90–91.

[39] Irvine and Sarkar, *Later Mughals*, I:30–32; S. A. A. Rizvi concludes that though Bahadur Shah was "innocent" in intention, he had "failed to recognize" that Lahore had developed into a center of Sunni orthodoxy. He attributes this to the displacements caused by the Sikh uprising in the region. Rizvi, *A Socio-Intellectual History of the Isnā 'Asharī Shī'īs in India*, I:40–41. As we have seen, however, the common folk of Lahore were already well noted for their unusual proficiency in matters of theology and law from the second half of the seventeenth century onwards.

[40] See, for instance, the brutally hostile account of the ruthless suppression of the Sikhs in Warid, "Mīrāt-i Wāridāt," fols. 114a–120a.

to his sainted father Aurangzeb.[41] Iradat Khan, who had served as a minor nobleman at Bahadur Shah's court, praised his piety and theological acumen, and defended him against the claims of "bigoted and evil-natured folk" who claimed the king wished to tamper with established traditions of faith (*mazhab*).[42] One such critic was the later hagiographer of the Naqshbandi Shah Muhammad Zubair, who accused Bahadur Shah of flirting with sacrilegious ideas, such as re-collating the Qur'an's chapters in a new order.[43]

The more banal heresy for which Bahadur Shah was remembered was his attempted alteration of the Friday sermon (*khutba*). The two-part sermon, uttered in Arabic by a prayer-leader (*khatīb*) before the main prayer (*salāt*), customarily included prayer for the Prophet and the ruling king, admonitions to piety, and recitation of the Qur'an, and was supposed to be uttered in every mosque across the realm.[44] Its recital, along with the minting of coin in the king's name, was an essential expression of sovereignty. According to his critics, Bahadur Shah wished to change the text of the sermon as it had been recited in Aurangzeb's reign by interpolating the word "heir" (*wasī*) as an epithet for ʿAli. Such an interpolation would imply that Bahadur Shah had broken with the Sunni piety of his father and embraced the Shiʿi doctrine that regarded ʿAli as Muhammad's designated successor.

Historians unsympathetic to Bahadur Shah described the righteous theologians of Lahore stoutly resisting the king's innovations. Such accounts involve descriptions of disputations between Bahadur Shah and the theologians, in which the king attempted to prove that ʿAli had the "right" (*haqq*) of inheritance through his expert quotations of the reports of the prophet (*hadīs*). Lahore's scholars, who perceived the dangers of yielding on this point, initially prevaricated. Under sustained pressure, they defied the king outright. In the inventive memory of the lowly hagiographer, they even informed the king that he would be "liable to death" for such claims. Infuriated, Bahadur Shah promised the resistant theologians that they would eat out of the same bowls as his hounds if they continued to obstruct him; but they did not yield, and were duly imprisoned. The king's effort was resisted on all sides. The vizier instructed the prayer-leader to recite the sermon as

[41] Anonymous, "Risāla-yi Muhammad Shāh," fols. 24b–25a.
[42] Wazih, *Tārīkh-i Irādat Khān*, 77–80; Wazih, *Memoirs of Eradut Khan*, 48–50.
[43] Ihsan, *Rauzat-i Qaiyūmiyya*, IV:84.
[44] Wensinck, "K͟huṭba."

formerly, "because this is Hindustan, and not Iran"—implying thereby that the realm was a land of Sunni, not Shiʿi, dominance. It was claimed that Bahadur Shah's sons threatened to rebel against him if he imposed the sermon on the empire. Likewise, on being unable to pray in their mosques, ordinary people bitterly cursed the king.[45]

It is then that Bahadur Shah is said to have lost his mind. Some claimed that howling dogs on rainy nights drove the king to distraction, or, more ominously, that he was haunted by apocalyptic nightmares, in which the people suffered torments and he himself was beset by barking dogs who sank their fangs in his flesh. On waking, the king is supposed to have given the order for the killing of all the stray mongrels in his camp. several observers attributed this to madness, and reported observing the camp's mutts swimming en masse across the river Ravi to safety on the other shore. Soon thereafter, Bahadur Shah died of an "inverted abscess" in his belly caused by the reproaches of the pious. In typical fashion, the lowly hagiographer attributed Bahadur Shah's death to his own teacher's spiritual exertions: so that after the king's death, vast crowds came to serve the master, reciting poetry in praise of his efforts to restore the faith and the law (*dīn, sharīʿat*).[46]

In the perspective of these chroniclers and hagiographers, the people who gathered to protest Bahadur Shah's innovation shrink to caricatures of the thwarted pious, or the servile followers of spiritual leaders who are only capable of expressing their gratitude. In fact, the popular insurgency against the sermon was more complex and deep-rooted than the chronicles suggest, and cannot be simply subsumed within the category of sectarian controversy. In order to understand the violence that rocked Lahore in 1711, we must therefore unearth the significance of the gesture of protest itself, which was the disruption of the recital of the sermon in the mosque on Friday.

45 Khan, "Tazkīrāt al-Mulūk," fols. 115b–6a; Ihsan, *Rauzat-i Qaiyūmiyya*, IV:85–86.

46 Khan and Yar, "Inshā-yi Dilkushā," fol. 10b; Khwush Hal, "Nādir al-Zamānī [B]," fol. 46b; Ihsan, *Rauzat-i Qaiyūmiyya*, IV:90; Khan, "Tazkīrāt al-Mulūk," fol. 116a. The point that such tropic narratives cannot be taken to represent historic reality is made sharply evident by the unnamed author of the *Touchstone of Conduct* who was both personally loyal to Bahadur Shah and fiercely opposed to Shiʿa "dissemblers." Such a contradictory position led to a certain degree of contortion in his account of the king. While he admitted that Bahadur Shah had become susceptible to Shiʿi influences, it was only because his uncles had become Shiʿa sectarians and he kept company with base men. The blame for the arrest of the scholars of Lahore in this narrative is transferred almost completely onto the previous administrator of the city, and there is no mention of any popular rebellion. Anonymous, "Mihakk al-Sulūk," fols. 480a–495b.

The Meaning of the Sermon

We are fortunate in that a version of the proclamation is recorded in original and interlinear translation in a history written for the orientalist James Fraser by his teacher Shaikh Muhammad Murad of Cambay (Khambayat) in the province of Gujarat.[47] The Shaikh noted that the new sermon made two significant changes, abbreviating the titles of the four "pillars of the faith," while expanding the epithets and attributes of the king himself.[48] A comparison of the text with a recording of Aurangzeb's sermon, also recorded in the same collection of works for Fraser, shows that Bahadur Shah's new sermon varied significantly from the older version.[49] The text of the new sermon begins with an exhortation in praise of God, the Prophet Muhammad, the four righteous Caliphs, Abu Bakr, ʿUmar, ʿUsman, and ʿAli "the heir" and son of the uncle of the Prophet. All four caliphs are designated as leaders of the faithful (*amīr al-muʾminīn*). The two sons of ʿAli, Hasan and Husain, and their mother Fatima are praised before the mention of the Prophet's uncles Hamza and ʿAbbas, and his companions and followers.

The sermon now continues with the prayer to god, seeking his mercy for the 'Community of Muslims,' living and dead *(al-muminīn w'al-muʾamināt w'al-muslimīn w'al-muslimāt al-ahayyāʾ minhum al-amawwāt)*, before a more fulsome invocation of the names of the emperors Shah Jahan and Aurangzeb, which are recited in their fullest amplitude. The attributes of the present monarch, which are granted to him by God, are next enumerated: he is excellent, perfect, the leader (*al-imām*), the dispenser of justice, humble (and in fact "very humble"), penitent, knowledgeable in the way and the book of God, and cognizant of the subtleties of the truths of God's word; he speaks to the people with truth and virtue, is granted victory by God, and exalted by divine decree. His every action is conducted with the assent of God and the Prophet; he smites rebels and infidels with the naked sword of God. By God's grace the king has been endowed with bravery, munificence, justice, greatness and goodness. He rules with virtue, prohibits the wrong, and refreshes the faith in conformance with the Prophet's

[47] The proclamation is recorded in Murad, "History of Aurangzeb," fols. 85b–92a. While the present manuscript is undated, it cannot be later than 1748, when Fraser returned from his second trip to India; it may indeed date from his return in 1740 from the first voyage, for the manuscript ends with an account of Nadir Shah's actions about 1738–1739. See Macdonell, "Fraser, James (1712/13–1754)."

[48] Murad, "History of Aurangzeb," fol. 85a.

[49] Cf. the text of Aurangzeb's Friday sermon in Various, "Khutba and Farmans . . . ," fols. 5a–14a.

predictions, and provides the benefits of justice and leadership according to the law of the prophets. He is the Caliph of God and his shadow on the earth, the son and the grandson of an emperor. He is, in short, "the Father of Victory and the Axis of the Faith" Muhammad Muʿazzam Shah ʿAlam Bahadur Shah al-Ghazi. Having announced the king's name, the sermon now exhorts the community to pray for him: may God extend his life and preserve his body "so that he lives for a hundred and twenty years, in fact even longer, much, much, much longer than this, and may his ending be better than his beginning." Because God has appointed him to perform works sacral and secular (*al-dīn wa al-dunya*), may his dominion be rendered strong in the way that it is of fortunate rulers, and his honor and dignity endure. With further such pleas, the sermon concludes.

The substance of the sermon resists easy classification into the sectarian categories of Shiʿi or Sunni. While Bahadur Shah's variant designates ʿAli the heir of Muhammad, it nevertheless regards all four caliphs as "commanders of the faithful": a title now conventionally associated only with ʿAli. In its praise of the Prophet and his family the proclamation cleaves unambiguously to a Sunni view. While the inclusion of the epithet "heir" for ʿAli might signal Tafzili or Shiʿi infringement for some, the proclamation overall strikes a maximalist position, incorporating and validating claims that run across the spectrum of opinion about the contested question of succession to the prophet's mantle.[50] The sermon's intention to transcend all divisions in the 'Community of Muslims' is completely consonant with its main assertion—that of the king's absolute authority over his realm. It is significant that while approximately three pages of the sermon are devoted to the section on Muhammad and his family, some ten pages are devoted to enumerating the qualities and attributes of the king. Those who heard the sermon would learn that the king, a hereditary ruler, had perfect, God-given dominion over the earth. To oppose the commands of the perfectly godly emperor is just the same as rebelling against God. Therefore it is to cut down "rebels and infidels" (in that order) that the emperor is given God's naked sword to wield. His tasks are only to rule, which is to lead and command, and to give justice. And what is the place of the people, the 'Community of Muslims' over whom the king looms so great? They are enjoined only to obey, and to pray earnestly for a 120-year lifespan for their ruler.

[50] I am grateful to Professor Hossein Kamaly for making this point to me.

In its evocation of the divine status of the ruler, his absolute authority and virtue, his commitment to justice, the Friday sermon presents a crystalline enunciation of the imperial discourse of sovereignty to its subjects at large. Its contents suggest that the obligatory Friday prayers also served as a powerful and repeated statement of the absolute authority of the king at the core communal site of the mosque. While it is difficult to assess just how frequently and widely the text was recited in this form, the fundamental importance of the sermon as constitutive of sovereignty was widely recognized. Indeed, the establishment of a king's rule was generally referred to by the pithy phrase of "*khutba o sikka*," alluding to the ruler's act of issuing a sermon and minting coin. Of currency we can say with certainty that a new king's regnal verses were rapidly proliferated across the empire, and that coinage was updated in even the most distant mints within weeks.[51] If Mughal administrators took the circulation of the sermon as seriously as they regarded the proper minting of coin, then the recital of the sermon would have been widespread indeed. Across the breadth of the empire, the Friday sermon would have been the only way in which the empire's denizens heard their king's name, and heard how he related the realm of the sacral to the earthly. And, in consonance with the discourse of sovereignty, the sermon demanded nothing more or less than the passive obedience of the crowds who streamed in to hear it every Friday.

Recognizing the Friday sermon as a central political articulation of the relationship between ruler and ruled is therefore key to understanding the little wave of rebellion that swept the empire's cities in 1711. For, while some chroniclers claimed that the thwarted prayers of the pious were enough to topple Bahadur Shah, the historian Khwafi Khan discerned a less subtle cause in the protests that roiled Friday services in mosques in Delhi, Agra, Lahore, and elsewhere. When the sermon was read out in Ahmedabad, related Khwafi Khan, Punjabis, and Mughal Turanis challenged the prayer-leader, who defended himself as acting on the orders of the king, the governor, and the judge. On the next Friday, the word "heir" had barely escaped the prayer-leader's lips when he was pulled down from the pulpit by the hem of his gown and stabbed in the belly. His body was dragged to the mosque's courtyard, where the irate crowd beat it with their shoes; his descendants did not dare

[51] Rafiʿ al-Darajat's brief reign of three months and nine days nevertheless saw the minting of coin in his name from Kabul, Lahore, Multan, Delhi, Agra, Gwalior, Etawah, Muazzamabad, Kora, Patna, Burhanpur, and Sirhind. Irvine remarks, "It is curious that in such a short reign a distant province like Kabul should have issued any coin." See Irvine and Sarkar, *Later Mughals*, I:418–19.

to reclaim his battered corpse for more than a day.[52] In Lahore, Khwafi Khan identified the leader of the protests as a certain Haji Yar Muhammad, who "gathered a common crowd" and led them to encircle the house of the city's judge. When Bahadur Shah sought to punish him, the crowds rose to his defense; Bahadur Shah gave the order that the sermon be recited as formerly, but that the "seditious mob" was not to enter the mosque or hinder the sermon. The mob nevertheless entered the mosque and remained threatening until the sermon was recited in the fashion they desired. And in describing this mob as having "neither head nor feet," Khwafi Khan acknowledged that ordinary people were the prime movers of the disturbance.[53]

Popular Protest and the *Khutba*

The records of Bahadur Shah's court cast a different light on the events described by the chroniclers, revealing how popular resistance to the king's new sermon troubled him more greatly than the objections of a few theologians. The king and his enormous entourage arrived in the vicinity of Lahore at the end of August 1711, when 900 tent-makers and 1,500 porters labored for two weeks to set up camp near the river, at the outskirts of the city.[54] No hint of trouble appears in the official records until September 19, when the king declared that the prayer-leader of Lahore's congregational mosque was "seditious" (*sharīr*), and to be imprisoned in Agra fort. On the 21st, the nobleman Islam Khan was ordered to proceed to the congregational mosque on the upcoming Friday with "the entire imperial artillery" and have the appointed sermon read out: whoever among the "barbarous" resisted was to be "taught manners."[55] On the next day, mace-bearers were appointed to take a certain Haji Yar Baig, "the leader of the community of the learned" (*fuzalā*ʾ), to be imprisoned in the fort in Agra for "prevaricating" in reciting the Friday sermon.[56] On September 30, Islam Khan was ordered to proceed to the city's main mosque with the military judge (*qāzī-yi askar*), the city's judge, the chief and city almoners, the sermon-leader, soldiers of the Fifth Guard, and armed retainers to read the sermon in the established

52 Khwafi Khan, *The Muntakhab Al-Lubáb [Fa]*, 1874, 3:664–65; Khan, *Mirat [En]*, 338.
53 Khwafi Khan, *The Muntakhab Al-Lubáb [Fa]*, 1874, 3:682.
54 Khan, *Tazkirat us-Salatin*, 130.
55 Khan, *Tazkirat us-Salatin*, 131.
56 Anonymous, "Akhbārāt, Bahādur Shāh, RY 5-6/II," 344.

fashion; riotous folk were to be kept from entering the mosque and the city's inhabitants were to be directed to other mosques for the prayer.[57]

On Thursday, October 1, the king did not hold a public council. He emerged from his private quarters in the morning and ordered Islam Khan and the others to proceed to the congregational mosque in Lahore and recite the sermon; the people of the city were not to be troubled, but the forty learned men of the city who were imprisoned in the police station were to be "whipped a few times" to encourage them to read the sermon as ordered. It was reported that although the men had been punished they refused to comply, and a person arrived at the police station and "expressed his view that tyranny was being exercised" (*izhār mīkard ki zulm mīshawad*).[58] When the officials of the police station had sought to arrest him, he pulled out a dagger; the police were unable to arrest him because of the vast crowds. The city's people were running out of their houses, and traders were refusing to open their shops, and the time of prayer was delayed. It is only now, at a moment of a rising and possibly uncontrollable popular insurgency, that Bahadur Shah changed his mind and declared that his name ("with *daulat*") was to be read in the sermon as customarily recited in his father Aurangzeb's reign.[59]

While it is true that the title of "heir" applied to ʿAli unveiled significant theological implications, Bahadur Shah's rapid withdrawal from the position suggests that the king did not attach as much importance to the matter as the later chroniclers reported.[60] The emperor had many other things on his mind, including the continuing Sikh uprising and near-mutinous soldiers of the artillery who loudly demanded their pay. More personal annoyances included

[57] Anonymous, "Akhbārāt, Bahādur Shāh, RY 5-6/II," 355; the text reads "*panj chawkī*" (fifth guard), which is unusual. Mughal sources from the period frequently mention the "*haft chawkī*" (seventh guard). The composition, nature, and function of this unit remains shrouded in mystery. Irvine thinks of it as a personal guard for the emperor. Sarkar on the other hand considers it to be a personal bodyguard that rotated every day of the week, thus accounting for seven guards. The existence of a "fifth guard" might imply instead the existence of cordons of guards, this being the fifth of seven. Irvine and Sarkar, *Later Mughals*, I:331; Sarkar, *History of Aurangzib, Based on Original Sources*, V:87.

[58] My reading regarding the refusal of the doctors to comply is doubtful. The text reads "*Hukm shud ki . . . dar khutba hazrat murtazá aʿlá ʿAlī karam Allāhū wajhahū rā wasī-yi mustafá sallā llāhu ʿalayhi ba/nakhwāhand.*" The interpretation of this line hinges on whether the emperor ordered the aforementioned to "not read" (*nakhwānand*) or "read" (*bakhwānand*). The text as it is written offers the former reading, but is perhaps a scribal error for the latter. Given the variable quality of the penmanship of the Sitamau transcripts, I am inclined to treat this is as a careless error (hardly isolated) on the part of the copyist. To read the text as suggesting that the emperor ordered the prisoners be beaten in order to "not read" the word "heir" in the sermon would imply the presence of a large countervailing Shiʿi opinion in Lahore, of which I have uncovered no corroborating textual trace. Anonymous, "Akhbārāt-i Darbār-i Muʿallā, Bahādur Shāh Regnal Years 5–6 Part II," 355.

[59] Anonymous, "Akhbārāt, Bahādur Shāh, RY 5-6/II," 355–56.

[60] For an overview of these implications, see Kohlberg, "Wasī."

a group of unruly musicians who noisily played musical instruments in the artillery lager, and who, together with loudly braying donkeys, disturbed the aged imperial ear in the late watches of the night. Bahadur Shah had both sets of noisemakers expelled.[61] And the king was hardly one to be dissuaded by the resistance of a few jumped-up theologians and the ruffianly mob of the city. On November 1, he ordered that the ceremonial drums were to remain silent on the martyrdom-anniversary of the "Leader of the Muslims" ʿAli.[62]

Yet matters had not been resolved so easily for the people of the city. While the courtly chronicler Kamwar Khan, ever unwilling to acknowledge resistance to his beloved king, passes over the next few days in calm descriptions of ceremony and order, the news reports of the court relate a different story. The people of the city had not been pacified by their victory. Five weeks later, on November 12, the king again instructed a bevy of noblemen and disciplinary officials to proceed to the mosque at the festival ground and offer prayers in the city, suggesting that he was aware of resistance even though the sermon was now recited in the unmodified form. When the prayer-leader reached the point in the sermon in praise of Hazrat ʿUmar, and called him "the leader of the faithful," a "Mughal Turani" unsheathed his sword and approached him. The prayer-leader tumbled to the ground, and the assembly of Muslims cried out to the Mughal that the sermon was being recited as it always had been. The Mughal protested that he knew that the name of ʿAli was to be recited first, sheathed his sword, and left the mosque. As the ranking nobleman Hamid al-Din Khan also arose, another person brandished a dagger at him. The police officers present rushed toward the Mughal, who drew his sword again and injured an officer before he was subdued.[63]

The emperor's punishment for these transgressions was swift and unflinching. The arrested Mughal was to be "cut apart at the joints" (*band az band judā sāzand*); the person who pulled the dagger on Hamid al-Din Khan Bahadur was also to be located and imprisoned.[64] On the next day, notes the news report, the emperor ordered that the people of Turan (*mardum-i Tūrāniyān*) were to be expelled from the city.[65] On November 14, 1711, the police chief reported that the Mughal who had come to the festival ground and caused mischief (*shūkhī*) had been executed and indeed "rent limb from

[61] Anonymous, "Akhbārāt, Bahādur Shāh, RY 5-6/II," 356, 357, 370, 429.
[62] Khan, *Tazkirat us-Salatin*, 132.
[63] Anonymous, "Akhbārāt, Bahādur Shāh, RY 5-6/II," 430–31.
[64] Anonymous, "Akhbārāt, Bahādur Shāh, RY 5-6/II," 430–31.
[65] Anonymous, "Akhbārāt, Bahādur Shāh, RY 5-6/II," 431.

limb." When the king asked to which community this man belonged, and whom he served, it was reported that he belonged to the "ruffians of Kabul" and lived in Lahore in the service of no one.[66] Yet the king was not utterly unrelenting. When, three weeks later, on December 5, the police chief reported that the person who had pulled the dagger on Hamid al-Din Khan had also been found and arrested, the king ordered imprisonment, not execution. Hamid al-Din Khan requested that his attacker should be released, and the emperor consented.[67] And finally, on January 7, the emperor dispatched a number of noblemen to commemorate his father's birthday at the mosque of Sharif Khan, who had served as Aurangzeb's preceptor. The nobility who went to the mosque distributed 2,000 rupees in cash for perfume (*khwushbū o ʿitr*). Prayers were said for the deceased emperor and food was offered to the learned men of the city, some of whom were perhaps still smarting from their recent floggings.[68]

Far indeed from the chroniclers' narrative of righteous Sunni resistance to Shiʿi encroachment, and the subsequent madness and death of the king, the reports from Bahadur Shah's court reveal that the king was less concerned by the resistance of the learned men of the city than by its ordinary denizens, who objected to any alteration of the sermon. And just as the sermon was more volubly a statement of royal power than a vehicle of theological chicanery, so is it striking that the language in which resistance to the sermon is described is curiously devoid of the emotive content generally associated with the Shiʿi-Sunni controversy that was hardly unknown in the realm.[69]

The disagreement between the Sunni theologians and the king, represented as one of emphasis and degree, does not appear to have animated much passion among the people, who simply objected to the interpolation of the word "heir" and wished matters to continue as they had formerly. More than the addition of a single word, the many changes from Aurangzeb's longstanding sermon marked an innovation in the expression of sovereignty which was important enough to arouse widespread resentment. We cannot discount the disapproval of some to the seeming encroachment of Shiʿi influence. But, as we have seen, others perceived no such thing. No public clashes, no symbolically charged gestures of contest, assertion, or humiliation between Shiʿa and Sunni are recorded in the aftermath of the event. To the reporters who

[66] Anonymous, "Akhbārāt, Bahādur Shāh, RY 5-6/II," 433.
[67] Anonymous, "Akhbārāt, Bahādur Shāh, RY 5-6/II," 435.
[68] Anonymous, "Akhbārāt, Bahādur Shāh, RY 5-6/II," 525.
[69] Sarkar, *History of Aurangzib Mainly Based on Original Sources*, V:346–49.

hurriedly scribbled down the news as it was reported to the king, the crowds that rose up against Bahadur Shah's infringement bore no sectarian markings at all: they were simply the people as such, expressing their resistance to the king's changing enunciation of sovereignty.

Conclusion: The Legacy of the Friday Disturbances

It is because interruptions of the Friday sermon had a wider relevance than sectarian assertion when used against the king that we find them repeatedly employed in ensuing years in urban political conflicts. Indeed such interruptions became for a while the central gesture in the language of popular politics constituted by the practices of Islam.

A classic instance that demonstrates this contention is the near-riot that wracked Delhi in 1725 over the question of conversion.[70] The facts of the case are complex, and difficult to establish. In that year, according to the historian Kamwar Khan, one Ramji, a scribe at the imperial court, declared before chief judge (*qāzī al-quzzāt*) Mustafiz Khan that he had converted to Islam some years previously.[71] He now claimed that because his daughter was a minor at the time of his conversion, she should by rights have been involuntarily also converted to Islam as his dependent. On the basis of conflicting testimony about the appearance of "signs of puberty" given by the young woman under duress, the chief judge decided that she had been a minor at the time of her father's conversion to Islam, and so was perforce a Muslim. But when this decision caused the "Hindus of the Urdu Bazar" to seek personal redressal from the Emperor at the window of presentation, the matter was assigned to the chief jurisprudent (*sadr al-sudūr*) for review. In a tense debate that ensued within the Wooden Mosque in the fort, the chief jurisprudent, the highest legal authority in the empire, argued that the onset of menstruation was not the only sign of puberty; because of the doubt about her adult status, she could not be regarded a Muslim. Despite the furious dissent

[70] Irvine and Sarkar, *Later Mughals*, I:126–27. I have based this account on Irvine's published version and consulted his transcription of a variant of Kamwar's chronicle. This is appended in an inlay to the British Library APAC IO Islamic 3918, ff. 7–8.

[71] A Ramji, son of Vir Mal, is described as owning a house in the neighborhood of Tandanwara, in the "Old City" of Delhi, from a sale deed dated 1726. Tirmizi, Perti, and National Archives of India, *Calendar of Acquired Documents, 1352-1754*, 67, doc. 141, no. 2450. A Ramji is again mentioned as holding a minor land grant in the province of Malwa in 1735. Tirmizi, Perti, and National Archives of India, *Calendar of Acquired Documents, 1352–1754*, 106, doc. 202, no. 2504.

of the chief judge and a jurisprudent (*muftī*) named Daulat, the woman in question was now handed over to a Hindu cloth-merchant named Jiwan Das for safekeeping.

On the next day, which was a Friday, some "sixty thousand" Muslims gathered at the congregational mosque. The unruly mob hindered the recital of the Friday sermon (*khutba*). "Two or three" Hindus were seized by artisans (*ahl-i hirfa*) and "forcibly circumcised." Because a "great riot" was on the verge of breaking out, the king deputed the high nobleman Raushan al-Daula to bring the judge and the jurisprudents to the imperial court; Irvine presents us with the fate of the girl in a direct quotation: "To make a long story short, she was killed, otherwise there would have been many headaches and vexation."[72] The poll tax (*jizya*) that had been abolished some years ago was proclaimed reinstituted; but in a week, the judge was removed, and new jurisprudents were appointed.

This picture is complicated by the fact that Shahabadi, the only other chronicler to describe the event, does so very differently. This author makes no mention of a woman, and describes only a controversy around the conversion of a person of the Hindu community (*qaum-i hunūd*). In this account, the chief jurisprudent forbade the conversion on the "instigation" of the community; the chief judge, concerned for the "honor" (*ghairat*) of Islam, gathered the "people of Islam," marched to the congregational mosque on Friday, and prevented the recital of the sermon. Noblemen and commoners gathered for the "defense of Islam." Helpless in the face of this popular uprising, the king conciliated the chief judge and even asked his forgiveness. The Hindu was immediately converted to Islam. The venal jurisprudent (who accepted bribes from "the chambers of hell") was removed, but so was the upright chief judge.[73]

At first glance, the stories described by the two chroniclers appear to refer to different events. For the logical and patient Kamwar, the rationality of the chief jurisprudent is contrasted with his hot-headed subordinate Daulat and the judge, Mustafiz Khan. For Shahabadi, it was the jurisprudent who was corrupt and disloyal to Islam, and the judge upright. The complex legalities surrounding the involuntary conversion of a young woman in Kamwar are reduced to a simple matter of a nameless individual's conversion in Shahabadi. The riotous mob that, according to Kamwar, compelled the king

72 Irvine and Sarkar, *Later Mughals*, II.127

73 Shahabadi, "Tārīkh-i Hindī," fol. 254a–b.

to send a conciliation by way of his minister, appears as a righteous gathering of Muslims in Shahabadi of whom the king must himself seek forgiveness. The unfortunate woman at the center of Kamwar's tale is simply absent from Shahabadi's account, as are the Hindu plaintiffs who seek justice from Muhammad Shah at the fort's window of presentation.

Nevertheless, the shared features of both accounts reveal the dispute's origins within a family, over a question of conversion. But conversion here has nothing to do with an individual's changing beliefs. It appears as a question in a court of law, where it is cast in terms of the thorny problem of a child's status on the conversion of a parent.[74] Questions of conversion and the status of children must have been commonplace problems in the Mughal empire of the eighteenth century. Their routine nature is suggested by a book of formulaic legal judgments, no doubt assembled to aid a judge through the everyday tasks of the courthouse. Among its transactions of property, marriage, and divorce, we also find included a generic order regarding a "Lady Bhagwati, daughter of so-and-so" who has approached "The Sublime House of Justice" to embrace Islam, and is given custody of her infant daughter.[75]

The object of legal contestation in Kamwar's account is the body of a woman, and the technicality on which its status will be determined is that of the signs of adulthood. Here, the workings of a conservative Islamic legalism serve to restrict—and not enable—conversion.[76] The inability of the state's officers to offer a cohesive judgment provokes a variety of responses from the people of the city. Some gather as Hindus to directly petition the emperor, invoking his place as a divinely endowed arbiter of justice in the discourse of sovereignty. Those who gather as Muslims at the mosque make two symbolic gestures: in inflicting penile violence on "two or three" Hindu passersby, some among the crowds reassert the theoretical privileges of the 'Community of Muslims' at a moment when they appear under threat. In interrupting the Friday sermon, the crowds demand the king accede to their view, which was at variance from the learned majority opinion of the king's expert adjudicants. In this way the crowds asserted the supremacy of the law—as *they* saw it—over the king's justice.

[74] On the diverse views this question occasioned, see the discussion in Friedmann, *Tolerance and Coercion in Islam*, 113–15.
[75] Khan, "Tārīkh," fol. 132a.
[76] For an Ottoman parallel, see Peirce, *Morality Tales: Law and Gender in the Ottoman Court of Aintab*, chap. 8.

Faced with this political challenge, imperial administrators offered a pragmatic political response, in which procedural niceties were forsaken in the service of the restoration of order. This is why the unfortunate woman who was caught between two communities had to be killed, so that there was neither a body to leave the Hindu fold nor one to be denied inclusion among Muslims. The poll tax was declared reinstated because it marked the formal supremacy of the 'Community of Muslims.' But these were passing declarations, and the imperial court reasserted its superior authority in expediently dismissing the troublemaking judge.

Historians have regarded such events as instances of "communal violence" in the contemporary sense of the term.[77] Certainly the heat of sectarian passion may have driven the actions of some participants. But it is noteworthy that such conflict was symbolic, limited in scope, and did not devolve into mass violence. In the same way, it is surely the case the artisans at the forefront of the agitation may have shared the widespread resentment of the growing clout of Hindu financiers and traders. But economic motives do not explain the gesture at the center of the protest: the disorderly mass gathering in the mosque and the hindering of the sermon's recital. The recent origins of this gesture in a Sunni-Shiʿi sectarian controversy were by now forgotten. Its deployment signaled a political assertion by urbanites, who claimed the privileges of the 'Community of Muslims.' In asserting their interpretation of justice according to the law, and in threatening the legitimacy of the king, the people no longer supplicated but rather coerced the ruler into action. The court's actions, which were designed to first settle the disorder and then reassert its authority, likewise constituted a political response. The language in which subjects waged a local political struggle against their masters was provided by the practices and gestures of Islam. To discern the fullest possibilities—and limits—of this language of popular politics is the object of the next chapter.

[77] Rizvi, *Shah Wali-Allah and His Times*, 199–200.

7

The Shoemakers' Riot and the Limits of Popular Politics

In March 1729, a minor scuffle between the retainers of a Hindu jeweler and a group of Muslim shoemakers in Delhi spiraled out of control. A retainer who had been disarmed by the shoemakers returned with a party later that night to seek revenge and killed an elderly shoemaker. Joined by the city's Arabs and Abyssinians, the shoemakers gathered around their elder's corpse and demanded justice from the judge, the police chief, and the emperor Muhammad Shah. When no justice was forthcoming, the shoemakers and their allies resolved to interrupt the recital of the Friday sermon in the congregational mosque. On Friday, the shoemakers and their allies came to the mosque's courtyard with weapons drawn. When the king's servants arrived to dissuade them from their belligerence, the enraged shoemakers hurled their shoes at the assembled nobility's heads. A general melee ensued in which the vizier's Mughal retainers ended up battling the nobleman Raushan al-Daula's Afghan soldiers. By the end of the affair, the mosque's courtyard was strewn with broken bodies and the shoemakers had vanished.

The significance of the soiled shoes dislodging the gold-fringed turbans was not lost on its elite observers, who regarded the turmoil in the city with a horrid fascination. Though the historian Khwush Hal thought this "unusual popular tumult" as unpalatable to write about as to read, he nevertheless felt compelled to describe it as "one of the strange events of the era."[1] As his words remind us, the shoemakers were not graciously ushered to their proper place on history's page. They erupted on it, against the chronicler's will, by the force of their assertion. The historical accounts of the shoemakers' riot carry within their own narrative structures the trace of the dramatic clash between high and low in the city. For, just as the shoemakers forcibly represented themselves against the city's high and mighty, so too did elite chroniclers labor to tame the subversiveness of the lowly folk's gesture by how they related

[1] Khwush Hal, "Nādir al-Zamānī [B]," fol. 222a.

The King and The People. Abhishek Kaicker, Oxford University Press (2020). © Oxford University Press.
DOI: 10.1093/oso/9780190070670.001.0001

it. The ripple of turmoil this contest produced in the practiced cadences of the chronicler's literary prose signaled a deeper churning: despite their artifactual nature, accounts of the riot thus offer us invaluable insight into the actions and intentions of the city's lowest inhabitants at a moment of urban crisis.

While there was general agreement over the broad outlines of what had happened, there was no unanimity as to its significance. Disturbed by the intensity of the rebellion, the bureaucrat and historian Khwush Hal hinted at noble conspiracies and the fanaticism of the bigoted. For an anonymous but sophisticated courtly writer who dismissed all conspiracy theories and sneered at invocations of piety, the uprising served as an amusing incident worthy of literary aestheticization, through which the shoemakers were put back in their lowly place. By contrast, the educated but embittered Muhammad Shafiʿ Warid regarded the shoemakers as rightfully seeking justice and exulted in the humiliation of the nobility. Muhammad Ihsan, the hagiographer of the Naqshbandi mystic Muhammad Zubair, claimed the course of events as a vindication of his master's spiritual prowess. Finally, writing half a century later, the historian Muhammad Bakhsh Ashob would refashion the anonymous courtly narrative into an account of the triumph of the 'Community of Muslims' over its prideful Hindu foes.

The lack of consensus among these chroniclers about the meaning of the event illustrates the complexity and polyvocality of the urban sphere in the early eighteenth century. To make sense of obscure events such as this one, modern historians have sought to reconcile diverse accounts into a seamless and uniform narrative of the historical past. Yet such narratives flatten the telling variations in the perceptions of the observers who occupied different vantage points in social space and historical time. By contrast, our goal in the historical reconstruction that follows will be to illuminate the tangled happenings of March 1729, while still preserving the multiplicity of meanings assigned to them. In doing so, we will find that the shoemakers' agitation cannot be neatly subsumed within the standard categories of economic conflict or sectarian hatred that have given us the conventional understanding of the period. Instead of closing the meanings of the event in narratives of "larger significance," the pages that follow attempt to behold the city of the eighteenth century from the eyes of the shoemaker.

Seen from this perspective, the shoemakers' action marks the most vivid instance of the use of Islam by the city's lowly as a language of politics to both invoke and challenge the imperial discourse of sovereignty. At first glance, the riot reflects the familiar elements of a classic urban conflict: a clash between two parties led to the invocation of the 'Community of Muslims' and the assertion of its rights, and the demand for justice was accompanied by a powerful symbolic challenge through the newly-developed gesture of the interruption of the Friday sermon. But there is more to the story. The shoemakers hurled their shoes at the heads of the empire's assembled nobility, giving the event a piquancy derived from the dishonorable and contaminated status of their profession. By their act of inversion, the shoemakers flexed the social order almost to its breaking point. Through the remarkable capability of the language of popular politics, even the lowliest inhabitants of the city now directly challenged the authority of the king and his nobility, which had been so carefully cultivated through the discourse of sovereignty. What the shoemakers' riot offers us, therefore, is an opportunity to explore the range of urban popular politics in the era before colonial rule.

The Evening of Tuesday, March 16: Origins

The origins of the tumult were unexceptional. The possibility of disorder had emerged from the coincidence of the Shab-i Baraʿat festival (14 Shaʿban 1141AH), determined by the Islamic calendar, with that of Holi, fixed by the Vikram calendar (24 Phalgun 1785VS). While Holi celebrations involved the rude inversion of the everyday order, Shab-i Baraʿat served as a moment of both pious celebration and ritualized aggression. An early-nineteenth-century compendium of Muslim customs and practices in southern India disapprovingly listed the heteropraxic accretions on the popular celebration: though from a later period, it is suggestive of the atmosphere of Delhi in 1729.[2] Festivities for Shab-i Baraʿat would have begun earlier in the week, with food and sweets being prepared and distributed in memory of deceased family members. For days before the festival, boys began to go about "beating small drums"; parents made votives—"figures of elephants" for sons and "lamps of clay" for daughters—to keep in an illuminated bamboo frame over which prayers were recited for Muhammad, ʿAli, or Fatima. Presents were exchanged, and on the night of the 14th of Shaʿban—which in 1729 fell on March 16—fireworks were gifted and set off among friends. These festivities had a distinctly rowdy aspect, for celebrants engaged in "sham battles by

[2] Sharif, *Islam in India*, 203–04.

letting off fireworks at each other, which occasionally end in clothes being burnt or people being killed or injured."[3] The anonymous courtly writer alluded to this potential for conflict when he observed that the "excessive gatherings" of both "sects" (*farīqain*) of Hindus and Muslims were "busily observing their customs of throwing colors and lighting firecrackers."[4]

Into the celebrating crowds ventured the procession of Subh Karan, sometimes misleadingly described in the chronicles as a jeweler (*jauhari*). While the jeweler's was a specialized and important profession in Delhi, most of the skilled craftsmen it employed would have been humble folk. A late nineteenth-century account of "native manufactures" describes the city as a historic center of the jewelry manufacture. The profession was well-organized. Atop the workshop sat a head jeweler, who designed the ornament; below him came the goldsmith, followed by the embossers and chasers, enamellers and inlayers.[5] Workmen, such as those involved in the production of the "thorny" (*khārgār*) golden items for which the city was famed, might in the late nineteenth century have earned as much as 3 rupees for producing a unit-measure of jewelry in which gold worth 14 rupees was used, indicating the value of skilled jewelers even in a market ravaged by the Rebellion of 1857.[6]

But even the most skilled jewelers of the early eighteenth century would not have enjoyed Subh Karan's palanquin or his armed retinue. Subh Karan derived his status from his service as an "appraiser" or "broker" (*muqīm*) in the imperial jewel-house (*jawāhirkhāna*).[7] His work would have included assessing the quality and value of jewelry bought and sold between palace and city. Such work was sensitive, for the process was subjective and the valuation of items determined the wealth of their possessors. By the mid seventeenth century, merchants, brokers, and appraisers of jewels—such as the famed Shantidas Jhaveri (d.1660)—had become prized servants of the empire.[8]

Skilled appraisers were equally valuable in Delhi. The financial reconsolidation of the imperial establishment spearheaded by Lutf Allah Khan in the

[3] Sharif, *Islam in India*, 203.

[4] Anonymous, "Sahīfa-yi Iqbāl [A]," fol. 48a.

[5] Baden-Powell, *Manufactures and Arts of the Punjab*, 184.

[6] Baden-Powell, *Manufactures and Arts of the Punjab*, 187.

[7] Warid, "Mīrāt-i Wāridāt," fol. 172b; Anonymous, "Sahīfa-yi Iqbāl [A]," fol. 48b; Ashob, "Tārīkh-i Shahādat [B]," fol. 56b.

[8] Siebenhuener, "Precious Things in Motion." On Shantidas see Mehta, *Indian Merchants and Entrepreneurs in Historical Perspective*, chap. 6; see also Tripathi and Mehta, "The Nagarsheth of Ahmedabad." For his relations with Dara Shukoh, see Faruqui, *Princes*, 164–65.

early 1730s, according to his son, depended on a systematic reappraisal of the treasures stored in the palace warehouses, a process that required the expert services of a team of "jewelers, goldsmiths and inlay-workers."[9] Due to the systematic undervaluing of plundered items from both the palace and the people of the city, Nadir Shah's exactions in Delhi in 1739 cut more deeply. As an appraiser or broker at the imperial court, Subh Karan thus occupied a position of great privilege. According to Ashob, Subh Karan's position derived from his association with the palace eunuchs Hafiz Jawahir Khan and Hafiz Khidmatgar Khan, who were responsible for managing the palace's jewelry collections and harem affairs respectively. They provided access to the lord-chamberlain (*khān-i sāmān*) ʿIzzat al-Daula, who oversaw the king's household. Finally, Subh Karan also had connections with the Harem (*maʿman*) ("impenetrable to all injunctions"), which appears to have emerged as an autonomous center of power under the queen mother, Nawwab Qudsiyya.[10]

The motley crowds through which his procession waded on Saʿd Allah Khan Square occupied the opposite end of the social spectrum. Unlike Moonlight Avenue, occupied by jewelers and financiers, Saʿd Allah Khan Square had a more plebeian character. In 1663, the Parisian Francois Bernier likened Saʿd Allah Khan Square to the Pont-Neuf: it was "the rendez-vous for all sorts of mountebanks and jugglers" and the home of false astrologers ("Mahometan and Gentile") who offered nonsensical advice to common folk for a trifle.[11] Some seventy-five years later, Dargah Quli Khan was likewise entranced by the square's diverse storytellers; mimes; astrologers; soothsayers; metalsmiths; vendors of liquor, birds, and weapons; and quacks who peddled aphrodisiacs and remedies for venereal diseases. The heterogeneity of the space is evident in the presence of both popular preachers, whose simple sermons had a powerful effect on the rustics who gathered to listen to them, and dancing boys (*amrād*), who trapped even the "seasoned hunters" they encountered there.[12]

Though the shoemakers of the square were too base for Dargah Quli Khan to mention, Ashob remembered how they set up stalls to hawk their wares on both sides of the passage, extending as far as a bow-shot south of the Red Fort. Their community consisted of devout, observant Muslims from Lahore; their elders, respectable and bearded, had memorized the Qurʾan

[9] Khan, "Hadīqa," fol. 141b.
[10] Ashob, "Tārīkh-i Shahādat [B]," fol. 58b.
[11] Bernier, Brock, and Constable, *Travels in the Mogul Empire, A.D. 1656–1668*, 243–44.
[12] Khan, *Muraqqaʿ-yi Dihlī*, 60–61.

and were versed in "jurisprudential affairs" (*masla o masāyil-i fiqhī*).[13] It is not surprising that the visible and assertive commitments to Islamic piety of the Punjabi shoemakers counterbalanced their extremely low social position. While we have no direct evidence for their beliefs or affiliations, a biographical compendium from a slightly earlier period mentions Punjabi shoemakers who were affiliated with the Naqshbandi way.[14] The Naqshbandi acceptance of craft (*kasb*) as a means of pious livelihood would have been attractive for artisans. But the leather-worker's embrace of piety would not let him transcend the boundary of contamination within which he was inevitably viewed. Thus the account of a certain "Maulana ʿInayat, the shoemaker" praises him for practicing his "contemptible profession" (*kasb-i dūn*) in ascetic solitude, which in his case involved quietly accepting any job given to him; for accepting whatever was offered without any haggling beforehand; and for spending some of his gains on charity for mendicants.

The compiler also includes a firsthand report of a senior mystic from a well-to-do background who encountered this shoemaker. In this remarkable narrative, despite the obvious mediating influence of the writer, we can hear the shoemaker speak something of his lot in life. The senior mystic met Maulana ʿInayat the shoemaker outside the Sar Jalal Inn, on the road from Attock to Lahore. The choice of place was strategic, for, as the shoemaker said, whoever traveled to or from Hindustan, Khurasan, and Turkistan had to pass before him (and we are reminded that shoemakers' trade required him to inhabit places of social intersection). A sense of hierarchy and social distance pervades the account of this encounter. The mystic reports his disciple's strange fancies without commenting on them: the shoemaker said that he knew the mystic had been praying for abundance, but the lack of famine meant that people ate well and so, forgetting God, gave themselves up to iniquity and debauchery. He also knew, he said, that the mystic had been praying for the people of Attock to travel easily by sea to the holy land. As a result, the people of Attock now took boats to Mecca, and he too planned to do the same.

As the mystic and the shoemaker conversed, a female traveler arrived in a litter (*mihaffat*). One of the porters came up to the shoemaker and said, "Stitch my shoe." The shoemaker took his shoe and instead hurled it as far as he could. The porter began to argue with the shoemaker and offered him

[13] Ashob, "Tārīkh-i Shahādat [B]," fol. 56b.
[14] The following discussion is based on ʿUmar, "Zawāhir al-Saraʾir," fol. 181a–b.

twice the going rate; but, despite the implorations of the gathering crowd, the shoemaker obstinately refused to serve him. The cause of the shoemaker's action was not, as we might think, the peremptoriness of the porter's request. When the mystic quizzed him, the shoemaker said he refused because the porter was "a bastard, a product of fornication" (*harāmī o walīd al-zinā*). Shocked by these violent sentiments, the mystic reproved the shoemaker: what sort of piety did he hope to achieve by revealing the private affairs of another person? The shoemaker was suitably contrite, and promised to never do so again, while still refusing to fix his shoe. He then reported that his comely wife had been taken away by another man to Lahore by force, and pleaded with the mystic to recover her. The mystic does not report taking any action to help him.

As the incident suggests, the fierce piety—and perhaps even bigotry—of the shoemaker was difficult to separate from his social marginality. To have the uncleanest of objects thrust into his face, and to be spoken to in the imperative, was the fate of the shoemaker. Yet, shoemakers occupied places of social interconnection, which brought them into regular contact with different groups. Their lack of formal education did not deprive them of the opportunity to develop pious inclinations. Even the formally illiterate might develop a robust sense of the principles of the faith from the simple catechistic poems that listed the duties and obligations of Islam in the Hindi vernacular and were in circulation by the early eighteenth century.[15] A knowledge of Islamic law might likewise be acquired by the perusal of legal compendia such as the *Plain Digest*, compiled by the author after a dream of the Prophet, "in the Persian language, which is unknown to no-one," for the "common good" (*fā'ida-yi ʿāmm*).[16] And the deepening connections of the region to the world of the Indian Ocean—the ever-present threats of European pirates notwithstanding—meant that even such marginal figures could visit the holy lands, and so claim the pious status that came with the pilgrimage.[17]

To return to the Delhi shoemakers of 1729: whether their devoutness derived from their origins in Lahore (which, as we have seen, was a center of popular engagement with theology and jurisprudence), or whether it was acquired by osmosis from the discipleship of mystics or the homilies of popular preachers in the square, the shoemakers' marks of devotion did not shield

[15] See, for instance, the short text of the "Masnawi." I thank Saqib Baburi for the reference.
[16] Anonymous, "Fatāwá-yi Birahna," fol. 1b.
[17] Farooqi, "Moguls, Ottomans, and Pilgrims."

them from the contempt of their betters. "Only the dog and the shoemaker who know what's in the leathern sack," spitefully commented a courtly observer of the riot, expressing not just a common proverb [indicating an obscure conflict][18] but also a distinctly Indic prejudice against the leather-worker's caste (*chamār*), "defiled" by his work as a tanner or his proximity to one.

A nineteenth-century colonial ethnographer noted that the lot of the *jatiya* subcaste of leather-workers, which inhabited the region of Delhi, was "all of the rough work in the village [and] . . . a certain amount of forced labor"; they made (but did not mend) shoes. Within the same rubric of the leather-workers' caste fell the "*Mochi* or cobbler who is generally a Muhammadan."[19] It was the tanner's job to skin the buffalo, goat, or camel; to soak the skin in lime water for days; to scrape the skin of loosened hair, and finally to sew up the skin as a "sack," fill it with tree bark, and water it repeatedly.[20] Whether they tanned the skins themselves or purchased tanned hides from the chamars of the city, whether they were shoemakers or shoe sellers only (as they were sometimes called), whether they were unlettered or piously orthopraxic *mochi*-s, it is certain that the shoe sellers were the lowest of the low, "deeply contaminated" (*shadīd palīd*) in the eyes of those who purchased their wares.[21] It may be these shoemakers, or other equally lowly artisans, who appear in the untitled painting of Saʿd Allah Khan Square (Fig. 7.1). In contrast to the colonnades filled with well-appointed traders and bedecked with wares, the shoe sellers' humble wood-and-thatch stalls were no doubt seen as the "encroachments" that the censor (*muhtasib*) was enjoined to remove from the city's public paths.[22]

Though lowly in status, the shoemakers who celebrated Shab-i Baraʿat in Saʿd Allah Khan Square would not have been impoverished. Evidence from the early eighteenth century is scarce, but in the late nineteenth century a colonial civil servant remarked that "Delhi is the great place . . . principally for ornamental shoes," in particular the *ghetta* (or *ghetla*), "very gaudy with gold thread and red leather . . . ornamented with silvered leather." Such fine

[18] Anonymous, "Sahīfa-yi Iqbāl [A]," fol. 53a; Dihkhuda, *Amsāl va ḥikam*, 984; Roebuck, *Proverbs, and Proverbial Phrases*, 32. I thank Hadi Jorati and Dan Sheffield for these references.

[19] Crooke, *An Ethnographical Handbook for the N.-W. Provinces and Oudh*, 63–64.

[20] Baden-Powell, *Manufactures and Arts of the Punjab*, 121.

[21] Anonymous, "Sahīfa-yi Iqbāl [A]," fol. 52b.

[22] The censor is advised: "If, in a wide area, someone seizes place to build a shop in a public thoroughfare, they are to be enjoined to desist; and that which is constructed contrary to regulation is to be demolished, so that no one produces a fresh innovation (*bidʿat-i tāza*)." Hidāyat Allāh, "Hidāyat al-Qawāʿid," fol. 21b.

Figure 7.1. High and low in the square.
(Credit: Rampur Raza Library, Rampur. Detail.)

slippers, a far cry from the rude footwear made of grass, wheat, or leather worn in the surrounding regions of the city, were, even as late as the 1860s, crafted by a hundred-odd families in Delhi and traded across the country.[23] Another valued product was the *kafsh*, a broad-toed backless slipper with a high and narrow iron-shod heel. "It is exceedingly difficult for one unaccustomed to walk with *kafsh* to move steadily while wearing them," complained a nineteenth-century colonial magistrate of Lucknow, further suggesting that it was chiefly worn by "sanctimonious maulvis [theologians]" because the "shaky movement characteristic of old age" caused by the shoe simulated venerability. In the late nineteenth century, when a simple pair of shoes might cost a quarter rupee, a fancy *kafsh* could cost two and a half rupees, and a premier *ghetta* even more. Prices may not have changed much since the late seventeenth century.[24] Although making shoes, even fancy ones, was unlikely to have been a greatly profitable business, in the buzzing commercial economy of eighteenth-century Delhi, even shoemakers could splurge on the fireworks their ancestors had only witnessed as displays of royal munificence. Given playful names like "parrot," "mole," and "little mouse,"[25] such fireworks would have been inexpensive; even a century later, a European observer noted that since saltpeter was cheap, fireworks were sold "for a small price" and particularly used on the festivals of Holi and Shab-i Bara'at.[26]

Given the conjunction of the two festivals in 1729, the courtly chronicler was unsure whether "first the 'little mouse' of discord was set afire by the Muslims, or whether the hand of the Hindus scattered the color of tumult"; he noted many conflicting explanations.[27] But Ashob was certain that a "disastrous" squib had fallen into Subh Karan's palanquin and burned his court robes. What happened next followed the script of urban conflict: the "harsh exchange of words," of "contumely and abuse," pushing and shoving, kicks and blows. Although Subh Karan's retainers were armed, they were quickly outnumbered by the gathering shoemakers. Though all are agreed that one of Subh Karan's men was deprived of his sword and shield in the affray, what happened next is unclear. Some say

[23] Baden-Powell, *Manufactures and Arts of the Punjab*, 135.

[24] Hoey, *A Monograph on Trade and Manufactures in Northern India*, 127. Writing around the end of the seventeenth century, Manuzzi describes shoes offered to the imprisoned Shah Jahan as ranging in price from half a rupee to eight rupees. Manucci, *Storia Do Mogor*, 2:77.

[25] Ashob, "Tārīkh-i Shahādat [B]," fol. 56b.

[26] 'Ali, *Observations on the Mussulmauns of India*, 237–38.

[27] Anonymous, "Sahīfa-yi Iqbāl [A]," 48a–b; Anonymous, "Sahīfa-yi Iqbāl [B]," 249b–250.

that the humiliated retainer decided to seek revenge of his own accord, but Ashob suggests that Subh Karan felt "dishonor and defamation" at being dragged into a quarrel on the street. When he reproved his servants, they protested their innocence; the battered retainer was compelled to return and seek revenge. Whatever the case, sides emerged, and large groups of people became involved.

Looking back from the 1780s, the aged Ashob cast the conflict half a century earlier as a sectarian one at its outset. Thus he relates how a gathering of "impudent villains" returned to the shoemakers in the night. The mob first encountered a small child, who was cowardly beaten to death. On hearing the child's cries, Haji Hafiz, a white-bearded and devout elder of the shoemakers' community (*tā'ifa*), rose from his string bed and, rushed barefoot to investigate. He too was struck down by the "infidel sword." Its lust for vengeance quenched, the mob returned home, leaving the Haji's corpse in the filth of the street.[28] Ashob offered a simple account of the conflict's origins. An act of Hindu "tyranny" provoked a righteous Muslim response. This narrative also appears in twisted form by the biographer of Muhammad Zubair, the Appointed One, who is unique in laying the blame on the jeweler. In this unlikely version, Subh Karan accidentally spilled saffron color onto the clothes of the pious shoemaker, a disciple of Muhammad Zubair. When the shoemaker properly and sharply reproved the jeweler, the latter had the temerity to respond in kind; and it was the shoemaker who was stabbed in the back in the ensuing fighting![29]

But not all commentators saw the matter as a sectarian dispute. In recounting the story, the contemporary chronicler Warid, for instance, did not mention the death of a small child before Haji Hafiz. The courtly writer simply tells us that the retainer returned and contended with a devout shoemaker, who was killed. Ashob, who drew on this narrative, embellished it with the additional death of a child (unmentioned anywhere else) to establish the unrighteousness of the Hindu mob. Yet for the contemporary observer Warid, the killing of a Punjabi shoe seller by a servant of an imperial appraiser was not a moment of Hindu aggression, but just another instance of the "daily occurrence of murder" in Muhammad Shah's "negligent reign." Warid thus turned the killing of Haji Hafiz into a rebuke against

[28] Ashob, "Tārīkh-i Shahādat [B]," fol. 57a–b.
[29] Ihsan, *Rauzat-i Qaiyūmiyya*, IV:186.

the claims of imperial justice which constituted so integral a feature of the king's right to rule.[30]

Wednesday to Thursday: The Defense of Islam

Did the strong trample the weak so fearlessly in Muhammad Shah's Delhi, as Warid suggested, that Subh Karan's men expected no retaliation for the killing of Haji Hafiz? It seems difficult to imagine that Subh Karan sanctioned his men's act, let alone encouraged them to kill a shoemaker in cold blood. Even so, when commentators remarked that the jeweler's men had feared no revenge from so base a group as the city's shoemakers, it is clear they were projecting their own expectations onto Subh Karan. The appraiser may not have been so sanguine, for at this moment he vanishes from the historical record. Our chroniclers' attention is now fixed on the thoroughfare where the murdered shoemaker's body lies, and it is now that the struggle takes a new form. It was no longer a dispute between a jeweler and some shoemakers: the defense of the faith was invoked.

Thus Ashob recalled that, by sunrise, shoe sellers from the entire city had begun to assemble around the murdered body and had resolved to leave the body unburied until vengeance was theirs. The courtly chronicler on whom he based his account had seen it more cynically. He remarked that the shoemakers "put on the clog of the defense of the faith," wryly suggesting that they treated the honor of Islam like footwear, to be worn or discarded at will. But both agreed on the diversity of the crowds who rallied to the shoemakers' mourning. In accounts of this variegated "Muslim rabble" of Arabs, ʿAjamis, Turks, Tajiks, Abyssinians, Rumis, Mughals, and Hindustanis who gathered around the shoemakers, the cosmopolitanism that had marked the greatness of empire in Shah Jahan's Delhi had come to assume a darker aspect in the increasingly disorderly city.[31]

The "clog of the defense of the faith" was not immediately donned. The first course of action for the shoemakers and their allies would have been to approach a judge or the police chief; but the city's administrators appear only as a negative presence in the chronicles. According to Muhammad Zubair's hagiographer, after the people approached the mystic for assistance, he sternly

[30] Warid, "Mīrāt-i Wāridāt," fol. 172b.

[31] Anonymous, "Sahīfa-yi Iqbāl [A]," fol. 48b; Ashob, "Tārīkh-i Shahādat [A]," fol. 58a.

instructed the judge to produce the culprit and to give legal recourse to the aggrieved party.[32] This seems unlikely, given Muhammad Zubair's obscurity and lack of mention in other historical accounts. Nevertheless, judicial officers were widely regarded as incapable of imposing the law in this situation: Warid pithily dismissed the judge as "the leader of the gang of thieves of the [nearby] town of Palwal."[33] Even Khwush Hal Chand, not a supporter of the shoemakers' cause, admitted that the judge and the police chief were unhelpful in resolving the dispute.[34]

The widely derided inability of the authorities to bring the murderer to justice was not due to any inherent inefficacy but because the now-vanished Subh Karan was known to have powerful protectors. Who these were is disputed. Some, like the hagiographer Ihsan, thought it was the high nobleman Raushan al-Daula.[35] Ashob named the grandee ʿIzzat al-Daula, an ally of Raushan al-Daula and a relative by marriage, adding that both abided by the chivalric code of the ethnically North Indian nobility, which required the granting of protection to anyone who sought it.[36] Warid went further, accusing not only ʿIzzat al-Daula but even the king of protecting Subh Karan, and claiming the appraiser had been hidden away in the Fort.[37] The courtly author vigorously denied such contentions, and insisted the "popular notion" that ʿIzzat al-Daula was to blame was a calumny against the chivalry and nobility of the great man, elsewhere lauded as a "fiery leopard" and a "crocodile from the land-ocean of Panipat."[38] Yet, while not otherwise sympathetic to the shoemakers, this author nevertheless gave grounds for their frustration. Over the course of the two days, it became clear that the murderer had absconded, his principal Subh Karan was in hiding, and his protectors (whoever they were) had sided with the appraiser, having accepted weighty bribes from him.[39]

This frustration with administrative corruption caused the shoemakers to "unfurl a chessboard of another kind," as the courtly chronicler put it.[40] This was a strikingly profound observation: unable to contest the game of urban politics by its established rules, the shoemakers changed the game

[32] Ihsan, *Rauzat-i Qaiyūmiyya*, IV:187.
[33] Warid, "Mīrāt-i Wāridāt," fol. 173a.
[34] Khwush Hal, "Nādir al-Zamānī [B]," fol. 152b.
[35] Ihsan, *Rauzat-i Qaiyūmiyya*, IV:187.
[36] Ashob, "Tārīkh-i Shahādat [B]," fol. 58a.
[37] Warid, "Mīrāt-i Wāridāt," fol. 172b.
[38] Anonymous, "Sahīfa-yi Iqbāl [A]," fol. 50a-b.
[39] Anonymous, "Sahīfa-yi Iqbāl [A]," fol. 49a.
[40] Anonymous, "Sahīfa-yi Iqbāl [A]," fol. 49a.

itself. This alternate game of urban politics required the mobilization of Islam as a language of politics. The first move was to rally the community of Muslims around the body of the deceased shoemaker, and to make it a symbol of injustice through which the reigning order would be critiqued. As it became clear that Subh Karan was untouchable, the shoemakers and their allies began by refusing to perform the requisite funeral rites for their martyred leader.

The significance of this gesture escaped no one. In a short essay on funerary rites, a Lahori theologian stressed the importance of the timely and proper cleansing of the body, which made it fit to await resurrection.[41] Though it claimed to have been written in the aftermath of a plague in which so many died that confusion about the rites of death arose, this treatise and others like it were written not to educate scholars but more probably to circulate among communities of the pious such as the shoemakers of Delhi, whose Lahori origins, devoutness, and theological interests we have already noted. The Lahori theologian strictly forbade the clamorous proclamation of a death in public, for such was the way of "infidels," not Muslims.[42] So genteel observers were horrified to report that the shoemakers and their allies gathered *en masse* to carry the martyr's corpse on a string bed to Subh Karan's door, shouting "The Faith! The Faith!" (*dīn gūyand*). In conspicuously denying the mandated treatment to a Muslim corpse, the shoemakers turned it into a symbol of the injustice and oppression they had suffered as a community.

This turning of a practice of piety against power was universally condemned by all observers, who were, however, not unacquainted with the popular uses of corpses for contestations. In 1668/1669, for instance, musicians were reported to have conducted a clamorous "burial procession" of their musical instruments when the emperor Aurangzeb banned the practice of music in 1668/1669.[43] In the anti-Shiʿa disturbances of 1711, the corpse of a murdered imperial sermonizer was left lying outside the mosque, and the people prevented his heirs from taking it away for a day. Urbanites were known to carry the body of a wrongfully killed person to the local administrator, demanding restitution or compensation.[44] In leaving the bloodied body of Haji Hafiz at Subh Karan's door, the shoemakers thus

[41] Lahori, "Risāla-yi Mayyat," fol. 4a.

[42] Lahori, Risāla-yi Mayyat," fol. 3a.

[43] Brown, "Did Aurangzeb Ban Music?"

[44] See, for instance, the "joke" about the prostitute raped to death, whose heirs "placed her on a bed and covered her with a shawl, and brought her body to the commander" of the unit whose men had assaulted her and loudly demanded recompense. Mukhlis, *Chamanistan*, 20–21.

employed a familiar tactic that asserted blame and demanded justice, casting the appraiser as the principal (*āmir*) who was as responsible as the murderer (*qātil*). It was the "vileness" of this move, recalled Ashob, that caused Subh Karan to flee his house.[45]

On Thursday, as the king returned from the garden of Ja'far Khan, his procession was accosted by the shoemakers and their allies, shouting "The Faith! The Faith!" and "Justice! Justice!" To approach the king directly for justice was an established popular practice that drew on the imperial discourse of sovereignty, but the people's cries also signaled that they were invoking the privileges of the 'Community of Muslims.' Playing his assigned part, Muhammad Shah ordered the vizier I'timad al-Daula to dispatch a "stern officer" to find the malefactor and produce him in court, so that the matter might be settled according to the "commandments of the resplendent law" (*hukm-i sharī'at-i ghurā*).[46] Most observers thought that "no great efforts were made" to arrest Subh Karan because of his service as an appraiser in the Harem, though Khwush Hal intriguingly suggested that the king ignored their complaint, because he recognized their culpability with his "all-seeing eye and all-knowing intellect." As the matter remained unresolved, the martyred Haji Hafiz's body continued to lie outside Subh Karan's door, and "tumultuous folk" began to gather.[47]

Even as the agitators approached the king, they also prepared to challenge his legitimacy directly through the language of Islam if justice according to their terms was not granted. As all by now expected, the key articulation of this challenge would be the disruption of the Friday sermon. Khwush Hal noted that the fractious folk had come to oppose his beloved emperor, "the shadow of God," saying that the king had turned away from Muhammad's faith (*dīn-i Muhammadī*) and that he nurtured infidelity; they resolved to prevent the prayer-leader from reciting the sermon in the congregational mosque on Friday. The author particularly noted the role in the agitation of the "unshaven, whose work is hair-splitting": a reference to those Muslims who indicated their piety by leaving their beards unshorn, in defiance of the prevailing fashion, and who indulged in controversy and disputation.[48]

45 Ashob, "Tārīkh-i Shahādat [B]," fol. 58a.
46 Anonymous, "Sahīfa-yi Iqbāl [A]," fol. 49a.
47 Anonymous, "Sahīfa-yi Iqbāl [A]," fol. 49a; Ashob, "Tārīkh-i Shahādat [B]," fol. 58b; Khwush Hal, "Nādir al-Zamānī [B]," fol. 152b.
48 Khwush Hal, "Nādir al-Zamānī [B]," fol. 152b.

Though Khwush Hal does not elaborate, it would seem he referred to the city's popular preachers. This was an attribution of leadership that Muhammad Zubair's hagiographer would have welcomed, for he naturally ascribed the course of events to the divine's spiritual exertions. The hagiographer's exaggerations give a sense of the heated deliberations that preceded the events on Friday. In this version, when the city's officers refused to heed the mystic's injunctions to turn over the murderer, he sent instructions to the city's theologians to prevent the recitation of the Friday sermon if the matter were not favorably settled before then. When the Muslims united behind him, Muhammad Zubair began to pray for the "strengthening of Islam and the humiliation of infidelity." After long meditation, he announced to the people that by the grace of God, Islam was going to win the contest, and so "all the Muslims" went to the mosque with his support.[49] Though Muhammad Zubair may have played only a peripheral role (if any) in rousing the people, both accounts suggest that by Thursday evening the collective intention to disrupt the Friday prayers had become widespread. They also index the transformation of the gesture. Shorn of the sectarian signification of its origins in Lahore two decades before, the act of interruption now simply expressed popular defiance and opposition to the king himself.

Friday, March 9: Confrontation, Negotiation, Escalation

Ashob remembered that Friday morning dawned with the shoemakers and "common mendicants" (*faqīr-i ʿāmm*) inciting the riotous in the defense of Islam. Vast numbers of the city's Muslims responded. They resolved to protect the faith by assisting the opponents of the "accursed infidel" (*kāfir-i laʿīn*) and began to gather at the congregational mosque.[50] The shoemakers had been planning for the confrontation, for they arrived at the mosque with the iron heel-pieces (*naʿlī-hā*) that gave the *kafsh*—the shoe that produced the quavering walk of the pious doctors—its distinct attributes. They also brought brickbats and stones in the hems of their long skirts. And the shoemakers carried the object of their trade and livelihood, which also marked them as demeaned and symbolized their oppression: their shoes.[51]

[49] Ihsan, *Rauzat-i Qaiyūmiyya*, IV:187.
[50] Ashob, "Tārīkh-i Shahādat [A]," fol. 59a.
[51] Ashob, "Tārīkh-i Shahādat [A]," fols. 60b–61a.

Their preparations to interrupt the prayer reveal their certainty in the fact of their injustice, the truth of their interpretation of the law, and the belief that all others—even the king—were in the wrong.

The elite chroniclers perceived this sense of rectitude perfectly well. As the courtly chronicler noted, the shoemakers marched to the mosque to defy the king and his nobility on the basis of the Qur'anic verse: "*Hence if anyone has been slain wrongly, We have empowered the defender of his rights.*" This sense of divine sanction, which united the shoemakers with their allies, the "Muslim riff-raff," was however regarded by the courtly observer as carrying "insolence and fearlessness beyond the limit of estimation."[52] Ashob describes this crowd as including soldiers serving the artillery captains Rumi Khan and Sayyid ʿArab ʿAli Khan, whose names betoken their leadership of ethnic groups: Ottoman (*rūmī*), Abyssinian and Arab soldiers, who arrived at the mosque with their flintlock muskets, pistols, and European guns, loaded and at the ready.[53]

Where and how did these expatriates come to embrace the shoemakers' cause? Had they come to know each other through intermingling in the shops of Saʿd Allah Khan Square? Did they pray next to each other at the congregational mosque or attend the same gatherings of lowly preachers like Muhammad Zubair? Whatever the case, even as sympathetic an observer as Ashob disapproved strongly of these refractory soldiers; he observed sarcastically that they imagined their support of the wronged shoemakers to be an article of faith and the courtyard of the congregational mosque to be a battleground of holy war (*ghazā, jihād*). Crowding around the pulpit and the alcove with matchlocks primed and arrows nocked, the shoemakers and their allies warned the preacher not to read the Friday sermon and loudly and impertinently accused the judge, the jurisprudent, and other officers of "siding with infidels."[54]

The significance of the potential interruption of the Friday sermon did not escape the court, which had been receiving reports of the multitudes streaming into the mosque. The king was dissuaded from going to offer prayers with the congregation of Muslims and to hear the Friday proclamation in his name, as was customary. Instead he dispatched the vizier and the minister Raushan al-Daula to proceed to the mosque and, as Khwush Hal

[52] Qur'ān 17:33; Anonymous, "Sahīfa-yi Iqbāl [A]," fol. 49a.
[53] Ashob, "Tārīkh-i Shahādat [A]," fol. 61b.
[54] Ashob, "Tārīkh-i Shahādat [A]," fol. 59a; Anonymous, "Sahīfa-yi Iqbāl [A]," fol. 49a.

punned darkly, to "relieve whoever raised their head in rebellion of its weight from their shoulders."[55]

In fact, the agents of state tried to quell the disorder by recourse to both conciliation and coercion. The vizier, Raushan al-Daula, and ʿIzzat al-Daula reached the mosque with their retinues, each group entering it from a separate side. According to Ashob, by the time the vizier arrived in the mosque's courtyard through the northern gate, matters had already escalated. The infuriated crowds had turned upon the magistrate and his son, who had been beaten within an inch of their lives. The prayer-leader, trapped near the pulpit with guns pointed at him, was being dared to recite the Friday sermon.[56] The vizier proceeded toward the pulpit and began to search for the prayer-leader (*pesh-namāzī*) and the sermon-reader, who were lost in the crowds.

For Ashob, this tense moment now became the scene of an artful negotiation between the rulers and the ruled. On approaching the crowds gathered around the pulpit, the vizier attempted to assuage the crowds by adopting their own language of Islam: he "declared himself firmly in accord with the Muslims in the claim for vengeance for the martyred and oppressed Haji Hafiz against that tyrannical infidel" and his "smooth-tongued words doused the fire of tumult." For their part, some of the assembled expressed "contrition and repentance" for their disrespectful violence against the judge. "In reality," adds Ashob, "the expression of support by such a high nobleman only increased their dissension." [57]

In fact, precisely the opposite happened. Both sides drew on the language of vengeance against tyrannical infidels, but the pantomime of the protestors' subservience incorporated at least some of the vizier's troops to their cause. For as the vizier engaged in this act of last-minute conciliation, Raushan al-Daula entered the mosque through its eastern imperial gate with his own contingent of Afghan troops, the "barbarous and brave" residents of the nearby regions of Khurja and Sikandra (which Ashob regarded as "an Afghanistan in India").[58] Shortly thereafter, ʿIzzat al-Daula entered the mosque through its southern gate. And as Raushan al-Daula and ʿIzzat al-Daula's troops arrived, it seemed to them as if the vizier's forces were arrayed with the "foreigners."[59] As with their appeals to the defense of the faith as

[55] Khwush Hal, "Nādir al-Zamānī [B]," fol. 152b.

[56] The courtly chronicler, however, thought that the sermon-reader had also been beaten, and fled. Anonymous, "Sahīfa-yi Iqbāl [A]," fol. 49b.

[57] Ashob, "Tārīkh-i Shahādat [A]," fol. 60a; Anonymous, "Sahīfa-yi Iqbāl [A]," fol. 50a; Anonymous, "Sahīfa-yi Iqbāl [B]," fol. 251b.

[58] Ashob, "Tārīkh-i Shahādat [A]," fol. 60a–b.

[59] Anonymous, "Sahīfa-yi Iqbāl [A]," fol. 51a.

their show of repentance, the shoemakers and their allies thus seem to have outmaneuvered the nobility, producing divisions between and among the agents of state and their soldiers.

According to Warid, the vizier had counseled Raushan al-Daula and ʿIzzat al-Daula that only "humility and conciliation" would pacify the "utterly enraged ruffians." But the two noblemen, confident in their Afghan soldiers and artillery, rejected this advice, and responded roughly to the complainants.[60] Now that the agitators were hemmed in on all sides, Raushan al-Daula instructed his men to close the gates. Though he did so to prevent other unruly folk from entering the mosque, this action was seen as the mistake that precipitated the violence and matters spun out of hand. The courtly chronicler sarcastically commented on its wisdom in verse:

> He said, "A hundred Afghans are to close each gate of thought."
> No better key than this to unlock this diabolical inspiration![61]

The crowd's mood turned. This was the moment they had feared, prepared, and perhaps longed for. The agents of state were arrayed against the people, whom they had planned to crush all along. In response, the shoemakers began to fling their shoes at ʿIzzat al-Daula, doubtless because he was believed to have given shelter to Subh Karan. The courtly chronicler compared the salvo of shoes to the vast flocks of pigeons that suddenly arise and wheel over the mosque's courtyard:

> Towards the mosque they came, shoe atop shoe
> Into the air they suddenly flew like a rank of pigeons[62]

To be struck by a shoe was a pointed act of humiliation, all the more so when the shoe was flung by the most contemptible at the most honorable.[63] But when the Afghan retainers of ʿIzzat al-Daula and Raushan al-Daula moved to "dissuade" the shoemakers from this "short-sighted course of action,"

[60] Warid, "Mīrāt-i Wāridāt," fol. 173a.

[61] Anonymous, "Sahīfa-yi Iqbāl [A]," fol. 50a. The literary skills of our author are here as elsewhere manifest in his delight in referentiality: a "Qufl-i waswās" is a specific reference to "[a]n intricate kind of lock." Steingass, Johnson, and Richardson, *A Comprehensive Persian-English Dictionary*, 981.

[62] Anonymous, "Sahīfa-yi Iqbāl [A]," fol. 50b; Anonymous, "Sahīfa-yi Iqbāl [B]," fol. 252a.

[63] Thus the many idiomatic phrases: "Jūtiyāṅ khānā, v.n., to suffer a shoe-beating; to suffer indignity or humiliation; to remain in an abject state of submission; jūtiyāṅ mārnā (-par), to give (one) a shoe-beating; to treat contemptuously, to disdain; to revile, taunt." Platts, *A Dictionary of Urdu, Classical Hindi, and English*, 396.

one of their Abyssinian allies fired his musket in the direction of the two noblemen. The Afghans fell on upon the shoemakers, and the vizier's Mughal troops fell upon the Afghans. Why this happened the courtly author does not say, instead simply stating that "slowly the affair became a fight between Mughals and Afghans."[64] In his version, Ashob blamed the proverbial fractiousness of the Mughals, who threw off their military discipline and joined their compatriots under attack by the Afghans. The Mughals received reinforcements from their compatriots outside the mosque, who seized its gates from the Afghans and brought in their own guns and light artillery on camelback. The unarmed shoemakers, comparatively few in number, vanished in the smoke and fury of the battle between the Mughal and Afghan contingents.[65] Despite their valiant efforts, the Afghans were ultimately defeated. Surrounding their leaders Raushan al-Daula and ʿIzzat al-Daula, the Afghans retreated to the nearby mansion of the latter's elder brother Diler Dil Khan. The vizier's Mughal troops were only restrained with the greatest difficulty from following the defeated party to the mansion and burning it down. Noblemen without retainers were left to fend for themselves; they jumped off the mosque's high walls and scurried ignominiously through the city's alleys to their own homes.[66]

As the disorder began to subside by the time of the afternoon prayers, agents of state set about restoring order and reasserting their legitimacy, again in the language of Islam. The first goal was to re-establish control over the mosque. Mace-bearers were deployed to disperse rioters, and armed guards were stationed at its gates. Because the bloody courtyard was hardly fit for worship, the late afternoon prayers were held at the Enclosure of the Relics just to the west of the city. According to Ashob, a special thanksgiving prayer was offered for the "divine victory" (*fath-i ghaʾibī*), though who or what was defeated is not stated.[67] Gifts were offered to the caretakers of the relics "by way of gratitude" to the Prophet. Muhammad Shah, without blaming any nobleman, sent a special turban, in the fashion of his own, to the vizier.[68] Such a gesture not only reaffirmed that the vizier was considered blameless in inciting the agitators but also reiterated the king's professed sympathy with the wronged Muslims. By containing the strife within a broad

64 Anonymous, "Sahīfa-yi Iqbāl [A]," fol. 51b.
65 Ashob, "Tārīkh-i Shahādat [A]," fols. 61b–62a.
66 Ashob, "Tārīkh-i Shahādat [A]," fols. 62b–63a; Warid, "Mīrāt-i Wāridāt," fol. 174a.
67 Ashob, "Tārīkh-i Shahādat [A]," fol. 64a.
68 Anonymous, "Sahīfa-yi Iqbāl [A]," fol. 53b.

if vague claim of the triumph of Islam, the king's agents sought to wrest away the narrative of righteous resistance from the shoemakers and reassert the leadership of the imperial elite.

What were the consequences for the disputants? Ashob thought the shoemakers' protest had a happy ending, that they and their allies were dispatched "victorious and triumphant, happy and laughing" by the vizier.[69] This seems unlikely. The courtly chronicler on whom Ashob based his account simply noted that they were routed and vanished in the first shock of combat.[70] According to Warid, the usual attempts were made to discover the hidden hand behind the uprising, but despite the slaying of fifty of Raushan al-Daula's Afghan retainers, the organizer of this "minor day of resurrection" remained untraceable.[71] Though the Afghans were universally lauded for their bravery, Ashob thought that the city's Mughals gained popularity among the city's people for their defense of Islam.[72] Khwush Hal added a laconic sentence to conclude his brief account: "[T]hat group, which originated the strife, agreed to bury their deceased in the house of Subh Karan; thus it was likewise enacted."[73]

It is certain that the shoemakers did not enjoy a total victory. The fact that Subh Karan escaped with his life, as even the fanatical biographer of Muhammad Zubair acknowledged, indicates that the court acted forcefully to reestablish its authority in the days after the event. A measure of the suppression that followed the riot can be discerned from the hagiography of Muhammad Zubair. Immediately after describing the "victory of Islam," the hagiographer describes a convoluted conspiracy against the mystic. First, Muhammad Zubair was forced by one ʿAbd al-Hakim, a noted theologian, to affix his seal to a declaration (*mazhar*) that found the king lax in the affairs of Islam, enjoined him to collect the poll tax, and demanded he conduct himself in accordance with past precedent. Muhammad Zubair only acceded (with the greatest reluctance) to this hostile move against the court, and only because it might help enforce legal obligations (*ahkām-i sharʿī*). The king's advisers were outraged and produced a "forged" declaration in which the mystic claimed that the king, having abandoned Islam, was unworthy of the mantle of rulership. The forged document further claimed that

[69] Ashob, "Tārīkh-i Shahādat [A]," fol. 64b.
[70] Anonymous, "Sahīfa-yi Iqbāl [A]," fol. 53a.
[71] Warid, "Mīrāt-i Wāridāt," fol. 175b.
[72] Ashob, "Tārīkh-i Shahādat [A]," fol. 63a.
[73] Khwush Hal, "Nādir al-Zamānī [B]," fol. 153a.

the prophet Muhammad had instructed its supposed author Muhammad Zubair to become the "Surety of the Caliphate" and to become king himself, so that the "orthodox" faith might flourish once again. Then these courtly conspirators spread the word that the king had ordered his army to attack Muhammad Zubair's hospice. In response, thousands of his disciples, particularly Mughals, gathered in his defense. Ultimately, the vizier effected a reconciliation. Though hurt by Muhammad Shah's fickleness, Muhammad Zubair continued to profess his support of the king, likening their relationship to that between Khwaja Baha᾿ al-Din, the founder of the Naqshbandi Way, and Amir Timur, the king's venerable ancestor.[74]

In relaying a confused account of real and false declarations, half-hearted endorsements, potential conflicts, and disaster averted, the hagiographer Muhammad Ihsan sought to weave his object of adulation, an otherwise insignificant mystic, into the high political dramas of the city's life. But the outlines of a more banal conflict are readily apparent beneath the hagiographer's artless obfuscations. The picture that emerges is one of a heightened frenzy of urban politics in the aftermath of the uprising, in which Muhammad Zubair, like other equally obscure divines, was now mobilizing popular opinion against the king and seeking support for himself.

Such challenges to the king were not without consequences. Because of Muhammad Zubair's affiliations with the city's Mughals, who as we have seen were partly blamed for the events in the mosque, royal power began to make itself felt at the mystic's hospice. According to his hagiographer, it was feared that the king's spies had infiltrated the divine's establishment and were sending "false reports" to the court. When, in the resulting paranoia, an innocent visitor was beaten up on suspicion of being a spy, Muhammad Zubair pointed out the *real* mole, who shamefacedly promised to send only accurate reports to his masters at court. Another secret agent who dispatched false reports found his face swollen and was rendered speechless. Despite these demonstrations of his supernatural power, the divine quickly bent at the knee when the court demanded. Though the hagiographer does his best to sugarcoat it, he relates how Muhammad Shah "humbly implored" the Appointed One to give a Friday sermon to the Mughals and other Muslims, instructing them to fall in line. When Muhammad Zubair graciously acceded to this "request" and gave a sermon urging his congregants to "obey the reigning emperor of the era," all willingly

[74] Ihsan, *Rauzat-i Qaiyūmiyya*, IV:188–98, quote on 191.

accepted these pronouncements, and so peace was finally re-established.[75] This exercise of quiet influence suggests that the court was cognizant of the popular challenge to its authority and able to mitigate it. Nevertheless it is an inescapable fact that the event of the uprising changed the structure of the king's relations with his subjects. Where, once upon a time, the emperor magnanimously welcomed pleaders at his window of presentation, now even his lowliest subjects demanded justice at the mosque by challenging his very right to rule.[76]

What the Riot Signified

In the eyes of historians of the past century who have examined the event, the riot signified the disorder of a society in the midst of imperial decline. For William Irvine, its value was as "conducing to the downfall of the group of palace favorites," and more generally "as a picture of turbulence of the capital."[77] Sayyid Athar Abbas Rizvi, subsuming the uprising in his five pages on "Hindu-Muslim riots" of the eighteenth century, found the violence symptomatic of an economic crisis. Blaming the "Afghans of Delhi, who were very easily excited and provoked into fighting," he described these men as "retainers of Rohēllas and Bangash adventurers . . . but most of them were unemployed."[78] In doing so, Rizvi made a move characteristic of post-independence Indian historians, whose fear of the "fissiparous tendencies" of the infant republic of India routinely led them to seek an economic basis for what appeared all too familiar in their present: interreligious conflict caused by the blind passions of the irrational mob. This led Rizvi, like others, to excise the language of zeal for the faith and hostility to the infidel from his rendition of the riot. But Muhammad Bakhsh Ashob, on whose account Irvine, Rizvi, and I too have relied, experienced no psychic schism or contradiction in relating an analytical historical account in terms of a struggle between the defenders of the "martyred and oppressed" Muslim shoemaker and the "accursed and oppressive" infidel. In studding his depiction with these words of confrontation—*shahīd, jihād, kāfir*—Ashob forged a polarized vision that evoked a language of urban popular politics in which he was fully versed. But,

[75] Ihsan, *Rauzat-i Qaiyūmiyya*, IV:224–25.
[76] Ihsan, *Rauzat-i Qaiyūmiyya*, IV:225–26.
[77] Irvine and Sarkar, *Later Mughals*, I:257–63.
[78] Rizvi, *Shah Wali-Allah and His Times*, 197–202, quote on 201–2.

as we have argued in previous pages, representations that drew on the language of Islam were the textual register of a corresponding political struggle that evoked the community and asserted its place on the basis of the imperial discourse of sovereignty. Nor were Ashob's views representative of any popular consensus: by his later years, Ashob, had acquired a reputation for "fanaticism" which even caused his acquaintances to write rude chronograms noting his death.[79]

It is therefore unsurprising that Ashob's polarized vision was not shared by contemporary observers, including the courtly account on which he relied and which he frequently reproduced verbatim and without attribution within his own. In defining the struggle as one between rightful Muslims and infidels, Ashob's words embodied a popular perspective that the courtly chronicler had found repugnant and repeatedly mocked. For the courtly chronicler, the people who marched through the city to the cries of "The Faith! The Faith! Muhammad!" were not righteous subjects but an ignorant and uncontrolled mob. In a manner reminiscent of Niʿmat Khan-i ʿAli's satires, the author sharpened his critique of the shoemakers by casually demonstrating his mastery of the Qurʾan as he rebuked them for claiming the mantle of religion. Thus the shoemakers were represented as invoking Qurʾanic verses in demanding retribution (2:179) and in justifying their own actions (17:33).[80] The result of this righteous agitation, however, was "insolence and temerity . . . disobedience . . . impertinence" (*shokhī o bī-bākī . . . pechish . . . nasazā*).[81] When hurling shoes at the nobility, the shoemakers were passingly likened to the birds who dropped pellets on enemy elephants mentioned in the Qurʾan; but they were summarily assigned all the blame for the events in the mosque and dismissed, simply, as "curs."[82] For contemporaries, the shoemakers' resistance did not uphold Islam, but, in violating the sanctity of the mosque, defiled it. In this vein, Warid sanctimoniously observed that the mosque was not a battleground, while others circulated verses to the effect that even the mosque's pulpit cried out in shame and pain from the fighting.[83]

For the courtly author, the events of the mosque were seen not as a moment to celebrate the successful defense of Islam by the city's lowly but rather as an opportunity for literary jest which cloaked a higher meaning

[79] Khan, "Khulāsat al-Afkār," fols. 357b–358a.
[80] Anonymous, "Sahīfa-yi Iqbāl [A]," fols. 48b, 49a.
[81] Anonymous, "Sahīfa-yi Iqbāl [A]," fol. 49a.
[82] Anonymous, "Sahīfa-yi Iqbāl [A]," fols. 49b, 53a.
[83] Warid, "Mīrāt-i Wāridāt," fol. 175a; Anonymous, "Sahīfa-yi Iqbāl [A]," fol. 53a.

in a "modern veil" (*niqāb-i tarz-i jadīd*).[84] Despite these puffed-up claims, no greater literary signification is apparent in his description. The uprising served a novel opportunity to demonstrate the author's literary virtuosity in terms familiar from the culture of satire prevalent among the city's elites. Thus slurs are casually aimed at the shoemakers' allies. The Abyssinian who first fired on the noblemen was described as "dark-hearted, black within as without." His supporters were described as the "barbaric common refractory Mughals" and the "wicked mouse-eating Arabs," the latter presented as proof of the Qur'anic verse that "the Arabs are more obstinate in their refusal to acknowledge the truth, and in their hypocrisy [than settled people]."[85] The greatest contempt, of course, was reserved for the shoemakers, who despite their claim to the honor of Islam, were linked repeatedly to their dishonorable profession. At the very outset, for instance, the author confessed that the tumult (*shorish*) was so weird that "the fitting of the shoe of description and narration on the foot-mold of writing is too tight."[86] And the bodily denigration of the shoemakers is made clear in a remarkable paragraph:

> The strangest thing of all was the action of the heavily contaminated community of the evil and unworthy shoemakers. Because their hand's reach did not extend beyond footwear, they used them; [but] just as at first they made such a powerful gesture at the heads of those present, the same blow of the hand left them bewildered, unable to discern their hands from their feet. The thread of the battle loosened from their hands; and with heads erect they confusedly (*sarāsima*) placed their feet in the valley of escape, when officers, on whose knowledgeable heads fell the task, quickly rendered them worn-out and non-existent.[87]

Though this translation does scant justice to the dexterousness of the original, the repeated emphasis on heads and feet locates the shoemakers at the bottom of the body social even as it acknowledges the significance of their transgression, which it seeks to limit through the deployment of aestheticized narrative. Elsewhere, too, the courtly author insisted that the shoemakers were incapable of confronting steadfast soldiers: "[T]hus of necessity greatness decided the day and took pity on the smallness of the shoemakers."[88] As

[84] Anonymous, "Sahīfa-yi Iqbāl [A]," fol. 48a.
[85] Anonymous, "Sahīfa-yi Iqbāl [A]," fol. 51a–b; Qur'an 9.97.
[86] Anonymous, "Sahīfa-yi Iqbāl [A]," fol. 48a.
[87] Anonymous, "Sahīfa-yi Iqbāl [A]," fols. 52b–53a.
[88] Anonymous, "Sahīfa-yi Iqbāl [A]," fol. 52a.

the spectacle was cast in the terms of the amusements of the cultured, so too was the usual order of society reasserted.

Another position was presented by the chronicler Warid. Like the courtly writer, Warid also delighted in the literary possibilities of the spectacle. His sympathies, however, rested not with the nobility but the shoemakers. Yet Warid did not regard the events in sectarian terms. In his account, the shoemakers are cast not as righteous Muslims battling infidels but rather as a community of the wrongfully oppressed fighting the king's injustice. Their agitation afforded Warid an opportunity to criticize the emperor Muhammad Shah for failing to enact the role assigned to him in the imperial discourse of sovereignty. This was a somewhat radical position. While it was possible to criticize the conduct of previous emperors, observers generally desisted from critiquing the reigning ruler. But Warid is perhaps unique in putting on paper the omens of fire and plague, which he read as indicating heaven's disfavor with the reigning king.[89]

In this context, Warid did not present the killing of the shoemaker as an instance of Hindu oppression but rather as among the "daily murders" that dotted this "reign conjoined with negligence." He particularly blamed the king's spiritual preceptor Shah ʿAbd al-Ghafur, whose "sword of injustice" fell daily on the humble and the poor, so that the custom of "man-slaughtering" had become a tradition in Delhi, and most days saw news of five killed here or ten there. "But in these ten years of the Muhammad Shahi reign," wrote Warid, "on no day was it ever heard that the imperial sword of justice might slay the murderer in retribution. The emperor remains unaware of the traces of the sighs of the oppressed."[90] This was the tradition of injustice and oppression against which Warid saw the shoemakers rebelling.

Though the humiliation of the great was not without its pleasures for all observers, Warid's schadenfreude reached, even for him, an extreme pitch. We are told that the people settled the affairs of the judge, whom Warid elsewhere accuses of leading an exurban gang of thieves, "according to the dictates of the law": the judge's "beard did not remain save for a few hairs, and the clothes he wore on his back were likewise taken away, shred by shred, as sacred relics." This assault on the honor of Muhammad Shah was followed by the disgrace of his assembled courtiers:

[89] Warid, "Mīrāt-i Wāridāt," fol. 174ab.
[90] Warid, "Mīrāt-i Wāridāt," fol. 172b.

> On that day, the eagle of the shoe flew in such a way that the heron of the turban could not keep to the nest of distinction atop the heads of the nobility . . . wherever the gaze alighted, suddenly the turban of the greatest grandees, endowed with large retinues [but] no honor, had come to serve as the door-mat for the shoe.[91]

Warid joyfully articulates the profound symbolic significance of the gesture. The highest, their great honor symbolized by the turban, were now debased by the uncleanest objects of the low. The specter of defilement, which hung over even the most professedly pious shoemaker, remained his most potent weapon. In a society obsessed with the proper order of head and foot, there could be no more charged challenge than a shoe displacing a turban.

Warid's spite is reminiscent of that of a talented elite who has gone unrecognized and turned against the imperial order.[92] But it is surely this embitterment and distance from court that helped him recognize the shoemakers' assault as a direct challenge to the imperial discourse of sovereignty. He makes this apparent in his description of the nobleman Raushan al-Daula in the midst of the battle. Now wearing the shoes of the people of the bazar instead of the distinctive eagle's feather in his turban—a symbol of the inversion of the body politic—Raushan al-Daula is made to utter a remarkable monologue at his Afghan retainers before their ignominious flight from the mosque:

> O Companions! Under no circumstances does exalted and praiseworthy God, who is the perfectly independent doctor (*hakīm*), grant *daulat* to anyone by mistaken grace. Be it certain that although perfect intellect and senses are not manifest in this infirm slave, he has not reached the apogee of stateliness and leadership, which is the inhabiting of high office in the imperial administration, by way of street-walking and aimless wandering (*kūcha-gardī o pādo'ī*). And so my nature must be regarded just as that of Aristotle, the vizier of Alexander. To this effect it is established that whenever one of the four humors (*khiltī az ikhlāt-i arba'a*) in the bodies of the tribe of Noah raises the standard of rebellion, it overshadows the flag of the good life (*rāyat-i zindagānī-yi nekū*). What we witness now is the mutual

[91] Warid, fol. 173b.

[92] A perhaps comparable case is that discussed in Fleischer, *Bureaucrat and Intellectual in the Ottoman Empire*.

> opposition of the constitutive elements of humanity. Thus, the self-willed wind of fate has turned against one, and is sprinkling shoes clotted with the dirt of desolation on one's head and face; and the watermark of the sword is so close as to pass the head; and the fire-spurting gun and the life-taking rocket (*bān*) are hotly engaged in shooting forth lightning . . .
>
> For sensible folk to remain here in such discordant conditions is to give one's head to the wind of annihilation . . . Therefore, you all must transport my life, which has no equal or match, which comes before all victory and is more precious than name and honor, from this ocean of bloodlust to the shore of safety.[93]

Warid's sarcastic diatribe is significant for several reasons. It directly, if fleetingly, invokes the philosophical tradition of the ethical literature (*akhlāq*) that undergirded the discourse of imperial sovereignty. The words placed in the mouth of Raushan al-Daula refract the ideas of the Arabic philosopher al-Farabi (d. 950–951), who, in the words of one commentator "carries over the Galenic medical analogy from ethics to politics, comparing the ideal ruler to a doctor who looks after the souls of his people."[94] Because God, as the perfect doctor, could not have granted *daulat* to him by accident, Raushan al-Daula imagines himself to be a philosophical ruler (rather than a petty vagabond and sycophant as is slyly suggested), who now beholds the good life as being overwhelmed by the humoral imbalance of a primeval social conflict in the mosque. Blaming fate (and not himself) for this disorder, the cowardly nobleman beseeches his retainers to save his life, even at the cost of his honor. At the same time, the ethical and philosophical tradition that undergirds the discourse of sovereignty is mocked for its hollowness in the face of popular rejection.

For Warid, the events in the mosque thus served to critique the nobility, personified in Raushan al-Daula. Whether the *daulat* was granted the nobleman by heavenly oversight or in accordance with some inscrutable purpose, Raushan al-Daula, and presumably others like him, were unworthy of it. It is true that Raushan al-Daula was blamed for the happenings in the mosque and that his unpopularity may have been connected to his fall from grace shortly thereafter. The courtly writer, otherwise circumspect about mocking members of the nobility, bizarrely insists on referring to the

93 Warid, "Mīrāt-i Wāridāt," fols. 173b–174a.

94 Peter Adamson, "Ethics in Philosophy."

nobleman Raushan al-Daula ("Luster of *Daulat*") as Rauzan al-Daula ("The Chimney of *Daulat*"), the putatively popular pronunciation of his title, and blames him for precipitating the riot.[95] Khwush Hal, by contrast, wondered if the vizier joined with the fractious folk in the mosque in order to cut his rival Raushan al-Daula down to size.[96] Such varied criticism of the nobility surely reflected both the range of opinions that circulated in the city, and the frustrating inability of elites to locate the true origin of the riot. But more likely than any such conspiracy theory is what Warid had himself discerned: the shoemakers had acted autonomously, and their gestures expressed a direct challenge to the legitimacy of the political order upheld by the king and his nobility.

Publication and Circulation

The variety of views on the causes, victims, culprits, and meanings of the shoemakers' riot cannot easily be reconciled. This diversity signals an urban culture in which public opinion was heterogeneous and fractured. The impulses that led observers to aestheticize their accounts of the disorder not only restrained the transgression in prose, but also made it fit to be read, enjoyed, and circulated by others. Yet, as we have seen, the networks of elite circulation in the city were also closely linked to a correspondingly developed realm of popular communication in which political opinions were formed and shared. The courtly writer reveals his awareness of the vitality of this realm in expressing his surprise at the number of charming but contentious poems and chronograms in Persian, Hindi, and Rekhta, which garnered widespread fame and enrichment for their authors. Those censured by such popular writers, he protests, were in fact faultless. While he probably refers here to the nobleman ʿIzzat al-Daula, whom he elsewhere defends, the author's concluding wish is undoubtedly meant for the nobility as a whole:

> May the True Protector give refuge to our contemporaries from the evil of the tongues of the people, who are like animals, for:
> It is possible to shut up the gate of the city,
> But not the mouths of opponents.[97]

[95] Anonymous, "Sahīfa-yi Iqbāl [A]," fols. 49b–50a.
[96] Khwush Hal, "Nādir al-Zamānī [B]," fol. 153a.
[97] Anonymous, "Sahīfa-yi Iqbāl [A]," 53a.

But that this feared popular chatter only intensified as time went by is apparent in Ashob's account. Writing decades later, he still remembered the strangeness of this "admonition-increasing" (*ʿibrat-afzā*) event, about which partisan accounts of "blame and schadenfreude" (*malāmat o shamātat*) were widely written and circulated. In fact it had become a literary topos, so that poets "opened the doors of gladness" for listeners with many kinds of poetry composed about the event.[98] The same process of urban circulation is evident in the much-repeated story of the portly nobleman Aʿzam Khan, who became entangled in the thatched roof of a simple potter's shop in his attempt to flee the fighting and was sorely beaten by the enraged potter as a result.[99]

Perhaps because such poems and anecdotes circulated in the oral and popular realm of the city's streets, they have left almost no trace in the archive. But one such poem, written in the "mixed language" of Rekhta, was unearthed and published by the great scholar of early Urdu literature Hafiz Mahmud Sherani. This work, titled "Quintets in Censure of Turra Baz Khan [Raushan al-Daula]," was written by the poet Benawa ("The Unfortunate"), an immigrant from the small town of Sunam in Punjab and a marginal figure in the literary scene of Delhi under Muhammad Shah. Though otherwise obscure, Benawa was recorded as a "witty and ingenious" (*shokh-chashm o zarīf*) person who produced "jests" (*latīfa*). Indeed, Sherani tells us that the poet Shauq, writing in 1785, noted that Benawa's *Quintets* were still "on the lips of the people" of his day.[100]

The continued circulation of the *Quintets* marks the fixing of the event in popular memory almost half a century later, when only a few firsthand observers would have remained. But while the poem's persistence in the oral sphere thus indicates the enduring significance of the uprising in the mosque, it was written by Benawa not chiefly as a means of memorialization for the future but primarily as an intervention in the politics of the poet's present. His poem was precisely the kind of widely popular work against which the courtly writer hoped vainly to shut his ears. We should imagine the *Quintets* as one among the many poems recited by minstrels, bards, storytellers, and mimes (*mīrāsī*-s, *bhāt*-s, *naqqāl*-s) who roamed the city's streets and occupied its squares, rewarded with small money by the folk who would in turn recite stanzas to their neighbors or murmur snippets to themselves. The *Quintets*, I am therefore suggesting, was not an "expression" of "popular opinion" as

[98] Ashob, "Tārīkh-i Shahādat [A]," fols. 64b–65a.
[99] Ashob, "Tārīkh-i Shahādat [A]," fol. 63a–b.
[100] The following discussion is based on my translation of Shirani, *Maqalat-i Hafiz Mahmud Shirani*, II:130–45.

much an artifact built for widespread circulation, its success in shaping and reflecting people's views indicated by its continued repetition.

Sharing only the broad outlines of the elite narratives of the disturbance, the *Quintets* offer a perspective remarkably different from those encountered above. Most significantly, what the *Quintets* commemorate is not the dispute between "Islam" and "infidelity" but the clash between the lowly and the high. Thus the poem is almost completely focused on the confrontation in the mosque on the Friday, to the exclusion of surrounding events. While Subh Karan is alluded to by name as "crushing the dazzling ruby with the mortar of oppression," no mention is made of the slaying of the Haji, the casting of his body at Subh Karan's door, or the eventual demolition of his house. Instead, the language of Islam is immediately invoked to rally the community around the victims, who are "shoe-sellers, Muslim men, and devout." The word to gather together (*ikatthā*) occurs four times in the second and third quintets, emphasizing the rapid forging of solidarity between various groups, first cobblers and vagabonds, later joined by Abyssinians and Arabs. Before that, however, the cobblers and vagabonds "recollect God"; they futilely approach the judge and police chief; they do not plead but demand "their justice" from the king.

Crucial to this assertive solidarity is the idea of a righteous war (*jihād*) against infidelity (*kufr*), so that the rallying cry of "The Faith! The Faith! Muhammad!" is preserved forever. But once the community has assembled, the question of the defense of Islam falls away. What is warmly anticipated now is the forceful opposition to the agents of the state. As in the elite narratives, there is sardonic amusement expressed at the beatings inflicted on the judge and jurisprudent. Earthy metaphors derived at the confectioner's shop express the sweetness of their humiliation: the judge has his "*halwā* stirred" by the gathered crowds, and the jurisprudent has his "*peth* crushed." Thousands gather to prevent the prayer, and Abyssinians and Arabs have surrounded the pulpit with their weapons unsheathed. At this moment, the nobleman Raushan al-Daula arrives and peremptorily orders the agitators to pray, to obey God, and to respect the judge, who is the "deputy of the Prophet." If Raushan al-Daula was popular for his public generosity, in this moment of confrontation no memory of past kindness quells the people's rage. In response to his words, the shoemakers discharge a prolific volley of shoes, the varieties of which the poet revels in naming: the *saif-khānī, ghitlī, ganwārū, charan-manda, bhatta-dār*. The nobleman Raushan al-Daula, mockingly called "gold robes," acknowledges his humiliation and turns to flee.

Unlike the elite narrators, united in their disapproval of the violence in the mosque, the poet exults in the bloody clash that follows. Day turns to night with the crack and flash of muskets. Angels descend from on high, urging Mughals, Afghans, villainous soldiers, and noble lords alike to smite one another. The "thundering clouds of battle pour down streams of blood." The Afghans, who are blamed for the battle, are defeated. The poet mourns the death of the many "valorous and brave" who "loved the Right," criticizes the cowardly "not-men" who fled the battlefield, and sympathizes with the plight of the innocent poor who were caught in the crossfire. But the victors are unambiguously the poor, who are lauded for their exceptional bravery in fighting and granted the "Victory of the Justice of the Right" (*fath-i dād-i haqq*) by God. The clear loser is Raushan al-Daula, whose crested turban was blown away by the fusillade of shoes and whose estate was overturned by the popular uprising. It was therefore the humiliation of the nobility, and the memorable retribution against them for their condoning of injustice, rather than the defeat of infidelity, that the author of the *Quintets* hoped would be remembered until the day of resurrection.

Conclusion

As a solitary artifact from the range of popular poetry said to have circulated in the aftermath of the riot, the *Quintets* can offer us only limited insight into popular perceptions of the event. Other groups or communities among the city's lowly may have favored narratives emphasizing other features, such as the martyrdom of the slain Haji, the defense or the victory of Islam, or perhaps even the sense of injustice and oppression felt by the jeweler who became the object of popular fury. If such perspectives were enshrined and circulated in verse, however, they have yet to be unearthed. Although it represents only one among what must undoubtedly have been many perspectives, it is still striking that the poem valorizes not the martyrdom of the shoemaker but rather the resistance to, and victory over, the king and his nobility.

This disjuncture is most profoundly evident in the exclusion from the *Quintets* of the end of the narrative for elite chroniclers: the act of the demolition of Subh Karan's house, the building of a mosque on the site, and the burial of the shoemaker within it. By contrast, the demolition was the logical culmination of the story for both Khwush Hal and Ashob. In this respect, Ashob considerably embellished the courtly writer's account, who had chosen to remain silent on this last matter:

> And after permission they set about conducting the funerary rites of the three-day-old corpse of that martyr. A tumultuous gathering demolished the house of the killer, although he eluded their grasp. The murdered martyr was buried in that very place. After a little while that mine of infidelity was made an abode of Islam. A mosque was built at his tomb, and it was made strong and firm with the rubble of that very mansion. A well was also dug in its courtyard, and made to serve as a place of rest and washing and purification for worshipers. [Though] the event surrounding it has been generally forgotten, that mosque and that well is a place of worship for the people of Islam, and used for ablutions by elites and commoners alike. The author has passed through that lane many times and washed himself in that well, and read prayers in that mosque, and prayed at the grave of the martyred Haji for his forgiveness.[101]

Ashob's words remind us that the shoemakers' riot did not end with the fighting in the mosque, as it did for the author of the *Quintets*. The actual circumstances of the destruction of Subh Karan's house remain a mystery—perhaps it was demanded by the shoemakers or offered as a solution by the city authorities; perhaps it was authorized by the king or the vizier. It is also unclear if such an attempt to mollify the sentiments of the shoemakers was accompanied by punitive force directed against them.

But in excluding these details, Ashob's narrative subsumes the shoemakers' protest into a larger history of the dominion of Islam in India, established long ago by force and now, in the face of the infidel's challenge, reasserted by righteous violence. This is why he lingers on the violent conversion of space, on how the rubble of "that very mansion" was used to establish a "bastion of Islam." Yet this textual evocation of the language of Islam, which recalls the mythopoeticizing writing in which the emperor Aurangzeb's many acts of temple destruction were rhapsodized by his courtly admirers, does not quite capture the events of 1729.[102] In this instance, the "Abode of Islam" was built

[101] Ashob, "Tārīkh-i Shahādat [A]," fol. 63b.

[102] Sarkar, *History of Aurangzib, Based on Original Sources*, III:319–24. The most convincing explanation for such acts remains Eaton, "Temple Desecration and Indo-Muslim States"; Eaton, *Temple Desecration and Muslim States in Medieval India*.

from no "mine of infidelity" but merely a jeweler's place of dwelling. Perhaps for this reason the house demolition was only a trivial (if not embarrassing) outcome of the far more gripping disturbances, not worthy of mention by the majority of chroniclers. And if the *Quintets* is any measure of a shared memory of the event, the exclusion of the house demolition from its narrative indicates only the popular indifference to the larger narrative of the victory of Islam which Ashob favored. For while the poem invokes the language of holy war against infidelity, it is unmarked by any trace of sectarian hatred against any community of faith—Subh Karan is mentioned only once, and diatribes against "Hindus" find no place in the text.

The *Quintets* offer us a unique opportunity to reflect on both the limits and the possibilities of Islam as a language of popular politics. It is true that the vision of the *Quintets* is essentially conservative and limited. While the intensity with which the shoemakers rallied in defense of the right and the pursuit of justice bespeaks a remarkable clarity of political consciousness and vision, the agitating masses did not upend or transform the order of their world. Instead, as we have seen, the same people who opposed the king in 1729 would rise up to defend his right to rule only ten years later. Unlike the rebellion led by Patrona Halil in Istanbul in 1730, the shoemakers' uprising did not widen into a generalized revolt against the king.[103] And unlike in the rebellion of 1703, no figure like the Janissary Çalık Ahmed, who supposedly advocated the overthrow of the Ottoman dynasty and its replacement by a "people's republic and collective *devlet* [*daulat*]," is known to have arisen.[104] The Ottoman comparison is not, in any case, a hopeful one, for, as Cemal Kafadar notes, even the leaders of successful revolts were "accepted, promoted, assimilated, and eventually executed through the orders of the new ruler enthroned by the rebels."[105]

Even by this not very high standard, the denizens of Delhi are destined to disappoint. If the discourse of Mughal sovereignty was auratic, no popular leader arose to partake of it; the riot produced no golden halo around the heads of the faceless protestors.[106] Despite the drama of the interrupted

[103] Olson, "The Esnaf and the Patrona Halil Rebellion of 1730"; Konrad, "Coping with 'the Riff-Raff and Mob.' "

[104] The phrase is that of the chronicler Mustafa Na'ima: "cumhur cem'iyeti ve tecemmu' devleti." Kafadar, "Janissaries and Other Riffraff of Ottoman Istanbul: Rebels without a Cause?," 133. Kafadar wonders whether the proponent had a "Janissary oligarchy in mind." Tezcan interprets this phrase as a "people's—read janissaries'—republic." Tezcan, *The Second Ottoman Empire*, 222–24, quote at 223.

[105] Kafadar, "Janissaries and Other Riffraff of Ottoman Istanbul: Rebels without a Cause?," 133.

[106] I am grateful to Dipesh Chakrabarty for making this point to me.

Friday sermon, no general rebellion erupted against the king, no new vision of politics was enunciated, no alternative regime of power established. But the implicit comparisons in such judgments are always haunted by the specter of the other popular eighteenth-century revolutions that established the regimes constitutive of our political modernity. In this light, it is worth lingering on the difficulty in situating the shoemakers' riot in the established narratives of Indian history. For even if no painter would ever memorialize the urban "mob" in action, the act of the popular protest represented itself. The smooth rapidity with which the city's lowliest artisans rallied in defense of the right and in the pursuit of justice remains as much a cause for marvel now as it was to contemporary observers. The adeptness of the city's diverse populace in using the practices, symbols, and gestures of Islam to invoke a form of community and assert its rights likewise betrays a sophisticated understanding of the claims of imperial sovereignty and an agile engagement with its practices of authority. That humble and nameless urbanites led an action so disruptive as to force its way into the polished prose of elite chronicles is perhaps the most enduring mark of the popular appropriation of power in a history that was by, for, and of elites. Certainly the imperial court understood the magnitude of the challenge from its subjects: when in 1731 a certain Sayyid Miran went to the mosque to prevent the Friday sermon in order to "give justice to the wronged," he was summarily "martyred" by the king's artillerymen.[107] We are reminded that behind the rulers' mockeries of the lowly for "donning the clog of the faith" in pursuit of their objectives, always lies the sharp fear of the moment, however short-lived, when the shoe is on the other foot.

[107] Shahabadi, "Tārīkh-i Hindī," fol. 259a; Muhammad, *Tārīkh-i Muhammadī*, 76.

Epilogue

On January 1922, as Jadunath Sarkar prepared for his lectures on Nadir Shah and Gandhi's non-cooperation movement raged across North India, in London the historian F. W. Buckler arose to read a paper at a meeting of the Royal Historical Society titled "The Political Theory of the Indian Mutiny."[1] Buckler's argument was straightforward. He believed that the East India Company had willfully misunderstood the features of Mughal sovereignty, which allowed it "to assume an imperialistic role, and claim to have acquired territory for the nation."[2] The mutiny of the East India Company's sepoy army of 1857, in this light, was not an unlawful revolt but a legitimate uprising by Indians in defense of their established sovereign. Buckler's words touched a raw political nerve in England, and appear to have been greeted with immediate consternation. A little more than a year and a half later, two long-serving members of the Indian Civil Service produced a dismissive response that upheld the established view of the uprising and indeed the company's conquest of India. The dispute hinged on the question of Mughal sovereignty. Buckler's detractors did not believe that any such thing existed:

> We do not know whether any Mogul philosopher ever gave a definition of a sovereign. Had, however, the average man in India been asked in the eighteenth century to define a sovereign, he would probably have compared such a being to the top dog in a dog-fight! Probably the majority of the Emperors of India had used the murdered bodies of their rivals as stepping-stones to the throne.[3]

Furthermore, they argued that the king of Delhi, as he was slightingly described after the company's conquest of the city in 1803, was not recognized as a sovereign by his subjects (though it is perhaps telling that all the

[1] Buckler, "The Political Theory of the Indian Mutiny."
[2] Buckler, "The Political Theory of the Indian Mutiny," 73.
[3] Dewar, Garrett, and Buckler, "Reply and Rejoinder," 152.

The King and The People. Abhishek Kaicker, Oxford University Press (2020). © Oxford University Press.
DOI: 10.1093/oso/9780190070670.001.0001

contemptuous accounts of the king they reproduce are provided by English observers).[4]

The debate in the Royal Historical Society appears to have ended with this exchange, but its bitterness indicates its stakes. For Buckler as for his critics, the question of the relation between the figure of the sovereign and the politics of the people was one of central importance not only in understanding the causes of the mutiny, but the entire sweep of British rule in India, from Clive's conquest of Bengal to the anticolonial movement of their present day. As Buckler declared in his rejoinder, "[t]he present state of affairs in India gives no room for trifling with any serious attempt to what has happened in the past. The movements making for unrest in India to-day have their roots in the sixteenth and seventeenth century."[5] In other words, suggested Buckler, the groundswell of support for the anticolonial movement under Gandhi's leadership derived from some much older popular conception of, and investment in, sovereign authority. In arguing that there had never been any such indigenous conceptions, by contrast, his critics negated all possibility of the attainment of sovereignty by any sort of popular entity in India.

While we shall return presently to the question of the mutiny around which this debate was staged, it has been a central contention of this work that Mughal rule was indeed animated by a sophisticated discourse of imperial sovereignty that operated in relation to the figure of a quiescent people. The scalar intensification of already-existing forces and trends in the seventeenth century created the conditions for the unintended growth and development of a robust practice of popular politics in the eighteenth century. Nowhere perhaps was this process of evolution more visible than in Delhi. Shah Jahan's construction of an imperial metropolis in his own name, which embodied his ideas of rule, set the stage for the birth of a new urban public. Designed to serve as a site of imperial power, commercial prosperity, urbane pleasure, and Islamic piety, the city created a stratified society in which a large urban population expected proximate access to the highest power in the realm.

Unlike in the case of the secluded rulers of Tokugawa Japan or the Ottoman empire, the Mughal capital served as a great stage for the performance of the kingly body, sanctified in the eyes of ideologues by the mystical ideals of

[4] "Another fact indicating the unimportance of the later kings of Delhi," write Dewar and Garrett "is that neither Akbar Shah nor Bahadur Shah finds a place in Buckland's Dictionary of Indian Biography." "Reply and Rejoinder," 156.

[5] Dewar, Garrett, and Buckler, "Reply and Rejoinder," 164.

daulat, which channeled heavenly justice to the people at large. While the people in this conception of sovereignty were to be the inert objects of kingly rule, a political sensibility is evident among the newly built city's residents, who by 1659 were already "voting from the rooftops" (in Rousseau's memorable phrase) in the matter of kingly succession.[6] This was surely not the first occasion on which brickbats were hurled at the despised agents of a ruler in an Indian city. This book has made no claims for the absolute novelty of such forms of action; they clearly represented an elaboration of older forms and techniques of popular protest and violence into a direct popular response to the particular Mughal claims to sovereignty.

It has been a running contention of this work that we cannot begin to see the workings of this politics until we place in abeyance the analytical frameworks that judge their actions and motivations by categorical distinctions between "religion," and "politics."[7] This is not to deny the everyday utility of such conceptual domains, or to suggest that premodern people were unable to experience faith in all its fullness, or lacked an understanding of money and power in social relations. It has rather been to argue that in the Mughal empire, as perhaps elsewhere, the symbols, gestures, rituals, and practices of faith were frictionlessly employed in the service of the familiar political processes of "brokerage" and "boundary activation" as in the language of historical sociology.[8] Given our examination of popular protests in Delhi and other cities of the Mughal empire, we have pleaded that in continuing to see Islam only as a "religion"—with all the conceptual and ideological baggage and the imputation of textual dogmatism and irrational compulsion entailed by that term—we blind ourselves to the means by which those who were seen as passive subjects began to create new solidarities and exercise power against their rulers. It is to overcome these modern conceptual divides that this book has pointed to the workings of Islam as a *language* in which elite conceptions posed the category of the 'Community of Muslims'; and in which those who were expected to inhabit the category began to assert themselves against kingly power.

Aurangzeb's reign was of transformative significance in this regard. Again, we cannot make sense of the king's unprecedented interventions in Mughal society unless we acknowledge the inseparability of his personal

[6] Rousseau, *On the Social Contract*, 74.
[7] For a similar argument I have found helpful, see Fancy, *The Mercenary Mediterranean*.
[8] Tilly, *The Politics of Collective Violence*.

piety from his practices of power, without yet privileging commitments to either. Aurangzeb's sovereignty was accordingly expressed in a new idiom that diverged from his predecessors in emphasizing commitment to *sharīʿa* over the possession of heavenly *daulat* as the fount of legitimacy. This directed Aurangzeb to develop the bureaucratic sinews of state to tame a diverse and fractious populace into an ideal 'Community of Muslims' through the increasing application of the law as it was available to him. As we have seen, Aurangzeb's enunciation of sovereignty was rather more productive than he could have imagined, and not in the ways he would have appreciated. For one, it invited the ire of courtly satirists, whose biting sarcasms and parodies—sometimes mockingly inverting the pious language favored by the king—spread widely through the streets and markets of Delhi and beyond. In the same way, the king's public embrace of a particular form of Islamic orthopraxy, coupled with the increasingly impersonal administrative systems of the empire, unintentionally granted the people a voice in which to not only invoke but also argue against imperial power.

In seeking to enact a vision of the 'Community of Muslims' obedient to his rule, Aurangzeb thus created the possibility for new forms of alliance across lines of ethnicity and community in the city. In this way, the grand mosque at the heart of the city no longer served only to frame the pleasing vista of an obedient community praying behind their king, but became repurposed into a site in which flexible coalitions could be forged in the heat of urban agitations. Likewise, in his unprecedented imposition of law, and in his creation of a juridical infrastructure, Aurangzeb opened the opportunity for new groups to challenge imperial acts by asserting their own understanding and interpretation of what was right and just. In the hands of lowly preachers and artisans who had been educated in the seminaries and schoolhouses built in Aurangzeb's reign, the practices of Islam became the means to "unroll a chessboard of another kind" in urban struggles for justice. They enabled ordinary folk who had no political standing – vagrants, mendicants, artisans, and soldiers who comprised "the people of the street and the bazar" – to articulate *their* own understanding of justice according to *their* interpretation of the law; to build alliances that would fuse communities across ethnic and sectarian divides; and to both invoke and challenge the powers that be in terms of their own purposes.

This practice of politics, increasingly apparent in Delhi and in other urban centers across North India in the second half of the seventeenth century, received a tremendous fillip in the disordered years after the death of

Aurangzeb. As we have seen, a catalytic moment in this regard was that of the disturbances around Bahadur Shah's attempted change of the Friday sermon (*khutba*) in 1711. Though perhaps set off by doctrinal controversy, the widespread agitation marked a popular intervention against any change in an established compact of sovereignty by those who had no right to object. But such resistance was only one aspect of the people's growing political ability, because ordinary urbanites were just as capable of rising to defend the ruler when the entire order was threatened. Farrukh Siyar's regicide in 1719 was again a powerful moment of inflection in this process, for it led Delhi's denizens to directly assert themselves in the question of whether *daulat* was the inalienable possession of the king alone, or whether it might now be claimed by his nobility. Though the people of the city were ultimately unable to preserve the conception of kingship from injury, their aggressiveness surely gave the nobility pause, and may have restrained them from contemplating more radical measures such as ending the dynasty. Similar considerations—and the bracing taste of urban revolt—guided Nadir Shah's careful restoration of the Mughal ruler after his departure from India in 1739. This developing capacity of the city's urbanites to both contest the ruler in everyday affairs and defend him at exceptional moments represents their creeping appropriation of imperial power.

Yet although *daulat* may have left the king's body, it would not fall so low as the shoemaker's. The repeated public display of dead kings did not kill the very idea of kingship as it would in France later that century.[9] Neither the uprisings in defense of the Mughal sovereign nor the challenges to him appear to have provoked a thoroughgoing reconceptualization of the relationship between sovereign power and its subjects. Though they recognized the dispersal of imperial *daulat* in the hands of many claimants, poets and philosophers do not appear to have suggested that the source of legitimacy to rule might come to rest among the great mass of the ruled.

Despite the symbolic richness, intense violence, and massive scale of protest, the people's politics was essentially conservative, not radical. It sought to preserve imperial sovereignty and to prevent the alteration of the compact which bound the king to the people through the principle of justice. This continuing relation enabled the people to insist ever more forcefully on their understanding of right and justice according to the law, against the settled wisdom of the king and his theologians. The act of interrupting the Friday

[9] Walzer, *Regicide and Revolution*.

sermon acquires a critical significance in this regard. In literally halting the enunciation of sovereignty, the people implied themselves not merely its audience but its precondition. The Friday sermon's interruption thus raised the possibility that the assent of the ruled might be a prerequisite of the claim to rule. Even so, for the people of the city, absolute authority would not be allowed to depart the body of the king because he represented the order of justice in their world. This is why the figure of the king came to be both protected and contested by the city's lowly folk, and the touch of divinely granted authority stubbornly adhered to the Mughal ruler's body despite the calamities of the period after Nadir Shah's withdrawal in 1739.

As this book has argued, the dual politics of the people that permitted both the invocation of, and opposition against, imperial power was thus the accretive result of enunciations of sovereignty against the backdrop of the commercial prosperity of the city. While the people had not taken the mantle of sovereignty on themselves by the time Nadir Shah arrived at Delhi's gates, we cannot predict how the relation between king and people would have unfolded if the conjuncture described in this book might have been maintained. In any event, Nadir Shah's occupation of Delhi and his departure with Shah Jahan's Peacock Throne inaugurated an era of repeated invasion, war, famine, and displacement. But what was forged in Delhi would not perish with the city's destruction. In these final pages we can accordingly do no more than gesture to continuing relation between sovereign power and the practices of popular politics until the forcible termination of Mughal kingship in 1857.

Sovereignty

To interpret the higher significance of what Nadir Shah had accomplished in Delhi, the chronicler Khwush Hal turned, as if by instinct, to the Mahabharata epic, which he regarded as "the most esteemed history and guardian-text (*pāsbān-nāma*) of India." The remarkable story he stages in it as an admonition to the "blindly ignorant" people of his day jumps far back in time, from 1739 to the mythical past of Raja Indar, the founder of the first city of Delhi named Indarpat. Khwush Hal relates how one day, as Raja Indar arose from his prostrations before the ascending sun during his ritual ablutions at the banks of the Ganges, he espied a radiant being in the sky.

This bejeweled figure, seated on a water lily throne and accompanied by an entourage of dancing girls (*lūlī zanān*), revealed herself on inquiry to be "The World" (*dunya*), and named Daulat. Raja Indar offered her the appropriate courtesies and politely inquired why she had come to him. Daulat offered a long oration in response:

> In all the three realms (*mulk*) . . . I have manifested from the lotus which has blossomed from the sun in aid of succoring the people. I am a woman who bears the necklace of lilies. I am the world (*dunya*). I am the substance of creation (*sāmān-i khalq*) and the degree and trust of men, and the strength of the wise. I am the power of creation (*qawām-i khalq*) and the independence of affairs (*istiqlāl-i muhimm*), and the means of reaching gifts to kings, and to the spirits of the elders. I am the fortune and power of those who are the comprehending. I dwell in the standards of the imperial armies who triumph over enemies. I find rest in the lands and cities of the well-advised, and among the brave, and am the companion of those who do not flee in battle. Formerly I dwelled among the Gods (*dēvān*) because of their wisdom and truthfulness. But now having seen a change in the conditions of that community, I have departed from them and come to you.[10]

Khwush Hal's story is a narrative of the origins of Delhi, related at the moment of the city's destruction. It restates the familiar general precepts of the Persian ethical literature with an Indic twist, carefully plotting them in a language that is equally compatible with Hindu or Muslim beliefs. It is also a reflection on sovereignty: once, at the dawn of the historical era, fortune came to Delhi's founder because its previous possessors, the gods, had disgraced themselves. Now, by implication, Nadir Shah's invasion showed how *daulat*, the fortune to rule, had left the possessors of Delhi's throne. But this conception also reflects the indigenization of *daulat*. For Khwush Hal, *daulat* is the same thing as "the world" in a material sense, which is also the same thing as "money" in an abstract sense: the heavenly being who arrives before Indar is marked by her lotus as being none other than Lakshmi, the goddess of wealth.

The emphasis on wealth in the conception of *daulat* marks a shift in the discourse of sovereignty from its earlier incarnations. It was not Shah Jahan's

[10] Khwush Hal, "Nādir al-Zamānī [B]," fols. 209b–210a.

wealth, after all, that had enabled him to rule, but God's favor that manifested in his fortune. But for Khwush Hal the command of a fortune now bestowed the fortune to command. This shifting emphasis is apparent in a deliberately ambiguous line of verse by the early-eighteenth-century poet Khwaja ʿAbd Allah "Sami":

> The *daulat*-seeker cannot escape
> Gold's impress, by kingship
> He's caught like a fish in money's tight net
> In the sea of worldly desire.[11]

Sami seems to imply that kingship will not free one who seeks *daulat* by minting coin, or is perhaps fettered by the desire for gold; he is instead ensnared in the web of small money (*dām-i fulūs*). But *daulat* here, as in his verses elsewhere, is now far from the absolutist ideal enunciated at Shah Jahan's court, and now appears to drift in meaning towards *wealth* as such. At much the same time, even as "the political-ideological leverage of the universal Empire of the Mughals was entirely preserved" in the rising Maratha power in the Deccan, *daulat* came to refer to a landed revenue estate ("dominion").[12] This confusion of the effects of God's favor with its causes would become deeply rooted, for even towards the end of the eighteenth century we see a Mughal prince receiving a vision of the goddess Lakshmi—that is, *daulat*—declaring her imminent arrival.[13]

Courtly writers continued to describe even the feeble Mughal rulers of the later eighteenth century in a language that echoed the classical discourse of sovereignty.[14] But the mid-century intellectuals who observed the collapse of the Safavid and Mughal polities also began to imagine kingly power in new ways. Thus the Safavid loyalist and émigré Shaikh ʿAli Hazin (d.

[11] I thank Sunil Sharma for discussing these verses with me. Given their ambiguity, I reproduce them below. *Shikanja-yi zar* straightforwardly implies "fetters of gold," but perhaps also refers to a coin press. I have tried to capture both meanings with the word "impress." *Dām-i fulūs* suggests "fishnet" but both words refer to small money. The word *birūn* may also be an allusion to small money.

> *Daulat-talab az shikanja-yi zar*
> *Birūn narawad zi bādshāhī*
> *Uftād ba bahr-i hars-i dunya*
> *Dar dām-i fulūs hamchū māhī*
> Sami, "Dīwān-i Sāmī," fol. 143a.

[12] Wink, *Land and Sovereignty in India*, 38 for usages; 57, 124, 137, 139 passim.

[13] Alam and Subrahmanyam, "Envisioning Power," 152; Azfari Gurgani, *Wāqiʿāt-i Azfarī*, 35.

[14] Alam and Subrahmanyam, "Eighteenth-Century Historiography," 418; Firaqi, *Waqāʾiʿ-yi ʿĀlam Shāhī*.

1766) thought a king's primary role was to dispel rebellion from the realm. But the qualities of rulership were not granted by heaven. They derived from philosophical self control. A possessor of *daulat (sāhib-i daulat)* was therefore one "who begins with himself, and removes unpleasant qualities and unlaudable attributes from himself."[15] Of course, Hazin quickly disclaimed the implication that self-improvement might allow the lowly to rule by recoursing to the familiar language of head and feet: "[O]ne must know that it is not appropriate to fasten a head-dress on the feet, to hang the covering of the feet on the head." Nevertheless, in acknowledging the validity of criticism (*mazammat*) of the king by those who did not receive his justice, Hazin also opens the possibility that the consent of the ruled was not without relevance to the business of kingship.[16]

At the other end of the philosophical spectrum, the religious scholar Shah Wali Allah (d. 1762) blamed economic forces for the disorder he saw in Delhi.[17] Faced with the contradiction between his approval of the arrangements that enabled the higher stages of city life and the inevitable degeneration of morality that commercial relations seemed to produce, Shah Wali Allah's solution was to reassert the legal discipline of Aurangzeb's age. His ideal Muslim ruler, who was dubbed the "Common Caliph" (*khalīfa-yi ʿāmm*), was to wage war against all enemies and to "amputate" the "incurably diseased limb" of rebels in the interests of the body of the people. Importantly, Wali Allah also emphasized the conditions under which it was permissible to rebel against the Caliph—for instance, if he violated the laws of the faith.[18] To this end, Wali Allah did not regard it necessary for the Common Caliph to derive from any particular family. This is why, by 1757, Wali Allah was writing exhortations not to the hapless king in Delhi, but to the invading Afghan ruler Ahmad Shah Abdali, imploring him to lead a righteous war (*jihād*) against the encroachments of the Jats and Marathas to restore the 'Community of Muslims' to its rightful dominance.[19]

Such theoretical innovations aside, the discourse of sovereignty was reanimated in the provinces, to represent the claims of the governors who threw off the Mughal yoke in all but name. Take the case of Siraj al-Daula ("Lamp of *Daulat*"), the twenty-three-year-old governor of Bengal who ruled

15 Hazin, "Risāla-yi dastūr al-ʿuqalāʾ," fol. 39b.
16 Hazin, "Risāla-yi dastūr al-ʿuqalāʾ," fols. 48a–49a, quote on 48a.
17 Syros, "An Early Modern South Asian Thinker on the Rise and Decline of Empires."
18 Rizvi, *Shah Wali-Allah and His Times*, 290–91.
19 Rizvi, *Shah Wali-Allah and His Times*, 304–05.

briefly in 1756–1757. His encomiast, the prolific author Mir Muhammad Taqi "Khayal" shed much ink in describing him as the "the pearl of the crown of *daulat* and felicity" without however ascribing kingship to him. At the same time Khayal only barely alluded to the actual Mughal king whose *daulat* Siraj al-Daula supposedly radiated. In praising him as the "strength of the arm of the resplendent Law" (*sharī'at-i ghurā*) and the "bright star of the radiant community" (*farūgh-i akhtar-i millat-i baizā'*), the encomiast evoked the familiar language of Islamic rule for the young governor (albeit here garbed in Shi'i allusions). Siraj al-Daula was commended for dealing with "mischief of the European infidels" (*shukhī o sharārat-i kuffār-i firang*) who had settled as traders in Calcutta, by invading their city and killing or capturing them. The sign of victory was the construction of a mosque, and the author produced the expected chronogram: "The predominance of Islam" (*ghalba'i Islām*).[20]

Finishing this volume on September 13, 1756, Khayal expressed his intention of next producing a history of Bengal, in which he would record the present "era of the *daulat*" of Siraj al-Daula.[21] Such a history would never come to be, for within the year Siraj al-Daula was to be killed by a British-led force in the aftermath of the battle of Plassey (Palashi), and a "revolution" would make the gentlemen of the East India Company the *de facto* masters of Bengal. Khayal could never have anticipated how rapidly and completely *daulat* would be wrested from the Nawwabs of Bengal and fall in the hands of Robert Clive and his compatriots, making them nabobs in England.

Prosperity

The continuing economic vitality of the Mughal heartland in the decades after Nadir Shah's raid discerned by some recent scholarship would come as cold comfort to the residents of Delhi, who watched their city repeatedly raided and plundered by Afghans and Marathas in the same period.[22] Returning to Delhi after 1757, the poet Gulshan produced a lament (*shahr āshob*), which neatly inverts the recent poetry of praise or disturbance at the

[20] Khayal, "Bustān-i Khayāl," fols. 467b–468b.

[21] Khayal, "Bustān-i Khayāl," fols. 469b–470a.

[22] Bayly, *Rulers, Townsmen, and Bazaars*; Bayly, "Delhi and Other Cities of North India during the 'Twilight'"; for countervailing views, see Malik, "The Core and the Periphery"; Chandra, *The 18th Century in India*; Ali, "The Mughal Polity: A Critique of Revisionist Approaches"; Habib, "The Eighteenth Century in Indian Economic History." An eyewitness account of events in Delhi during the period that details the city's destruction is Anonymous, "Delhi Chronicle."

city's great wealth. Gulshan now found a Delhi in which bread was expensive, and life cheap. He observed that the imperial canal that watered the city had run dry. Like the poets who had so recently described the city's bustling bazars, Gulshan too listed the professions, but now all in ruin. He saw that nothing remained in the city's markets other than the tools of trouble and strife. The money-changers once mocked for playing all day with their gold and silver now only possessed wounded hearts; once-uppity traders now struck their heads with their weights in their sorrow. Haughty jewelers and querulous shoemakers were both laid low:

> The jeweler joins and counts under the same head
> the ruby of his liver's flesh, and the tears of jewels shed
> . . .
> Since no one buys from the shoemaker's stall
> In grief he beats his breast with his awl[23]

Gulshan's contemporary Muhammad Basiti likewise thought that Shahjahanabad had become a "place of admonition" (*ʿibrat-gāh*).[24] Among its now-vanished splendors he counted the hubbub of conversation among friends in places such the magical Princess's Garden in the heart of the city, or the Tal Katora lake gardens, and the half-completed riverside Qudsiyya Garden of the queen mother which had been a "public gift" (*faiz . . . ʿāmm*). He rued how the city's singers, dancers, and courtesans had all been scattered to the winds (though he was not sorry for the loss of the city's offensive *naqqāl*-s). He described the desolation of the city's schools and seminaries, its soup kitchen and hospital, its inns and hunting grounds and streets. The ruling dynasty had lost their realms and riches, and all that remained of their inheritance was now the grave.[25]

These lamentations, of course, were just as stylized as the literary artifacts that had praised Delhi's thriving commerce or expressed dismay at its rich upstarts. Nevertheless, such visions of ruin indicate that the physical destruction of Shahjahanabad, the disruption of long-distance trade, and the reduction in the resources of the city's nobility all depleted the vitality of the urban sphere. They also mark the recognition that the discourse of sovereignty that

[23] Jaunpuri, "Sūrat-i Hāl," fol. 61a.
[24] Basiti, "Bayāz-i Bāsitī," fol. 153b.
[25] Basiti, "Bayāz-i Bāsitī," fols. 153b–156a.

had animated Shahjahanabad could no longer be expressed in the same way as before. Basiti typically described this in terms of the vanishing of *daulat* from the site of its most audible enunciation, the hall of the imperial ceremonial music (*naqqāra khāna*) in the Red Fort:

> There's nothing but trifling sounds in the music hall
> Since *daulat* has sounded there the drums of departure
> The drums here have remained here with *daulat*
> [But] *daulat* itself has been passed around[26]

Basiti's words draw a connection between the collapse of the urban sphere and the dispersal of Mughal kingship. No Mughal ruler was present in the city for the twelve years after the assassination of ʿAlamgir II in 1759; the return of Shah ʿAlam II to Delhi in 1772 brought decades of fragile and frequently violated stability. The dynamics of city life in mid-century Delhi are yet obscure, but much of its vibrant urban life was dispersed as the coffeehouses vanished from Moonlight Avenue and its glittering waters ran dry. The next generation of Delhi's poets—such as Sauda—would carry their satirical chronograms and rhyming complaints against rivals and police chiefs to new elites in other cities.[27]

Popular Politics

What, then, became of the practices of popular politics in Delhi in the years after 1739? The sad state of the city is palpable in the laconic prose of the anonymous chronicler who leaves us with the barest outline of events in these decades. In 1754, another Deccani army stood outside Delhi's gates, ready to overthrow the king. But unlike in 1719 or 1739, the people no longer seemed to have the capacity to resist. The previous year had seen the soldiers of the imperial paymaster and the vizier engage in pitched battles around the city. The Jats who lived down the river from Delhi plundered the Old City for a week. Anand Ram did not live to see his neighborhood of Wakilpura

[26] Basiti, "Bayāz-i Bāsitī," fol. 161a.

[27] Russell and Islam, *Three Mughal Poets: Mir, Sauda, Mir Hasan; Kullīyāt-i Saudā* (satires against a police-chief: 378–81; chronogrammatic wedding satire: 400–01; counter-satire on behalf of a patron: 410–16).

"completely ruined" in the Maratha and Jat raids that followed, having died a few years previously.[28]

Much of the everyday disorder in the city was produced by soldiers—particularly Turani Mughals—agitating for pay: 1754 alone was marked by six military revolts. When the imperial paymaster died in 1756, his Mughal Turani retainers did not allow his corpse to be removed until they were promised their pay.[29] With the arrival of an Afghan army led by Ahmad Shah Abdali, the year of 1757 saw a more intense repetition of the events of 1739. This time, the city's nobility did not linger to see what would happen. The families of Khwush Hal and Jugal Kishor had both fled before the Friday sermon was read in the name of Ahmad Shah. The chronicler of the city recorded a "great tumult" and "cries of distress" audible all day and night. Many of the city's neighborhoods burned, though again some remained safe through the resistance of their inhabitants, who threw stones from rooftops.[30] Besides these calamities, the anonymous chronicler repeatedly reported markets plundered by rampaging soldiers, slaughters in the street, and raging fires.[31]

And yet, the practices of popular politics did not die in the flames that engulfed Delhi and other North Indian cities in the same period. In 1747, aggravated by the unjust exactions of a market supervisor, the city's shopkeepers staged a total shut-down of its markets, protested vociferously before the king, and even "acted tumultuously" on the sandy bank of the river in front of the fort's imperial window of presentation. This time the chronicler Khwush Hal had no patience for the feeble Muhammad Shah's emollient words, which did nothing to quell the "mass uprising" until the offender was forced to resign his post. Instead, the chronicler hinted broadly that the king ought to "give more food to dervishes" so that even "insurmountable problems" would "resolve of their own accord": sentiments that suggest his sympathy for the city's lowly and a concern with redistribution.[32] In 1769, a doctor (*maulawī*) named Nazar Muhammad was implicated in an urban struggle over a (nameless) Khatri woman, who was "forcibly made a Muslim" in defiance of the city's judge and administrator. There was no king in the city at the time, but the ruling authorities responded with a practiced pragmatism. After first acceding, the nobleman Najib al-Daula expelled the

[28] Malik, "The Core and the Periphery," 15; Anonymous, "Delhi Chronicle," 23, 41–42.
[29] Anonymous, "Delhi Chronicle," 73–74.
[30] Anonymous, "Delhi Chronicle," 75–76, 83–85.
[31] Anonymous, "Delhi Chronicle," 61–62.
[32] Khwush Hal, "Tārīkh-i Muhammad Shāhī [B]," fols. 196a–198a.

turbulent doctor from Delhi when tempers had cooled with a message saying that he was "not in the service of the city" and did not do well to raise a disorder.[33] Similarly, in 1789, one Hafiz Ibrahim led some "ten thousand" of the city's Muslims from the congregational mosque to the residence of the ascetic warlord Himmat Bahadur, to liberate a kidnapped trader. Confronted by the people who were united "in the defense of Islam," Himmat Bahadur evacuated the city, sending his prisoners and the city's judicial officials with a deed of settlement to the mosque so that the crowds could be appeased.[34] It is noteworthy that in neither occasion are the people of the city recorded as interrupting the Friday sermon. It could be that the gesture had lost its potency as the king's power waned to nothingness. The king's relative irrelevance in these agitations, however, only serves to illustrate the continuing vitality of the language of popular politics.

The Last Resurrection of Mughal Sovereignty: 1857

It is in light of this relationship between the discourse of sovereignty and popular politics that we must revisit the debate between Buckler and his critics on the nature of the mutiny. In a recent essay, Azfar Moin partially agrees with Buckler's claim that "the Company's growing insults to Mughal sovereignty had caused Indian soldiers to come their emperor's defense." He asserts, however, that "a deeply and collectively held perversion—felt as bodily pollution, social disorder, and cosmic chaos—at the new sovereign order ushered in by the company" drove the rebellion.[35] In another vein, Faisal Devji has argued that it was not the "much-tarnished sanctity of [the last Mughal emperor] Bahadur Shah's dynasty that lent him any superstitious legitimacy, but what we might perhaps call the constitutional position he occupied, one that was augmented by his very powerlessness," and that the king crafted a novel and indeed modern political authority.[36]

[33] Anonymous, "Delhi Chronicle," 221–22. We know nothing about this figure, but a document of appointment for a new public-crier (*mu'azzin*) for the central mosque of Lahore in 1757 notes the previous occupant of the office, named Nazar Muhammad, "had run away." Perhaps this was the same turbulent doctor, who, having come into conflict with the city authorities of Lahore, was now raking up trouble in Delhi. Vogel, *Catalogue of the Delhi Museum of Archaeology*, 28.

[34] Ilahabadi, "'Ibratnāma," fols. 212b–213a. I am grateful to Hasan Siddiqui for pointing me to this incident. See also Pinch, "Who Was Himmat Bahadur?"; Pinch, *Warrior Ascetics and Indian Empires*.

[35] Moin, "The 'Millennium' of 1857," 337.

[36] Devji, "The Mutiny to Come," 426.

The arguments of this book suggest another genealogy for the uprising, at least as it was played out in Delhi. As much scholarship has shown, there were many disparate origins of the fury that erupted into ferocious violence against Europeans and Christians in 1857.[37] But, despite the dramatic changes wrought under the supremacy of the East India Company's occupation of Delhi since 1803, the figure of the king was still remembered by ordinary people as the highest guarantor of justice and order in the realm. In this sense, the mutineers were not so much rebelling unconsciously against an "inexplicable and unbearable dispensation" (in Moin's suggestive phrase), as purposefully resurrecting a ghostly but still evocative memory of Mughal sovereignty to consciously mobilize popular support for a political struggle of their own making.[38] Thus, a later report of a conversation between two mutineers after the outbreak of violence described their deliberate intention to march on Delhi because "the possession of the [gunpowder] magazine, and the person of the King, for future operations, were highly beneficial . . . they would hold Delhie against the English for months, during which time, the name of the King will work like a magic and induce the distant stations to mutiny."[39] Such views represent a clear-eyed sense of the importance of the figure of the king to a popular sensibility, which endured despite his evident powerlessness.

It is likewise significant that when, on May 11, the arriving rebel army found the gates of Delhi shut to them, they rode to the window of presentation (*jharoka*) where the Mughal emperors appeared to hear petitioners. Invoking the standard script of popular appeals to the ruler, they described themselves as complainants fighting for "the faith."[40] Such loaded gestures were immediately successful in forging a solidarity between the rebels and the city's lowly folk, in contrast to its elites, who tried to stay aloof from the uprising.[41] Thus we hear that the city's gates were first opened to the rebels by the "Mahomedans of the Thauba-Bazaar [Darya Ganj] . . . . As they rode on, with the cry of "Deen Deen!" they were followed by an excited Mahomedan rabble."[42] A witness later described their number and emphatically demarcated them from the city's well-to-do:

[37] Stokes and Bayly, *The Peasant Armed: The Indian Revolt of 1857*; Bates et al., *Mutiny at the Margins*.
[38] Moin, "The 'Millenium' of 1857," 337.
[39] Cited in Wagner, *The Great Fear of 1857*, 186.
[40] Wagner, *The Great Fear of 1857*, 191–92.
[41] Dalrymple, *The Last Mughal*, 154; Wagner, *The Great Fear of 1857*, 197.
[42] Kaye, *A History of the Sepoy War in India, 1857–58*, II:76–77.

> These rebels and rioters were the rebellious soldiers, the criminals who had been freed from the jail and the *chamars* [untouchables and sweepers], loafers, *dhobis* [laundrymen], barbers, butchers and the paper makers of the Kaghazi Gali, pick-pockets, wrestlers and other vagabonds. No person from a decent family was a part of this crowd of rioters, for the respectable people of the city were all locked inside their houses, and were quite unaware of what was going on in the city.[43]

It is likewise important that the city's "budmashes" (*bad-maʿāsh*, "lowlifes") directed the sepoys in the initial outbreak of violence against the Europeans, which saw looting and acts of symbolic violence against the bank and the church. Again, solidarities of faith were inevitably critical in shaping these actions. Yet, it was not a sectarian hatred of the tenets of Christianity that drove the sepoys to massacre the city's Indian Christians; it was rather that lines of sect were symbolically invoked because they were fundamental to the imagination of political community (thus the few reports of British or Anglo-Indians who fought willingly or under duress for the rebels having converted to Islam).[44]

If the Europeans were now described as "infidels" to be massacred wherever encountered, the king, by virtue of his historic "constitutional neutrality," was critically important in joining both Hindus and Muslims to this cause.[45] Such efforts were not always successful, and the symbols of Hindu-Muslim alliance would crack as the tide turned against the rebels.[46] But the king was not merely a figurehead of Hindu-Muslim unity. He was also crucial for the rebels because the city's people were the principal object of their regime, who had be to be placated, persuaded, marshalled, or impressed into the war effort. As the reams of petitions from ordinary urbanites held in the *Mutiny Papers* at the National Archives of India show, the king served as a crucial intermediary between competing groups and as the provider of redress for the city's harried population.[47]

Yet the uprising did not mark a restoration of Mughal kingship. Rather, it represented the efforts of a junta attempting to organize and maintain a

[43] Zahir Dihlawi, cited in Dalrymple, *The Last Mughal*, 258.
[44] Llewellyn-Jones, *The Great Uprising in India, 1857–58*, 60–63.
[45] Devji, "The Mutiny to Come," 426.
[46] Llewellyn-Jones, *The Great Uprising in India, 1857–58*, 58–59.
[47] Thus we find the numerous complaints of urbanites against soldiers who looted and invaded civilian houses, or pleas for compensation from war-widows. Farooqui, *Besieged*, 171, 173, 177, 192, etc.; *Press-List*.

disparate military force under conditions of war and scarcity in a city in which the people were not unequivocally committed to the rebel cause. As scholars have noted, the regime they erected was marked by modernizing innovations that reflected the effects of many decades of colonial rule. Thus the establishment of a "court administration"—a committee of ten, of which six derived from the army and four from civilians—that was concerned with the collection of taxes and the judicial supervision of the army. Its twelve-point "constitution" began from the definition of its name, purpose, organization, and titles (president, vice-president, secretary), mode of election, and rules of procedure.[48] This was a remarkable innovation, all the more so considering that the senior leadership of the Delhi rebels were long-serving subalterns who had little if any formal exposure to the administrative practices of the upper echelons that were reserved for whites.

Although the workings of the court administration were dictated by the exigencies of a desperate wartime mobilization, the principles of its establishment reflect a vision of a new distribution of power that did not derive solely from older forms.[49] Though it is perhaps going too far to see "incipient republicanism" in the Delhi regime, as some have, the court administration marks another stage in the movement of sovereignty from the king towards the people.[50] But even as it is easy to imagine the momentous and world-historical consequences of the rebellion's success, I do not wish to paint it as a stage in the emergence of popular sovereignty in India. To do so would be to chain it in a teleology towards some universal significance of European provenance. The rebellion, after all, was crushed with the utmost application of cruelty. If anything, it only demonstrates again how the possibilities of the most creative moments of popular action in India have been inevitably foreclosed by mass bloodshed.

But even in the grip of the bloodlust that marked their recapture of Delhi, the British did not stray from the cultural logic of Mughal sovereignty. Thus, on the one hand, the British were careful to show that the captured person of the last Mughal ruler was treated without injury, in this way acknowledging his inviolable status. On the other, in capturing, stripping, and shooting the princes who might have inherited the throne, and in leaving their bodies for display outside the police station for several days (a classic touch), the English

[48] Farooqui, *Besieged*, 53–58.
[49] Habib, "The Coming of 1857," 13–14.
[50] Samaddar, "The Heterogeneous World of the Citizen."

officer Hodson betrayed his fluency in the proper forms of violence exercised by those who claimed sovereignty against their contenders.[51] The captured king's subsequent trial, a sort of sham intended to demonstrate the superiority of British law over the "Shadow of God," was fatally undercut by this inability of the British to execute or imprison him. In deporting him alive to just outside the farthest reaches of the former Mughal dominion, the British paradoxically recognized the divine claims of the discourse of Mughal sovereignty, as one that could not be extinguished but perhaps only displaced. In any case, the extirpation of Bahadur Shah's line has not halted successive claimants to the Mughal legacy. Nor would the British imperial establishment long resist the seduction of posing the royal family at the Red Fort's window of public presentation for the adulation of their Indian subjects.[52]

The nominal claim to sovereignty would not formally descend upon the people until the adoption of the Constitution of India, ninety-three years after the rebellion of 1857. And yet, as Buckler astutely noted, the practices of popular politics forged in the encounter between Mughal monarchs and their subjects enjoyed a long afterlife. As in the classic trope of the folk tales recorded from Mughal India, the body of the people would lurch on long after its head had been removed. The legacy of Mughal sovereignty, as of colonial authority, and the innovations of the rebellion of 1857 all point to a complicated path towards popular sovereignty and the politics of the present that is yet to be charted. But, as much in the satirical rhymes about politicians circulated on messaging platforms as in the acts of mass violence meant to challengingly invoke the highest power in the land, the traces of the politics of Delhi's long-dead urbanites may even now be discernible beneath what is left of the veneer of liberal democracy around us today.

[51] Kaye, *A History of the Sepoy War in India, 1857–58*, III:647–54.

[52] Trevithick, "Some Structural and Sequential Aspects of the British Imperial Assemblages at Delhi"; Codell, *Power and Resistance*.

Bibliography

Primary Sources

Documents, Oriental Records Reading Room, National Archives of India, Delhi.

ʿAbd al-Karim, ʿAqibat Mahmud Kashmiri. *Bayān-i wāqiʿ: sarguzasht-i aḥvāl-i Nādir Shāh va safarhā-yi muṣannif Khvājah ʿAbd al-Karīm ibn Khvājah ʿĀqibat Maḥmud Kashmīrī*. Idarah-i Tahqiqat-i Pakistan, Danishgah-i Panjab, 1970.

ʿAbd al-Rasul. *Nairang-i Zamāna*. Lahore: Panjabi Adabi Academy, 1960.

Abu al-Fazl. *The History of Akbar*. Translated by W. M. Thackston. Vol. I. MCLI. Cambridge, MA: Harvard University Press, 2015.

Ahmad, Bashiruddin. *Farāmīn-i salātīn*. Dihli: Dilli Printing Press, 1926.

Ahsan, Zafar Khan Ahsan Allah. "Jalwa-yi Nāz/Wasf-i Kashmīr," n.d. Bibliotheque Nationale de Paris, SP 505.

Ahsan, Zafar Khan Ahsan Allah. "Kitāb-i Masnawīyyāt-i Zafar Khān," ca 1661. Royal Asiatic Society Persian Ms. 310. https://cudl.lib.cam.ac.uk/view/MS-RAS-00310/134.

ʿAli, Mrs. Mir Hasan. *Observations on the Mussulmauns of India: Descriptive of Their Manners, Customs, Habits and Religious Opinions, Made During a Twelve Years' Residence in Their Immediate Society*. London: Humphrey Milford, 1917.

ʿAli, Niʿmat Khan. "Bahādur Shāh-Nāma," pre-1712. Oxford University, Bodleian Library, Oxford, Persian Mss. Elliot 20.

ʿAli, Niʿmat Khan. *Chronicles of the Seige of Golkonda Fort: An Abridged Translation of the Waqāʾiʿ of Niʿmat Khanʾ ʿĀli*. Translated by Nurulhasan Ansari. Delhi: Idarah-i Adabiyat-i Delhi, 1975.

ʿAli, Niʿmat Khan. *Dīwān-i ʿĀlī*. Lakhnau: Nawal Kishor, 1881.

ʿAli, Niʿmat Khan. *Ruqqāt o Muzhikāt*. Lakhnau: Matba'-yi Sangin, 1845.

ʿAli, Niʿmat Khan. *Waqʿiʾ-yi Niʿmat Khān-i ʿĀlī*. Lakhnau: Nawal Kishor, 1928.

Amar. "Hālāt-i Nādir Shāh," n.d. British Library, London, APAC Or. 4008.

Anonymous. "Ajāʾib al-Āfāq," n.d. British Library, London, APAC Or. 1776.

Anonymous. "Akhbārāt of the Reign of Aurangzeb and Bahadur Shah (Transcripts)," n.d. National Library of India, Delhi, Jadunath Sarkar Collection #36.

Anonymous. "Akhbārāt-i Darbār-i Muʿallā, Aurangzeb, Regnal Years 36-40," 1935. Sri Natnagar Shodh Samsthan, Sitamau.

Anonymous. "Akhbārāt-i Darbār-i Muʿallā, Bahādur Shāh Regnal Years 5-6 Part II," 1937. Sri Natnagar Shodh Samsthan, Sitamau.

Anonymous. "Akhbārāt-i Darbār-i Muʿallā, Jahāndār Shāh," 1937. Sri Natnagar Shodh Samsthan, Sitamau.

Anonymous. "Akhbārāt-i Darbār-i Muʿallā, Farrukh Siyar, Regnal Year 1-2," 1937. Sri Natnagar Shodh Samsthan, Sitamau.

Anonymous. "Akhbārāt-i Darbār-i Muʿallā, Farrukh Siyar, Regnal Year 1-2 Part II," 1937. Sri Natnagar Shodh Samsthan, Sitamau.

Anonymous. "Akhbārāt-i Darbār-i Mu'allā, Farrukh Siyar, Regnal Year 6-7," 1937. Sri Natnagar Shodh Samsthan, Sitamau.

Anonymous. "Akhbārāt-i Darbār-i Mu'allā, Farrukh Siyar, Regnal Year 6-7 Part II," 1937. Sri Natnagar Shodh Samsthan, Sitamau.

Anonymous. "Akhbārāt-i Darbār-i Mu'allā, Farrukh Siyar, Regnal Year 7," 1939. Sri Natnagar Shodh Samsthan, Sitamau.

Anonymous. "Bayāz-i Yūsufī," n.d. Khuda Bakhsh Oriental Public Library, Patna, HL 864.

Anonymous. "Collection of Essays in Verse and Prose," n.d. Staatsbibliothek zu Berlin, Ms. Sprenger 1641–42.

Anonymous. "Commentary on 'Verses on the Marriage of Kamgar Khan,'" n.d. British Library, London, APAC, I.O. Islamic 1359, ff. 188a–196b.

Anonymous. "Copies of Persian Letters, accounts, etc." Royal Asiatic Society, London, Persian Ms., n.d. 173.

Anonymous. "Delhi Chronicle," pre-1800. National Library of India, Delhi, Jadunath Sarkar Collection #37.

Anonymous. "Fatāwá-yi Birahna," 1716. University of Manchester, John Rylands Library, Manchester, Pers. Ms. 750.

Anonymous. "Hādisa-yi Nādir Shāhī," n.d. Andhra Pradesh Government Oriental Manuscripts Library, Hyderabad, #777, Dakhila number 12150.

Anonymous. "Hikāyat-i Latīf," n.d. Khuda Bakhsh Oriental Public Library, Patna, HL 2344.

Anonymous. "Lughat-i Mullā Do-piyāza," n.d. Asiatic Society of Bengal, Curzon Collection, Kolkata, Ms. No. 676.

Anonymous. "Masnawi," October 18, 1703. British Library, London, APAC Delhi Persian 744A.

Anonymous. "Mihakk al-Sulūk o Mislaqat al-Nufūs," 1720. British Library, London, APAC I.O. Islamic 1012.

Anonymous. "Muhāriba-yi Nādir Shāh," n.d. University of Edinburgh Library, Edinburgh, Ms. Or. 227.

Anonymous. "Risāla-yi Muhammad Shāh Bādshāh Ghāzī wa Ahwāl-i Khān-i Daurān Khān Nawwāb," 1788. British Library, London, APAC Or. 180.

Anonymous. "Sahīfa-yi Iqbāl [A]," pre-1739. British Library, London, APAC Or. 1900.

Anonymous. "Sahīfa-yi Iqbāl [B]," pre-1739. British Library, London, APAC I.O. Islamic 3934D.

Anonymous. "Transcripts from Jaipur State Archives, Years 36-40 of Aurangzeb's Reign," n.d. Sri Natnagar Shodh Samsthan, Sitamau.

Anonymous. "Waqā'i'-yi Kharābī-yi Dihlī," n.d. Andhra Pradesh Government Oriental Manuscripts Library, Hyderabad, No. 779, Dakhila number 12152.

'Aqil, Hunarwar Khan. "Jalwa-yi Dīdār," July 1706. Telangana State Archives, Hyderabad, Tarnaka Ms. 130.

Arzu, Siraj al-Din 'Ali Khan. *Majma' al-Nafā'is: Bakhsh-i Mu'āsirān*. Edited by Mir Hashim Muhaddis. Tihran: Anjuman-i Asar va Mafakhir-i Farhangi, 2006.

Arzu, Siraj al-Din 'Ali Khan. "Tārīkh-i Istīsāl-i Sādāt-i Bārhā," pre-1739. British Library, London, APAC I.O. Islamic 4002.

Ashob, Mirza Muhammad Bakhsh. "Sawānih-i 'Umrī-yi Mirzā Muhammad Bakhsh Mutakhallis bi Āshob wa Khāndān-i ū,"1780s. British Library, London, APAC Or. 4034.

Ashob, Mirza Muhammad Bakhsh. "Tārīkh-i Shahādat-i Farrukh Siyār wa Julūs-i Muhammad Shāh [A]," 1782. British Library, London, APAC I.O. Islamic 250 Vol. II.

Ashob, Mirza Muhammad Bakhsh. "Tārīkh-i Shahādat-i Farrukh Siyār wa Julūs-i Muhammad Shāh [B]," 1782. British Library, London, APAC Or. 1832.

ʿAsi, Jiwan Ram. "Bahr Al-Maʿāni," July 14, 1733. Salar Jung Museum, Hyderabad, A/ N 13.

Astarabadi, Mahdi Khan. *Tārīkh-i Jahāngushā-yi Nādirī*. Bombay, 1875.

Aurangabadi, Muhammad Qasim. "Ahwāl al-Khawāqīn," 1738/39. British Library, London, APAC Add. 26, 244.

Aurangabadi, Shah Nawaz Khan. *Maʾāsir al-Umarāʾ [En]*. Edited by Baini Prasad. 2 vols. Calcutta: Asiatic Society, 1952; Patna: Janaki Prakashan, 1979.

Aurangabadi, Shah Nawaz Khan. *Maʾāsir al-Umarāʾ [Fa]*. Edited by ʿAbd al-Rahim and Ashraf ʿAli. 3 vols. Calcutta: Asiatic Society, 1888.

Aurangzeb, Muhyī al-Dīn Muhammad. "ʿAhdnāma-yi ʿĀlamgīr wa Murād Bakhsh," n.d. British Library, London, APAC I.O. Islamic 3997.

Azfari Gurgani, Mirza ʿAli Bakht Bahadur Muhammad Zahir al-Din. *Wāqiʿāt-i Azfarī*. Edited by T. Chandrasekharan. Madras, Nuri Press: 1957.

Babur, Zahir al-Din Muhammad. *The Baburnama: Memoirs of Babur, Prince and Emperor*. Edited by W. M. Thackston. New York: Modern Library, 2002.

Badaʾuni, ʿAbd al-Qadir ibn Muluk Shah. *Muntakhab Ut-Tawārikh*. Translated by George S. A Ranking, W. H. Lowe, and Wolseley Haig. 3 vols. Calcutta: Asiatic Society of Bengal, 1898.

Baig, Mirza Sangin. *Sair al-manāzil*. Edited and translated by Sharif Husain Qasimi. Aligarh: Adabi Akademi, 1980.

Balmukund, Mehta. *Letters of a King-Maker of the Eighteenth Century (Balmukund Nama)*. Edited by Satish Chandra. Aligarh: Dept. of History, Aligarh Muslim University, Asia Pub. House, 1972.

Barani, Ziyaʾ al-Din. *Fatāwā-yi Jahāndārī*. Edited by Afsar Saleem Khan. Lahawr: Idarah-'i Tahqiqat-i Pakistan, Danishgah-i Panjab, 1972.

Barani, Ziyaʾ al-Din. *Tārīkh-i Fīroz Shāhī*. Edited by Maulawi Sayyid Ahmad Khan Sahib. Calcutta: Asiatic Society of Bengal, 1862.

Basiti, Sayyid Muhammad ʿAli. "Bayāz-i Bāsitī," before 1764. Khuda Bakhsh Oriental Public Library, Patna, HL 1/3830.

Bedil, ʿAbd al-Qadir. *Kullīyāt-i Bedil*. 4 vols. Kabul: Dipuhini matba'ah, 1962.

Bernier, François, Irving Brock, and Archibald Constable. *Travels in the Mogul Empire, AD 1656–1668*. Delhi: S. Chand, 1968.

Bhandari, Sujan Rai. *The Khulasatu-t-Tawarikh*. Edited by M. Zafar Hasan. 1690. Reprint, Delhi, 1918.

Bilgrami, Mir Azmat Allah "Bikhabar." "Safīna-yi Bīkhabar,"n.d. Maulana Azad Library, Aligarh Muslim University, Aligarh, Ahsan Farsiyya 920/8.

Bilgrami, Mir Ghulam ʿAli Azad. *Khazāna-yi ʿĀmira*. Kanpur: Nawal Kishor, 1871.

Bilgrami, Mir Ghulam ʿAli Azad. *Maʾāṣir al-Kirām*. Vol. II. Hyderabad and Lahore: Kutubkhana-yi Asafiya, 1913.

Bilgrami, Mir Ghulam ʿAli Azad. *Sharh-i Qitʿa-i Niʿmat Khān-i ʿĀli*. Delhi? Unknown, 1844.

Bilgrami, ʿAbd al-Jalil. *Inshāʾ-yi Jalīl*. Edited by Amir Haidar Bilgrami. Lakhnau: Maulawi Masih al-Zaman, 1852.

Bilgrami, ʿAbd al-Jalil. *Maṣnawī-yi Mīr ʿAbd al-Jalīl Bilgrāmī*. Lakhnau: Nawal Kishor, 1882.

Bilgrami, ʿAbd al-Jalil. "Original Letters, &c." in *The Oriental Miscellany Consisting of Original Productions and Translations*. Vol. 1., compiled by Francis Gladwin. Calcutta: ?, 1798: 133–293.

Brahman, Candar Bhan. *Chahar chaman*. Dihli-i Naw: Markaz-i Tahqiqat-i Farsi-i Rayzani-i Farhangi-i Jumhuri-i Islami-i Iran, 2007.

Brahman, Candar Bhan. "Tārīkh-i Rājāhā-yi Dihlī-yi Hindūstān," n.d. Gujarat Vidya Sabha, Ahmadabad, Main Catalog #46.

Das, Har Charan. "Chahār Gulzār-i Shujāʿī," n.d. British Library, London, APAC, Or. 1732.

Daulat Raʾi. *Inshā-yi Daulat Rām [Sic]*. Kanpur: Nawal Kishor, 1880.

Dihlawi, Shah Wali Allah. *Anfās al-ʿArifīn*. Delhi: Matba'-yi Ahmad, 1897.

Dihlawi, ʿAbd-al-Haqq Miskin. *Risāla-i Nūrīyya-i Sultāniyya*. Edited by Muhammad Saleem Akhtar. Islamabad, Pakistan: Markaz-i Tahqiqat-i Farsi-i Iran wa Pakistan, 1985.

Fazil, Mir Muhammad. "Wisātat al-ʿIqd," 1699. University of Manchester, John Rylands Library, Manchester, Pers. Ms. 793.

Faʾiz, Sadr al-Din. "Kulliyāt-i Fāʾiz," n.d. Oxford University, Bodleian Library, Oxford, Persian Mss. Ouseley Add. 182.

Firaqi, Prem Kishor. *Waqāʾiʿ-yi ʿĀlam Shāhī*. Edited by Imtiyaz ʿAli Khan ʿArshi. Rampur: Hindustan Press, 1949.

Fraser, James. *The History of Nadir Shah, Formerly Called Thamas Kuli Khan, the Present Emperor of Persia, [James Fraser]. To Which Is Prefix'd, A Short History of the Moghol Emperors. At the End Is Inserted, A Catalogue of about Two Hundred Manuscripts in the Persic and Other Oriental Languages, Collected in the East*. London, W. Straban: 1742.

Ghalib, ʿAbd al-Ghalib. "Sharh-i Dīwān-i Ghālib," 1672. Salar Jung Museum, Hyderabad, AC 2359.

Hasan, Muhammad. "Guldasta-yi Bustān-i Khayāl," 1723. Oxford University, Bodleian Library, Oxford, Persian Ms. Whinfield 25.

Hatim, Muhammad. "Abr-i Faiz," 1692. British Library, London, APAC Delhi Persian 495a.

Hatim, Shaikh Zuhur al-Din. *Dīwān-zāda*. Edited by Abdul Haq. New Delhi: National Mission for Manuscripts, Dilli Kitab Ghar, 2011.

Hazin, Shaikh Muhammad ʿAli. "Risāla-yi Dastūr al-ʿUqalāʾ," December 16, 1753. British Library, London, APAC Delhi Persian 1207b.

Hidayat Allah. "Hidāyat al-Qawāʾid," 1708. Maulana Azad Library, Aligarh Muslim University, Abd al-Salam 379/149.

Husain, Mawlavi M. Hidayat. "The Mīrzā Nāmah (The Book of the Perfect Gentleman) of Mīrzā Kāmrān with an English Translation." *Journal of the Asiatic Society of Bengal New Series* IX (1913): 1–13.

Husaini, Mir Muhammad Sharif. "Kulliyāt-i Husainī," June 22, 1754. Khuda Bakhsh Oriental Public Library, Patna, HL 671.

Ihsan, Muhammad. "Rauzat-i Qaiyūmiyya," 1803. Asiatic Society of Bengal, Curzon Collection, Ms. No. P82.

Ihsan, Muhammad. *Rauzat-i Qaiyūmiyya*. Translated by Iqbal Ahmad Faruqi. Vol. IV. 1786. Reprint, Lahore: Maktaba-yi Nabuwiyya, 2002.

Ijad, Mir Muhammad Ihsan. "Farrukh Siyar-nāma [A]," pre-1720. Cambridge University Library, Cambridge, Eton 15.1.

Ijad, Mir Muhammad Ihsan. "Farrukh Siyar-Nāma [B]," pre-1720. British Library, London, APAC Or. 25.

Ilahabadi, Khair al-Din Muhammad. "ʿIbratnāma," after 1791. British Library, London, APAC Or. 1932.

Isfahani, Muhammad Sadiq. "Shāhid-i Sādiq," 1646. British Library, London, APAC Or. 1626.

Jahangir, Nur al-Din Muhammad. *Jahāngīrnāma*. Edited by Mohammad Hashem. Teheran: Bonyad Farhang Iran, 1981.

Jaunpuri, Gulshan. "Sūrat-i Hāl," post-1762. British Library, London, APAC Add. 16, 805.

Kam Raj. "ʿIbratnāma," n.d. British Library, London, APAC, I.O. Islamic 1534.

Kambuh, Muhammad Salih. *ʿAmal-i Ṣāliḥ al-mawsūm bih Shāhjahānnāmah*. Tabʿ-i 2. Lahaur: Majlis-i Taraqqi Adab, 1967.

Kamgar, Muhammad. *Majālis-i Kalīmī*. Edited by ʿAbd al-Aziz Sahir. Islamabad, Pakistan: Idarah-i Furugh-i Muʿarifat-i Nizamiya, 2017.

al-Kashifi, Mulla Husain bin Ali al-Waʾiz. *The Anwár-i-Suhailí: Or, Lights of Canopus, Commonly Known as Kalílah and Damnah*. Translated by Arthur Wollaston. London: W. H. Allen & Company, 1877.

Kazim, Muhammad. *The Álamgír námah*. Edited by Khadim Husain, Abd al-Hayy, and W. Nassau Lees. Calcutta: College Press, 1868.

Khair Allah, Haji. *Anecdotes of Aurangzib: English Translation of Ahkam-i-Alamgiri*. Translated by Jadunath Sarkar. 2nd ed. Calcutta: M. C. Sarkar & Sons, 1949.

Khair Allah, Haji. *Anecdotes of Aurangzib, Translated into English with Notes and Historical Essays*. Translated by Jadunath Sarkar. Calcutta: M. C. Sarkar, 1917.

Khair Allah, Haji. "Tausīf-i Dār al-Khilāfat Shāhjahānābād." 2nd rev. ed. June 13, 1722. British Library, London, APAC I.O. Islamic 2678.

Khalil, Khwaja. "Tārīkh-i Shāhanshāhī," June 21, 1716. National Library of India, Delhi, Buhar 79.

Khan, ʿAbd al-Rahman Bakhtawar. "Sāqī-nāma," n.d. Salar Jung Museum, Hyderabad, A/N 367, Acc. No. 3469.

Khan, Abu Talib. "Khulāsat al-Afkār," 1791. British Library, London, APAC, Add. 18, 542.

Khan, ʿAli Muhammad. *Mirāt-i Ahmadī [Fa]*. 2 vols. Bambay: Fath al-Karim, 1889.

Khan, ʿAli Muhammad. *Mirat-i-Ahmadi: A Persian history of Gujarat*. Translated by M. F. Lokhandwala. Baroda: Oriental Institute, 1965.

Khan, ʿAli Muhammad. *Mirat-i-Ahmadi: Supplement (Persian Text) of Ali Muhammad Khan Bahadur*. Baroda: Oriental Institute, 1928.

Khan, Amin al-Din and Shaikh Allah Yar. "Inshā-yi Dilkushā," n.d. Cambridge University Library, Cambridge, Add. Ms. 439.

Khan, Dargah Quli. *Muraqqaʿ-yi Dihlī*. Edited by Nurulhasan Ansari. Dihli: Shuʿbah-i Urdu, Dihli Yunivarsiti, 1982.

Khan, Ghulam Husain. *Siyar al-Mutaʾakhkhirīn*. Edited by ʿAbd al-Majid. Calcutta: Fort William, 1832.

Khan, Ghulam Husain, and Haji Mustepha. *A Translation of the Sëir Mutaqherin; or View of Modern Times, Being an History of India, from the Year 1118 to Year 1194 (This Year Answers to the Christian Year 1781–82) of the Hidjrah, Containing, in General, the Reigns of the Seven Last Emperors of Hindostan, and in Particular, an Account of the English Wars in Bengal . . . To Which the Author Has Added Critical Examination of the English Government and Policy in Those Countries, down to the Year 1783*. Calcutta: J. White, 1789.

Khan, Hamid al-Din. *Ahkām-i ʿĀlamgīrī*. Edited by Jadunath Sarkar. 2nd rev. ed.. Calcutta: M. C. Sarkar & Sons, 1926.

Khan, Iʿtimad ʿAli. "Majmaʿ al-Fawāʾid / Masdar-i Akhbār," 1726. Oxford University, Bodleian Library, Oxford, Persian Mss. Fraser 124.

Khan, ʿIzzat. "Mirʾāt al-Masāʾil-i Muhammad Shāhī," March 3, 1843. Salar Jung Museum, Hyderabad, AC 2693. [Pre-1748].

Khan, Mir Ahmad ʿAli. "Akhlāq-i Muhammad Shāhī," 1721. Oxford University, Bodleian Library, Oxford, Ms. Elliott 6.

Khan, Muhammad Hadi Kamwar. *Tazkirat us-Salatin Chaghta: a Mughal chronicle of post-Aurangzeb period, 1707–1724*. Edited by Muzaffar Alam. Bombay: Asia, 1980.

Khan, Muhammad Saqi Mustaʿidd. *Maʾāsir-i ʿĀlamgīrī [EN]*. Translated by Jadunath Sarkar. Calcutta: Royal Asiatic Society of Bengal, 1947.

Khan, Muhammad Saqi Mustaʿidd. *The Maásir i 'Álamgírí [FA]*. Edited by Ahmad ʿAli. Calcutta: Baptist Mission Press, 1870.

Khan, Shakir. "Hadīqa-yi Hādiq wa Ganjīna-yi Sādiq," n.d. British Library, London, APAC, I.O. Islamic 1781.

Khan, Shakir. "Tārīkh-i Shākir Khānī," n.d. British Library, London, APAC Add. 6585.

Khan Yahya. "Tazkīrāt al-Mulūk," n.d. British Library, London, APAC I.O. Islamic 1147.

Khayal, Mir Muhammad Taqi al-Jaʿfari al-Husaini. "Bustān-i Khayāl," September 13, 1756. University of Manchester, John Rylands Library, Manchester, Pers. Ms. 905.

Khwafi Khan, Muhammad Hashim. *Muntakhab al-lubāb: Mughaliyah daur-i ḥukūmat*. Karaci: Nafis Akaidemi, 1985.

Khwafi Khan, Muhammad Hashim. *The Muntakhab Al-Lubáb [Fa]*. Edited by Kabir al-Din Ahmad. Vol. 1. Calcutta: Asiatic Society of Bengal, 1869.

Khwush Hal. "Tārīkh-i Muhammad Shahī / Nādir al-Zamānī [Berlin]," n.d. Staatsbibliothek zu Berlin Ms. Or. Fol. 222 (Sprenger 495).

Khwush Hal. "Tārīkh-i Muhammad Shāhī [B]," n.d. British Library, London, APAC, Or. 1844.

Khwushgu, Bindraban Das. *Safina-yi Khwushgu*. Edited by S. M. Ataur Rahman. Patna: Institute of Post Graduate Studies & Research in Arabic & Persian, 1959.

Kishor, Raja Jugal. "Rūydād-i Nādir Shāh," n.d. National Archives of India, Delhi, Ac. 324.

Lahori, Abu Bakr al-Faʾiz. "Risāla-yi Mayyat," n.d. Khuda Bakhsh Oriental Public Library, Patna, No. 1663.

Lahori, Muhammad Qasim. *ʿIbratnāma*. Lahore: Idarah-i Tahqiqat-i Pakistan, 1977.

Lahori, Mulla ʿAbd al-Hamid. *Bādshāhnāma*. Edited by Maulawi Kabir al-Din Ahmad and Maulawi ʿAbd al-Rahim. Vol. I. Calcutta: College Press, 1867.

Lakhnavi, Shiv Das. *Shāhnāma-yi Munawwar Kalām*. Translated by Hasan Askari. Patna: Janaki Prakashan, 1980.

Manucci, Niccolao. *Storia Do Mogor*. Edited by William Irvine. London: J. Murray, 1907.

Mashhadi, Mulla Tughra. "Julūsiyya-Yi Tughrā." In *Rasāʾil-i Tughrā*, 130–48. 1667. Kanpur: Matbaʿ-yi Mustafaʾi, 1864.

Mir, Mir Muhammad Taqi. *Tazkīra-yi Nikāt al-Shuʿarā*. Lakhnau: Uttar Pradesh Urdu Akadmi, 1984.

Mir, Mir Muhammad Taqi. *Zikr-i Mir: The Autobiography of the Eighteenth Century Mughal Poet, Mir Muhammad Taqi 'Mir', 1723–1810*. Edited by C. M. Naim. New Delhi and New York: Oxford University Press, 1999.

Muhammad, Mirza. "Tārīkh-i Muhammadi," n.d. British Library, London, APAC I.O. Islamic 813.

Muhammad, Mirza. *Tārīkh-i Muhammadī: jild-i 2, hissah-i 6, 1101-61 H*. Edited by Imtiyaz ʿAli Khan ʿArshi. Aligarh: AMU, 1973.

Muhammad, Mirza. "ʿIbratnāma," n.d. British Library, London, APAC, I.O. Islamic 50 (2).
Mukhlis, Anand Ram. *Chamanistan*. Lakhnau: Nawal Kishor, 1877.
Mukhlis, Anand Ram. "Waqāʾiʿ-yi Ānand Rām Mukhlis," n.d. National Library of India, Delhi, Jadunath Sarkar Collection #201.
Multani, Nur al-Din Faruqi. "Jahāndār Nāmā," n.d. British Library, London, APAC, IO Islamic 3988.
Murad, Shaikh Muhammad. "History of Aurangzeb," n.d. Oxford University, Bodleian Library, Oxford, Persian Mss. Fraser 122.
Mutalliʿ. "Dīwān-Mutalliʿ," before 1712. Asiatic Society of Bengal, Kolkata, Persian Second Collection, Ms. No. 825.
Najm-Sani, Muhammad Baqir. *Advice on the Art of Governance: An Indo-Islamic Mirror for Princes: Mauʿiẓah-i Jahāngīrī of Muḥammad Bāqir Najm-i S̱ānī*. Edited by Sajida Sultana Alvi. Albany: State University of New York Press, 1989.
Nik Raʾi. "Tazkīrat al-Safar wa Tuhfat al-Zafar," n.d. Salar Jung Museum, Hyderabad, Ac. no. 4519.
Qalandar, Munshi Yar Muhammad. *Dastūr al-Inshā*. Calcutta: Islami Press, 1853.
Qazwini, Muhammad Amin, "Pādishāhnāma." Undated. Retrieved from the Library of Congress, https://www.loc.gov/item/50045639/.
Rai, Dalpat. "Malāhat-i Maqal," pre-1768. British Library, London, APAC Or. 1828.
Ram, Lal. "Tuhfat al-Hind." 1735. British Library, London, APAC Add. 6583, 6584.
Rasa, Izid Bakhsh. "Bayāz-i Īzid Bakhsh 'Rasa,'" n.d. British Library, London, APAC I.O. Islamic 4014C.
Sami, Khwaja ʿAbd Allah. "Dīwān-i Sāmī," n.d. Salar Jung Museum, AC 2293.
Sarkhwush, Muhammad Afzal. *Kalimāt al-Shuʿarāʾ*. Edited by ʿAli Raza Qazwah. Tihran: Markaz-i Pazuhish Kitabkhana, Maza wa Markaz-i Isnad-i Majlis-i Shuraʾi-yi Islami, 2011.
Sarkhwush, Muhammad Afzal. "Kalimāt al-Shuʿarāʾ," n.d. British Library, London, APAC Or. 5882.
Sauda, Mirza Muhammad Rafiʿ. *Kullīyāt-i Saudā*. Lakhnau: Nawal Kishor, 1932.
Shahabadi, Rustam ʿAli Khan. "Tārīkh-i Hindī," 1741. British Library, London, APAC Or. 1628.
Shahjahanabadi Chishti, Kalim Allah. *Maktūbāt-i Kalīmī*. Edited by Muhammad Qasīm ʿAli Kalimi. Dihli: Matbaʿ-yi Yusufi, 1883.
Sharif, Jaʿfar. *Islam in India; or, the Qanuni-Islam: The Customs of Musulmans of India, Comprising a Full and Exact Account of Their Various Rites and Ceremonies from the Moment of Birth to the Hour of Death*. Edited by William Crooke. Translated by Herklots. Humphrey Milford: London, 1921.
Siddiqi, Muhammad Muhsin. "Jauhar-i Samsām," 1740. British Library, London, APAC Or. 1898.
Singh, Zorawar. "Masnawī-yi Muhammad Amīn Khān Wazīr wa Muhammad Shāh," 1720s. Bibliotheque Nationale de Paris, SP 508.
Tihrani, Muhammad Quli Salim. *Dīwān-i kāmil-i Muḥammad Qulī Salīm Tihrānī*. Edited by Raḥīm Rida. Tihran: Insisarat-i Ibn Sini, 1970.
ʿUmar, Muhammad. "Zawāhir al-Sarāʾir," 1700. Oxford University, Bodleian Library, Oxford, Persian Mss. Pers. d. 101.
Various. "Historical and Geographical Extracts," n.d. British Library, London, APAC I.O. Islamic 611.
Various. "Khutba and Farmans . . . ," n.d. Oxford University, Bodleian Library, Oxford, Persian Mss. Fraser 228.

Warid, Muhammad Shafiʿ. "Mīrāt-i Wāridāt," pre-1739. British Library, London, APAC Add. 6579.

Warid, Muhammad Shafiʿ. *Tārīkh-i Nādirshāhī: Nadir'nāmah*. Edited by Riza Shaʾbani. Chap-i 1. Tehran: Muʾassasah-ʾi Mutalaʿat va Tahqiqat-i Farhangi, 1990.

Waris, Muhammad. "Bādshāhnāma (Vol. III)," 1656. British Library, London, APAC I.O. Islamic 324.

Wazih, Iradat Khan. *A Translation of the Memoirs of Eradut Khan a Nobleman of Hindostan: Containing Interesting Anecdotes of the Emperor Aulumgeer Aurungzebe, and of His Successors, Shaw Aulum and Jehaundar Shaw: In Which Are Displayed the Causes of the Very Precipitate Decline of the Mogul Empire in India. By Jonathan Scott, Captain in the Service of the Honourable East-India Company, and Private Persian Translator to Warren Hastings, Esquire, Late Governor-General of Bengal, &c. &c. &c.* Translated by Jonathan Scott. London: Stockdale, 1786.

Wazih, Iradat Khan. *Tārīkh-i Irādat Khān*. Edited by Ghulam Rasul Mihr. Lahore: Idarah-'i Tahqiqat-i Pakistan Danishgah-i Punjab, 1971.

Wazih, Iradat Khan. "Tārīkh-i Irādat Khānī," n.d. Salar Jung Museum, Hyderabad, AC 3808.

Yaqin, Shah ʿAbd Allah. "Tārīkh al-Sābit / Khilsī-yi Zubda," 1721. British Library, London, APAC Delhi Persian 614.

Zatalli, Mir Ja'far. *Zatal Namah*. Edited by Rasheed Hasan Khan. Na'i Dihli : Anjuman Taraqqi-i Urdu (Hind), 2003.

Secondary Sources

Ahmad, Aziz. "The British Museum Mīrzānāma and the Seventeenth Century Mīrzā in India." *Iran* 13 (January 1, 1975): 99–110.

Ahmad, Bashiruddin. *Vaqi'at-i mamlakat-i Bijapur*. Agra: Matbaʿ-yi Mufid-i ʿAmm, 1915.

Alam, Muzaffar. *The Crisis of Empire in Mughal North India: Awadh and the Punjab, 1707–1748*. 2nd ed. Oxford India Perennials. New Delhi: Oxford University Press, 2013.

Alam, Muzaffar. *The Languages of Political Islam: India, 1200–1800*. Chicago: University of Chicago Press, 2004.

Alam, Muzaffar. "A Muslim State in a Non-Muslim Context: The Mughal Case." In *Mirror for the Muslim Prince: Islam and the Theory of Statecraft*. Edited by Mehrzad Boroujerdi, 160–90. Syracuse: Syracuse University Press, 2013.

Alam, Muzaffar. "State Building under the Mughals: Religion, Culture and Politics." *Cahiers d'Asie Centrale*, no. 3/4 (October 1, 1997): 105–28.

Alam, Muzaffar. "Trade, State Policy and Regional Change: Aspects of Mughal-Uzbek Commercial Relations, c. 1550–1750." *Journal of the Economic and Social History of the Orient* 37, no. 3 (1994): 202–27.

Alam, Muzaffar, and Sanjay Subrahmanyam. "Eighteenth-Century Historiography and the World of the Mughal Munshi." In *Writing the Mughal World: Studies on Culture and Politics*. New York: Columbia University Press, 2011: 393–423.

Alam, Muzaffar, and Sanjay Subrahmanyam. "Envisioning Power: The Political Thought of a Late Eighteenth-Century Mughal Prince." *Indian Economic Social History Review* 43, no. 2 (2006): 131–61.

Alam, Muzaffar, and Sanjay Subrahmanyam. *Indo-Persian Travels in the Age of Discoveries, 1400–1800*. Cambridge, UK and New York: Cambridge University Press, 2007.

Alam, Muzaffar, and Sanjay Subrahmanyam. "Introduction." In *The Mughal State, 1526–1750*, 1–71. New Delhi and Oxford: Oxford University Press, 1999.

Alam, Muzaffar, and Sanjay Subrahmanyam. "The Making of a Munshi." *Comparative Studies of South Asia, Africa and the Middle East* 24, no. 2 (January 1, 2004): 61–72.

Alavi, Seema, ed. *The Eighteenth Century in India*. New Delhi and New York: Oxford University Press, 2002.

Ali, Daud. "Rethinking the History of the 'Kāma' World in Early India." *Journal of Indian Philosophy* 39, no. 1 (2011): 1–13.

Ali, M. Athar. *The Mughal Nobility under Aurangzeb*. Bombay and New York: Asia Publishing House, 1966.

Ali, M. Athar. "The Mughal Polity: A Critique of Revisionist Approaches." *Modern Asian Studies* 27, no. 4 (1993): 699–710.

Alvi, Sajida S. "The Historians of Awrangzeb: A Comparative Study of Three Primary Sources." In *Essays on Islamic Civilization: Presented to Niyazi Berkes*, edited by Donald P. Little, 57–73. Leiden: Brill, 1976.

Amin, Shahid. *Conquest and Community: The Afterlife of Warrior Saint Ghazi Miyan*. Chicago: Chicago University Press, 2016.

Anastasopoulos, Antonis, ed. *Political Initiatives "from the Bottom up" in the Ottoman Empire: Halcyon Days in Crete VII, a Symposium Held in Rethymno 9–11 January 2009*. Rethymno: Crete University Press, 2012.

Andaya, Barbara Watson, and Leonard Y. Andaya. *A History of Early Modern Southeast Asia, 1400–1830*. Cambridge: Cambridge University Press, 2015.

Anooshahr, Ali. "On the Imperial Discourse of the Delhi Sultanate and Early Mughal India." *Journal of Persianate Studies* 7, no. 2 (November 5, 2014): 157–76.

Anooshahr, Ali. "Muslims among Non-Muslims: Creating Islamic Identity through Law." In *Law Addressing Diversity: Pre-Modern Europe and India in Comparison (13th to 18th Centuries)*, edited by Thomas Ertl and Gijs Kruijtzer, 19–31. Germany: De Gruyter Oldenbourg, 2017.

Ansari, A. S. Bazmee. "Ba<u>kh</u>tāwar <u>Kh</u>ān." In *Encyclopaedia of Islam*. 2nd ed., edited by P. Bearman, Th. Bianquis, C. E. Bosworth, E. van Donzel, and W. P. Heinrichs. Brill Online, 2016.

Asher, Catherine B. *Architecture of Mughal India*. Cambridge: Cambridge University Press, 1992.

Asher, Catherine B. "A Ray from the Sun: Mughal Ideology and the Visual Construction of the Divine." In *The Presence of Light: Divine Radiance and Religious Experience*, edited by Matthew T. Kapstein, 161–95. Chicago: University of Chicago Press, 2004.

Asher, Catherine B. "Sub-Imperial Palaces: Power and Authority in Mughal India." *Ars Orientalis* 23 (January 1, 1993): 281–302.

Askari, Syed Hasan. "A Contemporary Correspondence Describing the Events at Delhi at the Time of Nadir Shah's Invasion." *Proceedings of the Indian History Congress* 10 (1947): 357–66.

Ataullah. "Jafar Zatalli and the Historical Context." *Proceedings of the Indian History Congress* 69 (2008): 447–54.

Atkinson, Edward. *Descriptive and Historical Account of the Aligarh District*. Allahabad: North-Western Provinces Government Press, 1875.

Aubin, Jean. "Comment Tamerlan Prenait Les Villes." *Studia Islamica*, no. 19 (1963): 83–122.

Azizuddin Husain, S. M. "Religious Policy of Aurangzeb during the Later Part of His Reign—An Examination." *Proceedings of the Indian History Congress* 57 (1996): 394–96.

Azizuddin Husain, S. M. *Structure of politics under Aurangzeb, 1658–1707*. New Delhi: Kanishka Publishers, Distributors, 2002.

al-Azmeh, Aziz. *Muslim Kingship: Power and the Sacred in Muslim, Christian and Pagan Polities*. London and New York: I. B. Tauris, 1997.

Baden-Powell, B. H. *Hand-Book of the Manufactures and Arts of the Punjab with a Combined Glossary and Index of Vernacular Trades and Technical Terms, &c. &c.: Forming Vol. II to the "Hand-Book of the Economic Products of the Punjab."* Lahore: Punjab Printing Company, 1872.

Badiou, Alain, Pierre Bourdieu, Judith Butler, Georges Didi-Huberman, Sadri Khiari, and Jacques Rancière. *What Is a People?* Translated by Joy Gladding. New York: Columbia University Press, 2016.

Baer, Marc David. *Honored by the Glory of Islam: Conversion and Conquest in Ottoman Europe*. New York: Oxford University Press, 2008.

Baker, Keith Michael. "A Script for a French Revolution: The Political Consciousness of the Abbé Mably." In *Inventing the French Revolution: Essays on French Political Culture in the Eighteenth Century*, 86–109. Cambridge, UK and New York: Cambridge University Press, 1990.

Baker, Keith Michael, and Dan Edelstein. *Scripting Revolution: A Historical Approach to the Comparative Study of Revolutions*. Stanford, CA: Stanford University Press, 2015.

Balabanlilar, Lisa. "The Emperor Jahangir and the Pursuit of Pleasure." *Journal of the Royal Asiatic Society* 19, no. 2 (2009): 173–86.

Barnett, Richard B. *Rethinking Early Modern India*. New Delhi: Manohar Publishers & Distributors, 2002.

Bates, Crispin, Marina Carter, Andrea Major, and Gavin Rand. *Mutiny at the Margins. New Perspectives on the Indian Uprising of 1857*. 7 vols. NewDelhi: Sage Publications, 2017.

Bayly, Christopher Alan. "Delhi and Other Cities of North India during the 'Twilight.'" In *Delhi through the Ages: Essays in Urban History, Culture, and Society*, edited by Robert Eric Frykenberg, 221–36. Delhi and New York: Oxford University Press, 1986.

Bayly, Christopher Alan. *Empire and Information: Intelligence Gathering and Social Communication in India, 1780–1870*. Cambridge, UK and New York: Cambridge University Press, 1996.

Bayly, Christopher Alan. *Origins of Nationality in South Asia: Patriotism and Ethical Government in the Making of Modern India*. Delhi and New York: Oxford University Press, 1998.

Bayly, Christopher Alan. "The Pre-History of 'Communalism'? Religious Conflict in India, 1700–1860." *Modern Asian Studies* 19, no. 2 (January 1, 1985): 177–203.

Bayly, Christopher Alan. *Rulers, Townsmen, and Bazaars: North Indian Society in the Age of British Expansion, 1770–1870*. Cambridge, UK and New York: Cambridge University Press, 1983.

Ben-Dor Benite, Zvi, Stefanos Geroulanos, and Nicole Jerr. *The Scaffolding of Sovereignty: Global and Aesthetic Perspectives on the History of a Concept*. New York: Columbia University Press, 2017.

Berg, Maxine, Felicia Gottmann, Hanna Hodacs, and Chris Nierstrasz. *Goods from the East, 1600–1800: Trading Eurasia*. Houndmills, Basingstoke, Hampshire: Palgrave Macmillan,, 2015.

Berthels, E. "Niʿmat Kh̲ān, Called ʿĀlī." In *Encyclopaedia of Islam*. 2nd ed., edited by P. Bearman, Th. Bianquis, C. E. Bosworth, E. van Donzel, and W. P. Heinrichs. Brill Online, 2012.

Bhardwaj, Suraj Bhan. *Contestations and Accommodations: Mewat and Meos in Mughal India*. New Delhi: Oxford University Press, 2016.

Bhatt, S. K. "Two Persian Documents Relating to the Religious Policy of the Mughals: A Parwanah of Aurangzeb, 1112 AH and a Parwanah of Muhammad Shah, 13 Julus." *Proceedings of the Indian History Congress* 36 (1975): 358–61.

Blake, Stephen P. "The Khanah Bagh in Mughal India: House Gardens in the Palaces and Mansions of the Great Men of Shahjahanabad." In *Mughal Gardens: Sources, Places, Representations, and Prospects*, edited by James L Wescoat and Joachim Wolschke Bulmahn, 171–89. Washington, DC: Dumbarton Oaks Trustees for Harvard University, 1996.

Blake, Stephen P. *Shahjahanabad: The Sovereign City in Mughal India, 1639–1739*. Cambridge, UK and New York: Cambridge University Press, 1991.

de Boer, Tj., "Faiḍ," in: *Encyclopaedia of Islam, First Edition (1913–1936)*, Edited by M. Th. Houtsma, T.W. Arnold, R. Basset, R. Hartmann. Brill Online, 2012.

Bourke, Richard, and Quentin Skinner. *Popular Sovereignty in Historical Perspective*. Cambridge: Cambridge University Press., 2016.

Böwering, Gerhard, and Patricia Crone. *The Princeton Encyclopedia of Islamic Political Thought*. Princeton: Princeton University Press, 2013.

Brass, Paul R. *The Production of Hindu-Muslim Violence in Contemporary India*. New Delhi: Oxford University Press, 2003.

Brook, Timothy. *The Confusions of Pleasure: Commerce and Culture in Ming China*. Berkeley: University of California Press, 1998.

Brown, Katherine Butler. "Did Aurangzeb Ban Music? Questions for the Historiography of His Reign." *Modern Asian Studies* 41, no. 1 (2007): 77–120.

Buckler, F. W. "A New Interpretation of Akbar's 'Infallibility' Decree of 1579." *The Journal of the Royal Asiatic Society of Great Britain and Ireland*, no. 4 (1924): 591–608.

Buckler, F. W. "The Political Theory of the Indian Mutiny." *Transactions of the Royal Historical Society* 5 (January 1, 1922): 71–100.

Burak, Guy. *The Second Formation of Islamic Law: The Ḥanafī School in the Early Modern Ottoman Empire*. Cambridge: Cambridge University Press, 2017.

Busch, Allison. *Poetry of Kings: The Classical Hindi Literature of Mughal India*. New York: Oxford University Press, 2011.

Canbakal, Hülya. *Society and Politics in an Ottoman Town: ʾAyntāb in the 17th Century*. Leiden: Brill, 2007.

Carroll, Stuart. *Blood and Violence in Early Modern France*. Oxford: Oxford University Press, 2006.

Chaghtai, M. Abdullah. "A Family of Great Mughal Architects." *Islamic Culture* 11 (1937): 200–211.

Chakrabarty, Dipesh. *The Calling of History: Sir Jadunath Sarkar and His Empire of Truth*. Chicago: University of Chicago Press, 2015.

Chakrabarty, Dipesh. "The Muddle of Modernity." *The American Historical Review* 116, no. 3 (June 1, 2011): 663–75.

Chandra, Satish. "Cultural and Political Role of Delhi, 1675–1725." In *Delhi Through the Ages: Selected Essays in Urban History, Culture and Society*, edited by Robert Eric Frykenberg, 104–18. Delhi and New York: Oxford University Press, 1986.

Chandra, Satish. *The 18th Century in India: Its Economy and the Role of the Marathas, the Jats, the Sikhs, and the Afghans*. Sakharam Ganesh Deuskar Lectures on Indian History 1982. Calcutta: Published for Centre for Studies in Social Sciences, Calcutta by K.P. Bagchi & Co, 1986.

Chandra, Satish. "Jizyah and the State in India during the 17th Century." *Journal of the Economic and Social History of the Orient* 12, no. 3 (1969): 322–40.

Chandra, Satish. "Jizyah in the Post-Aurangzeb Period." In *Essays in Medieval Indian Economic History*, 345–53. New Delhi: Munshiram Manoharlal, 1987.

Chandra, Satish. *Medieval India: From Sultanat to the Mughals*. New Delhi: Har Anand Publications, 1997.

Chandra, Satish. *Parties and Politics at the Mughal Court, 1707–1740*. 4th ed. New Delhi and New York: Oxford University Press, 2002.

Chandra, Satish. "Some Considerations on the Religious Policy of Aurangzeb during the Latter Part of His Reign." *Proceedings of the Indian History Congress* 47 (1986): 369–81.

Chatterjee, Partha. *Nationalist Thought and the Colonial World: A Derivative Discourse?* London, UK: Zed Books, 1986.

Chaudhuri, K. N. "Some Reflections on the Town and Country in Mughal India." *Modern Asian Studies* 12, no. 1 (1978): 77–96.

Chenoy, Shama Mitra. *Shahjahanabad, a City of Delhi, 1638–1857*. New Delhi: Munshiram Manoharlal Publishers, 1998.

Chenoy, Shama Mitra. *Shahjahanabad: Seventeenth and Eighteenth Centuries Symphony, Identities, Plurality*. NMML Monograph, 8. New Delhi: Nehru Memorial Museum and Library, 2004.

Codell, Julie F. *Power and Resistance: The Delhi Coronation Durbars, 1877, 1903, 1911*. New Delhi: Mapin, 2012.

Colvin, John. "On the Restoration of the Ancient Canals in the Delhi Territory." *Journal of the Asiatic Society of Bengal* 2 (1833): 105–27. Corboz, André. "The Land as Palimpsest." *Diogenes* 31, no. 121 (March 1, 1983): 12–34.

Crone, Patricia. *God's Rule: Government and Islam*. New York: Columbia University Press, 2004.

Crooke, William. *An Ethnographical Handbook for the N.-W. Provinces and Oudh*. Allahabad: North-Western Provinces and Oudh Government Press, 1890.

Crooke, William. "The Holi: A Vernal Festival of the Hindus." *Folklore* 25, no. 1 (1914): 55–83.

Crooke, William. *The Tribes and Castes of the North-Western Provinces and Oudh*. XX: Office of the Superintendent of Government Printing, 1896.

Dadlani, Chanchal. "The City Built, the City Rendered: Locating Urban Subjectivity in Eighteenth-Century Mughal Delhi." *Affect, Emotion, and Subjectivity in Early Modern Muslim Empires: New Studies in Ottoman, Safavid, and Mughal Art and Culture*, October 19, 2017, 148–67.

Dale, Stephen Frederic. *The Garden of the Eight Paradises: Babur and the Culture of Empire in Central Asia, Afghanistan and India (1483–1530)*. Leiden and Boston: Brill, 2004.

Dale, Stephen Frederic. *Indian Merchants and Eurasian Trade, 1600–1750*. Cambridge, UK and New York: Cambridge University Press, 1994.

Dalrymple, William. *The Last Mughal: The Fall of Delhi, 1857*. London: Bloomsbury, 2009.

Dames, M. Longworth. "Khwādja Khiḍr." In *Encyclopaedia of Islam*. 2nd ed., edited by P. Bearman, Th. Bianquis, C. E. Bosworth, E. van Donzel, and W. P. Heinrichs. Brill Online, 2012.

Darling, Linda T. "'Do Justice, Do Justice, for That Is Paradise': Middle Eastern Advice for Indian Muslim Rulers." *Comparative Studies of South Asia, Africa and the Middle East* 22, no. 1 (2002): 3–19.

Darling, Linda T. *A History of Social Justice and Political Power in the Middle East : The Circle of Justice From Mesopotamia to Globalization*. London, New York: Routledge, 2013.

Darnton, Robert. *The Great Cat Massacre and Other Episodes in French Cultural History*. New York: Basic Books, 1984.

Darnton, Robert. *Poetry and the Police: Communication Networks in Eighteenth-Century Paris*. Cambridge, MA: Belknap Press of Harvard University Press, 2010.

Das Gupta, Ashin. *Indian Merchants and the Decline of Surat: C. 1700–1750*. Wiesbaden: Steiner, 1979.

Das Gupta, Ashin. "Trade and Politics in Eighteenth Century India." In *The Mughal State, 1526–1750*, edited by Muzaffar Alam and Sanjay Subrahmanyam, 361–98. New Delhi and Oxford: Oxford University Press, 1999.

Davis, Dick. "Tūrān." In *Encyclopaedia of Islam, Second Edition*, edited by P. Bearman, Th. Bianquis, C. E. Bosworth, E. van Donzel, and W. P. Heinrichs. Brill Online, 2012.

Davis, Natalie Zemon. "The Rites of Violence: Religious Riot in Sixteenth-Century France." *Past & Present*, no. 59 (May 1, 1973): 51–91.

Davis, Natalie Zemon. "The Sacred and the Body Social in Sixteenth-Century Lyon." *Past & Present*, no. 90 (February 1, 1981): 40–70.

Devji, Faisal. "The Mutiny to Come." *New Literary History* 40, no. 2 (2009): 411–30.

Dewar, Douglas, H. L. Garrett, and F. W. Buckler. "The Political Theory of the Indian Mutiny: A Reply and with a Rejoinder." *Transactions of the Royal Historical Society* 7 (1924): 131–65.

Dhavan, Purnima. *When Sparrows Became Hawks: The Making of the Sikh Warrior Tradition, 1699–1799*. New York: Oxford University Press, 2011.

Digby, Simon. "Encounters with Jogis in Sufi Hagiography." Unpublished paper, School of Oriental and African Studies, London, 1970.

Dihkhuda, ʿAli Akbar. *Amsāl va ḥikam*. Tihrān: Amir Kabir, 1984.

Eaton, Richard Maxwell. "Approaches to the Study of Conversion to Islam in India." In *Approaches to Islam in Religious Studies*, edited by Richard C. Martin. Tucson: University of Arizona Press, 1985: 106–23.

Eaton, Richard Maxwell. *The Rise of Islam and the Bengal Frontier, 1204–1760*. Berkeley: University of California Press, 1993.

Eaton, Richard Maxwell. "Shrines, Cultivators, and Muslim 'Conversion' in Punjab and Bengal, 1300–1700." *The Medieval History Journal* 12, no. 2 (2009): 191–220.

Eaton, Richard Maxwell. *Sufis of Bijapur, 1300–1700: Social Roles of Sufis in Medieval India*. Princeton, NJ: Princeton University Press, 1978.

Eaton, Richard Maxwell. "Temple Desecration and Indo-Muslim States." In *Beyond Turk and Hindu: Rethinking Religious Identities in Islamicate South Asia*, edited by David Gilmartin and Bruce Lawrence, 246–81. Gainesville: University Press of Florida, 2000.

Eaton, Richard Maxwell. *Temple Desecration and Muslim States in Medieval India*. Gurgaon: Hope India Publications, 2004.

Ehlers, Eckart, and Thomas Krafft. *Shâhjahânâbâd, Old Delhi: Tradition and Colonial Change*. Stuttgart: F. Steiner, 1993.

Elbendary, Amina. *Crowds and Sultans: Urban Protest in Late Medieval Egypt and Syria.* New York: American University in Cairo Press, 2016.

Elliot, H. M., and J. Dowson. *The History of India as Told by Its Own Historians: The Muhammadan Period.* Vol. I. London : Trübner & Co, 1867.

Ernst, Carl W. "Muslim Studies of Hinduism? A Reconsideration of Arabic and Persian Translations from Indian Languages." *Iranian Studies* 36, no. 2 (2003): 173–95.

Fallon, S. W. *A New English-Hindustani Dictionary, with Illus. from English Literature and Colloquial English Translated into Hindustani.* Banaras: Medical Hall Press, 1883.

Fancy, Hussein. "Of Sovereigns, Sacred Kings, and Polemics." *History and Theory* 56, no. 1 (March 1, 2017): 61–70.

Fancy, Hussein. *The Mercenary Mediterranean: Sovereignty, Religion and Violence in the Medieval Crown of Aragon.* Chicago and London: University of Chicago Press, 2016.

Farooqi, Naimur Rahman. "Moguls, Ottomans, and Pilgrims: Protecting the Routes to Mecca in the Sixteenth and Seventeenth Centuries." *The International History Review* 10, no. 2 (1988): 198–220.

Farooqi, Naimur Rahman. *Mughal-Ottoman Relations: A Study of Political & Diplomatic Relations between Mughal India and the Ottoman Empire, 1556–1748.* Delhi: Idarah-i Adabiyat-i Delli, 1989.

Farooqui, Mahmood. *Besieged: Voices from Delhi, 1857.* New Delhi: Penguin Viking, 2010.

Faruqi, Shamsur Rahman. "A Long History of Urdu Literary Culture, Part I: Naming and Placing a Literary Culture." In *Literary Cultures in History: Reconstructions from South Asia,* edited by Sheldon I. Pollock, 805–64. Berkeley: University of California Press, 2003.

Faruqui, Munis D. "Awrangzīb." In *Encyclopaedia of Islam, THREE,* edited by Kate Fleet, Gudrun Krämer, Denis Matringe, John Nawas, and Everett Rowson. Brill Online, 2011.

Faruqui, Munis D. *Princes of the Mughal Empire, 1504–1719.* Cambridge, UK and New York: Cambridge University Press, 2012.

Feuillebois, Ève. "Firdawsī, Abū l-Qāsim, and the Shāhnāma." In *Encyclopaedia of Islam, THREE,* edited by Kate Fleet, Gudrun Krämer, Denis Matringe, John Nawas, and Everett Rowson. Brill Online, 2017.

Fierro, Ma Isabel, and Christian Lange. *Public Violence in Islamic Societies: Power, Discipline, and the Construction of the Public Sphere, 7th–19th Centuries CE.* Edinburgh: Edinburgh University Press, 2009.

Fink, H. R. "The Hindu Custom of 'Sitting Dharna.'" *The Calcutta Review* LXII (1876): 37–52.

Fleischer, Cornell H. *Bureaucrat and Intellectual in the Ottoman Empire: The Historian Mustafa Âli (1541–1600).* Princeton, NJ: Princeton University Press, 1986.

Flood, Finbarr Barry. *Objects of Translation: Material Culture and Medieval "Hindu-Muslim" Encounter.* Princeton, NJ: Princeton University Press, 2009.

Flores, Jorge. "'I Will Do as My Father Did': On Portuguese and Other European Views of Mughal Succession Crises." *e-JPH* 3, no. 2 (Winter 2005). http://www.brown.edu/Departments/Portuguese_Brazilian_Studies/ejph/html/issue6/html/flores_main.html.

Flores, Jorge, and Sanjay Subrahmanyam. "The Shadow Sultan: Succession and Imposture in the Mughal Empire, 1628–1640." *Journal of the Economic and Social History of the Orient* 47, no. 1 (March 1, 2004): 80–121.

Foltz, Richard. "Central Asians in the Administration of Mughal India." *Journal of Asian History* 31, no. 2 (1997): 139–54.

Foltz, Richard. "Cultural Contacts Between Central Asia and Mughal India." *Central Asiatic Journal* 42, no. 1 (1998): 44–65.

Franke, Heike. "Emperors of Ṣūrat and Maʿnī: Jahangir and Shah Jahan as Temporal and Spiritual Rulers." *Muqarnas* 31 (2014): 123–49.

Freitag, Sandria B. *Culture and Power in Banaras: Community, Performance, and Environment, 1800–1980*. Berkeley: University of California Press, 1989.

Friedmann, Yohanan. *Tolerance and Coercion in Islam: Interfaith Relations in the Muslim Tradition*. Cambridge Studies in Islamic Civilization. New York: Cambridge University Press, 2003.

Friedrichs, Christopher R. "What Made the Eurasian City Work? Urban Political Cultures in Early Modern Europe and Asia." In *City Limits: Perspectives on the Historical European City*, edited by Glenn Clark, Judith Owens, and Greg T. Smith, 29–64. Montreal and Kingston: McGill-Queen's University Press, 2010.

Frykenberg, Robert Eric, ed. *Delhi through the Ages: Essays in Urban History, Culture, and Society*. Delhi and New York: Oxford University Press, 1986.

Gara, Eleni, M. Erdem Kabadayi, and Christoph K Neumann. *Popular Protest and Political Participation in the Ottoman Empire: Studies in Honor of Suraiya Faroqhi*. Istanbul: Bilgi İletişim GrubuYayincilik Müzik Yapim ve Haber Ajansi Ltd., 2011.

Gilchrist, John Borthwick. *The Oriental Linguist: An Easy and Familiar Introduction to the Hindoostanee, or Grand Popular Language of Hindoostan (Vulgarly, but Improperly, Called the Moors). By the Author of the English and Hindóostanee Dictionary [J. B. Gilchrist]*. 2nd ed., rev. and altered. Calcutta: Ferris and Co., 1798.

Gillion, Kenneth L. *Ahmedabad: A Study in Indian Urban History*. Berkeley and Los Angeles: University of California Press, 1968.

Gilmartin, David. "Imperial Sovereignty in Mughal and British Forms." *History and Theory* 56, no. 1 (March 1, 2017): 80–88.

Gokhale, Balkrishna Govind. *Poona in the Eighteenth Century: An Urban History*. New Delhi: Oxford University Press, 1988.

Gokhale, Balkrishna Govind. *Surat in the Seventeenth Century: A Study of Urban History of Pre-Modern India*. London: Curzon Press, 1979.

Gommans, Jos J. L. *Mughal Warfare: Indian Frontiers and Highroads to Empire 1500–1700*. London: Routledge, 2003.

Gommans, Jos J. L. *The Rise of the Indo-Afghan Empire, c.1710–1780*. Leiden and New York: E.J. Brill, 1995.

Gordon, Stewart. *Robes of Honour: Khil'at in Pre-Colonial and Colonial India*. New Delhi: Oxford University Press, 2003.

Gordon, Stewart. "Robes of Honour: A 'transactional' Kingly Ceremony." *The Indian Economic and Social History Review.* 33, no. 3 (1996): 225.

Goswamy, B. N., and J. S. Grewal. *The Mughals and the Jogis of Jakhbar: Some Madad-i-Ma`ash and Other Documents*. Simla: Indian Institute of Advanced Study, 1967.

Grewal, J. S., India Banga, India University Grants Commission., and Guru Nanak Dev University. *Studies in Urban History*. Amritsar: Dept. of History, Guru Nanak Dev University, 1981.

Guha, Ranajit. *Elementary Aspects of Peasant Insurgency in Colonial India*. Delhi: Oxford, 1983.

Gupta, Narayani. *Delhi between Two Empires, 1803–1931: Society, Government and Urban Growth*. Delhi: Oxford University Press, 1981.

Habib, Irfan. *The Agrarian System of Mughal India, 1556–1707*. 3rd ed. Delhi and Oxford: Oxford, 2000.

Habib, Irfan. "Barani's Theory of the History of the Delhi Sultanate." *Indian Historical Review* VII (1981): 99–115.

Habib, Irfan. "The Eighteenth Century in Indian Economic History." In *The Eighteenth Century in India*, edited by Seema Alavi, 57–84. New Delhi and New York: Oxford University Press, 2002.

Habib, Irfan. "Forms of Class Struggle in Mughal India." In *Essays in Indian History: Towards a Marxist Perception*, 233–59. Anthem South Asian Studies. London: Anthem Press, 2002.

Habib, Irfan. "The Mercantile Classes of India During the Period of the Delhi Sultanate." *Proceedings of the Indian History Congress* 69 (2008): 297–308.

Habib, Irfan. "Merchant Communities in Precolonial India." In *The Rise of Merchant Empires: Long-Distance Trade in the Early Modern World*, 371–99. Cambridge, UK and New York: Cambridge, 1993.

Habib, Irfan. "Notes on the Economic and Social Aspects of Mughal Gardens." In *Mughal Gardens: Sources, Places, Representations, and Prospects*, edited by James L Wescoat and Joachim Wolschke Bulmahn, 127–39. Washington, DC: Dumbarton Oaks Trustees for Harvard University, 1996.

Habib, Irfan. "Peasant and Artisan Resistance in Mughal India." *McGill Studies in International Development*, no. 34 (July 1984).

Habib, Irfan. "Persian Book Writing and Book Use in the Pre-Printing Age." Proceedings of the Indian History Congress 66 (2005): 514–37.

Habib, Irfan. "Population." In *The Cambridge Economic History of India: Volume 1, C.1200-c.1750*, edited by Tapan Raychaudhuri, Irfan Habib, and Dharma Kumar, 163–72. Cambridge, UK: Cambridge University Press, 1982.

Haider, Najaf. "A Holi Riot of 1714: Versions from Ahmadabad and Delhi." In *Living Together Separately: Cultural India in History and Politics*, edited by Mushirul Hasan and Asim Roy, 127–44. New Delhi: Oxford University Press, 2005.

Haider, Najaf. "Justice and Political Authority in Medieval Indian Islam." In *Justice: Political, Social, Juridical*, edited by Rajeev Bhargava, Michael Dusche, and Helmut Reifeld, 75–93. SAGE Publishing India, 2008.

Haider, Najaf. "Precious Metal Flows and Currency Circulation in the Mughal Empire." *Journal of the Economic and Social History of the Orient* 39, no. 3 (1996): 298–364.

Hakala, Walter N. "A Sultan in the Realm of Passion: Coffee in Eighteenth-Century Delhi." *Eighteenth-Century Studies* 47, no. 4 (2014): 371–88.

Hallaq, Wael B. *Sharī'a: Theory, Practice, Transformations*. Cambridge, UK and New York: Cambridge University Press, 2009.

Hamadeh, Shirine. *The City's Pleasures: Istanbul in the Eighteenth Century*. Seattle: University of Washington Press, 2008.

Hambly, Gavin. *Cities of Mughul India: Delhi, Agra, and Fatehpur Sikri*. New York: Putnam, 1968.

Hambly, Gavin. "Towns and Cities." In *The Cambridge Economic History of India*. Vol. 1, c.1200–c.1750, edited by Tapan Raychaudhuri, Irfan Habib, and Dharma Kumar, 434–52. Cambridge, UK: Cambridge University Press, 1982.

Hansen, Thomas Blom, and Finn Stepputat. "Sovereignty Revisited." *Annual Review of Anthropology* 35 (January 1, 2006): 295–315.

Hardy, Peter. "Modern European and Muslim Explanations of Conversion to Islam in South Asia: A Preliminary Survey of the Literature." *Journal of the Royal Asiatic Society of Great Britain and Ireland*, no. 2 (1977): 177–206.

Harris, Tim, ed. *The Politics of the Excluded, c. 1500–1850*. Houndmills and Basingstoke: Palgrave, 2001.

Hasan, Farhat. "Forms of Civility and Publicness in Pre-British India." In *Civil Society, Public Sphere, and Citizenship: Dialogues and Perceptions*, edited by Rajeev Bhargava and Helmut Reifeld, 84–105. New Delhi: Sage, 2005.

Hasan, Farhat. *State and Locality in Mughal India: Power Relations in Western India, c. 1572–1730*. Cambridge, UK and New York: Cambridge University Press, 2004.

Hasan, Hadi. *Mughal Poetry: Its Cultural and Historical Value*. Madras: Islamic Literature Society, 1952.

Hasan, S. Nurul. "The Morphology of a Mediaeval Indian City: A Case Study of Shahjahanabad in the 18th and Early 19th Century." *Proceedings of the Indian History Congress* 43 (1982): 307–17.

Hasan, S. Nurul. "Zamindars under the Mughals." In *The Mughal State, 1526–1750*, edited by Muzaffar Alam and Sanjay Subrahmanyam, 284–301. New Delhi and Oxford: Oxford University Press, 1999.

Hattox, Ralph S. *Coffee and Coffeehouses: The Origins of a Social Beverage in the Medieval Near East*. Seattle: University of Washington Press, 2002.

Heim, Maria. *Theories of the Gift in Medieval South Asia: Hindu, Buddhist and Jain Reflections on Dana*. London: Routledge, 2004.

Hodivala, Shahpurshah Hormasji. *Historical Studies in Mughal Numismatics*. 1923. Reprint, Varanasi: Numismatic Society of India, 1976.

Hoey, William. *A Monograph on Trade and Manufactures in Northern India*. Lucknow: American Methodist Mission Press, 1880.

Huart, Cl. and H. Massé. "Firdawsī." In *Encyclopaedia of Islam*. 2nd ed., edited by P. Bearman, Th. Bianquis, C. E. Bosworth, E. van Donzel, and W. P. Heinrichs. Brill Online, 2012.

Hunt, Lynn. *Politics, Culture, and Class in the French Revolution*. Berkeley: University of California Press, 1984.

Imperial Record Department, India. *Press-List of "Mutiny Papers" 1857: Being a Colection of the Correspondence of the Mutineers at Delhi, Reports of Spies to English Officials and Other Miscellaneous Papers*. Calcutta: Superintendent, Government Printing, India, 1921.

Inalcik, Halil. "The Ottoman Succession and Its Relation to the Turkish Concept of Sovereignty." In *The Middle East and the Balkans under the Ottoman Empire: Essays on Economy and Society*, 37–70. Bloomington: Indiana University Press, 1993.

Irvine, William. *The Army of the Indian Moghuls: Its Organization and Administration*. London: Luzac, 1903.

Irvine, William. "Nādir Shāh and Muhammād Shāh, a Hindi Poem by Tilok Dās." *Journal of the Asiatic Society of Bengal* (1897): 24–62.

Irvine, William. "Two Proposed Corrections in the 'Catalogue of Persian MSS in the British Museum' of Dr. C. Rieu." *Journal of the Royal Asiatic Society (New Series)* 30, no. 2 (1898): 373–75.

Irvine, William, and Jadunath Sarkar. *Later Mughals*. Vol. I. Calcutta: M. C. Sarkar & Sons, 1921.

Jacob, Margaret C., and Catherine Secretan. *In Praise of Ordinary People: Early Modern Britain and the Dutch Republic*. New York: Palgrave Macmillan, 2013.

Jalal, Ayesha. "Exploding Communalism: The Politics of Muslim Identity in South Asia." In *Nationalism, Democracy and Development: State and Politics in India*, edited by Sugata Bose and Ayesha Jalal, 76–103. New Delhi: Oxford University Press, 2009.

Jha, D. N. "Against Communalising History." *Social Scientist* 26, no. 9/10 (1998): 52–62.

Jha, Kalpana. *Urbanisation in Early Medieval North India: An Analysis of the Samaraichchakaha*. Patna: Janaki Prakashan, 1990.

Jones, Linda G. *The Power of Oratory in the Medieval Muslim World*. Cambridge, UK: Cambridge University Press, 2012.

Kafadar, Cemal. "How Dark Is the History of the Night, How Black the Story of Coffee, How Bitter the Tale of Love: The Changing Measure of Leisure and Pleasure in Early Modern Istanbul." In *Medieval and Early Modern Performance in the Eastern Mediterranean*, edited by Arzu Öztürkmen and Evelyn Birge Vitz, 243–69. Turnhout: Brepols, 2014.

Kafadar, Cemal. "Janissaries and Other Riffraff of Ottoman Istanbul: Rebels without a Cause?" *International Journal of Turkish Studies* 13, no. 1 & 2 (2007): 113–34.

Kaicker, Abhishek. "Unquiet City: Making and Unmaking Politics in Mughal Delhi, 1707–39." PhD diss., Columbia University, 2014.

Kaye, John William. *A History of the Sepoy War in India, 1857–58*. 3 vols. London and New York: Longmans, Green and Co., 1896.

Keegan, John. *The Face of Battle*. New York: Viking Press, 1976.

Khan, Iqtidar Alam. "Muskets in the Mawas: Instruments of Peasant Resistance." In *The Making of History: Essays Presented to Irfan Habib*, edited by K. N. Panikkar, T. J. Byres, and Utsa Patnaik, 81–103. London: Anthem Press, 2002.

Khan, Iqtidar Alam. "The Middle Classes in the Mughal Empire." *Social Scientist* 5, no. 1 (1976): 28–49.

Khan, Mohammad Afzal. "Glimpses of the Administration of Agra under Muhammad Shah [Based on News Reports from The City]." *Proceedings of the Indian History Congress* 54 (1993): 200–07.

Khan, Mohammad Afzal. "Local Administration in Agra: Archival Evidence from Muhammad Shah's Reign." *Proceedings of the Indian History* Congress 55 (1994): 255–61.

Khare, G. H. "Emblems of Royalty in Art and Literature." *Annals of the Bhandarkar Oriental Research Institute* 58/59 (1977): 683–89.

Khuda Bakhsh Oriental Public Library. *Catalogue of the Arabic and Persian Manuscripts in the Khuda Bakhsh Oriental Public Library at Patna*. Vol. VII. Calcutta: Baptist Mission Press, 1921.

Khuda Bakhsh Oriental Public Library. *The Muntakhab Al-Lubáb [Fa]*. Edited by Kabir al-Din Ahmad. Vol. 3. Calcutta: Asiatic Society of Bengal, 1874.

Kia, Mana. "Adab as Literary Form and Social Conduct: Reading the Gulistan in Late Mughal India." In *"No Tapping Around Philology": A Festschrift in Celebration and Honor of Wheeler McIntosh Thackston Jr.'s 70th Birthday*, edited by A. Korangy and D. Sheffield, 281–308. Wiesbaden: Harrassowitz Verlag, 2014.

Kia, Mana. "Contours of Persianate Community, 1722–1835." PhD diss., Harvard University, 2011.

Kinra, Rajeev. *Writing Self, Writing Empire: Chandar Bhan Brahman and the Cultural World of the Indo-Persian State Secretary*. South Asia across the Disciplines. Oakland: University of California Press, 2015.

Kinra, Rajeev. *Writing Self, Writing Empire: Chandar Bhan Brahman and the Cultural World of the Indo-Persian State Secretary*. Oakland, CA: University of California Press, 2015.

Koch, Ebba. "Agra." In *Encyclopaedia of Islam, THREE*, edited by Kate Fleet, John Nawas, Everett Rowson, Gudrun Krämer, and Denis Matringe, n.d. Accessed February 19, 2018.

Koch, Ebba. "The Delhi of the Mughals Prior to Shahjahanabad as Reflected in the Patterns of Imperial Visits." In *Mughal Art and Imperial Ideology: Collected Essays*, 163–83. New Delhi and New York: Oxford University Press, 2001.

Koch, Ebba. "Diwan-i ʿAmm and Chihil Sutun: The Audience Halls of Shah Jahan." *Muqarnas* 11 (1994): 143–65.

Koch, Ebba. "The Hierarchical Principles of Shah Jahani Painting." In *Mughal Art and Imperial Ideology: Collected Essays*, 130–62. New Delhi and New York: Oxford University Press, 2001.

Koch, Ebba. "Mughal Agra: A Riverfront Garden City." In *The City in the Islamic World, Volume 94/1 & 94/2*, edited by Salma K. Jayyusi, Renata Holod, Attilio Petruccioli, and Andre Raymond, 555–88. Leiden; Boston: Brill, 2008.

Koch, Ebba. "The Mughal Emperor as Solomon, Majnun, and Orpheus, or the Album as a Think Tank for Allegory." *Muqarnas* 27 (2010): 277–311.

Koch, Ebba. "Mughal Palace Gardens from Babur to Shah Jahan (1526–1648)." *Muqarnas* 14 (1997): 143–65.

Koch, Ebba. "Shah Jahan and Orpheus: The Pietre Dure Decoration and the Programme of the Throne in the Hall of Public Audiences at the Red Fort of Delhi." In *Mughal Art and Imperial Ideology: Collected Essays*, 61–130. Delhi: Oxford University Press, 2001.

Kohlberg, E. "Wasī." In *Encyclopaedia of Islam*, 2nd ed., edited by P. Bearman, Th. Bianquis, C. E. Bosworth, E. van Donzel, and W. P. Heinrichs. Brill Online, 2016.

Kolff, D. H. A. *Naukar, Rajput, and Sepoy: The Ethnohistory of the Military Labour Market in Hindustan, 1450–1850*. Cambridge, UK and New York: Cambridge University Press, 1990.

Konrad, Felix. "Coping with 'the Riff-Raff and Mob': Representations of Order and Disorder in the Patrona Halil Rebellion (1730)." *Die Welt Des Islams* 54, nos. 3–4 (December 2, 2014): 363–98.

Koselleck, Reinhart. *Futures Past: On the Semantics of Historical Time*. New York: Columbia University Press, 2004.

Kruijtzer, Gijs. *Xenophobia in Seventeenth-Century India*. Amsterdam: Leiden University Press, 2009.

Kumar, Dharma. "Left Secularists and Communalism." *Economic and Political Weekly* 29, no. 28 (1994): 1803–09.

Kumar, Sunil. *The Emergence of the Delhi Sultanate, 1192–1286*. New Delhi and Bangalore: Permanent Black, Distributed by Orient Longman, 2007.

Lal, Ruby. *Domesticity and Power in the Early Mughal World*. Cambridge, UK: Cambridge University Press, 2005.

Lal, Ruby. "Settled, Sacred and All-Powerful: Making of New Genealogies and Traditions of Empire under Akbar." *Economic and Political Weekly* 36, no. 11 (2001): 941–58.

Lambton, Ann K. S. *State and Government in Medieval Islam: An Introduction to the Study of Islamic Political Theory: The Jurists*. Oxford and New York: Oxford University Press, 1981.

Llewellyn-Jones, Rosie. *The Great Uprising in India, 1857–58: Untold Stories, Indian and British*. Woodbridge and Suffolk: Boydell Press, 2007.

Lockhart, Laurence. "De Voulton's Noticia." Edited by De Voulton. *Bulletin of the School of Oriental Studies, University of London* 4, no. 2 (January 1, 1926): 223–45.

Lockhart, Laurence. *Nadir Shah: A Critical Study Based Mainly upon Contemporary Sources*. London: Luzac, 1938.

Lorenzen, David N., ed. *Bhakti Religion in North India: Community Identity and Political Action*. Albany: SUNY Press, 1995.

Losensky, Paul. "Coordinates in Time and Space: Architectural Chronograms in Safavid Iran." In *New Perspectives on Safavid Iran: Empire and Society*, edited by Colin Paul Mitchell, 198–219. Milton Park and Abingdon: Routledge, 2011.

Losensky, Paul. "Mādda Tāriḵ." In *Encyclopædia Iranica*, December 5, 2006.

Losensky, Paul. "Qodsi Mashadi." In *Encyclopædia Iranica*, December 5, 2006.

Losty, Jeremiah P. "Delineating Delhi: Images of the Mughal Capital." In *Delhi: Red Fort to Raisina*, edited by Pramod Kapoor and Jeremiah P Losty, 14–87. New Delhi: Lustre Press, 2012.

Macdonell, A. A. "Fraser, James (1712/13–1754)." In *Oxford Dictionary of National Biography*, revised by P. J. Marshall. Oxford: Oxford University Press, 2004. http://www.oxforddnb.com/view/article/10107.

Malik, Zahiruddin. "The Core and the Periphery: A Contribution to the Debate on the Eighteenth Century." *Social Scientist* 18, nos. 11/12 (November 1, 1990): 3–35.

Malik, Zahiruddin. *A Mughal Statesman of the Eighteenth Century: Khan-i-Dauran, Mir Bakshi of Muhammad Shah, 1719–1739*. Aligarh: Asia Publishing House, 1973.

Malik, Zahiruddin. *The Reign of Muhammad Shah, 1717–1748*. New Delhi: Icon Publications, 2006.

Maloni, Ruby. "The Monetary Realm of Surat in the Seventeenth Century." *Proceedings of the Indian History Congress* 63 (2002): 359–68.

Mangalam, S. J. "Tulāpurusha Mahādāna." *Bulletin of the Deccan College Research Institute* 36, no. 1/4 (1976): 89–96.

Markiewicz, Christopher Andrew. "The Crisis of Rule in Late Medieval Islam: A Study of Idrīs Bidlīsī (861–926/1457–1520) and Kingship at the Turn of the Sixteenth Century." PhD diss., University of Chicago, 2015.

Marshall, Sir John. *Taxila: An Illustrated Account of Archaeological Excavations*. Vol. I. Cambridge, UK: Cambridge University Press, 1951.

Matthee, Rudi. "Coffee in Safavid Iran: Commerce and Consumption." *Journal of the Economic and Social History of the Orient* 37, no. 1 (1994): 1–32.

Matthee, Rudi. "Nādir Shāh in Iranian Historiography: Warlord or National Hero?" In *Studying the Near and Middle East at the Institute for Advanced Study, Princeton (1935–2018)*, edited by Sabine Schmidtke, 467–74. Piscataway: Georgias Press, 2018.

Matthee, Rudi, and Willem Floor. *The Monetary History of Iran: From the Safavids to the Qajars*. London, New York: I. B. Tauris, 2013.

Mayaram, Shail. *Against History, Against State: Counterperspectives from the Margins*. New York: Columbia University Press, 2003.

McHugh, James. "The Incense Trees of the Land of Emeralds: The Exotic Material Culture of 'Kāmaśāstra.'" *Journal of Indian Philosophy* 39, no. 1 (2011): 63–100.

Mehta, Makrand. *Indian Merchants and Entrepreneurs in Historical Perspective: With Special Reference to Shroffs of Gujarat, 17th to 19th Centuries*. Delhi: Academic Foundation, 1991.

Meisami, Julie Scott. "Khāqānī, Elegy on Madā'in." In *Qasida Poetry in Islamic Asia and Africa II: Eulogy's Bounty, Meaning's Abundance. An Anthology*, edited by Stefan Sperl and Christopher Shackle, 162–69. Leiden: Brill, 1996.

Meisami, Julie Scott. *Persian Historiography to the End of the Twelfth Century*. Edinburgh: Edinburgh University Press, 1999.

Menon, M. U. "ʿĀlī, Neʿmat Khan." In *Encyclopædia Iranica*, August 1, 2011.

Minissale, Gregory. *Images of Thought Visuality in Islamic India, 1550–1750*. Newcastle: Cambridge Scholars, 2009.

Modi, Jivanji Jamshedji. *Asiatic Papers*. Part IV. Bombay: Times of India Press, 1929.

Moin, A. Azfar. *The Millennial Sovereign: Sacred Kingship and Sainthood in Islam*. New York: Columbia University Press, 2012.

Moin, A. Azfar. "Millennial Sovereignty, Total Religion, and Total Politics." *History and Theory* 56, no. 1 (March 1, 2017): 89–97.

Moin, A. Azfar. "The 'Millennium' of 1857: The Last Performance of the Great Mughal." In *The Scaffolding of Sovereignty: Global and Aesthetic Perspectives on the History of a Concept*, edited by Zvi Ben-Dor Benite, Stefanos Geroulanos, and Nicole Jerr, 322–39. New York: Columbia University Press, 2017.

Moosvi, Shireen. "Expenditure on Buildings under Shahjahan–A Chapter of Imperial Financial History." *Proceedings of the Indian History Congress* 46 (1985): 285–99.

Moosvi, Shireen. "The Silver Influx, Money Supply, Prices and Revenue-Extraction in Mughal India." *Journal of the Economic and Social History of the Orient* 30, no. 1 (1987): 47–94.

Moosvi, Shireen. "Urban Houses and Building: Use in Mughal India." *Proceedings of the Indian History Congress* 72 (2011): 423–32.

Mottahedeh, Roy. "Some Islamic Views of the Pre-Islamic Past." *Harvard Middle Eastern and Islamic Review* 1, no. 1 (1994): 17–26.

Moy, Timothy, J. "The 'Sejarah Melayu' Tradition of Power and Political Structure: An Assessment of Relevant Sections of the 'Tuhfat Al-Nafis.'" *Journal of the Malaysian Branch of the Royal Asiatic Society* 48, no. 2 (228) (1975): 64–78.

Naim, C. M. "Popular Jokes and Political History: The Case of Akbar, Birbal and Mulla Do-Piyaza." *Economic and Political Weekly* 30, no. 24 (1995): 1456–64.

Narayana Rao, Velcheru, David Dean Shulman, and Sanjay Subrahmanyam. *Textures of Time: Writing History in South India*. New York: Other Press, 2003.

Nevill, H. R. *Meerut: A Gazetteer, Being Volume IV of the District Gazetteers of the United Provinces of Agra and Oudh*. Allahabad: Government Press, 1904.

Nirenberg, David. *Communities of Violence: Persecution of Minorities in the Middle Ages*. Princeton, NJ: Princeton University Press, 1996.

Nussdorfer, Laurie. "Politics and the People of Rome." In *Rome—Amsterdam*. Edited by Peter van Kessel and Elisja Schulte, 146–55. Amsterdam: Amsterdam University Press, 1997.

Oesterheld, Christina. "Humor and Satire: Precolonial, Colonial, and Postcolonial." *Annual of Urdu Studies* (2011): 64–86.

Oesterheld, Christina. "Satirizing the Late Mughals: The Works of Mīr Jaʿfar 'Zaṭallī." In *Indian Satire in the Period of First Modernity*, edited by Monika Thiel-Horstmann and Heidi Rika Maria Pauwels, 135–53. Wiesbaden: Harrassowitz, 2012.

O'Hanlon, Rosalind. "Manliness and Imperial Service in Mughal North India." *Journal of the Economic and Social History of the Orient* 42, no. 1 (1999): 47–93.

Olson, Robert W. "The Esnaf and the Patrona Halil Rebellion of 1730: A Realignment in Ottoman Politics?" *Journal of the Economic and Social History of the Orient* 17, no. 3 (1974): 329–44.

Pamment, Claire. *Comic Performance in Pakistan: The Bhānd*. London: Palgrave Macmillan, 2017.

Pandey, Gyanendra. *The Construction of Communalism in Colonial North India*. Delhi and New York: Oxford University Press, 1990.

Parihar, Subhash. *Land Transport in Mughal India: Agra-Lahore Mughal Highway and Its Architectural Remains*. New Delhi: Aryan Books International, 2008.

Parker, Charles H. *Global Interactions in the Early Modern Age*. Cambridge, UK and New York: Cambridge University Press, 2010.

Pathak, Padmesh. "Ziyauddin Barani's Theory of Price Control—A Critical Estimate." *Proceedings of the Indian History Congress* 45 (1984): 296–305.

Peirce, Leslie P. *Morality Tales: Law and Gender in the Ottoman Court of Aintab*. Berkeley: University of California Press, 2003.

Péri, Benedek. "A Turkic Clan in Mughal India: The Qaqshals in Akbar's Service." *Acta Orientalia Academiae Scientiarum Hungaricae* 60, no. 4 (2007): 363–98.

Perlin, Frank. "Growth of Money Economy and Some Questions of Transitions in Late Pre-Colonial India." *Social Scientist* 11, no. 10 (1983): 27–38.

Pernau, Margrit. *Ashraf into Middle Classes: Muslims in Nineteenth-Century Delhi*. New Delhi: Oxford University Press, 2013.

Peter Adamson. "Ethics in Philosophy." In *Encyclopaedia of Islam, THREE*, edited by Kate Fleet, Gudrun Krämer, Denis Matringe, John Nawas, and Everett Rowson. Brill Online, 2015.

Pinch, William R. *Warrior Ascetics and Indian Empires*. Cambridge, UK and New York: Cambridge University Press, 2006.

Pinch, William R. "Who Was Himmat Bahadur? Gosains, Rajputs and the British in Bundelkhand, ca. 1800." *The Indian Economic & Social History Review* 35, no. 3 (September 1, 1998): 293–335.

Pincus, Steven C. A. *1688: The First Modern Revolution*. New Haven, CT: Yale University Press, 2009.

Platts, John T. *A Dictionary of Urdu, Classical Hindi, and English*. London: Oxford University Press, 1960.

Pocock, J. G. A. "On the Unglobality of Contexts: Cambridge Methods and the History of Political Thought." *Global Intellectual History* (2019): 1–14.

Prior, Katherine. "Making History: The State's Intervention in Urban Religious Disputes in the North-Western Provinces in the Early Nineteenth Century." *Modern Asian Studies* 27, no. 1 (1993): 179–203.

Raychaudhuri, Tapan, Irfan Habib, and Dharma Kumar. *The Cambridge Economic History of India*. Vol. 1, c.1200–c.1750. Cambridge, UK: Cambridge University Press, 1982.

Rezavi, Syed Ali Nadeem. "Bazars and Markets in Medieval India." *Studies in People's History* 2, no. 1 (June 1, 2015): 61–70.

Rezavi, Syed Ali Nadeem. "The Dynamics of Composite Culture: Evolution of an Urban Social Identity in Mughal India." *Proceedings of the Indian History Congress* 72 (2011): 408–22.

Rezavi, Syed Ali Nadeem. "Mercantile Life in Mughal India." *Proceedings of the Indian History Congress* 65 (2004): 277–303.

Rezavi, Syed Ali Nadeem. "'The Mighty Defensive Fort': Red Fort At Delhi Under Shahjahan—Its Plan And Structures As Described By Muhammad Waris." *Proceedings of the Indian History Congress* 71 (2010): 1108–21.

Rezavi, Syed Ali Nadeem. "Representation of Middle Class Professionals in Mughal Visual Art." In *The Varied Facets of History: Essays in Honour of Aniruddha Ray*, edited by Ishrat Alam and Sayyid Ejaz Hussain, 159–93. Delhi: Primus Books, 2011.

Richards, John F. *Document Forms for Official Orders of Appointment in the Mughal Empire: Translation, Notes and Text*. Cambridge, UK: Trustees of the E. J. W. Gibb Memorial, 1986.

Richards, John F. "Early Modern India and World History." *Journal of World History* 8, no. 2 (1997): 197–209.

Richards, John F. "The Formulation of Imperial Authority under Akbar and Jahangir." In *Kingship and Authority in South Asia*, edited by John F. Richards, 285–327. Madison: South Asian Studies, University of Wisconsin, 1981.

Richards, John F. *The Imperial Monetary System of Mughal India*. Delhi: Oxford University Press, 1987.

Richards, John F. *Mughal Administration in Golconda*. Oxford: Clarendon Press, 1975.

Richards, John F. *The Mughal Empire*. Cambridge, UK and New York: Cambridge University Press, 1993.

Richards, John F. "The Seventeenth-Century Crisis in South Asia." *Modern Asian Studies* 24, no. 4 (October 1, 1990): 625–38.

Rizvi, Saiyid Athar Abbas. *Shah Wali-Allah and His Times: A Study of Eighteenth Century Islam, Politics, and Society in India*. Canberra: Marifat Pub., 1980.

Rizvi, Saiyid Athar Abbas. *A Socio-Intellectual History of the Isnā 'Asharī Shī'īs in India*. Vol. I. New Delhi: Munshiram Manoharlal, 1986.

Roebuck, Thomas. *A Collection of Proverbs, and Proverbial Phrases in the Persian and Hindoostanee Languages: Persian*. Calcutta: Hindoostanee Press, 1824.

Rose, H. A. *A Glossary of the Tribes and Castes of the Punjab and North-West Frontier Province*. 3 vols. Lahore: Civil and Military Gazette Press, 1911.

Rouighi, Ramzi. *The Making of a Mediterranean Emirate: Ifriqiya and Its Andalusis, 1200–1400*. Philadelphia: University of Pennsylvania Press, 2011.

Rousseau, Jean-Jacques. *On the Social Contract*. Indianapolis: Hackett Publishing, 1988.

Roy, Sourin. "A Rare Document on Delhi Wheat-Prices 1763–1835." *Indian Economic & Social History Review* 9, no. 1 (January 1, 1972): 91–99.

Rudé, George F. E. *Paris and London in the Eighteenth Century: Studies in Popular Protest*. New York: Viking Press, 1971.

Russell, Ralph, and Khurshidul Islam. *Three Mughal Poets: Mir, Sauda, Mir Hasan*. Cambridge, MA: Harvard University Press, 1968.

Sajdi, Dana. *The Barber of Damascus: Nouveau Literacy in the Eighteenth-Century Ottoman Levant*. Stanford: Stanford University Press, 2013.

Samaddar, Ranabir. "The Heterogeneous World of the Citizen." *Citizenship Studies* 16, nos. 5–6 (August 1, 2012): 839–49.

Sangar, Satya Prakash. "The Procedure of Work in the Courts of Aurangzeb (as Mentioned in the Akhbarat-i-Darbar-i-Mu'alla)." *Proceedings of the Indian History Congress* 28 (1966): 211–17.

Sariyannis, Marinos. "Mob, Scamps and Rebels in Seventeenth-Century Istanbul: Some Remarks on Ottoman Social Vocabulary." *International Journal of Turkish Studies* 11, nos. 1–2 (2005): 1–15.

Sariyannis, Marinos. "Ruler and State, State and Society in Ottoman Political Thought." *Turkish Historical Review* 4 (2013): 92–126.

Sarkar, Jadunath. *Fall of the Mughal Empire*. 4 vols. Calcutta: M.C. Sarkar & sons, 1932.

Sarkar, Jadunath. *History of Aurangzib, Based on Original Sources*. 5 vols. Calcutta: M. C. Sarkar & Sons, 1912–1952.

Sarkar, Jadunath. *A History of Jaipur: C. 1503–1938*. New Delhi: Orient Blackswan, 1994.

Sarkar, Jadunath. *The Mughal Administration: Six Lectures*. Patna: Superintendent, Government Printing, Bihar and Orissa, 1920.

Sarkar, Jadunath. *Nadir Shah in India [Six Lectures Delivered in 1922, Compressed and Re-Arranged]*. Patna: Patna University, 1925.

Sarkar, Jadunath. *Studies in Mughal India*. London and New York: Longmans, Green and Co., 1920.

Sarkar, Nilanjan. "An Urban Imaginaire, ca. 1350: The Capital City in Ziya' Barani's Fatawa-i Jahandari." *The Indian Economic & Social History Review* 48, no. 3 (2011): 407–24.

Satyal, Amita. "The Mughal Empire, Overland Trade, and Merchants of Northern India, 1526–1707." Berkeley: University of California, 2008.

Schimmel, Annemarie, and Carl W. Ernst. *Mystical Dimensions of Islam*. Chapel Hill: University of North Carolina Press, 2011.

Schimmel, Annemarie, and Burzine K Waghmar. *The Empire of the Great Mughals: History, Art and Culture*. London: Reaktion Books, 2004.

Schmitz, Barbara and Ziyaud-Din A. Desai. *Mughal and Persian Paintings and Illustrated Manuscripts in the Raza Rampur Library, Rampur*. New Delhi: IGNCA, Raza Rampur Library, Aryan Books International, 2006.

Seyller, John. "The Inspection and Valuation of Manuscripts in the Imperial Mughal Library." *Artibusasiae Artibus Asiae* 57, no. 3–4 (1997): 243–349.

Shagan, Ethan H. *Popular Politics and the English Reformation*. Cambridge, UK: Cambridge University Press, 2003.

Shagan, Ethan H. "Rumours and Popular Politics in the Reign of Henry VIII." In *The Politics of the Excluded, c. 1500–1800*, edited by Tim Harris, 30–67. New York: Palgrave Macmillan, 2001.

Sharma, Sri Ram. *The Religious Policy of the Mughal Emperors*. 2nd ed. London and Bombay: Asia Publishing House, 1962.

Sharma, Sunil. "The City of Beauties in Indo-Persian Poetic Landscape." *Comparative Studies of South Asia, Africa and the Middle East* 24, no. 2 (2004): 73–81.

Sharma, Sunil. *Mughal Arcadia: Persian Literature in an Indian Court*. Cambridge, MA: Harvard University Press, 2017.

Sharma, Yogesh, and Pius Malekandathil. *Cities in Medieval India*. New Delhi: Primus Books, 2014.

Sheehan, James J. "The Problem of Sovereignty in European History." *The American Historical Review* 111, no. 1 (February 1, 2006): 1–15.

Sheikh, Samira. "Aurangzeb as Seen from Gujarat: Shi'i and Millenarian Challenges to Mughal Sovereignty." *Journal of the Royal Asiatic Society* (April 2018): 1–25.

Shirani, Mahmud. *Maqalat-i Hafiz Mahmud Shirani*. Edited by Mazhar Mahmud Shirani. Vol. II. Lahaur: Majlis Tarraqi-yi Adab, 1966.

Siddiqi, Iqtidar Husain. *Delhi Sultanate: Urbanization and Social Change*. New Delhi: Viva Books, 2009.

Siddiqi, Jamal Muhammad. *Aligarh District: A History Survey, from Ancient Times to 1803 AD*. Munshiram Manoharlal, 1981.

Siddiqi, Muhammad Zameeruddin. "The Muhtasib under Aurangzeb." *Medieval India Quarterly* 5 (1963): 113–19.

Siddiqui, Iqtidar Husain. "Water Works and Irrigation System in India during Pre-Mughal Times." *Journal of the Economic and Social History of the Orient* 29, no. 1 (1986): 52–77.

Siebenhuener, Kim. "Precious Things in Motion: Luxury and the Circulation of Jewels in Mughal India." In *Luxury in Global Perspective: Objects and Practices, 1600–2000*, edited by Bernd-Stefan Grewe and Karin Hofmeester, 27–54. Studies in Comparative World History. New York: Cambridge University Press, 2016.

Singh, Chetan. *Region and Empire: Panjab in the Seventeenth Century*. Delhi and New York: Oxford University Press, 1991.

Singh, M. P. *Town, Market, Mint, and Port in the Mughal Empire, 1556–1707: An Administrative-Cum-Economic Study*. New Delhi: Adam Publishers & Distributors, 1985.

Singh, Upinder. *Political Violence in Ancient India*. Cambridge, MA: Harvard University Press, 2017.

Smith, George, ed. *Alexander Grant, Physician and Friend: His Autobiography and His Letters from the Marquis of Dalhousie*. London: Murray, 1902.

Smith, Wilfred Cantwell. "The Crystallization of Religious Communities in Mughul India." In *Yād-nāme-ye-Īrānī-ye Minorsky*, edited by Mujtaba Minovi and Iraj Afshar, 197–220. Ganjine-ye-Tahqiqat-e Irani no. 57; Publications of Tehran University, no. 1241. Tehran: Intisharat Daneshgah, 1969.

Smith, Wilfred Cantwell. "Lower-Class Uprisings in the Mughal Empire." In *The Mughal State, 1526–1750*, edited by Muzaffar Alam and Sanjay Subrahmanyam, 323–46. New Delhi and Oxford: Oxford University Press, 1999.

Smith, Wilfred Cantwell. "The 'Ulamā' in Indian Politics." In *On Understanding Islam: Selected Studies*, 197–213. Den Haag: Mouton, 1981.

Soja, Edward W. "Cities and States in Geohistory." *Theory and Society* 39, nos. 3/4 (2010): 361–76.

Spear, Thomas George Percival. *Twilight of the Mughuls: Studies in Late Mughul Delhi*. Cambridge, UK: Cambridge University Press, 1951.

Srivastava, Ashirbadi Lal. *The First Two Nawabs of Oudh: A Critical Study Based on Original Sources*. Lucknow: Upper India Pub. House, 1933.

Steingass, F., Francis Johnson, and John Richardson. *A Comprehensive Persian-English Dictionary: Including the Arabic Words and Phrases to Be Met with in Persian Literature*. London: Routledge & K. Paul, 1892.

Stewart, Tony K. "In Search of Equivalence: Conceiving Muslim-Hindu Encounter through Translation Theory." *History of Religions* 40, no. 3 (2001): 260–87.

Stokes, Eric, and Christopher Alan Bayly. *The Peasant Armed: The Indian Revolt of 1857*. Oxford and New York: Oxford University Press, 1986.

Stronge, Susan. *Painting for the Mughal Emperor: The Art of the Book, 1560–1660*. London: Victoria & Albert Publications, 2002.

Subrahmanyam, Sanjay. "Before the Leviathan: Sectarian Violence and the State in Pre-Colonial India." In *Unravelling the Nation: Sectarian Conflict and India's Secular Identity*, edited by Kaushik Basu and Sanjay Subrahmanyam, 44–80. Delhi: Penguin Books, 1996.

Subrahmanyam, Sanjay. "Connected Histories: Notes towards a Reconfiguration of Early Modern Eurasia." *Modern Asian Studies* 31, no. 3 (July 1, 1997): 735–62.

Subrahmanyam, Sanjay. *Courtly Encounters: Translating Courtliness and Violence in Early Modern Eurasia*. Cambridge, MA: Harvard University Press, 2012.

Subrahmanyam, Sanjay. *Europe's India: Words, People, Empires, 1500–1800*. Cambridge, MA: Harvard University Press, 2017.

Subrahmanyam, Sanjay. *Money and the Market in India, 1100–1700*. Delhi and Oxford: Oxford University Press, 1998.

Subrahmanyam, Sanjay. "The Mughal State—Structure or Process? Reflections on Recent Western Historiography." *Indian Economic & Social History Review* 29, no. 3 (September 1, 1992): 291–321.

Subrahmanyam, Sanjay. "Of Imarat and Tijarat: Asian Merchants and State Power in the Western Indian Ocean, 1400 to 1750." *Comparative Studies in Society and History* 37, no. 4 (1995): 750–80.

Subrahmanyam, Sanjay. "Parody and Public Space in an Early Modern Society." In *Penumbral Visions: The Making of Polities in Early Modern South India*, 220–52. Delhi and Oxford: Oxford University Press, 2000.

Subrahmanyam, Sanjay. "Un Grand Dérangement: Dreaming an Indo-Persian Empire in South Asia, 1740–1800." *Journal of Early Modern History* 4, no. 3–1 (January 1, 2000): 337–78.

Subrahmanyam, Sanjay. "Violence, Grievance and Memory in Early Modern South Asia." In *From the Tagus to the Ganges*, 80–102. New Delhi: Oxford University Press, 2005.

Subrahmanyam, Sanjay. "Waiting for the Simorgh: Comparisons, Connections, and the 'Early Modern.'" In *Delimiting Modernities: Conceptual Challenges and Regional Responses*, edited by Sven Trakulhun and Ralph Weber, 99–122. Lanham, Maryland: Lexington Books, 2015.

Subrahmanyam, Sanjay, and Christopher Alan Bayly. "Portfolio Capitalists and the Political Economy of Early Modern India." *Indian Economic & Social History Review* 25, no. 4 (December 1, 1988): 401–24.

Syed, Anees Jahan. *Aurangzeb in Muntakhab-Al Lubab*. Bombay: Somaiya Publications, 1977.

Syros, Vasileios. "An Early Modern South Asian Thinker on the Rise and Decline of Empires: Shāh Walī Allāh of Delhi, the Mughals, and the Byzantines." *Journal of World History* 23, no. 4 (2012): 793–840.

Talbot, Cynthia. "Becoming Turk the Rajput Way: Conversion and Identity in an Indian Warrior Narrative." *Modern Asian Studies* 43, no. 1 (2009): 211–43.

Talbot, Cynthia. "Inscribing the Other, Inscribing the Self: Hindu-Muslim Identities in Pre-Colonial India." *Comparative Studies in Society and History* 37 (1995): 692–722.

Te Brake, Wayne. *Regents and Rebels: The Revolutionary World of an Eighteenth-Century Dutch City*. Studies in Social Discontinuity. Oxford and New York: Basil Blackwell, 1989.

Te Brake, Wayne. *Shaping History: Ordinary People in European Politics, 1500–1700*. Berkeley: University of California Press, 1998.

Terzioğlu, Derin. "How to Conceptualize Ottoman Sunnitization: A Historiographical Discussion." *Turcica* 44 (2013): 301–38.

Tezcan, Baki. *The Second Ottoman Empire: Political and Social Transformation in the Early Modern World*. Cambridge, UK: Cambridge University Press, 2010.

Thackston, W. M. *A Millennium of Classical Persian Poetry: A Guide to the Reading & Understanding of Persian Poetry from the Tenth to the Twentieth Century*. Bethesda, MD: Iranbooks, 1994.

The Asiatic Journal and Monthly Register for British and Foreign India, China, and Australia. London: Parbury, Allen, and Company, 1839.

Tilly, Charles. *The Politics of Collective Violence*. Cambridge Studies in Contentious Politics. Cambridge, UK and New York: Cambridge University Press, 2003.

Tirmizi, S. A. I., R. K. Perti, and National Archives of India. *Calendar of Acquired Documents. 1352–1754*. New Delhi: National Archives of India, 1986.

Travers, Robert. "The Connected Worlds of Haji Mustapha (c. 1730–91): A Eurasian Cosmopolitan in Eighteenth-Century Bengal." *Indian Economic & Social History Review* 52, no. 3 (July 1, 2015): 297–333.

Travers, Robert. "The Eighteenth Century in Indian History." Edited by Seema Alavi, Indrani Chatterjee, Rajat Datta, Rosie Llewellyn-Jones, P. J. Marshall, Prasannan Parthasarathi, Norbert Peabody, and Muzaffar Alam. *Eighteenth-Century Studies* 40, no. 3 (2007): 492–508.

Trevithick, Alan. "Some Structural and Sequential Aspects of the British Imperial Assemblages at Delhi: 1877–1911." *Modern Asian Studies* 24, no. 3 (1990): 561–78.

Tripathi, Dwijendra, and Makrand Mehta. "The Nagarsheth of Ahmedabad: The History of an Urban Institution in a Gujarat City." In *Essays in Medieval Indian Economic History*, edited by Satish Chandra, 262–75. New Delhi: Munshiram Manoharlal, 1987.

Tripathi, Ram Prasad. *Some Aspects of Muslim Administration*. Allahabad: Central Book Depot, 1966.

Truschke, Audrey. "The Mughal Book of War: A Persian Translation of the Sanskrit Mahabharata." *Comparative Studies of South Asia, Africa and the Middle East* 31, no. 2 (2011): 506–20.Tuck, Richard. *The Sleeping Sovereign: The Invention of Modern Democracy*, 2016.

Tucker, Ernest. "1739: History, Self, and Other in Afsharid Iran and Mughal India." *Iranian Studies* 31, no. 2 (1998): 207–17.

Tucker, Ernst. "Nāder Shah." In *Encyclopedia Iranica*, August 15, 2006. http://www.iranicaonline.org/articles/nader-shah.

Umar, Muhammad. *Islam in Northern India during the Eighteenth Century*. New Delhi: Munshiram Manoharlal, 1993.

Umar, Muhammad. *Muslim Society in Northern India during the Eighteenth Century*. New Delhi: Munshiram Manoharlal 1998.

Umar, Muhammad. *Urban Culture in Northern India during the Eighteenth Century*. New Delhi: Munshiram Manoharlal, 2001.

Veluthat, Kesavan. "The Status of the Monarch: A Note on the Rituals Pertaining to Kingship and Their Significance in the Tamil Country (AD 600–1200)." *Proceedings of the Indian History Congress* 43 (1982): 147–57.

Verma, Harish Chandra. *Dynamics of Urban Life in Pre-Mughal India*. New Delhi: Munshiram Manoharlal, 1986.

Vogel, Jean Philippe. *Catalogue of the Delhi Museum of Archaeology*. Calcutta: Baptist Mission Press, 1908.

Vries, Jan De. "The Limits of Globalization in the Early Modern World." *The Economic History Review*, New Series, 63, no. 3 (August 1, 2010): 710–33.

Wagner, Kim A. *The Great Fear of 1857: Rumours, Conspiracies and the Making of the Indian Uprising*. Oxford, UK: Peter Lang Ltd., 2010.

Walzer, Michael. *Regicide and Revolution: Speeches at the Trial of Louis XVI*. New York: Columbia University Press, 1993.

Weber, Max. "The Nature of the City." In *Classic Essays on the Culture of Cities*, edited by Richard Sennett, 23–46. New York: Appleton-Century-Crofts, 1969.

Welsford, Thomas. *Four Types of Loyalty in Early Modern Central Asia the Tūqāy-Timūrid Takeover of Greater Mā Warā Al-Nahr, 1598–1605*. Leiden and Boston: Brill, 2013.

Wensinck, A. J. "Khuṭba." In *Encyclopaedia of Islam*, 2nd ed., edited by P. Bearman, Th. Bianquis, C. E. Bosworth, E. van Donzel, and W. P. Heinrichs. Brill Online, 2016.

Wild, Antony. *Coffee: A Dark History*. London: Fourth Estate, 2004.

Wink, André. *Land and Sovereignty in India: Agrarian Society and Politics under the Eighteenth-Century Maratha Svarājya*. Cambridge, UK: Cambridge University Press, 1986.

Yılmaz, Hüseyin. *Caliphate Redefined: The Mystical Turn in Ottoman Political Thought*. Princeton: Princeton University Press, 2018.

Zafarul Islam. *Fatāwā Literature of the Sultanate Period*. New Delhi: Kanishka Publishers, Distributors, 2005.

Zaman, Muhammad Qasim, "Ahl al-ḥall wa-l-ʿaqd," in: *Encyclopaedia of Islam, THREE*, Edited by: Kate Fleet, Gudrun Krämer, Denis Matringe, John Nawas, Everett Rowson. Brill Online, 2019.

Zarinebaf, Fariba. *Crime and Punishment in Istanbul: 1700–1800*. Berkeley: University of California Press, 2011.

Index

Note: *For the benefit of digital users, indexed terms that span two pages (e.g., 52–53) may, on occasion, appear on only one of those pages.*